FROMMER'S

COMPREHENSIVE TRAVEL GUIDE

THE CAROLINAS & GEORGIA

2ND EDITION

by Dale Northrup

PRENTICE HALL TRAVEL

NEW YORK • LONDON • TORONTO • SYDNEY • TOKYO • SINGAPORE

FROMMER BOOKS

Published by Prentice Hall General Reference
A division of Simon & Schuster Inc.
15 Columbus Circle
New York, NY 10023

ISBN 0-671-79770-0
ISSN 1055-5420

Design by Robert Bull Design
Maps by Geografix Inc.

FROMMER'S EDITORIAL STAFF
Vice President/Editorial Director: Marilyn Wood
Senior Editor/Editorial Manager: Alice Fellows
Senior Editors: Sara Hinsey Raveret, Lisa Renaud
Editors: Charlotte Allstrom, Thomas F. Hirsch, Peter Katucki, Theodore Stavrou
Assistant Editors: Margaret Bowen, Christopher Hollander, Alice Thompson, Ian Wilker
Editorial Assistants: Gretchen Henderson, Bethany Jewett
Managing Editor: Leanne Coupe

SPECIAL SALES
Bulk purchases (10+ copies) of Frommer's Travel Guides are available to corporations at special discounts. The Special Sales Department can produce custom editions to be used as premiums and/or for sales promotion to suit individual needs. Existing editions can be produced with custom cover imprints, such as a corporate logo. For more information, write to Special Sales, Prentice Hall Travel, 15 Columbus Circle, New York, NY 10023.

Manufactured in the United States of America

CONTENTS

LIST OF MAPS

ACKNOWLEDGMENTS

Special thanks go to a number of folks who helped facilitate the work that follows, especially Bob Anderson, Amy Blyth, Karen Cook, Sara Hinsey Raveret, Heather Gatchell, Paige Gordon, Kim Myers, Cynthia Rand, Jenny Stacy, Ruth Sykes, Gary Wieland, and Julie Wright-Harkins. And to Margaret Northrup, who for ten years from coast to coast always said there's time to see one more hotel.

INVITATION TO THE READERS

In researching this book, I have come across many wonderful establishments, the best of which I have included here. I am sure that many of you will also come across appealing hotels, inns, restaurants, guesthouses, shops, and attractions. Please don't keep them to yourself. Share your experiences, especially if you want to comment on places that have been included in this edition that have changed for the worse. You can address your letters to:

Dale Northrup
Frommer's The Carolinas & Georgia, 2nd Edition
c/o Prentice Hall Travel
15 Columbus Circle
New York, NY 10023

A DISCLAIMER

Readers are advised that prices fluctuate in the course of time and travel information changes under the impact of the varied and volatile factors that affect the travel industry. Neither the author nor the publisher can be held responsible for the experiences of readers while traveling. Readers are invited to write to the publisher with ideas, comments, and suggestions for future editions.

SAFETY ADVISORY

Whenever you're traveling in an unfamiliar city or country, stay alert. Be aware of your immediate surroundings. Wear a moneybelt and keep a close eye on your possessions. Be particularly careful with cameras, purses, and wallets, all favorite targets of thieves and pickpockets.

CHAPTER 1

PLANNING A TRIP TO NORTH CAROLINA

Although Southerners have long known and enjoyed North Carolina's resorts, "Yankees," Midwesterners, and those from the West Coast have often thought of the state as merely a place to pass through on the way to points farther south. Yet, often to their delighted surprise, visitors find within its borders tourist and vacation attractions numerous and varied enough to appeal to almost any traveler.

Its beaches are a delight, with broad stretches of white sand, waves to challenge the most skillful surfer, and seaside resorts located on outer banks, peninsulas, and offshore islands, facing sounds and rivers as well as the Atlantic. Fishing, boating, waterskiing, sand-skiing, and even hang-gliding from gigantic dunes are all part of the fun up and down the coastline.

Tennis and golf lovers will find a home in the state too. Indeed, who doesn't equate the very word "golf" with Pinehurst? While no one would deny that the sport is at its best there, the rest of the excellent courses and courts scattered throughout the state should not be overlooked. Equestrians will find some of the country's finest horses in North Carolina, along with miles and miles of riding trails on the beaches, on sandy paths shaded by longleaf pines, and following ancient Native American routes through mountain passes.

Speaking of mountains, the peaks of North Carolina beckon hikers, climbers, skiers, and campers; then throw in Fontana, where square dancing and other old-time recreations still hold sway. Naturalists and others who'd rather bed down in a tent than in the fanciest resort hotel will find an embarrassment of riches in the Great Smoky Mountains National Park, as well as 2 national seashores, 4 national forests, 34 state parks and recreation areas, and 60 public and more than 300 privately owned campgrounds in the state.

WHAT'S SPECIAL ABOUT NORTH CAROLINA

Beaches

☐ The Outer Banks, a string of wide-strand beaches on offshore islands, stretching from Nags Head to Hatteras.

☐ Atlantic Beach, one of North Carolina's oldest seaside resorts, situated on a 24-mile stretch of Bogue Banks.

Mountains

☐ The Blue Ridge Mountains, from the Virginia border to the entrance of Great Smoky Mountains National Park.

☐ Grandfather Mountain with its mile-high swinging bridge and habitat for native wildlife.

Historic Sites

☐ Fort Raleigh National Historic Site, at Manteo, with restored earthworks of Sir Walter Raleigh's doomed colony.

☐ Old Salem, a cluster of fine old Moravian settler buildings in Winston-Salem dating back to 1753.

Literary Shrines

☐ The Thomas Wolfe Memorial State Historic Site, the Asheville home of the distinguished author.

☐ The Carl Sandburg Home National Memorial Site, where the author lived for nearly 22 years.

☐ The Greensboro Historical Museum, with a wonderful exhibit on one of its natives, short-story writer O. Henry (William Sidney Porter).

Museums

☐ The North Carolina Museum of History, in Raleigh, displaying the original Carolina Charter and exhibits that illuminate state history from the 16th century to the present.

☐ The Museum of the Cherokee Indians, in the town of Cherokee.

Outdoor Dramas

☐ *The Lost Colony*, Paul Green's stunning play, on Roanoke Island—the nation's first historical outdoor drama.

☐ *Unto These Hills*, in Cherokee, a moving play about the history of the Cherokees.

☐ *Horn in the West*, in Boone, the stirring story of Daniel Boone, who led a group of settlers from this area to the West.

1. GETTING TO KNOW NORTH CAROLINA

The people of North Carolina call themselves "Tarheels." It is said that Gen. Robert E. Lee originated the name when North Carolina troops stuck tenaciously in the front lines of battle during the Civil War. While the three geographical regions have produced certain "personality" characteristics in the natives, there are some traits that all North Carolinians share. Along with the courtesy and friendliness found among most Southern people, those in North Carolina possess an engaging lack of pretense and a delightful sense of humor. Resourcefulness and determination have, down

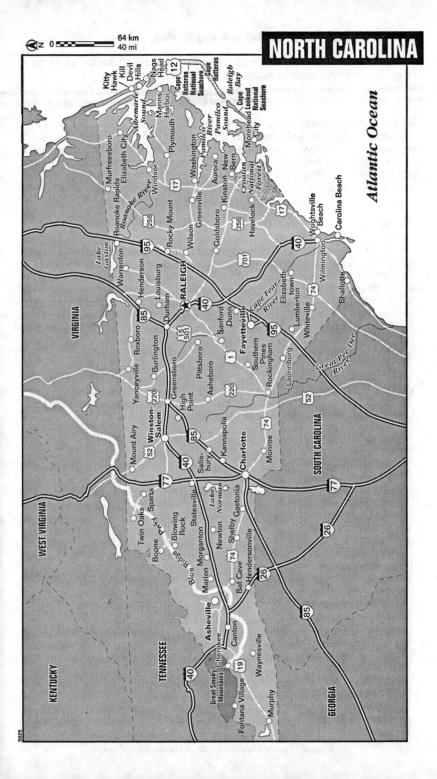

through the years, been responsible for North Carolina's position as one of the most progressive Southern states in industry, education, and agriculture.

GEOGRAPHY

Within its 48,843 square miles, North Carolina's geographical makeup divides into three distinct regions: the Coastal Plain, the Piedmont Plateau, and the mountains. A long, rather narrow state, its coast lies some 500 miles east of its mountains, which border neighboring Tennessee. From sea level along the Coastal Plain, the land gently rises to cross the rolling sandhills of the Piedmont Plateau to reach a top elevation of some 6,684 feet at Mt. Mitchell in the western Appalachian mountain range.

DATELINE

- **1585** First English colony in America founded on Roanoke Island, but abandoned the next year.
- **1587** Second colony established on Roanoke Island; first English child (Virginia Dare) born in the New World.
- **1663** Charles II grants a charter to the territory south of Virginia to eight lords proprietors.
- **1729** North Carolina becomes a royal province under George II.
- **1774** North Carolina elects delegates to First Continental Congress.
- **1789** North Carolina becomes 12th state to ratify the U.S. Constitution. General Assembly charters University of North Carolina at Chapel Hill.
- **1792** Raleigh becomes the state's permanent capital.

(continues)

HISTORY

There's history aplenty, for it was here, on tiny Roanoke Island, that Sir Walter Raleigh's colony of 150 English settlers was "lost" in 1587, a full 20 years before Englishmen arrived farther north in Virginia's Jamestown. What happened to them (including Virginia Dare, the first child born of English parents in the New World) remains a mystery, since the only clue—if that's what it is—to their fate is the word "Croatan" (the name of a tribe of friendly Native Americans) carved on a tree.

Along the coast are stately old plantation homes, some with formal gardens still lovingly tended and open to visitors. And farther inland, at Winston-Salem, an entire village—Old Salem—has been restored to depict the lifestyle of Moravians who arrived in 1753 and created a community that has lived here through the centuries.

To the west, in the mountains (the Blue Ridge, Great Smokies, Nantahalas, and others that form the southern Appalachians), history lives on in the form of the Cherokee reservation—teeming with residents whose ancestors were here eons before a white face appeared—and in towns like Boone (named for you-know-who) and Banner Elk, established by persevering westward settlers who cleared the way for those who followed, bringing "civilization" with them.

Some of the first Revolutionary War skirmishes were fought on North Carolina soil. During the War Between the States, Tarheel troops—who felt their state's rights were threatened when Federal troops fired on South Carolina's Fort Sumter—fought valiantly even though there were relatively few slaveowners among its citizens and it had recognized free blacks since 1860.

Twentieth-century history is represented at Kitty Hawk, where the Age of Flight began in 1903 when Wilbur and Orville Wright made the first machine-powered flight. And while for many years textiles and tobacco led the state's industrial growth, high-tech industries are now mushrooming in centers like the Raleigh/Durham/Chapel Hill Industrial Triangle. Tourism has also been given high development priority, with the result that first-class highways and airport hubs, accommodations, attractions, and eateries are now found throughout the state.

FAMOUS NORTH CAROLINIANS

Samuel James Ervin, Jr. (1896–1985), noted jurist and U.S. senator. His long and distinguished legal career in the North Carolina courts and his tenure in both the U.S. House of Representatives and the Senate brought him recognition as a leading authority on the U.S. Constitution. His public service was capped by chairmanship of the Senate committee investigating the Watergate affair. He waged a vigorous battle against President Nixon's use of executive privilege to withhold evidence, and his sense of humor and pithy observations won him great popularity with the public.

Andrew Jackson (1767–1845), seventh President of the United States, was born in Waxhaw, near the South Carolina border. Most of his early political life was spent in Tennessee, but he is remembered chiefly for his brilliant military leadership as a major general in campaigns against the British in the War of 1812 and the Creek Indians in Alabama. Nicknamed "Old Hickory," he was elected president in 1828; under his administration the national debt was retired and a sizable surplus distributed to the individual states.

Andrew Johnson (1808–1875), 17th President of the United States. Born in Raleigh, he early on showed signs of political ambition and became a public official in Greeneville, Tennessee, while working as a master tailor. He was Vice President of the U.S., and following the assassination of President Lincoln, he served as President from 1865 to 1869. As such, he headed the controversial years of Reconstruction of the Southern states following the Civil War, and ultimately became the only U.S. President to be impeached, although he was later acquitted of the charges.

Charles Kuralt (1934–), writer and television personality. Born in Wilmington, he was educated in Chapel Hill before joining CBS. For years, he traveled across the United States in search of human-interest stories for his popular "On The Road" television series. Although he has not resided in the state since 1957, he remains active in North Carolina affairs, and has strong ties to the Outer Banks, the present home of his parents.

James Knox Polk (1795–1849), 11th President of the United States, was born, the oldest of ten children, on a farm near Pineville in Mecklinburg County. After graduating at the head of his University of North Carolina class in 1818, he went to Tennessee to read law and became active in politics. After serving in the Tennessee House of Representatives and the U.S. House of Representatives, and one term as governor of Tennessee, he was elected President in 1845.

Thomas Clayton Wolfe (1900–1938), novelist. Born in Asheville, he struggled as a playwright in New York in the mid-1920s while teaching English at New York University. His *Look Homeward, Angel,* a massive novel based on his own rebellious and bitter Southern childhood, brought about his first association with noted editor Maxwell Perkins, who remained a major influence. Although the book created more than a little turbulence in Asheville, and much torment for Wolfe, he

DATELINE

- **1861** North Carolina secedes from the Union.
- **1868** North Carolina readmitted to the Union.
- **1903** The Wright brothers successfully fly the first powered aircraft.
- **1960** Black students from Greensboro's Black Agricultural and Technical College stage a sit-in at Woolworth's "whites-only" lunch counter.
- **1982** University of North Carolina at Chapel Hill wins NCAA basketball championship.
- **1983** North Carolina State University wins NCAA basketball championship.
- **1991** Duke University wins NCAA basketball championship.
- **1992** Duke University wins NCAA basketball championship.
- **1993** University of North Carolina at Chapel Hill wins NCAA basketball championship.

later added to his rather harrowing autobiographical work with *You Can't Go Home Again.*

RECOMMENDED BOOKS

For those of you who want a more detailed understanding of North Carolina's history and background, I list, below, some random selections of books.

ECONOMIC, POLITICAL & SOCIAL HISTORY

Kell, Jean B. *North Carolina's Coastal Carteret County During the American Revolution.*
Morton, Hugh M., and Edward L. Rankin, Jr. *Making a Difference in North Carolina.*
Powell, William S. *North Carolina: A History.*
Quinn, David Beers. *The Lost Colonists and Their Probable Fate.*
Yearns, W. Buck, and John G. Barret. *North Carolina Civil War Documentary.*

ARCHITECTURE & FICTION

Bishir, Catherine W. *North Carolina Architecture.*
Henry, O. (William Sidney Porter). Short stories including "An Unfinished Story," "Cabbages and Kings," "Gift of the Magi," and "Municipal Report."
Owen, Guy. *The Flim Flam Man and Other Stories.*
Walser, Richard Gaither. *North Carolina in the Short Story.*
Wolfe, Thomas. *Look Homeward, Angel* and *You Can't Go Home Again.*

2. INFORMATION & MONEY

INFORMATION

To receive a packet of specific information brochures and bulletins before coming to North Carolina, contact the **North Carolina Travel and Tourism Division,** 430 N. Salisbury St., Raleigh, NC 27611 (tel. 919/733-4171, or toll free 800/VISIT-NC). Whether you're interested in sightseeing, golf, or fishing, this packet is likely to provide very complete, thorough answers to your questions. There are also excellent visitors' centers located at state borders on most major highways, which can furnish detailed tourist information.

WHAT THINGS COST IN NORTH CAROLINA	U.S. $
Taxi from the airport to Raleigh city center	$15.00
Local telephone call	.25
Double at Raleigh Marriott Crabtree Valley (deluxe)	100.00
Double at Velvet Cloak Inn in Raleigh (moderate)	79.00
Double at Fairfield Inn in Raleigh (budget)	47.00
Lunch for one at Coopers Barbecue (moderate)	5.00

Lunch for one at K & W Cafeteria (budget)	4.00
Dinner for one, without wine, at Angus Barn in Raleigh (deluxe)	27.95
Dinner for one, without wine, at Longhorn's Steak Restaurant & Saloon in Charlotte (moderate)	14.00
Dinner for one, without wine, at Arthurs on Trade in Charlotte (budget)	6.00
Bottle of beer	2.00
Coca-Cola	.75
Roll of ASA 100 Kodachrome film, 36 exposures	5.79
Admission to NC Museum of Natural History	Free
Movie ticket	5.50
Ticket to NC Symphony concert	14.00

3. WHEN TO GO — CLIMATE & EVENTS

CLIMATE

North Carolina's climate is generally moderate, with winter temperatures on average in the 60s along the coast, the low 40s farther inland. Summer temperatures can rise to the high 90s in the interior of the state, but are cooled to the mid-60s to high 70s by mountain breezes in the west and sea breezes on the coast. The following are yearly mean highs and lows for various locations around the state:

NORTH CAROLINA AVERAGE TEMPERATURES [IN FAHRENHEIT]

	High	Low
Cape Hatteras	84	40
Raleigh	88	31
Winston-Salem	88	32
Asheville	85	30

NORTH CAROLINA CALENDAR OF EVENTS

JANUARY

☐ **Black American Arts Festival,** Greensboro. Many cultural and artistic events highlighting the achievements of America's black population. Early January to late March.

☐ **Martin Luther King, Jr., Community Celebration,** High Point Theatre, High Point. Celebrates the birthday of the slain civil rights leader with a variety of events. Mid-January.

FEBRUARY

☐ **Annual Winterfest Art & Craft Show,** in Asheville. Arts and crafts judging and sales at the Asheville Shopping Mall. February 7 to 11.

MARCH

☐ **Reenactments of the Battle of Guilford Courthouse,** in Tannenbaum Park, Greensboro. Celebrating this historic Revolutionary War engagement. Mid-March.

APRIL

☐ **North Carolina Azalea Festival,** in Wilmington, and spread over several locations in the area. Early April.
☐ **Festival of Flowers,** at the Biltmore Estate, Asheville. A billionaire showplace awash with color and special events. Mid-April to mid-May.
☐ **Old Salem Spring Festival,** in Winston-Salem. Workshops and fascinating exhibits and entertainment. Mid-April.

MAY

☐ **Fort Bragg Fair.** A carnival affair at the military base fairgrounds. May 3 to 20.
☐ **Annual Hang Gliding Spectacular,** at Jockey's Ridge State Park, Nags Head. Multilevel competitions. Mid-May.
☐ **Confederate Memorial Day,** in Capitol Square, Raleigh. A parade and memorial service to remember the boys in gray. Late May.

JUNE

☐ **Highland Heritage Art & Craft Show,** in the Asheville Shopping Mall. An opportunity to meet the area's leading craftspeople. Mid-June.
☐ **Eastern Music Festival,** headquartered at Greensboro's Guilford College, with events in High Point and Winston-Salem. Everything from Bach to show tunes. Late June to early August.
☐ **Brevard Music Festival,** at the Brevard Music Center. Concerts and other musical events. Last week in June to mid-August.

JULY

☐ **North Carolina State 4-H Horse Show,** at the State Fairgrounds in Raleigh. Second weekend in July.
☐ **Annual Highland Games,** atop Grandfather Mountain at MacRae Meadows. The magic of bagpipes and other age-old traditions brought by early Scottish settlers. Mid-July.

AUGUST

☐ **Shrimp Festival,** at Sneads Ferry (south of Jacksonville). A fishing village comes alive. Early August.

SEPTEMBER

☐ **Golden Gathering of Senior Adults,** in Maggie Valley. Features a golf tournament, among other events. Early September.

☐ **North Carolina Turkey Festival,** Raeford (Sandhills area). A parade down Main Street, street entertainment, and food stalls. Mid-September.

OCTOBER

☐ **Thomas Wolfe's birthday celebration,** in the writer's Asheville home. Early October.
☐ **Peanut Festival,** in Edenton. Entertainment, crafts, and homage to the lowly peanut, which is indigenous to this region.
☐ **North Carolina State Fair,** in Raleigh. One of the country's best, with a midway, horse shows, livestock events, and aromatic food stalls. October 12 to 21.

NOVEMBER

☐ **PGA World Golf Hall of Fame Pro-Am and Induction Ceremonies,** at the Pinehurst Hotel and Country Club. The world's leading golfers gather in Pinehurst. First weekend in November.
☐ **Thanksgiving Celebration,** in Blowing Rock. Bonfires, concerts, Christmas in the Park, and a host of other events. Thanksgiving weekend.

DECEMBER

☐ **Christmas Through the Ages,** at Poplar Grove Plantation, near Wilmington. Music, Victorian decorations, and crafts. December 1 to 2.
☐ **Moore County Junior Golf Classic,** Mid Pines Resort, in Southern Pines. Spotlights golfers 18 and under. December 8.
☐ **A Christmas Open House,** in Raleigh. Held in the governor's executive mansion. Early December.
☐ **Christmas Celebration** at Tyron Palace in New Bern. Traditional decorations, food, and special candlelight tours in this pre-Revolutionary mansion. December 10 to 22.

4. TIPS FOR THE DISABLED, SENIORS, SINGLES, FAMILIES & STUDENTS

FOR THE DISABLED Many hotels and restaurants in North Carolina now provide easy access for the handicapped, and some display the international wheelchair symbol in their brochures. It is always a good idea to call ahead to find out just what the situation is before you book.

The **Information Center for Individuals with Disabilities,** Fort Point Place, 27–43 Wormwood St., Boston, MA 02210 (tel. 617/727-5540), provides travel assistance and can also recommend tour operators; and **Mobility International USA,** Box 3551, Eugene, OR 97403 (tel. 503/343-1284), charges a small annual fee and provides travel information for those with disabilities. A useful book for handicapped travelers is *Access to the World, a Travel Guide for the Handicapped,* by Louise Weiss, which can be ordered from Henry Holt & Co. (tel. toll free 800/247-3912). Another useful book is the *World of Options for the 1990s* by Cindy Lewis and Susan Sygall with information about traveling with disabilities.

Amtrak will, with 24 hours' notice, provide porter service, special seating, and a substantial discount (tel. toll free 800/USA-RAIL). An organized tour package can make life on the road much easier, and two well-established firms that specialize in travel for the disabled are: **Whole Person Tours,** P.O. Box 1084, Bayonne, NJ 07002 (tel. 201/858-3400); and **Evergreen Travel Service/Wings on Wheels Tours,** 4114 198th Street, Suite 13, Lynnwood, WA 98036 (tel. 206/776-1184, or toll free 800/435-2288). Evergreen has many tours for the blind and others who want a slow-paced tour.

FOR SENIORS   Nearly all major U.S. hotel and motel chains now offer a senior citizen's discount, and you should be sure to ask for the reduction *when you make the reservation*—there may be restrictions during peak days—then be sure to carry proof of your age (driver's license, passport, etc.) when you check in. Among those chains that offer the best discounts are **Marriott Hotels** (tel. toll free 800/228-9290) for those 62 and over and **La Quinta Inns** (tel. toll free 800/531-5900) for ages 52 and over. You can save sightseeing dollars if you are 62 or over by picking up a **Golden Age Passport** from any federally operated park, recreation area, or monument. **Elderhostel,** 80 Boylston St., Boston, MA 02116 (tel. 617/426-7788 or 617/426-8056) also provides stimulating vacations at moderate prices for those over 60, with a balanced mix of learning, field trips, and free time for sightseeing. If you fancy organized tours, **AARP Travel Service** (see below) puts together terrific packages at moderate rates, and **Saga International Holidays,** 120 Boylston St., Boston, MA 02116 (tel. toll free 800/343-0273), arranges tours for single travelers over 60.

Membership in the following senior organizations also offers a wide variety of travel benefits: the **American Association of Retired Persons (AARP),** 1909 K St. NW, Washington, DC 20049 (tel. 202/662-4850); and the **National Council of Senior Citizens,** 1331 F St. NW, Washington, DC 20005 (tel. 202/347-8800).

Major sightseeing attractions and entertainments also often offer senior discounts—*be sure to ask when you buy your ticket.*

FOR SINGLES   Let's face it, if you're traveling on your own you will almost surely pay a single supplement for accommodations. One solution to the problem is to team up with another single to share a room at the doubles rate. An organization that can help with that solution is **Travel Companion Exchange,** P.O. Box 833, Amityville, NY 11701 (tel. 516/454-0880). Another solution is to book an organized tour and have the tour operator team you with another single traveler. RV vacationers can join **Loners on Wheels, Inc.,** 808 Lester St., Poplar Bluff, MO 63901 (tel. 314/785-2420), who organize caravans of singles only.

FOR FAMILIES   Amtrak offers family discount fares on specified days of the week, and in most major hotel and motel chains children below a certain age (ranging from 12 to 18) stay free when sharing a room with their parents. *Be sure to confirm this when making reservations.* Babysitters can usually be arranged by your hotel or motel, but again, you should check in advance. A useful newsletter for traveling parents is *Family Travel Times,* which publishes ten issues annually ($55) and has a call-in service for specific travel advice. Subscribe by contacting Travel with Your Children, 45 W. 18th St., New York, NY 10011 (tel. 212/206-0688). Also, be sure to ask about family discount tickets to sightseeing attractions.

Remember, also, that your trip will be a happier one if the youngsters are involved in the planning—a map and travel brochures will do wonders for a restless child! Bring along a few simple games or books to relieve boredom during long stretches of travel.

FOR STUDENTS   Before setting out, non-U.S. students should obtain an International Student Identity Card from the **Council on International Educational Exchange (CIEE),** 205 E. 42nd St., New York, NY 10017 (tel. 212/661-1414) or 312 Sutter St., Rm. 407, San Francisco, CA 94108 (tel. 415/421-3473). It will entitle you to several student discounts, although not as many as in many foreign countries. (U.S. students can't use the card in the United States.) For economical accommodations, as well as a great way to meet other traveling students, join **American Youth Hostels,** Box 37613, Washington, DC 20013-7613 (tel. 202/783-6161); for a $7 fee, they'll send a directory of all U.S. hostels. One of the leading student travel tour operators is **Contiki Holidays,** 1432 E. Katella Ave., Anaheim, CA 92805 (tel. 800/626-0611), for ages 18 through 35. **Arista Student Travel Association, Inc.,** 11 E. 44th St., New York, NY 10017 (tel. 212/687-5121, or toll free 800/356-8861), caters to ages 15 to 20. Remember, too, to *always* ask about student discount tickets to attractions.

5. ALTERNATIVE/ADVENTURE TRAVEL

Bicycle touring through a state or region is a delightful way to travel, if you have the stamina. Bikers can write for the free 50-page catalog of **Backroads Bicycle Touring,** 1516 5th St. Berkeley, CA 94710 (tel. 510/527-1555, or toll free 800/462-2848), a reliable firm organizing tours that provide a support van, lodging, and all meals. **Paradise Pedallers,** P.O. Box 34625, Charlotte, NC 28234 (tel. 704/335-8687, or toll free 800/992-3966) organizes moderately priced bicycle tours abroad and in North and South Carolina.

Camping and hiking also hold out great possibilities for the adventurous traveler. Contact the **Sierra Club,** Outing Dept., 730 Polk St., San Francisco, CA 94109 (tel. 415/776-2211), for a listing of their outings in this region. The **Appalachian Mountain Club,** 5 Joy St., Boston, MA 02108 (tel. 617/523-0636), is another good source of information.

If you plan an educational vacation, you'll reap benefits long after your return home. The **Vacation College of the University of North Carolina at Chapel Hill** provides a wide variety of study programs at moderate prices, with leading educators and lecturers. Contact Humanities Program, Campus Box 3425, University of North Carolina, Chapel Hill, NC 27599 (tel. 919/962-1544). An arts and crafts vacation can teach you a lasting skill. The **John C. Campbell Folk School,** Rt. 1, Box 14A, Dept. P.H.P., Brasstown, NC 28902 (tel. 704/837-2775, or toll free 800/562-2440), teaches traditional southern Appalachian crafts such as spinning, knitting, woodcarving, pottery, and quilting, all at moderate fees. Up in the Blue Ridge Mountains, **Penland School,** Penland, NC 28765 (tel. 704/765-2359), specializes in creating new American crafts, using the most advanced technology to create exciting objects of wood, clay, fibers, glass, iron and other metals, and paper.

For a vacation that will get you compliments galore, why not book a reducing center vacation. One of the most prominent is the **Duke University Diet and Fitness Center,** 804 W. Trinity Ave., Durham, NC 27701 (tel. 919/684-6331). Their well-respected program includes exercise, medical and psychological evaluations, swimming, gym work, classroom lectures, workshops, and all meals.

6. GETTING THERE

BY PLANE **United** (tel. toll free 800/241-6522), **Delta** (tel. toll free 800/221-1212), **American** (tel. toll free 800/433-7300), and **USAir** (tel. toll free 800/428-

4322) have direct flights into major North Carolina cities. USAir has the largest number of North Carolina destinations from out of state, though not all are direct.

While there are good regional airports, Raleigh/Durham and Charlotte airports have developed into major "hubs," with connecting flights to most major U.S. destinations.

BY TRAIN   North Carolina is on **Amtrak**'s New York–Miami and –Tampa runs, with stops in Raleigh, Hamlet, Southern Pines, Rocky Mount, and Fayetteville. The New York–Washington–New Orleans *Southern Crescent* stops in Greensboro, High Point, Salisbury, Charlotte, and Gastonia. Be sure to check for excursion fares or seasonal specials. For reservations and fare information, call toll free 800/USA-RAIL—be sure to ask about their money-saving "All Aboard America" regional fares or any other current fare specials. Amtrak also offers attractive rail/drive vacation packages in the Carolinas and Georgia.

BY BUS   **Greyhound/Trailways** has good direct service to major cities in North Carolina from out of state, with connections to almost any destination within the state. With 21-day advance purchase, they offer a discounted "Go Anywhere" fare (some day-of-the-week restrictions). For information and schedules, contact the Greyhound depot in your area; in Raleigh, 919/828-2567.

BY CAR   From Virginia and South Carolina, you can enter North Carolina on either I-95 or I-85, and I-27 and I-77 also lead in from South Carolina. The main Tennessee entry is I-40. All major border points have attractive, helpful welcome centers, some with cookout facilities and playground equipment in a parklike setting.

Before leaving home, it's a good idea to join the **American Automobile Association (AAA)**, 8111 Gatehouse Rd., Falls Church, VA 22047 (tel. 703/222-6000). For a very small fee, they provide a wide variety of services, including trip planning, accommodation and restaurant directories, and a 24-hour toll-free telephone number (800/336-4357) set up exclusively to deal with members' road emergencies.

Leading car-rental firms are represented in North Carolina's major cities and airports. For reservations and rate information, call the following toll-free telephone numbers: **Avis** (tel. toll free 800/331-1212), **Budget Car Rental** (tel. toll free 800/527-0700), **Hertz** (tel. toll free 800/654-3131), and **Thrifty Car Rental** (tel. toll free 800/367-2277).

7. GETTING AROUND

BY PLANE   **USAir** (tel. toll free 800/428-4322), has a number of in-state destinations, with connecting flights possible between most. See "Getting There," above, for destinations.

BY BUS   There are few places you can't reach by **Greyhound/Trailways** (see "Getting There," above). In Raleigh, the Greyhound Travel Information Center is at 314 W. Jones St., Raleigh, NC 27603-1391 (tel. 919/828-2567).

BY CAR   Driving is a pleasure on North Carolina's 76,000 miles of toll-free, well-maintained highways. Most interstate and U.S. highways and some state roads have rest areas with picnic tables and outdoor cooking facilities. Write to **Travel and Tourism NC,** Dept. of Commerce, 430 North Salisbury St., Raleigh, NC 27611, for the *Official North Carolina Highway Map and Guide to Points of Interest*—it's one of the easiest maps to use, plus it is filled with tourist information on the state.

Special Note: North Carolina law is quite specific that all traffic must come to a standstill when a school bus is stopped on a highway, and this is stringently enforced.

THE CAROLINAS DRIVING TIMES & DISTANCES

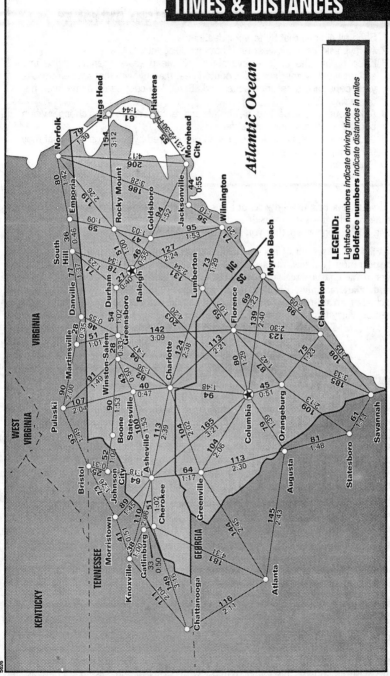

Atlantic Ocean

LEGEND:
Lightface numbers indicate driving times
Boldface numbers indicate distances in miles

FROMMER'S SMART TRAVELER: AIRFARES

1. Shop all airlines that fly to your destination.
2. Always ask for the *lowest* fare, not just discounts.
3. Keep calling the airline—availability of cheap seats changes daily, and airlines would rather sell a discounted seat than fly with that seat empty. As your departure date approaches, additional low-cost seats sometimes become available.
4. Ask about air/land packages—hotels and rental cars are often cheaper when booked in conjunction with airfares.
5. Look for special, limited-time promotions offered by major carriers that may fall within your travel period.
6. Plan ahead.

So if you see a bright-yellow school bus stopped—whether or not you see children getting on or off—save yourself a stiff fine and stop, regardless of whether you're facing it head-on or whether you're following behind it.

BY FERRY   I go out of my way just to travel on one of this state's most enjoyable transportation facilities, the system of toll-free auto ferries that ply the sounds and rivers of the coastal area. You can cross Currituck Sound from Currituck to Knotts Island, Hatteras Inlet, Pamlico River at Bayview, and Neuse River at Minnesott Beach. For an up-to-date printed ferry schedule before you leave home, write to: Director, Ferry Division, Room 120, Maritime Building, 113 Arendell St., Morehead City, NC 28557 (tel. 919/726-6446, fax 919/726-2903).

8. SUGGESTED ITINERARIES

Because it is so spread out (over 600 miles from the coast to Fontana on the Tennessee border), North Carolina invites holidays in one region at a time unless you have a minimum of three weeks in which to visit all regions. Your personal interests and time restraints will determine your own itinerary; the following are offered only as guidelines, using Raleigh, with its major airline hub, as a beginning point in the east, and Asheville, which also has good airline connections, in the west. These are *driving* itineraries and should be modified to allow more time if you're traveling by bus.

IF YOU HAVE ONE WEEK (NORTHERN COAST)

Days 1 and 2   Raleigh. Allow time for settling into your accommodations. Spend afternoon hours of the first day sightseeing in Raleigh's compact Capitol area, with its fine public buildings and museum. Your second day is ideal for a rambling trip to nearby Durham and Chapel Hill.

Days 3 and 4   Raleigh to Nags Head. Drive to Nags Head (197 miles), with a short stop in Edenton, where streets are lined with historic colonial homes. Next day, visit the Wright Brothers Memorial in Kill Devil Hills and take in the open-air drama *The Lost Colony* in Manteo on Roanoke Island.

Day 5   Nags Head to Beaufort (or Morehead City). With an early start, you can drive leisurely down the Outer Banks, with stops at villages like Hatteras and

Ocracoke, and reach Beaufort, with its quaint streets and colonial atmosphere, in time for late-afternoon sightseeing.

Day 6   Beaufort to New Bern. A short drive (35 miles) inland to New Bern allows a full day to visit Tryon Palace and Gardens and historic homes and public buildings.

Day 7   New Bern to Raleigh. Make the 112-mile journey a leisurely one through rich farmlands and prosperous towns (like Kinston and Goldsboro) of the Coastal Plain.

IF YOU HAVE ONE WEEK (SOUTHERN COAST)

Days 1 and 2   Raleigh. Same as above.

Days 3 through 5   Raleigh to Wilmington. The 123-mile drive takes you through typical rural North Carolina towns and fertile farmlands. Take a beach break in the late afternoon at nearby Wrightsville, Carolina, or Kure beaches. Devote Day 4 to Wilmington's delightful Cotton Exchange, Chandler's Wharf, and historic buildings, with perhaps a river cruise thrown in for good measure. The next day, visit Orton Plantation Gardens and Fort Fisher, with a beach stop at Kure Beach.

Day 6   Wilmington to New Bern. It's an 87-mile drive via Morehead City. Leave some sightseeing time in New Bern as suggested on Day 6 above.

Day 7   New Bern to Raleigh. Same as above.

IF YOU HAVE ONE WEEK (MOUNTAINS)

Days 1 and 2   Asheville. Allow time to settle in. Spend your second day exploring this mountain city, with a visit to the magnificent Biltmore Estate.

Days 3 and 4   Asheville Day Trips. Head for the hills via the Blue Ridge Parkway and take a short detour to visit the Folk Art Center, with its fine display of Appalachian arts and crafts and many entertainment programs. Off the parkway, take your pick and visit Mt. Mitchell, North Carolina's tallest mountain; Chimney Rock Park; Cherokee, the reservation home of this proud American Indian tribe; Maggie Valley and the Ghost Town in the Sky; Brevard, with its musical events; or Connemara Farm, longtime home of author Carl Sandburg.

Days 5 and 6   Asheville to Boone. It's a 95-mile drive through gorgeous mountain country, with plenty of time to stop in Burnsville for lunch and still arrive in time for the open-air drama *Horn in the West*. Next day, visit Blowing Rock and its Pioneer Museum and take time to ride the narrow-gauge Tweetsie Railroad.

Day 7   Boone to Asheville. Plenty of time to visit Grandfather Mountain en route.

IF YOU HAVE TWO WEEKS (SOUTHERN COAST AND MOUNTAINS)

Days 1 through 5   Raleigh to Wilmington. See "Southern Coast," above.

Day 6   Wilmington to Charlotte. Get an early start for this 345-mile drive and treat yourself to dinner in one of Charlotte's fine restaurants.

Day 7   Charlotte to Asheville. Spend an hour or two at Carowinds before setting off on the 115-mile drive, and plan a leisurely evening—you'll have done a lot of driving since leaving the coast!

Days 8 through 11   Asheville. Same as Days 1 through 4 in "Mountains," above.

Day 12   Asheville to Winston-Salem. After the 144-mile drive, spend the late afternoon or evening hours strolling the streets of historic Old Salem.

Day 13   Winston-Salem. Return to Old Salem to visit a building that may not have been open the evening before. Lunch on traditional Southern dishes in this interesting Moravian settlement.

Day 14   Winston-Salem to Raleigh. The 104-mile drive gives you time for a short detour from Greensboro to visit the Guilford County Courthouse National Military Park, site of one of the closing battles of the Revolutionary War.

IF YOU HAVE THREE WEEKS [COAST, MOUNTAINS, AND SANDHILLS]

Days 1 through 6   Raleigh to Nags Head to New Bern. See "Northern Coast," above.

Days 7 through 9   New Bern to Wilmington. See Days 3 through 5 of "Southern Coast," above.

Day 10   Wilmington to Charlotte. See Day 7 in "Southern Coast and Mountains," above.

Days 11 through 17   Charlotte to Asheville to Boone. See Days 1 through 4 of "Mountains," above. If it suits your fancy, spend one day mining for rubies in the Cowee Valley, just north of Franklin (about 50 miles south of Asheville).

Day 18   Boone to Winston-Salem. An 85-mile drive, with time in the afternoon and evening to explore Old Salem.

Days 19 and 20   Winston-Salem to Pinehurst or Southern Pines. The 93-mile drive takes you into the heart of the Sandhills, with a day for golfing or rambling through the rural potteries for which the area is noted.

Day 21   Pinehurst to Raleigh. A leisurely 71-mile drive, with time for afternoon sightseeing before leaving the state.

9. WHERE TO STAY & DINE

ACCOMMODATIONS

You can find hotel accommodations in just about any price range in Georgia and the Carolinas, from the most expensive chain hotels to a variety of budget motel chains. Aside from price, there is also a wide choice in your *type* of accommodation—country inns, mountain lodges, tourist homes, or motels and hotels with distinctive regional flavor.

When you're making your plans, consider reserving a spot in a hotel or inn representative of the area. That means a beachfront resort in Myrtle Beach, a delightful historic inn in Charleston, an uptown hostelry in Atlanta, or perhaps a room with a view in the Great Smoky Mountains or along North Carolina's Outer Banks. And, thankfully, you don't have to spend a fortune for a room; I've selected plenty of terrific value-minded operations in each area.

I've spared you the cheapest of the roadside lodgings—they're okay in a pinch, for a few hours of rest enroute to something better. You know their names: Super 8, Motel 6, Budgetel, and their clones. However, I do suggest a number of excellent budget choices. One of the best is **Fairfield Inn by Marriott** (tel. toll free

FROMMER'S SMART TRAVELER: HOTELS

VALUE-CONSCIOUS TRAVELERS SHOULD TAKE ADVANTAGE OF THE FOLLOWING:

1. Weekend rates, which at some locations cover Friday, Saturday, and Sunday nights, with reductions of 30% to 50%.
2. Off-season rate reductions at coastal and mountain resorts that are often as much as 50% to 70% lower than in-season rates.
3. Rate reductions for seniors, families, and active-duty military personnel.
4. Special-interest package rates, which sometimes include greens fees, entrance fees, and some meals.

800/228-2800); several are listed in the coming pages and even more are out there, so call ahead and see if one will fit into your itinerary. Another chain of well-respected inns, also by Marriott, is **Residence Inn** (tel. toll free 800/331-3131). These suite accommodations are equipped with separate living and sleeping areas, full kitchens with complete utensils, and often a fireplace or second bedroom. Also noteworthy are **Guest Quarters Suite Hotels** (tel. toll free 800/424-2900). They are the most upscale of the suite accommodations—although Embassy Suites will argue the point with some success.

Be sure to plan ahead. Many chains have advance (as much as 30 days) rates you should take advantage of. AAA also enjoys guaranteed rates at many hotels, so ask about that, too.

Campers will find very good facilities throughout North Carolina, with fees ranging from $9 to $14 per night. RV campers will, however, find hookups only at state recreation facilities. For detailed information, contact: Division of Parks & Recreation, Dept. of Environment, Health & Natural Resources, P.O. Box 27687, Raleigh, NC 27611 (tel. 919/733-4181). The excellent *Official North Carolina Highway Map and Guide to Points of Interest* (see "Getting Around," above) also has extensive information about national and state parks and forests.

A WORD OF WARNING Just because *you* may not have thought of North Carolina as a prime tourist area, don't be deceived into believing that you can come without reserving ahead. I once arrived "out of season" at the coast, only to find that the nearest room to be had was 40 miles inland—because of the annual mullet fishing tournament! So, no matter when you plan to travel in the state, do yourself a favor and reserve your accommodations.

 FROMMER'S SMART TRAVELER: RESTAURANTS

1. Plan your main meal at lunch—prices are lower than in the evening, and in many top restaurants the menu is much the same.
2. Take a picnic, with take-outs from fast-food shops or your own fixings from local grocers (a terrific way to meet the locals!).
3. Nothing runs up a restaurant bill as fast as wine or other alcoholic beverages. Save your alcoholic consumption for before the meal or afterward either from your own supply or in a bar, where prices are lower per drink.

DINING

Georgia and the Carolinas are known for good, home-cooked, "down-home" cuisine, and you'll find it in small roadside eateries, inner-city restaurants, and posh top-of-the-line restaurants. Prices at most are surprisingly moderate.

Restaurants range from fancy establishments that rival the best in New York to plain roadhouse cafés. At either end of the spectrum, you're likely to find well-prepared, tasty North Carolina specialties: barbecued pork (the spicy, minced-up kind that's unique to this state; the Parker's chain serves some of the best barbecue anywhere at very moderate prices); country ham; fresh seafood served with hush puppies (cornmeal batter-fried in deep fat); and always grits served with breakfast (don't knock them until you've tried them served with globs of melting butter). In the following chapters I've pointed out my own personal finds, but you stand a very good chance of finding a "special" place if you ask about local favorites.

 NORTH CAROLINA

American Express The main American Express Travel Agency is at 528 Forum VI, Northline Ave., Greensboro, NC (tel. 919/299-5922). Check local telephone directories for addresses and telephone numbers in Raleigh, Asheville, Greenville, and Charlotte.

Area Codes Raleigh, Winston-Salem, Nags Head, and Wilmington (Wrightsville Beach), 919; Asheville and Charlotte, 704.

Business Hours Banking hours are Monday to Friday 9am to 3pm; some also open for a half day on Saturday. Office hours are generally 9am to 5pm Monday to Friday, and shopping hours vary with location, usually 9 or 10am to 6pm, Monday to Saturday. Some shops remain open until 9pm or later (especially in shopping centers) on specified days of the week, and many are now open for shorter hours on Sunday. Post-office hours are Monday to Friday 8:30am to 5pm, 8:30am to noon on Saturday.

Climate See "When to Go—Climate and Events," earlier in this chapter.

Crime See "Safety," below.

Emergencies Dial 911 for police, medical, and other emergency services. You can also dial 0 and ask the operator to connect you to emergency services. Travelers Aid can also be helpful—check local telephone directories.

Etiquette Southerners are especially mindful of courteous behavior, and a gracious "Thank you" or "Please" will yield big dividends. Use good old common sense and all the manners you can remember.

Hitchhiking Illegal on state, U.S., and interstate highways.

Information See "Information," above.

Liquor Laws You must be 21 to order any alcoholic beverage. Beer and wine are sold in grocery stores, but all package liquor is sold through local government-controlled stores, commonly called "ABC" (Alcoholic Beverage Control Commission) stores. The availability of mixed drinks is determined by each county.

Maps As mentioned above, the *Official North Carolina Highway Map and Guide to Points of Interest* is great. You'll need to write to the Department of Commerce for a copy (see "Getting Around," above, for the address) or pick one up at a state visitors' center.

Newspapers/Magazines *The State* is a weekly magazine available at most newsstands, a folksy, down-home publication that reflects the Tarheel way of life; *North Carolina Folklore Journal,* is available by subscription (contact N.C.

Folklore Society, Dept. of English, Appalachian State University, Boone, NC 28608, for publication schedule and subscription rates). The state's major dailies are the *News & Observer* (Raleigh) and *The Charlotte Observer* (Charlotte) as well as local papers in Asheville, Durham, Fayetteville, Greensboro, and Winston-Salem.

Police See "Emergencies," above.

Safety Although rural areas and small towns in the southern United States are relatively safe, you should observe the same precautions in large cities that you would in any international metropolitan city: Do not leave valuables in an unlocked, parked car; avoid unlighted streets, public parks, and unattended parking lots after dark; when driving through depressed areas of large cities, be sure to lock your car doors; and *never* carry large sums of cash (use traveler's checks) or jewelry on your person.

Taxes North Carolina has a 6% sales tax.

Time North Carolina is on eastern standard time. Daylight saving time is in effect from April through October.

CHAPTER 2

THE NORTH CAROLINA COAST

1. **NAGS HEAD & ENVIRONS**

2. **CAPE HATTERAS NATIONAL SEASHORE**

3. **BEAUFORT, MOREHEAD CITY, NEW BERN & ENVIRONS**

4. **WILMINGTON & ENVIRONS**

The beaches along North Carolina's Atlantic coastline are, to say the least, unusual. Many of them, in fact, are offshore on the long string of narrow islands that make up the Outer Banks. And what beaches they are! Wide strands and breathtakingly high dunes interspersed with resort centers.

WHERE TO STAY Take your choice: headquarter in Nags Head or Duck, to explore the northern end of the coast; in historic old Beaufort, Morehead City, or along the string of beaches known collectively as Atlantic Beach, for New Bern and other area sightseeing; or in Wilmington, for plantation and garden sightseeing, a visit to Fort Fisher, and fine beaches. For a comprehensive listing of motels, accommodations (including campgrounds), restaurants, and attractions, write to individual tourist information agencies listed in each area.

Another option is camping. There are campgrounds at various spots, but you should know in advance that they're flat, sandy areas with no shade and that you'll need tent stakes longer than you'd normally use. Also, no hookups are provided. Sites are on a first-come, first-served basis, and the maximum stay is 14 days from mid-April through September 10. Fees are $11 nightly for up to six people at all sites.

For private campgrounds in the area, which do have hookups, call the tourist offices listed in each section below, and they'll supply full information.

1. NAGS HEAD & ENVIRONS

197 miles from Raleigh; 234 miles from Wilmington

GETTING THERE By Plane The nearest airport to Nags Head is 80 miles northwest at Norfolk, Va., serviced by **American** (tel. toll free 800/433-7300), **Continental** (tel. toll free 800/525-0280), **Delta** (tel. toll free 800/221-1212), **TWA** (tel. toll free 800/221-2000), and **USAir** (tel. toll free 800/428-4322).

By Train The nearest **Amtrak** (tel. toll free 800/USA-RAIL) stop is Raleigh, on its New York–Miami and –Tampa routes.

By Bus **Greyhound/Trailways** serves Elizabeth City, one hour away.

By Car From Virginia and points north, reach Nags Head via N.C. 156; from Raleigh, via N.C. 64; from Wilmington, via the Cedar Island ferry (see "Cape Hatteras National Seashore," below). N.C. 12 runs the length of the Outer Banks, from Ocracoke to Duck.

ESSENTIALS The **area code** is 919. For sightseeing particulars, contact the **Outer Banks Chamber of Commerce**, P.O. Box 1757, Kill Devil Hills, NC

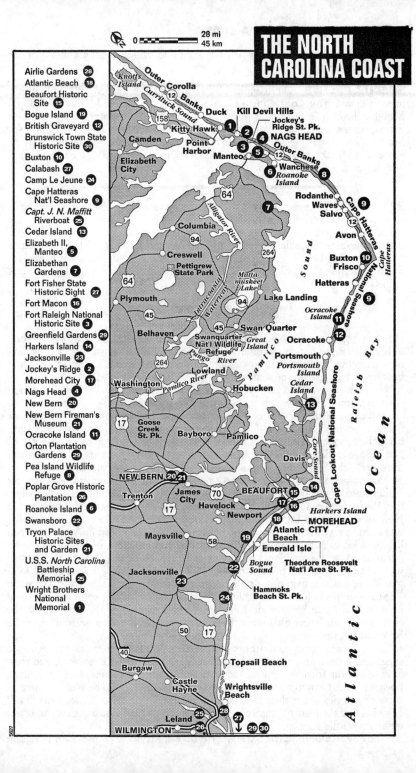

THE NORTH CAROLINA COAST

0   28 mi
     45 km

Knotts Island
Outer Corolla
Banks
Currituck Sound
Duck
Kill Devil Hills
158
Jockey's Ridge St. Pk.
Kitty Hawk
NAGS HEAD
Camden
Point Harbor
Manteo
Outer Banks
Elizabeth City
Wanchese
Roanoke Island
64
Columbia
Rodanthe
Waves
Salvo
Cape Hatteras
Avon
94
Creswell
Pettigrew State Park
Mattamuskeet Lake
Buxton
Frisco
Sound
Cape Hatteras
64
Plymouth
Lake Landing
Cape Hatteras National Seashore
45
94
Intracoastal Waterway
Ocracoke Island
Belhaven
45
Swan Quarter
Swanquarter Nat'l Wildlife Refuge
Great Island Ch.
Ocracoke
264
Pungo River
Pamlico
Portsmouth
Portsmouth Island
Lowland
Washington
Pamlico River
Hobucken
Cedar Island
Raleigh Bay
Goose Creek St. Pk.
17
Bayboro
Pamlico
Cape Lookout National Seashore
Core Sound
Davis
NEW BERN 20 21
Trenton
James City
70
BEAUFORT
17
Havelock
Harkers Island
Newport
MOREHEAD CITY
Atlantic Beach
Maysville
58
Emerald Isle
Theodore Roosevelt Nat'l Area St. Pk.
Jacksonville
Bogue Sound
Hammoks Beach St. Pk.
50
17
40
Burgaw
Topsail Beach
Castle Hayne
Wrightsville Beach
Leland
WILMINGTON

Atlantic Ocean

27948 (tel. 919/441-8144). They will also send information about accommodations and outdoor activities.

SPECIAL EVENTS   On Roanoke Island, where it all happened,   ✪ Paul Green's moving drama *The Lost Colony* is presented in the Waterside Theater, 8:30pm Monday through Saturday mid-June to late Aug. It's the country's oldest outdoor drama, running since 1937. All seats are reserved (Waterside Theater, P.O. Box 40, Manteo, NC 27954; tel. 919/473-3414, or toll free 800/488-5012 for VISA or MasterCard bookings) and cost about $10 for adults; $9 for seniors, the military, and handicapped; $4 for those under 12.

Nags Head is the largest resort in the Outer Banks area. Its odd name, according to local legend, comes from the practice of wily land pirates who in the old days would hang lanterns from the necks of ponies, parade them along the dunes at night, and lure unsuspecting ships onto shoals where they ran aground and had their cargos promptly stripped by the waiting robbers. Another theory holds that it was named for the highest point of Scilly Island, the last sight English colonists had of their homeland.

WHAT TO SEE & DO

However it got its name, Nags Head has been one of the most popular beach resorts in North Carolina for over a century. The town itself is a somewhat tacky collection of nondescript beach houses, motels, and modern hotels, but it has one of the finest beaches to be found in the state.

Needless to say, beach activities and fishing head the list here. Do exercise caution when swimming, however, for rip tides can be very strong in these parts.

Jockey's Ridge, north of Nags Head, is the highest sand dune on the East Coast. Its smooth, sandy, 138-foot-high slopes are popular with the sand-skiing and hang-gliding crowd, and since it is now a state park, it's open to all. Also north of Nags Head at **Kill Devil Hills** (named for a particularly potent rum once shipped from here), the Wright brothers made that historic first flight back in 1903.

Roanoke Island, between the Outer Banks and the mainland, is where Sir Walter Raleigh's colony of more than 100 men, women, and children settled when they landed here in 1585 in what was to be England's first permanent foothold in the New World. Virginia Dare, granddaughter of the little band's governor, John White, was born that year, the first child of English parents to be born in America. When White sailed back to England on the ships that had brought the settlers, it was his intention to secure additional provisions and perhaps more colonists, then return within the year. Instead, because of political events in England, it wasn't until 1590 that White was able to get back to Roanoke. And what he found there was a mystery: The rude houses he had helped build were all dismantled, and the entire area enclosed by a high palisade he later described as "very fortlike." At the entrance of the enclosure, crude letters spelled out the word "CROATAN" on a post from which the bark had been peeled.

Since their prearranged distress signal—a cross—was not there, and no evidence suggested violence, his conclusion was that those he'd left on Roanoke Island must have joined the friendly Croatan Indian tribe. An unhappy chain of circumstances, however, forced him to set sail for England before a search could be made. Despite all sorts of theories about their fate, no link was ever established between the "lost" colonists and the Native Americans, nor was there ever any clue unearthed to reveal exactly what did happen.

The **Fort Raleigh National Historic Site** at Roanoke was named in 1941, and its visitor center tells the story in exhibits and film. Paul Green's symphonic drama *The Lost Colony* brings it to life in the amphitheater that has been constructed at the edge of Roanoke Sound.

THE WRIGHT BROTHERS NATIONAL MEMORIAL   A little to the north, on U.S. 158 Bypass, at Kill Devil Hills, the   ✪ **Wright Brothers National Memorial** is open to the public for $2 per person or $4 a car; seniors and children under 16 are admitted for free. Both the hangar and Orville and Wilbur's living quarters have been restored, and the visitor center holds a replica of that first airplane, as well as exhibits that tell the story of the two brothers who came here on vacations from their Dayton, Ohio, bicycle business to turn their dream into reality.

MANTEO & ROANOKE ISLAND   From Whalebone Junction, U.S. 64-264 leads to   ✪ **Roanoke Island** and the village of **Manteo.** Four miles west, you'll reach **Fort Raleigh National Historic Site,** where the old fort has been excavated and reconstructed just as it stood in 1585 (see above). The visitor center (tel. 919/473-5772) is a fascinating first stop, with a museum and audiovisual program to acquaint visitors with the park story. From mid-June to late August it's open from 9am to 8pm; the rest of the year it closes at 5pm.

If at all possible, don't miss **The Lost Colony** at the Waterside Theater (see "Special Events," above). The nearby **Elizabethan Gardens,** as well as the Tudor-style auxiliary buildings, remind us that this was the first connection between Elizabethan England and what was to become the United States of America. There's a $2.50 charge to enter the gardens (tel. 919/473-3234), except for children under 12, who enter for free.

Also when you're in Manteo, don't miss one of North Carolina's newest state historic sites, the **Elizabeth II** (tel. 919/473-1144), moored across from the nicely renovated waterfront. This 69-foot-long three-masted bark, a composite design of 16th-century ships, was built with private funds for the 400th anniversary commemoration of the 1584 and 1587 Roanoke voyages in 1984. Before boarding her, enter the visitor center, where exhibits describe the tense political climate between Protestant England and Catholic Spain, as well as Native American life on the island. A slide presentation realistically depicts life aboard such a ship from the perspective of the voyagers. Tuesday through Saturday, mid-June to late August, living-history interpreters portray roles of colonists and mariners. The site is open April through October daily from 10am to 6pm, and November through March, Tuesday through Sunday from 10am to 4pm; it's closed on major holidays. Admission is $3 for adults, $2 for seniors, and $1.50 for students.

INLAND TO EDENTON   About an hour and a half away from Nags Head (take U.S. 64, turn right at N.C. 37, then left when you reach N.C. 32), a later phase of U.S. history is preserved at **Edenton,** a lovely old town whose streets are lined with homes built by the planters and merchants who settled along the Albemarle Sound. The women of Edenton held their own "tea party" in 1774, one of the first recorded instances of American women taking political action. Visit the new **Historic Edenton Visitor Center** (tel. 919/482-3663) at 108 North Broad Street (signs are posted throughout the town), to view a free 14-minute slide show, and purchase a historic-district map for a nominal fee. The visitor center is open Monday through Saturday from 9am to 5pm and Sunday from 1 to 5pm; it's closed on major holidays. Guided tours of four historic buildings—the 1767 Chowan County Courthouse, the 1725 Cupola House, the 1773 James Iredell House State Historic Site, and restored St. Paul's Episcopal Church—are conducted Monday through Saturday from 10am to 2:30pm, and Sunday at 2:30pm. The package tour is $5 for adults, $2.50 for ages 6 to 18; admission to individual buildings is $3 for adults, $1.50 for ages 6 to 18.

WHERE TO STAY

While the beaches are lined with cottage rentals, many of them are spoken for on a year-to-year basis, so it is absolutely essential to make your reservations well in advance. I'll list a few in the hotel-motel category in this area, but if you'd like to settle down for a week or more, your best bet is to write the **Outer Banks Chamber of Commerce** (see "Essentials," above). Nags Head, Kill Devil Hills, and Kitty Hawk are so close together that you can choose your accommodation by style and facilities rather than by location. Duck, about 18 miles north of Nags Head, is the site of an exceptional seaside hotel well worth the short drive.

Another option is camping (see introduction to this chapter). For information about private campgrounds in the area, contact the Outer Banks Chamber of Commerce (see "Essentials," above).

EXPENSIVE

SANDERLING INN RESORT, Box 319Y, Duck, NC 27949. Tel. 919/261-4111. 56 rms, 4 suites. A/C MINIBAR TV TEL **Directions:** 18 miles north of Nags Head on N.C. 12.
$ Rates (including continental breakfast and wine and hors d'oeuvre service): Winter, spring, fall, $90–$130 single or double; $200–$250 suite. Summer $145–$190 single or double; $200–$250 suite. DISC, MC, V. **Parking:** Free.

The Sanderling Inn is wishful thinking fulfilled for those of us who remember the Outer Banks as a haven of rambling wooden hotels with old-fashioned hospitality. It is surrounded only by sand dunes and a wide beachfront, with glimpses of private homes in the distance. Not a neon sign in sight, nor will there ever be, since the Sanderling is situated on 12 acres of a private residential community bordered by the 6,500-acre Audubon sanctuary to the north. Wide verandas wrap around both floors of the two-story wooden building, and rocking chairs aplenty invite leisurely hours of "rockin' and thinkin'."

Rooms are very spacious, all beautifully decorated and furnished. Public rooms, many with fireplaces, are graciously appointed, and the focal point of the Green Gallery is a magnificent portfolio of Audubon prints. Ramps provide wheelchair access to all facilities (including the beach), and there are periodic barbecues on a beachfront sundeck.

Sanderling restaurant and bar, adjacent to the inn itself, is a handsome 1899 building that was once a Coast Guard station, now a registered historic landmark.

Room, valet and concierge services, airport transportation; picnic lunches packed by the restaurant; organized sightseeing tours to Roanoke Island, Cape Hatteras, and Edenton; and a scenic cruise along the Outer Banks are all available. Other facilities include an outdoor and indoor swimming pool, sauna, steam room, fitness room, tennis courts, and membership to a nearby golf club.

MODERATE/BUDGET

BEACON MOTOR LODGE, 2617 S. Virginia Dare Trail (P.O. Box 729), Nags Head, NC 27959. Tel. 919/441-5501, or toll free 800/441-4804. 42 rms, 5 suites, 20 efficiencies (including some cottages and apartments). A/C TV TEL
$ Rates: In-season, $65–$85 single or double. Off-season, $35–$70 single or double. AE, MC, V. **Parking:** Free. **Closed:** Late Oct–late Mar.
The Beacon is a low, rambling complex offering rooms, efficiencies, cottages, and apartments. There are two swimming pools, and tennis and golf privileges at nearby

facilities. The comfortably furnished rooms are decorated in soft greens and blues and have refrigerators. There's a children's playground and coin-operated laundry; several restaurants are located nearby. All rooms have refrigerators and some have microwave ovens.

COMFORT INN, 8031 Old Oregon Inlet Rd., Nags Head, NC 27959. Tel. 919/441-6315; or toll free 800/334-3302 (direct to hotel), or 800/228-5150. 105 rms. A/C TV TEL
$ Rates (including continental breakfast): $34–$135 single or double. AE, CB, DC, DISC, MC, V.
Once a Best-Western affiliate, this new Comfort Inn offers fine value in a good locale. The hotel sits at the south end of Nags Head, where U.S. 158 and U.S. 64 meet. It's a seven-story hotel with some oceanfront accommodations. The restaurant wasn't operating when I visited, but you can get a cold beer and something light in the pub. The beach can be rather private, and there are tennis courts and a pool.

COMFORT INN–NORTH OCEANFRONT, Kill Devil Hills, NC 27948. Tel. 919/480-2600, or toll free 800/854-5286. Fax 919/480-2873. 122 rms. A/C TV TEL
$ Rates (including continental breakfast): $35–$135 single or double. AE, CB, DC, DISC, ER, MC, V.
A smart, moderate choice, this is in a three-story building featuring 16 oceanfront balconied rooms. There's a complimentary manager's cocktail party on Thursdays. Some rooms are reserved for nonsmokers, and a few are handicapped accessible. Rooms have one king-size or two double beds; some also have microwave ovens.

DAYS INN, 3919 Croatan Hwy., P.O. Box 1096, Kitty Hawk, NC 27949. Tel. 919/261-4888, or toll free 800/325-2525. 98 rms. A/C TV TEL **Directions:** Milepost 4.5, on U.S. 158 bypass.
$ Rates: $35–$95 single or double, depending on season. Discount for seniors. AE, DC, MC, V. **Parking:** Free.
One block from the ocean, its nicely appointed guest rooms have cable TV and in-room movies and are wheelchair-accessible. There's a small pool, and sightseeing is easy, with the Wright Brothers Memorial less than five miles away.

DAYS INN OCEANFRONT–WILBUR & ORVILLE WRIGHT, 101 N. Virginia Dare Trail (P.O. Box 3189), Kitty Hawk, NC 27948. Tel. 919/441-7211, or toll free 800/325-2525. 50 rms and efficiencies. A/C TV TEL **Directions:** Milepost 8.25 on N.C. 12.
$ Rates: May–Aug, $55–$125 single or double. Sept–Apr, $45–$85 single or double. Discounts for seniors. AE, DC, MC, V. **Parking:** Free.
This lovely oceanfront hotel has a cozy pine-paneled lobby, complete with fireplace. In addition to its private beach, there's a pool, and the attractive guest units are spacious and come with refrigerators. The staff is friendly and accommodating.

NAGS HEAD INN, 4701 S. Virginia Dare Trail (P.O. Box 1599), Nags Head, NC 27959. Tel. 919/441-0454. 100 rms, 1 suite. A/C TV TEL
$ Rates: May to early Sept, $65–$145 single or double. Early Sept to Apr, $35–$75 single or double. 10% discount for stays of 6 nights or more. MC, V.
This oceanfront motel has nicely done-up guestrooms with contemporary decor and furnishings. Those facing the water have balconies, and there's a small heated pool, a whirlpool, and golf privileges at nearby courses. Rooms have refrigerators and are wheelchair-accessible.

QUALITY INN JOHN YANCEY, P.O. Box 422, Kill Devil Hills, NC 27948.

Tel. 919/441-7141. Fax 919/441-4277. 108 rms. A/C TV TEL **Directions:** Milepost 10, on Beach Road.

$ Rates: $59 single or double. Extra person $10. Children under 12 stay free with parents. AE, DC, DISC, MC, V. **Parking:** Free.

⑤ The moderate price range is a joy at the John Yancey, as are the efficiencies, which come completely equipped, right down to the coffeepot. The rooms are cheerful, and guests can enjoy the swimming pool. The management here is especially friendly and helpful.

QUALITY INN SEA RANCH, P.O. Box 325, Kill Devil Hills, NC 27959.
Tel. 919/441-7126, or toll free 800/334-4737. Fax 919/441-3795. 50 rms, 28 timeshare units nearby. A/C TV TEL **Directions:** Milepost 7, on Beach Road.

$ Rates: Jun–Aug, $85–$125 single or double. Sept–May, $35–$60 single or double. AE, DC, DISC, MC, V.

The Sea Ranch has an oceanfront tower with glass-enclosed balconies and rooms decorated with flair. Each has two double beds or one king-size bed, and there are efficiencies with mini kitchens. Oceanfront apartments have two bedrooms, two baths (one with full Jacuzzi), full kitchens, and balconies. There's a beauty shop, Nautilus equipment, an enclosed pool with a sliding-glass roof, and an indoor tennis club. Golf is just minutes away on two 18-hole championship courses. Dinner is served by candlelight in the window-walled Top of the Dune dining room, and there's dancing and entertainment in the cocktail lounge. Lunch is not served at the property.

TRANQUIL HOUSE INN, Queen Elizabeth St. (P.O. Box 2045), Manteo, NC 27954. Tel. 919/473-1404, or toll free 800/458-7069. 26 rms, 2 suites. A/C TV TEL **Directions:** Whalebone Junction on N.C. 158 in South Nags Head is signposted for Manteo, six miles on Hwy. 64/264W. Inn is on the harborfront (turn right at first traffic light on Sir Walter Raleigh Street).

$ Rates: $59–$125 single or double; $59–$148 suite. Children under 16 stay free with parents. Senior discount and special package prices. AE, DC, MC, V.

This charming waterfront inn, built in recent years, would have felt right at home in 19th-century Manteo. Its front porches face the water, and there's even a lookout room. Rooms are spacious and furnished with reproductions of antiques, and guests are greeted with flowers and a complimentary bottle of wine. Each room also has a well-lighted desk and wheelchair access.

WHERE TO DINE

FISHERMAN'S WHARF, Wanchees. Tel. 473-5205.
Cuisine: SEAFOOD. **Reservations:** Not required.
$ Prices: Complete meals $11–$20. MC, V.
Open: Lunch Mon–Sat noon–3pm; dinner Mon–Sat 3–9pm.

This restaurant at the south end of Roanoke Island, on the waterfront, serves the freshest seafood, steaks, and chicken at moderate prices, and overlooks the harbor. It also has a connected retail seafood market.

GOOMBAY'S GRILLE & RAW BAR, Milepost 7.5, Kill Devil Hills. Tel. 441-6001.
Cuisine: SEAFOOD/CARIBBEAN. **Reservations:** Not required. **Directions:** Go one block south of Sea Ranch; look for mile markers.
$ Prices: Main courses $8.95–$11.95. DISC, MC, V.
Open: Daily 11:30am–2am.

This is one of the most fun places you'll find on the Outer Banks. The decor is lively with Caribbean colors, fish paintings, knotty pine tongue-and-groove walls, and fans hanging from the knotty pine ceiling. Adjoining the main dining room is a raw bar where you can order snow crab legs, a pile of crayfish, and spiced steamed shrimp. On the main menu are Hatteras chowder (a local clear broth with potatoes, onions, celery, and clams), johnnycakes stuffed with cheese, fried banana peppers served with spicy fruit chutney, and jalapeño crab balls. They smoke their own fish here. For lunch, consider the burger boat, a seafood taco, or West Indian curried chicken. If you're game, try the tender marinated alligator tail meat as an appetizer.

OWENS' RESTAURANT, Milepost 17, on Beach Rd., Nags Head. Tel. 441-7309.
 Cuisine: SEAFOOD/BEEF. **Reservations:** Not accepted.
$ **Prices:** Appetizers $6–$6.50; main courses $14–$19. AE, DC, MC, V.
 Open: Mid-Mar to Nov, daily 5–10pm. **Closed:** Thanksgiving Day.

The Owens family has owned and operated this excellent restaurant for over 40 years, and it is one of those local favorites that just keep getting better. This homey spot is decorated with nautical relics and artifacts from the Outer Banks' "olden days." They offer a children's menu. You can enjoy nightly entertainment and your favorite libation in the Station Keepers Lounge.

THE THAI ROOM, Milepost 8.5, on Beach Road, Nags Head. Tel. 441-1180.
 Cuisine: THAI/CHINESE. **Reservations:** Not required.
$ **Prices:** Complete meals $6–$15. AE, MC, V.
 Open: Lunch Mon–Sat noon–2:30pm; dinner daily 5–10pm. **Closed:** Jan–Feb, major holidays.
This small, charming restaurant has a delightful decor, and the atmosphere is casual. Asian specialties really star here, but steaks and chicken are also quite good. There's also a money-saving children's menu.

2. CAPE HATTERAS NATIONAL SEASHORE

From Whalebone Junction in South Nags Head, the Cape Hatteras National Seashore stretches 70 miles down the Outer Banks barrier islands. The drive along N.C. 12 (about 4½ hours) takes you through a wildlife refuge and pleasant villages, past gorgeous sand beaches, and on to Buxton and the Cape Hatteras Lighthouse, the tallest on the coast. The lighthouse has stood since 1870 as a beacon for ships passing through these treacherous waters, which have earned the title "Graveyard of the Atlantic," claiming more than 1,500 victims of foul weather, strong rip currents, and shifting shoals. This is where the ironclad Union gunboat *Monitor* went down in a storm in December 1862.

At the little village of Hatteras, a free auto ferry makes the 40-minute crossing to Ocracoke Island, where more than 5,000 acres, including 16 miles of beach, are preserved by the National Park Service for recreation. It's also where the pirate Edward Teach (Blackbeard) met his end. From the southern end of the island, a toll auto ferry takes you on a 2¼-hour voyage across Pamlico Sound to Cedar Island.

The National Seashore is best explored in an all-day trip, or several half-day trips, from a Nags Head base. Try to give yourself plenty of time for swimming, fishing, or just walking along the sand, and to take in the breathtaking view from the top of Cape Hatteras Lighthouse. Stop for lunch or to shop, and to get to know the marvelous people who call this necklace of sand home. The hardy "Bankers" can recount tales of heroism at sea, and tell you about the ghostly light that bobs over Teach's Hole, and the wild ponies that have roamed Ocracoke Island for over 400 years—all in a soft accent that some say harks back to Devon, England, home base of a band of shipwrecked sailors who came ashore here and stayed.

FROM NAGS HEAD TO HATTERAS

Turn left off N.C. 12 about eight miles south of U.S. 158 to reach **Coquina Beach,** where there are bath shelters, lifeguards (from mid-June to Labor Day), picnic shelters, and beach walks guided by National Parks Service naturalists.

Farther south, across Oregon Inlet, the **Pea Island Wildlife Refuge** attracts birdwatchers from all over the country to see the snow geese in winter, and the wading shore and upland birds in summer. There's a parking area and overlook.

All along N.C. 12, you'll see places to pull off and park to reach the beaches, which are hidden from view by huge protective sand dunes. A word of warning: *Don't* try to park anywhere else—the sands are very soft and it's easy to get stuck!

Note: Whether you're camping or just stopping at beaches where there are no lifeguards, remember that you should always keep in mind that tides and currents along the Outer Banks are *very* strong, and ocean swimming can be dangerous at times.

When you get to Buxton, turn left off N.C. 12 to see the **Cape Hatteras Lighthouse.** Its rotating duplex beacon has a 1,000-watt, 250,000-candlepower lamp in each side, and is visible for 20 miles.

The little village of ✪ **Hatteras** exists now, as it has from the 1700s, as a fishing center, and there are large commercial and sport fleets that operate from its docks and marinas. In the spring and fall the boats bring in catches of sea trout, king and Spanish mackerel, bluefish, red drum, and striped bass; in summer, most of the action is offshore, where blue marlin and other billfish are in plentiful supply. If you're interested in doing some fishing yourself, the Outer Banks Chamber of Commerce (see "Nags Head and Environs," above), can supply a list of charter boats available, as well as fishing information. Even if you don't fish, it's fun to watch the boats come in between 4 and 6pm.

WHERE TO STAY

COMFORT INN–HATTERAS ISLAND, 12th and Old Lighthouse Rd., Oceanside, Buxton, NC 27920. Tel. 919/995-6100, or toll free 800/228-5150. 60 rms. A/C TV TEL

$ Rates: $45–$85 single or double. AE, DC, DISC, MC, V.

This small, attractive hotel has several inviting features, such as a pool and laundry room. All the rooms have refrigerators and one king-size or two double beds.

WHERE TO DINE

THE CHANNEL BASS, N.C. 12, Hatteras. Tel. 986-2250.
 Cuisine: SEAFOOD. **Reservations:** Not required. **Directions:** Go 12 miles south of the lighthouse.
$ Prices: Appetizers $2.95–$8.95; main courses $8.95–$24.95. AE, MC, V.
Open: Apr–Nov, dinner daily 5–10pm.

The clam chowder here will have you calling for seconds. In fact, all their seafood is fresh and cooked to perfection. The menu is semi-à la carte, and portions are so ample that the steamed sampler appetizer (oysters, clams, and shrimp) could well do you as a full meal. A specialty is their fried or broiled fresh local fish.

OCRACOKE ISLAND

From Hatteras, a free auto ferry crosses the inlet to ✪ **Ocracoke Island** in 40 minutes; however, especially during the peak summer tourist season, be prepared to wait in line to board the ferry. Ocracoke has shown up on maps as far back as the late 1500s, when Sir Walter Raleigh's Roanoke Island party landed here. It is rumored to have been the last headquarters of Blackbeard, who was killed here. The wily pirate, after years of terrorizing merchant ships along the Atlantic Coast, had made his peace with the British Crown in 1712, and had received a full pardon from the king. Soon thereafter, however, he came out of retirement and began again preying on ships from the Caribbean to the Virginia Capes, working hand in glove with colonial governor Charles Eden and colonial secretary Tobias Knight. In 1718, Lt. Richard Maynard of the British Royal Navy captured Blackbeard's ship and crew in Ocracoke Inlet, and killed the pirate in a bloody duel. Maynard then sailed back to Virginia with Blackbeard's head mounted on his prow to let ships along the coast know that the sea lanes were safe once more. Tales persist to this day of treasure stashed away along the coast of North Carolina, but none has ever been found; it's likely that Blackbeard sold his spoils quickly and squandered the proceeds.

When Ocracoke Island was isolated from the mainland and few visitors came by boat, as many as a thousand wild ponies roamed its dunes. Where they came from—whether from shipwrecks, early Spanish explorers, or English settlers—is uncertain. Eventually, as more and more people traveled to and from the island, many ponies were rounded up and shipped to the mainland. The remnants of the herd—about a dozen—now live on a range seven miles north of Ocracoke village, where the National Park Service looks after them.

In a quiet little corner of Ocracoke Island, there's a bit of England: The **British Graveyard,** where four British navy seamen were buried after their bodies washed ashore when the H.M.S. *Bedfordshire* was torpedoed offshore by a German submarine in 1942. The graveyard is leased by the British government, but is lovingly tended by townspeople.

Ocracoke village has seen some changes since World War II, when the U.S. Navy dredged out Silver Lake harbor (still called "Cockle Creek" by many natives) and built a base here. They also brought the first public telephones and paved roads. In spite of the invasion of 20th-century improvements, Ocracoke is essentially what it has always been—a fishing village whose manners and speech reflect 17th-century ancestors. It is by far the most picturesque spot on the Outer Banks.

WHERE TO STAY & DINE

THE ISLAND INN, P.O. Box 9, Ocracoke Island, NC 27960. Tel. 919/ 928-4351. 35 rms, 4 cottages. A/C TV

$ Rates: $30–$90 single or double; $500–$600 per week cottages. Extra person $50. DISC, MC, V.

⭐ The Island Inn, on N.C. 12, has been here since 1901, when it housed the first public school on its ground floor. Over the years it has been moved across the street and been converted to a small inn, with new wings added to accommodate more travelers. It is now under the ownership of Claudia (Cee) and Bob Touley. (Cee and Bob had their first date on Ocracoke.) The inn has the island's only heated swimming pool. A hearty islander's breakfast ($3 to $5.25) is served from 7 to 11am; lunch ($4.25 to $11), served from 11am to 2pm, includes salads, sandwiches, and a couple of hot seafood platters; and for dinner ($9 to $16), served from 5 to 9pm, offerings include sautéed crabmeat, clam chowder, and an enormous seafood platter.

CEDAR ISLAND

To reach North Carolina's more southerly beaches, take the ferry from Ocracoke to Cedar Island. Not only is there a toll for the 2¼-hour trip; you have to make a reservation. Call within 30 days of departure and reserve space on one of the scheduled sailings. To sail from Cedar Island, call 919/225-3551; to sail from Ocracoke, call 919/928-3841. *Reservations are not honored if your car is not in the loading zone at least 30 minutes before departure time.* The fare is $10 per car and occupants, $2 per bicycle and rider, and $1 for pedestrians. It's a wonderful voyage.

For a complete list of ferries, schedules, and fares, write: Ferry Division, Department of Transportation, 113 Arendell St., Morehead City, NC 28557 (tel. 919/726-6446).

3. BEAUFORT, MOREHEAD CITY, NEW BERN & ENVIRONS

Morehead City is 147 miles SE of Raleigh; 3 miles W of Beaufort;
45 miles SE of New Bern; 87 miles NE of Wilmington

GETTING THERE   By Plane   The nearest airport is at New Bern, served by **American** (tel. toll free 800/433-7300) and **USAir** (tel. toll free 800/428-4322).

By Train   The nearest **Amtrak** (tel. toll free 800/USA-RAIL) stop is Raleigh, on its New York–Miami and –Tampa routes.

By Bus   Greyhound/Trailways serves Morehead City (tel. 919/726-3029) and New Bern (tel. 919/633-3100).

By Car   Beaufort, Morehead City, and New Bern are reached via U.S. 7; from the south, N.C. 24 reaches Morehead City.

ESSENTIALS   The **area code** is 919. For sightseeing and accommodation particulars, contact the **Carteret County Tourism Bureau,** P.O. Box 1406, Morehead City, NC 28557 (tel. 919/726-8148, or toll free 800/SUNNY NC).

From the Cedar Island ferry landing—where, incidentally, the **Pirate's Chest Restaurant** at the Driftwood Motel serves very good food at moderate prices—it's almost a 2-hour drive south to Beaufort. The distance isn't that far (about 35 miles), but the two-lane highway (U.S. 70) winds and curves through historic old fishing towns, like Atlantic and Sealevel, under huge old water oaks hung with Spanish moss, emerging at intervals for long, straight patches of marshy sea-grass savannahs.

Beaufort (pronounced "*Bo*-fort"), once a whaling center, is a quaint old seaport that seems frozen in time, with narrow streets lined by white frame houses built in a distinctive, almost Caribbean style. **Morehead City,** which has been an important port for oceangoing vessels since 1857, is the world's largest tobacco export terminal. **New Bern** was the capital city when North Carolina was a royal colony and again when it first attained statehood.

BEAUFORT

North Carolina's third-oldest town, Beaufort dates back to 1713 and still reflects its early history. Along its narrow streets are two 200-year-old houses, and more than a hundred houses over 100 years old. The last weekend in June, many residents open their homes for the annual Old Homes Tour. The **Beaufort Historic Site** in the 100 block of Turner Street includes the 1767 Joseph Bell House, the 1825 Josiah Bell House, the 1796 Carteret County Courthouse, the 1829 county jail, the 1859 apothecary shop and doctor's office, and the 1778 Samuel Leffers House, home of the town's first schoolmaster. The 1732 Rustell House also functions as an art gallery. Tours led by charming costumed guides are given Monday through Saturday from 9:30am to 4:30pm. Adults pay $5 for the tour, children $3.

A block away is the **Old Burying Ground,** dating from 1709 and listed on the National Register of Historic Places. Both self-guided and narrated tours are available. There also are narrated tours aboard an English double-decker bus on Wednesday and Saturday, April to October, for a $5-per-person fare. Complete sightseeing information is available at **Beaufort Historical Association Welcome Center,** 126 Turner St. (tel. 728-5225).

Don't miss the fine state-owned **North Carolina Maritime Museum,** 315 Front St. (tel. 728-7317). It has splendid natural and maritime history exhibits, ship models, and shell collections, and offers intriguing field trips, lectures, and programs for all ages. The Wooden Boat Show is held here annually the first weekend in May, and in August the museum is the site of one of the South's zaniest events, the Strange Seafood Festival—your golden opportunity to chow down on marinated octopus, squid, stingray casserole, and other delicacies. Admission is about $7, and it's so popular you must reserve in advance. Museum admission is free, and it's open Monday through Friday 9am to 5pm, Saturday 10am to 5pm, and Sunday 1 to 5pm; closed major holidays. Across the street is the museum's Watercraft Center, where they restore boats.

HARKERS ISLAND   If you're a boat owner, you could tie up across the sound from Beaufort at **Calico Jack's Marina** (tel. 728-3575) on Harkers Island. If you don't have your own boat, a Park Service ferry (tel. 728-3866) leaves from Calico Jack's for the 35-minute trip to Cape Lookout. (For details, call Calico Jack's Marina.) The ferry runs between April and December and the fare is $12 round-trip. At the cape, a jitney service roams between Cape Point and the lighthouse to move visitors from one spot to another. Bring a picnic, insect repellent, and your own water supply. The island atmosphere is perfect for anyone who likes sailboats, lots of sun, and miles and miles of sand beach, great for surf fishing or beachcombing. The unique diamond-patterned lighthouse has stood here since 1859.

WHERE TO STAY

BEAUFORT INN, 101 Ann St., Beaufort, NC 28516. Tel. 919/728-2600. 41 rms. A/C TV TEL
$ Rates (including breakfast): $44–$89 single or double, depending on season. AE, DC, DISC, MC, V.

Katie and Bruce Ethridge have managed to give their inn a historical feel, though it is of recent vintage. It's located in the Historic District, and its rooms are tastefully decorated, with lots of homey touches. Some 15 boat slips are provided for guests who arrive by water, and there are bicycles for rent. A scrumptious cooked breakfast is served in the beautiful dining area (don't miss Katie's breakfast pie of sausages, eggs, and cheese), and several good restaurants are within walking distance.

THE CEDARS INN, 305 Front St., Beaufort, NC 28516. Tel. 919/728-7036. 11 suites. A/C TV TEL
$ Rates (including breakfast): $79–$136 single or double, depending on season. Midweek packages available. MC, V.
This interesting house, built in the 1700s, was once the home of a shipbuilder. Its furnishings include many fine antique pieces, and suites, with private patios and balconies, provide every modern comfort in gracious surroundings. The restaurant (open for nonresidents) serves excellent continental cuisine, with a good wine list, in a lovely candlelit dining room, for around $25.

WHERE TO DINE

BEAUFORT HOUSE, 502 Front St. Tel. 728-7541.
Cuisine: SEAFOOD. **Reservations:** Not required.
$ Prices: Lunch $4–$7; dinner $9–$15; Sunday brunch $10. MC, V.
Open: Mar–Dec 21, lunch daily 11am–2:30pm; dinner daily 5–9pm. Hours may vary Nov–Dec.

On the boardwalk, overlooking the harbor, this is a relaxed sort of place, specializing in fresh seafood from local waters, but with a large menu that includes a wide variety of prime steaks and Southern-fried chicken. There's also an excellent salad bar, and breads are home-baked (do try Southern-style biscuits or cornbread). Service is friendly and efficient, and most main courses come with a choice of two fresh vegetables. Wine and beer are served, as are setups for mixed drinks. During the summer, there's live music on weekends.

THE SPOUTER INN, 218 Front St. Tel. 728-5190.
   Cuisine: SEAFOOD. **Reservations:** Recommended for dinner.
$ **Prices:** Lunch under $10; dinner $15–$18. MC, V.
   Open: Lunch daily 11:30am–2pm; dinner daily 5:30–9:30pm. **Closed:** Major holidays.
This casual place is popular with locals and visitors alike. You dine by candlelight in the evening from a menu that specializes in fresh seafood, but also has continental dishes that are rather rare in this region. Waterfront dining is available.

MOREHEAD CITY

Fishing is especially good here—the Gulf Stream brings in blue marlin, tarpon, and other prizes, in addition to inshore fish. There are some 80 miles of surf and 400 miles of protected waterways in this area. A near-perfect day or evening on the water can be arranged by contacting the *Carolina Princess,* 711 Shepherd St., Morehead City (tel. 726-5479, or toll free 800/682-3456). The *Princess* is a trim vessel that can accommodate up to 100 passengers and has a snack bar and a sundeck. Full-day deep-sea fishing trips run around $50 for adults, $30 for children, and there are coolers to hold the day's catch on ice. From May to October, dinner cruises are offered down Bogue Sound and the Inland Waterway for a seafood or steak dinner at the Galley Stack Restaurant, at prices of $25 for adults, $20 for children.

WHERE TO STAY

BEST WESTERN BUCCANEER MOTOR INN, 2806 Arendell St., Morehead City, NC 28557. Tel. 919/726-3115. 91 rms. A/C TV TEL
$ **Rates** (including breakfast): $35–$75 single; $38–$79 double. AE, DC, DISC, MC, V.
Recently remodeled, rooms are both attractive and comfortable; some have in-room whirlpools. Amenities include free coffee, free local telephone calls, and a pool. The Anchor Inn Restaurant, with two dining rooms and a lounge, specializes in seafood, steaks, and prime ribs, all at moderate prices.

COMFORT INN, 3100 Arendell St., Morehead City, NC 28557. Tel. 919/247-3434. 100 rms. A/C TV TEL **Directions:** Take U.S. 70 east across the causeway to Atlantic Beach.
$ **Rates** (including continental breakfast): $34–$69 single; $38–$72 double. Children under 16 stay free with parents. AE, DC, DISC, MC, V.
S The Comfort Inn is right at Morehead Plaza. Guest rooms are tastefully furnished; some have refrigerators, nine have in-room whirlpools. Golf privileges at nearby courses can be arranged for a small fee.

WHERE TO DINE

CAPTAIN BILL'S WATERFRONT RESTAURANT, 701 Evans St., Morehead City. Tel. 726-2166.
   Cuisine: SEAFOOD. **Reservations:** Recommended.

$ Prices: Lunch $4–$16; dinner $7–$16. MC, V.
   Open: Sun–Thurs 11am–9pm, Fri–Sat 11am–10pm.
Overlooking colorful fishing boats on Bogue Sound, this family-style restaurant
retains its popularity year after year. Locals look forward to the conch stew on
Wednesday and Saturday, as well as all-you-can-eat nightly seafood specials. Prices are
moderate to cheap, and if you're tired of seafood, you'll find a good selection of
nonfinny dishes. Desserts, sauces, and salad dressings are all homemade, and there's a
children's menu.

**MRS. WILLIS RESTAURANT, 3002 Bridges St., Morehead City. Tel.
726-3741.**
   Cuisine: SEAFOOD/PRIME RIB. **Reservations:** Recommended.
$ Prices: Appetizers $3–$4.50; main courses $6–$18. DISC, MC, V.
   Open: Daily 11:30am–9:30pm. **Closed:** Christmas week.
      Mrs. Russell Willis's family has been serving the public since 1952. There's
      seafood, as you'd expect in this fishing center, but in addition, you'll find prime
      ribs and choice charcoal steaks. It's a cozy place, rather rustic, with a fireplace,
      background music, and very friendly service. There's full bar service in addition
      to a good wine list.

**SANITARY FISH MARKET AND RESTAURANT, 501 Evans St.,
Morehead City. Tel. 247-3111.**
   Cuisine: SEAFOOD. **Reservations:** Not required.
$ Prices: Lunch $4–$17; dinner $5–$22. MC, V.
   Open: Feb–Nov, daily 11am–8:30pm.
      This has been family-owned and -operated since 1938. Located right on the
      waterfront, this large eatery (seating 550) offers 50 items on its menu, most—as
      you would expect—related to the waters just outside. Broiled and fried
      seafood, homemade clam chowder, and she-crab soup are local favorites.
      Steaks are new to the menu.

ATLANTIC BEACH & BOGUE BANKS

Atlantic Beach is the oldest of the resorts on the 24-mile stretch of Bogue Banks, and
most North Carolinians use the name Atlantic Beach to include the newer vacation
centers of Pine Knoll Shores, Indian Beach, Emerald Isle, and Salter Path. The long,
thin island began to develop back in 1927 when the first bridge was built across Bogue
Sound to Morehead City, and it is now one of the state's most popular coastal areas,
with fishing festivals and tournaments in early spring and late fall making it virtually a
year-round resort.
   When you begin to feel a bit waterlogged, plenty of sightseeing is within easy
reach. For instance, down at the very tip of Bogue Island (you're on it if you stay at
Atlantic Beach) sits **Fort Macon,** a Civil War landmark now restored and open
to the public at no charge. The jetties (designed by Robert E. Lee), moats, gun
emplacements, and dungeons make up terrific exploring territory. The museum is
quite good, though small, and the public beach has bathhouses, a snack bar, and
lifeguards.

WHERE TO STAY & DINE

Many of the hotels have dining rooms, but for fine restaurant dining your best bet is
the short drive to Morehead City or Beaufort (see above).

Motels

JOHN YANCEY MOTOR HOTEL, P.O. Box 790, Atlantic Beach, NC 28512. Tel. 919/726-5188; or toll free 800/533-3700, 800/682-3700 in North Carolina. 95 rms. A/C TV TEL **Directions:** Go three miles west of U.S. 70 on N.C. 58 to Pine Knoll Shores/Salter Path exit.

$ Rates: $35–$90 single or double. Senior discounts available. Children 18 and under stay free with parents. AE, DC, MC, V.

Facing 1,000 feet of broad ocean beach on Salter Path Road, this hotel has a games room, free coffee and doughnuts, a pool, and golf and tennis privileges at nearby facilities. The rates are modest. Some rooms have refrigerators.

OCEANA RESORT MOTEL, P.O. Box 250, Atlantic Beach, NC 28512. Tel. 919/726-4111. 109 rms and kitchen units. A/C TV TEL **Directions:** Go three miles south of U.S. 70 on N.C. 58.

$ Rates (including breakfast): $45–$70 single or double; $50–$95 kitchen units. MC, V. **Closed:** Nov–Mar.

This motel at Atlantic Beach proper, and right on the ocean has a free fishing pier for guests. If you want to turn the day's catch into the evening meal, you'll find grills and a supply of charcoal, starter fluid, and even ketchup and mustard out by the pool, and picnic tables nearby. For the small fry, there's a playground, and for vacationers of all ages, the semiweekly watermelon party out by the pool is a festive occasion. The tropical breakfast spread under an open poolside pavilion features more than 15 fresh fruits. The coffee shop is open from 5am to midnight, and there's a fast-food grill out by the fishing pier. Every room has a refrigerator, and some have stoves. Portable grills may be brought to the lawn area in front of your room (but not on upper-floor decks), so you can cook dinner right at your front door.

Campgrounds

The **Salter Path Campground,** Milepost 11.5, Salter Path Road (P.O. Box 232), Atlantic Beach, NC 28512 (tel. 919/247-3525), overlooks the ocean on one side, Bogue Sound on the other. There are full hookups, a boat ramp, bathhouses, and a playground. Rates are $18 and up. For reservations, call with a credit card.

Also on Salter Path Road, the **Arrowhead,** 1550 Salter Path Rd., Atlantic Beach, NC 28512 (tel. 919/247-3838), has showers, a store, pier fishing, a playground, drive-through waterfront sites, and golf nearby. Rates begin at $14.

NEW BERN

Less than 50 miles inland, on U.S. (Bus.) 70 and U.S. 17, New Bern was the colonial capital for several years. Swiss colonists gave the town its name, perhaps in a fit of homesickness. When William Tryon was royal governor, he built a splendid "palace" here, considered at the time the "most beautiful building in the New World." Both the palace and the gardens around it have been restored to their former splendor.

The **visitors' center,** 219 Pollock St. (tel. 637-9400), is located in an 1800s historic home, open Monday through Friday 8am to 5pm, Saturday 10am to 5pm, and Sunday and holidays 11am to 4pm. They can furnish detailed information on New Bern's sightseeing attractions.

WHAT TO SEE & DO

Historic **Christ Episcopal Church** at Middle and Pollock Streets, is among the many sites that may be visited in old New Bern. There are over 180 18th- and 19th-century structures in New Bern listed in the National Register of Historic Places. Among the highlights are the following:

TRYON PALACE HISTORIC SITES AND GARDENS, 613 Pollock St. Tel. 638-1560.

⭐ This 48-room museum, built in 1767–70, as both the capitol and residence for the royal governor, has been authentically restored. It's easy to see, walking through the elegant rooms, why this mansion was once called the most beautiful in America. The main building burned in 1798, and lay in ruins until the restoration in 1952–59. The handsome grounds and gardens surrounding Tryon Palace are designed in 18th-century style.

Two other landmarks in the 13-acre Tryon Palace complex are the **John Wright Stanly House** (1780), a sophisticated late-Georgian-style mansion with town-house gardens, and the **Stevenson House** (1805), built by a merchant and noted for its rare Federal antiques. On the grounds, craftspeople demonstrate 18th-century home arts. Historical dramas supplement the regular guided tours during the summer months. Special events, including candlelight tours of the complex, are held at Christmas and other seasons.

Admission: Combination ticket for tours, landmarks, and gardens, $12 adults, $6 children through high school; palace and gardens only, $8 adults, $4 children; landmark homes, $8 adults, $4 children; gardens only, $4 adults, $2 children.

Open: Guided tours Mon–Sat 9:30am–4pm, Sun 1:30–4pm. **Closed:** Major holidays.

NEW BERN FIREMEN'S MUSEUM, 410 Hancock St. Tel. 636-4020.

This museum is 2½ blocks from Tryon Palace. Firefighting equipment dating back to the early 19th century, memorabilia from the mother city of Bern, Switzerland, and Civil War artifacts make this a memorable, small museum.

Admission: $1 adults, 50¢ children.

Open: Tues–Sat 9:30am–noon and 1–5pm, Sun 1–6pm. **Closed:** Major holidays.

IN THE ENVIRONS

Along the coast southwest of Morehead City, the little town of **Swansboro,** bordering the White Oak River across from Cape Carteret, is a real charmer, with interesting little shops and renovated waterfront buildings and docks. The **Mullet Festival,** held here every October, draws huge crowds from around the Southeast. A free passenger ferry runs from Swansboro to **Bear Island,** where Hammocks Beach is a state park dominated by high sand dunes, a maritime forest, and more than four miles of unspoiled beach.

Almost due west of Swansboro, **Jacksonville** sits inland, but only a 20-minute drive from choice beaches. The focal point of the city is the adjacent New River Marine Base, on N.C. 24, universally known as **Camp LeJeune.** The 110,000-acre reservation is one of the world's most complete amphibious military training centers, and you can obtain a pass to drive through unrestricted parts of the grounds if you present your driver's license and car registration to personnel at the information center next to the main gate on N.C. 24. Organized tours can be arranged for groups, and in June, the Marine Corps Air Station stages a spectacular demonstration of parachuting and free-fall acrobatic skills. Call 919/451-2197 for exact dates and other details about the base.

For a true North Carolina coastal seafood experience, drive south of Jacksonville to the little fishing village of **Sneads Ferry,** which is loaded with eateries featuring right-off-the-boat choices, steamed, broiled, or fried to perfection.

For further information about the Swansboro/Jacksonville area, contact the **Greater Jacksonville/Onslow Chamber of Commerce,** 1 Marine Blvd. N., P.O. Box 765, Jacksonville, NC 28541-0165 (tel. 919/347-3141). They can also help you with accommodations and places to eat.

WHERE TO DINE NEAR SWANSBORO

THE TW OYSTER BAR AND RESTAURANT, 3231 N.C. 58 North,
Swansboro. Tel. 393-8838.
    Cuisine: SEAFOOD. **Reservations:** Not accepted. **Directions:** Go five miles
north of the Emerald Isle bridge on N.C. 58.
$ **Prices:** Appetizers $3.50–$5; main courses $6–$10. MC, V.
    Open: Dinner Mon–Sat 5–10pm, Sun noon–10pm.

    This place is definitely worth looking up. It looks like a country roadhouse
from the outside. Inside, however, the sloping, beamed ceiling and two large
dining rooms, each with a fireplace, have a simplicity bordering on sophistication. The oyster bar is very popular, with a half dozen on the half shell costing
only $3.50. Steamed oysters and clams are sold by the peck and half peck.
Dress is casual.

4. WILMINGTON & ENVIRONS

Wilmington is 123 miles SE of Raleigh; 87 miles S
of Morehead City; 234 miles S of Nags Head

GETTING THERE **By Plane**   Wilmington is served by **American** (tel. toll free
800/433-7300) and **USAir** (tel. toll free 800/428-4322).

By Train   **Amtrak**'s (tel. toll free 800/USA-RAIL) closest stop is Raleigh.

By Bus   **Greyhound/Trailways** serves Wilmington (tel. 919/762-6625) from all
major points.

By Car   Wilmington is reached via U.S. 117 and U.S. 40 from the northwest, and
U.S. 17 from the northeast and south.

ESSENTIALS   The **area code** is 919. The **Cape Fear Coast Convention and
Visitors Bureau,** 24 N. 3rd St., Wilmington, NC 28401 (tel. 919/341-4030; or toll
free 800/222-4757 in the U.S., or 800/457-8912 in Canada), offers free brochures on
the many attractions and accommodations of the Cape Fear coast. The efficient staff
can provide a self-guided walking tour map of historic Wilmington and background
details on other area attractions.

Near the southern end of North Carolina's coast is Wilmington, a city that has
figured prominently in the state's history since 1732. Known first as New
Carthage, then as New Liverpool, New Town, and Newton, in 1739 it was given its
present name in honor of the Earl of Wilmington. Technically it isn't even on the
coast—it's inland a bit, at the junction of the Cape Fear River's northeast and
northwest branches. Despite the treacherous shoals that guarded the mouth of the
Cape Fear when explorers first arrived in 1524, upriver Wilmington developed into an
important port for the movement of goods to and from Europe during colonial days.
Since then the town has grown steadily as a commercial shipping center.
    Remnants of the city's history are lovingly restored and maintained in the old
residential section of town (now an official "historic area"), the grounds of Orton
Plantation, the excavated foundations of Brunswick Town houses, and the blockade-
runner relics at Fort Fisher. And nearby on the coast is Wrightsville Beach (a
family-oriented resort for generations), the perfect place from which to explore the
whole region—unless, that is, you prefer swimming, beachcombing, fishing, sailing, or
just plain loafing.
    A BIT OF HISTORY   The first English settlers, from the Massachusetts Bay

Colony, actually landed on the west bank of the Cape Fear River in 1662, and they were followed shortly by another group from Barbados. But they suffered mightily from Indian conflicts and the depredations of pirates, who roamed the river freely. There wasn't much of a settlement until Brunswick Town was founded in 1725 about 16 miles south of Wilmington, where a fort was built to guard the passageway up Cape Fear. Soon surrounded by large, thriving plantations (some of them still intact today), Brunswick prospered until the British tried to destroy it by fire in 1776. It never really recovered, and ceased to exist as a town about 1830. It became a part of the Orton Plantation until it was named a state historic site in this century.

Wilmington, too, played a part in the Revolution. In 1765, eight years before the Boston Tea Party, patriots here refused to allow the unloading of stamps to implement the infamous Stamp Act, and forced the resignation of the stamp master. In 1780, the city fell to Lord Cornwallis, and he headquartered there (in a house still standing) all that winter before leaving for Yorktown and ultimate defeat.

This was one of the principal ports of the Confederacy during the Civil War, and many blockade runners, who eluded Northern ships that patrolled the coastline and the Cape Fear shoals to bring in supplies to the South, found a home berth here. Fort Fisher, on the eastern shore of the river, sustained one of the heaviest bombardments of the war, and fell just 90 days before the Confederacy met defeat.

During both world wars, Wilmington was a major port for naval supplies. Today the river is busier than ever with industrial shipping, and in recent years has seen a thriving industry develop—some 34 pictures have been shot here, including *Crimes of the Heart* and *Blue Velvet.*

WHAT TO SEE & DO

IN TOWN

To get a delightful overview of the historic Wilmington waterfront, hop aboard the ✪ *Capt. J. N. Maffitt* riverboat (tel. 343-1611), which departs from the foot of Market Street for a five-mile loop of the Cape Fear River. The 45-minute narrated cruise skirts the busy harbor, passes the Cotton Exchange renovation and the new Waterfront Park, and stops at the dock for passengers who wish to disembark to tour the battleship **U.S.S. *North Carolina*** (see below). Daily departure times for the riverboat are 11am and 3pm June through August, and at 3pm in May and September. Cost is $5 for adults, $3 for ages 1 to 12.

The **Cotton Exchange,** an in-town shopping center, is in the old cotton exchange with its two-foot-thick brick walls and hurricane rods. The small shops and restaurants are a delight, and the wrought-iron lanterns and benches add to the charm of the setting. It's right on the riverfront, just across from the Wilmington Hilton, and there's an ample parking deck adjacent.

Another "must" is ✪ **Chandler's Wharf,** also on the riverfront, at the southern end. It encompasses specialty shops in renovated and restored buildings. Across the street, two warehouses are home to more shops, galleries, and restaurants. Wooden sidewalks, white picket fences, and cobblestone alleyways lend the complex a distinctive 19th-century ambience.

In the Historic Wilmington old residential area, bounded roughly by Nun, Princess, Front, and 4th Streets, the **Burgwin-Wright House,** 224 Market St. (tel. 762-0570), was built in 1771 and used by Lord Cornwallis as his headquarters in 1781. The house was built over an abandoned city jail. It's a beautifully restored example of a colonial gentleman's town house. You can tour the interior Tuesday through Saturday from 10am to 4pm. Adults pay $3; children, $1.

Also at 3rd and Market is **St. James Episcopal Church,** erected in 1839 to replace a 1751 church which had been used by the British as a stable during the

Revolution. The Spanish painting *Ecce Homo* that hangs inside was taken from a captured pirate ship in 1748, and is estimated to be 400 to 600 years old.

The ✪ **New Hanover County Museum,** 814 Market St. (tel. 341-4350), showcases the lower Cape Fear region's social and natural history. Especially fascinating are the Civil War artifacts and dioramas from the former Blockade Runner Museum. Followers of fashion will appreciate the fine collection of 19th- and 20th-century costumes. The museum is free and open Tuesday through Saturday from 9am to 5pm, and Sunday from 2 to 5pm; closed major holidays.

NEARBY

U.S.S. *NORTH CAROLINA* BATTLESHIP MEMORIAL, Battleship Drive, Eagle Island. Tel. 251-5797.

✪ The *North Carolina* was commissioned in 1941, and is permanently berthed here as a memorial to the state's World War II dead. You can tour most of the ship, and the museum presents a pictorial history of the *North Carolina*'s Pacific campaigns. From early June through Labor Day, there's a 70-minute sound and light show, *The Immortal Showboat,* at 9pm every night, at a cost of $3.50 for adults, $1.75 for children. A visitor center has a large gift shop and snack bar, as well as an auditorium where a 10-minute orientation film is shown. *Note:* If you don't want to drive, take the river taxi from Waterfront Park Dock that runs every half hour from 10 to 11:30am and 3:30 to 5pm, with a $1 fare.

Admission: Tour of ship, $6 adults, $3 children 6–11.

Open: Daily 8am–sunset. **Directions:** Just across the river from downtown Wilmington, at junction of U.S. 17.

AIRLIE GARDENS, U.S. 76, Wilmington. Tel. 763-9991.

Once the plantation home of a wealthy rice planter, Airlie is surrounded by huge lawns, serene lakes, and wooded gardens that hold just about every kind of azalea in existence. The blooms are at their height in the early spring, but even when they've faded, this is a lovely spot.

Admission: $4 adults, $2 children.

Open: Mar–Apr, 8am–6pm; May–Oct, 9am–5pm. **Directions:** Take U.S. 76 toward beach.

POPLAR GROVE HISTORIC PLANTATION, Rte. 1, Wilmington. Tel. 686-9989.

✪ A restored Greek Revival manor house and estate dating from 1850. Outbuildings include a smokehouse, tenant house, and restored old kitchen, with demonstrations by a basket weaver, a fabric weaver, and a blacksmith. Moderately priced, country-style meals are served weekdays from 11am to 3pm and on Sunday from noon to 4pm in the Plantation Tea Room.

Admission (including tour): $6 adults, $5 seniors, $3 students, free for children 5 and under.

Open: "Living History" tours, Mon–Sat 9am–5pm, Sun noon–5pm. **Closed:** Jan–Feb. **Directions:** Go nine miles northeast of town on U.S. 17.

GREENFIELD GARDENS, U.S. 421 South, Wilmington. Tel. 341-7855.

Wilmington's largest municipal park is justly famous for its scenic millpond, a garden of native North Carolina flowers, and the Venus's-flytrap, which is native to the Carolinas and not found anywhere else in the world. In the spring and summer, camellias, azaleas, and roses bloom in profusion, and the five-mile drive around Greenfield Lake is beautiful any time of the year.

Admission: Free.

Open: Daily, dawn to dusk. **Directions:** Go 2½ miles from town on U.S. 421 South.

FORT FISHER STATE HISTORIC SITE, P.O. Box 68, Kure Beach. Tel. 458-5538.

⭐ One of the Confederacy's largest, most technically advanced forts, Fort Fisher protected blockade runners bringing in vital goods to the port of Wilmington. After withstanding two of the heaviest naval bombardments of the Civil War, the fort finally fell to Union forces in the conflict's largest land-sea battle. The visitor center exhibits artifacts of that era, and there's an audiovisual program as well. Costumed tour guides welcome visitors, and living-history events are depicted seasonally.

Admission: Free.
Open: Fort and visitors' center, Apr–Nov, Mon–Sat 9am–5pm, Sun 1–5pm; Dec–Mar, Tues–Sat 10am–4pm, Sun 1–4pm. **Directions:** Follow U.S. 421 South.

BRUNSWICK TOWN STATE HISTORIC SITE, Rte. 1, Winnabow. Tel. 371-6613.

The excavated home foundations have been left as archeological exhibits, and there are displays that re-create colonial life here. The walls of St. Philip's Anglican Church are still partially standing.

Admission: Free.
Open: Visitors' center, Apr–Oct, Mon–Sat 9am–5pm, Sun 1–5pm; Nov–Mar, Tues–Sat 10am–4pm, Sun 1–4pm. **Directions:** Take toll ($5 for car and passengers) ferry near Fort Fisher (see above) for the half-hour crossing of Cape Fear River to Southport. Turn north on N.C. 87, then left at N.C. 133. Or, driving south from Wilmington stay on N.C. 133.

ORTON PLANTATION GARDENS, RFD 1, Winnabow. Tel. 371-6851.

This private mansion is not open to the public, but the magnificent gardens, bordered by long avenues of live oak and planted with camellias, azaleas, and thousands of other ornamental plants, are a treat to visit. It's a lovely setting overlooking old rice fields and the Cape Fear River.

Admission: $7 adults, $3 children 6–12.
Open: Mar–Nov, daily 8am–5pm. **Directions:** Go to N.C. 133 between Wilmington and Southport.

AN EXCURSION TO BALD HEAD ISLAND

A 45-minute drive southeast from Wilmington on U.S. 17 South, with a left turn onto U.S. 87, will bring you to the little town of Southport, jumping-off point for the passenger ferry to ⭕ **Bald Head Island** (the terminal is at India Plantation). You must call ahead to book the ferry (tel. 919/457-5006); day-trippers pay $15.

For nature-lovers, it's a trip not to be missed, and Bald Head Island invites a much-longer-than-one-day visit. There are some 3,000 pristine acres, with 14 miles of sandy beachfront; miles and miles of salt marshes, tidal creeks, and maritime forests; as well as an 18-hole championship golf course and the village of Bald Head Island, with shops, restaurants, private homes, and condominiums. Activities on the island include swimming (there's a pool as well as all those miles of beaches), biking, tennis, golf, canoeing, fishing, and just plain beachcombing or birdwatching.

Still, human intrusion is kept to a minimum. No cars are permitted on the island—transportation is strictly provided by golf carts and jitneys, which are used to transport guests. Sea oats, yucca, beach grasses, live oak, red cedar trees, palmetto, sabal palms, loblolly pines, and a lovely yellow wildflower called galardia still thrive, seemingly undisturbed by the human touch. Such birds as the white ibis, great blue heron, snowy egret, black ducks, mallards, and pintails frequent the island, and a protected population of loggerhead sea turtles nests here. Bald Head Island takes its name from a high, bare dune that was a much-used lookout point during both the Revolutionary and the Civil wars.

Where to Stay

Private homes, as well as condominiums in communities with names like Swan's Quarter, Timber Creek, and Royal James Landing, are available as rentals, as are two historic cottages that were homes to lighthouse keepers and their families from 1903 to 1958. All units are beautifully furnished, with full kitchens, TVs, and other modern conveniences, and most rates include the use of one of the electric passenger carts. Daily rates are in the $150-to-$400 range during summer months, $90 to $350 other months; weekly rates run $750 to $2,400 in summer, $450 to $1,800 off-season. For full details and bookings, contact: Bald Head Island, P.O. Box 3069, Bald Head Island, NC 28461 (tel. 919/457-5000, or toll free 800/234-1666).

AN EXCURSION TO CALABASH

Sooner or later you're bound to hear the name ✪ **Calabash** in connection with food. This tiny town of 150 residents, about 35 miles south of Wilmington on U.S. 17, is renowned for its seafood restaurants—about 20 of them, vying with one another to serve the biggest and best platter of seafood at the lowest price. These eateries use family recipes handed down from generation to generation; in one recent year they served 1½ million people some 668,000 pounds of flounder and 378,000 pounds of shrimp, to say nothing of tons and tons of oysters, scallops, and other fish. Recommendations for specific restaurants? I wouldn't even try! And you won't need them—according to locals, you can't miss, no matter which one you choose.

AN EXCURSION TO MOORES CREEK

Twenty miles northwest of Wilmington, Moores Creek is the site of North Carolina's first battle of the Revolution, now a national battlefield. The victory of local patriots here squelched a Tory scheme to invade and seize all the Southern colonies. The earthworks and bridge have been reconstructed, and there's a visitor center and museum. To get there, take U.S. 421 and N.C. 210.

WHERE TO STAY

The **Cape Fear Coast Convention and Visitors Bureau** (see above) will do more than just send you their *Accommodations Guide*. If you're in the market for an apartment or cottage for a week or more (a dollar-saving approach that's hard to beat), write them well in advance, describing just what you have in mind. They'll circulate your requirements in a bulletin that goes to area owners and managers, who will then contact you directly.

If you're interested in camping, the **Camelot Campground**, 7415 Market St., Wilmington, NC 28405 (tel. 919/686-7705), sits on 43 wooded acres on U.S. 17. There's a pool, recreation room, playground, laundry, and grocery store, and propane gas is available for stoves. Rates range from $13 for tent sites to $19 for full hookups.

IN WILMINGTON

COAST LINE INN, 503 Nutt St., Wilmington, NC 28401. Tel. 919/763-2800. Fax 919/763-2785. 50 rms. A/C TV TEL
$ Rates (including continental breakfast): $69 single or double. AE, DC, MC, V.

Next door to the Coast Line Convention Center, this inn was designed to complement the restored historic rail depot for which it is named. Its adjacent full-service restaurant actually occupies one of the original railroad buildings, and, in addition to dinner service, has a nice bar and periodic live entertainment. The inn's rooms all have good views of the Cape Fear River, and suites afford two river views, as does the River's Edge Lounge. In decor, the Coast Line Inn features lots of mahogany, brass, and rich leather. Rooms adapted for the handicapped are available.

DAYS INN, 5040 Market St., Wilmington, NC 28405. Tel. 919/799-6300. 122 rms. A/C TV TEL
$ Rates: $33 single; $38 double. Extra person $5. AE, DC, DISC, MC, V.
The Days Inn offers some of Wilmington's most attractive budget priced guest rooms. There's a pool and an inexpensive restaurant on the premises.

WILMINGTON HILTON, 301 N. Water St., Wilmington, NC 28401. Tel. 919/763-5900, or toll free 800/662-9338. Fax 919/763-0038. 178 rms and suites. A/C TV TEL
$ Rates: $85–$105 single; $95–$110 double; $110–$275 suite. Luxury level, $105–$115 single; $115–$125 double; $250–$275 suite. Extra person $10. AE, DC, MC, V.
If you want to stay in Wilmington rather than at Wrightsville Beach, this waterfront Hilton offers superior accommodations: attractively decorated rooms, pool, whirlpool, and an exercise room. Luxury-level rooms and suites come with the services of a concierge, a continental breakfast, and a private lounge. For all guests, there's free airport transportation.

AT WRIGHTSVILLE BEACH

BLOCKADE RUNNER RESORT HOTEL & CONFERENCE CENTER, 275 Waynick Blvd. (P.O. Box 555), Wrightsville Beach, NC 28480. Tel. 919/256-2251. Fax 919/256-2251, ext. 7404. 150 rms. A/C TV TEL
$ Rates: Mid-May to mid-Sept, $89–$170 single or double. Mid-Sept to mid-May, $59–$81 single or double. AE, DC, MC, V.
At the tip of the island of Wrightsville Beach, with marvelous ocean and Wrightsville Sound views, this seven-story hotel has luxury rooms, a heated oceanside pool, a spa, an indoor health center, tennis, volleyball, a playground for children, comedy club or other nightly entertainment, and sailboats for rent. There are special programs for the young fry, and a sailing center for first-time sailors. Meeting facilities will accommodate up to 350. The bright, cheerful dining room serves continental cuisine at moderate prices.

HOLIDAY INN WRIGHTSVILLE BEACH HOTEL, 1706 N. Lumina Ave. (P.O. Box 599), Wrightsville Beach, NC 28480. Tel. 919/256-2231, or toll free 800/HOLIDAY. 147 rms. A/C TV TEL
$ Rates: June–Aug $95–$125 single or double. Sept–May, $50–$95 single or double. Extra person $10. AE, MC, V.
All of the guest rooms in this Holiday Inn have balconies or patios with an ocean view, and all are attractively furnished. Rooms facing the ocean are especially nice, with sliding doors opening directly onto the beach or to individual balconies. A large, oceanside pool has shady areas and a refreshment bar. The lounge offers dancing and seasonal entertainment. Dinners in the charming dining room are good and inexpensive ($10 and under at dinner). Guests enjoy golf privileges at a nearby private course, and sailboat rentals are available. The hotel will also arrange golf-package weekends and charter-boat fishing trips.

AT KURE BEACH

South of Wrightsville and Carolina beaches, en route to Fort Fisher, the little settlement of Kure Beach still retains much of its past. There's an aquarium in the immediate area, making this a good sightseeing base.

DOCKSIDER INN, 202 N. Rt. 421, P.O. Box 373, Kure Beach, NC 28449. Tel. 919/458-4200. 25 rms, 16 efficiencies. A/C TV

$ Rates: Summer $80–$100 for up to four persons. Fall–spring, $49–$82 for up to four persons. Extra person $5. Weekly rates available at a 10% discount. AE, CB, DC, DISC, MC, V.

The Dockside Inn offers the sort of low-key beach accommodations that fit right into the easygoing ambience of the area. The owner, personable Kip Darling, says he "psychologically retired" at the age of 38, fled the rigors of Chicago winters, and watched his blood pressure drop dramatically "the moment I drove into Kure Beach." The long, U-shaped structure has a dozen oceanfront rooms (all with private porches). All rooms are attractively decorated in beach colors, with lots of nautical items as well as original watercolors with beach themes. Each has a coffeepot and refrigerator. Efficiencies also have popcorn poppers, toasters, and all the tableware, cookware, and utensils you'll need for light snacking. For $10 above other rates, the star of the Docksider is the Captain's Cabin, with its queen-size bed romantically ensconced on a raised platform looking out to sea.

The pool is surrounded by a wooden deck, the setting for Sunday-morning coffee, juice, and doughnuts; the Sunketch, a topside sundeck, is the scene of frequent convivial gatherings. Golfers can choose among three superb local courses within a 15-minute drive.

WHERE TO DINE

As is true of so many coastal towns, Wilmington's best dining spots are at the beaches or on its fringes, and you'll find more seafood spots (most of them excellent) than you'll have time to sample.

IN WILMINGTON

BRIDGE TENDER, Airlie Rd. at Wrightsville Beach Bridge, Wilmington. Tel. 256-4519.
   Cuisine: SEAFOOD. **Reservations:** Not accepted.
$ Prices: Lunch $3.50–$8; dinner $14–$22. AE, DC, MC, V.
   Open: Lunch Mon–Fri 11:30am–2pm; dinner Sun–Thurs 5:30–10pm, Fri–Sat 5:30–11pm. **Closed:** Major holidays.

A native of Wilmington recommended the Bridge Tender to me: "It's reasonable," she said, "yet has an elegant feeling, and it's relaxing to watch the boats go past when the bridge is raised." I found this restaurant all of that—and the food is superb. A limited selection of top-quality meats and seafoods is prepared imaginatively by expert chefs. The Polynesian chicken is excellent. Desserts are made fresh daily.

PILOT HOUSE RESTAURANT, 2 Ann St., Wilmington. Tel. 343-0200.
   Cuisine: SEAFOOD/CONTINENTAL/PASTA. **Reservations:** Not required.
$ Prices: Lunch $5–$8; dinner $8–$18. AE, DISC, MC, V.
   Open: Lunch Mon–Sat 11am–3pm; dinner Mon–Sat 5–10pm.
This popular restaurant is comfortable and casual, with an emphasis on high-quality cuisine. It's quite lively at lunchtime, when shoppers, downtown workers, and tourists surge in for crab quiche or Carolina seafood chowder. Dinner specialties range from fresh local seafood to veal, beef, and fowl entrées, all prepared with deft special touches. Save room for the Caribbean fudge pie!

SKINNER & DANIELS, 5214 Market St., Wilmington. Tel. 799-1790.
   Cuisine: BARBECUE. **Reservations:** Not accepted.
$ Prices: Sandwiches $2–$3.75; barbecue plates and combinations $4–$10. No credit cards.
   Open: Mon–Sat 11am–9pm.

For distinctively North Carolinian barbecue, make a beeline for Skinner & Daniels. Its heaping plates of barbecued pork, chicken, beef, or short ribs—or its Brunswick stew—will satisfy the strongest appetites at amazingly modest cost. There's also a good selection of Southern vegetables (blackeyed peas, greens, and the like). You can place take-out orders until 9pm.

AT WRIGHTSVILLE BEACH

THE KING NEPTUNE, 11 N. Lumina St., Wrightsville Beach. Tel. 256-2525.

Cuisine: SEAFOOD/CONTINENTAL. **Reservations:** Not accepted.
$ Prices: Dinner $5.50–$18. AE, MC, V.
Open: Dinner daily 5–10pm.

Right in the center of Wrightsville Beach, it's a very informal, very nautical place with two large dining rooms and a lounge to one side. Pictures of Wrightsville Beach in the 1920s and 1930s adorn the walls. The atmosphere is lively, and the food is superb. In addition to seafood, there is also a good selection of beef and even a pizza.

THE RAW BAR, 13 E. Salisbury St., Wrightsville Beach. Tel. 256-2974.

Cuisine: SEAFOOD. **Reservations:** Not accepted.
$ Prices: Dinner $8–$13. AE, MC, V.
Open: Daily 5pm–1am.

Everybody in the area knows and loves the Raw Bar, located at the beach, right where U.S. 74 meets the ocean. This highly informal and often crowded restaurant serves oysters and clams, both on the half shell and steamed, as well as delicious seafood platters, either broiled or fried. Prices range from inexpensive to moderate.

CHAPTER 3

PIEDMONT NORTH CAROLINA

1. RALEIGH
2. DURHAM
3. CHAPEL HILL
4. GREENSBORO
5. WINSTON-SALEM
6. CHARLOTTE

Perhaps nowhere in the South do the old and the new come together quite so dramatically as in the section of North Carolina known as the Piedmont, lying between the coastal plains and the mountains. The contrast is especially marked in cities such as Winston-Salem, where the mammoth tobacco industry is represented by R. J. Reynolds Tobacco Company, and where the Stroh Brewery produces millions of barrels of beer each year—while across town the streets and buildings of Old Salem are perfectly restored to reflect the life of Moravians who planned the community in 1753.

The landscape itself is as varied as the industry, agriculture, and recreational opportunities. From the red clay hills around Raleigh and Greensboro, to the flat fields of tobacco, peanuts, and vegetables in the midlands, to the rolling sand dunes alive with longleaf pines and peach orchards in the Sandhills, there is a pleasant, ever-changing character to the countryside. The blossoms of dogwood, azaleas, camellias, and a host of summer-blooming flowers add to the visual beauty of this section of the state.

The Piedmont is also home to the "Research Triangle"—Duke University in Durham, the University of North Carolina in Chapel Hill, and North Carolina State University in Raleigh. Wake Forest University, founded in 1834 in the town of that name near Raleigh, and relocated to the western edge of Winston-Salem in the 1950s, is another leading educational institution in the region. Scores of small private colleges and junior colleges are also located throughout the area.

The Piedmont has sophisticated entertainment in its cities; the simplicity of outdoor life in fishing camps along three rivers; the excitement of intercollegiate sports competitions and the challenge of some of the world's greatest championship golf courses; and sightseeing trips to delight any history buff. This one 21,000-square-mile region fully justifies North Carolina's "Variety Vacationland" slogan.

1. RALEIGH

23 miles E of Durham; 28 miles E of Chapel Hill; 78 miles E of Greensboro; 104 miles E of Winston-Salem; and 143 miles NE of Charlotte

GETTING THERE By Plane The Raleigh/Durham International Airport is about 15 miles west of Raleigh, just off I-40. **American** (tel. toll free 800/433-7300), **Delta** (tel. toll free 800/221-1212), **Northwest** (tel. toll free 800/225-2525), **TWA** (tel. toll free 800/221-2000), **United** (tel. toll free 800/241-6522), and **USAir** (tel. toll free 800/428-4322) service the airport from out-of-state destinations; **American Eagle** (a division of American) and **USAir** provide regional service.

By Train **Amtrak** provides rail service from New York and Washington, D.C., to the north, and Florida to the south, with one train daily from each direction (tel. toll free 800/USA-RAIL).

By Bus   The **Greyhound/Trailways** bus station is at 321 W. Jones St. (tel. 919/828-2567).

By Car   U.S. 64 and U.S. 70 run east and west from Raleigh; U.S. 1 runs north and south, joining I-85, which runs northeast and is joined by I-40 to the west and I-95 to the east. U.S. 401 also runs northeast and southwest. The AAA is represented by the Carolina Motor Club, 2301 Blue Ridge Rd., Raleigh, NC 27605 (tel. 919/832-0543).

ESSENTIALS   The **area code** is 919. For tourist information, contact: **Greater Raleigh Convention and Visitors Bureau,** 225 Hillsborough St., Suite 400 (P.O. Box 1879), Raleigh, NC 27602 (tel. 919/834-5900, or toll free 800/849-8499). The **Raleigh Visitor Information Center,** 800 S. Salisbury St., Raleigh, NC 27602 (tel. 919/834-5900, or toll free 800/868-6666), is open weekdays from 8:30am to 5pm. The **Capital Area Visitor Center,** 301 N. Blount St., Raleigh, NC 27602 (tel. 919/733-3456), furnishes information about state government buildings and tours available on weekdays 8am to 5pm, Saturday 9am to 5pm, and Sunday 1 to 5pm. All three offices have city bus route information.

SPECIAL EVENTS   In mid-October, the **North Carolina State Fair** draws crowds from all over. Fairgrounds are located five miles west of town on I-440, then one mile west on N.C. 54. For exact dates, contact: North Carolina State Fair, 1025 Blue Ridge Blvd., Raleigh, NC 27607 (tel. 919/733-2145).

State government has been the principal business conducted in Raleigh since 1792, when it became the state's capital. A five-acre square that holds the state capitol is the focal point for a cluster of state office buildings in the heart of the city. From it radiate wide boulevards and lovely residential streets shaded by trees.

Downtown Raleigh has been transformed by an attractive pedestrian mall, where trees and fountains and statuary create a shopping oasis from the capitol to the civic center. No fewer than six college campuses dot the city streets with wide lawns and impressive brick buildings. The oldest, St. Mary's College, was founded in 1842; the youngest, North Carolina State University, in 1887. New suburbs and gigantic shopping centers dominate the outskirts, characterized by nicely designed homes blending into a landscape that retains much of its original wooded character.

Just prior to the Civil War, Raleigh was the setting for fiery legislative debate that led at last to North Carolina's secession from the Union in 1861. The city endured Union occupation by General Sherman in 1865, and during Reconstruction days it saw the west wing of its imposing Grecian Doric capitol building turned into a rowdy barroom by "carpetbagger" and "scalawag" legislators, its steps permanently nicked from whisky barrels rolling in and out of the building.

All of this, plus the abundance of good accommodations, makes Raleigh the ideal base from which to explore the Research Triangle area. Both Chapel Hill and Durham are within easy reach for day trips, and after a day of sightseeing, the capital city becomes an entertainment center for anything from smart, supper-club shows and dancing to Broadway theater to cultural events to intercollegiate sporting events (especially basketball, which is an abiding passion in this area).

WHAT TO SEE & DO

MAJOR ATTRACTIONS

For the best possible tour of the capital city, your first stop should be the **Capital Area Visitor Center** (see above). They'll start you off with an orientation film, arm you with brochures and loads of background information, and coordinate walking or driving tours of the area. Most of the attractions listed below are within easy walking distance of the state capitol and each other.

THE STATE CAPITOL, Capitol Square. Tel. 733-4994.

This stately Greek Revival structure (constructed 1833–1840) has been named a national historic landmark. All state business was conducted here until 1888. The building now contains the offices of the governor and lieutenant governor as well as restored legislative chambers. Beneath the awe-inspiring 97½-foot copper dome there's a duplicate of Antonio Canova's marble statue of George Washington dressed as a Roman general. The capitol takes about 30 to 45 minutes to tour.

Admission: Free.
Open: Mon–Fri 8am–5pm, Sat 9am–5pm, Sun 1–5pm.

NORTH CAROLINA STATE MUSEUM OF NATURAL SCIENCES, Museum Mall. Tel. 733-7450.

You'll need at least an hour here. Some outstanding displays are the fossil lab, where volunteers work on dinosaur bones; an exhibit featuring the state's gems; Bioscanner, an interactive exhibit of living animals shown enlarged on color video monitors; and the hands-on Discovery Room. There's even a bird hall and a live snake collection. Also on exhibit are four whale skeletons.

Admission: Free, but donations are appreciated.
Open: Mon–Sat 9am–5pm, Sun 1–5pm. **Closed:** Holidays.

THE LEGISLATIVE BUILDING, W. Jones St. Tel. 733-7928.

This striking contemporary building on the corner of Jones and Salisbury Streets was designed by Edward Durrell Stone, the architect for the Kennedy Center for the Performing Arts in Washington, D.C. Allow about 45 minutes to go through it—longer if you happen to be there when the legislature is in session, since you'll be able to watch the proceedings.

Admission: Free.
Open: Mon–Fri 8am–5pm, Sat 9am–5pm, Sun 1–5pm.

NORTH CAROLINA MUSEUM OF HISTORY, 109 E. Jones St. Tel. 733-3894.

The state's history is pictured in exhibits that tell the story of the Roanoke Island colonists and display relics of colonial Revolutionary, and Civil War eras. You'll want to spend about an hour and a half here, exploring costumes exhibits, shops, and period rooms. There's an interesting display tracing the developments of firearms, as well as changing exhibits in various areas. The museum will likely move to a new building in 1994.

Admission: Free.
Open: Tues–Sat 9am–5pm, Sun 1–6pm.

NORTH CAROLINA MUSEUM OF ART, 2110 Blue Ridge Rd. Tel. 833-1935.

This museum houses an important collection of European paintings, plus American, 20th-century, ancient, African, Oceanic, Judaica, and New World collections. A variety of special exhibitions and programs is offered. There's wheelchair access, and it's a good idea to plan for lunch in the **Museum Café** (tel. 833-3548), open Tuesday through Friday from 11:30am to 2:30pm, and Saturday and Sunday from 11am to 3pm.

Admission: Free.
Open: Tues–Thurs, Sat 9am–5pm; Fri 9am–9pm; Sun 11am–6pm.

RALEIGH–DURHAM AREA

0 — 3.5 km
2.1 mi

DURHAM

To Greensboro
To Chapel Hill
751 BYP
15
Erwin Rd.
BYP
501
Mud Creek
Sandy Creek
15 501
DURHAM
751
BUS 15
New Hope Creek
Old Chapel Hill Rd.
Garrett Rd.
Academy Rd.
Cameron Blvd.
Duke University Rd.
Anderson St.
Duke University W. Campus
Chapel Hill Rd.
BUS 501
Duke University E. Campus
University Dr.
Hope Valley Rd.
Cornwallis Rd.
751
Keene
40
Fayetteville Rd.
Old Durham Rd.
Apex Rd.
Fayetteville St.
Alston Ave.
Lawson St.
East-West Frwy.
55
147
Few
Bilboa
85
70
Hillsborough Rd.
Broad St.
Markham Ave.
Gregson St.
Duke Homestead Rd.
Duke Homestead State Historic Site
501
To Roxboro
BUS 501
BYP 501
Duke St.
Roxboro St.
147
BYP 70
Main St.
Angier Ave.
Magnum St.
Roxboro St.
Geer St.
Miami Blvd.
Briggs Ave.
55
15 85
To Henderson
BYP 70
BUS 70
Holloway St.
Oak Grove

To Airport
12 miles to Durham
12 miles to Raleigh

RALEIGH

12 miles to Durham
Asbury
To Airport
Edwards Mill Rd.
Mine Rd.
40
To Asheboro & Sanford
Western Blvd. Ext.
Hillsborough St.
Trinity Rd.
State Fair Grounds
Blue Ridge Rd.
Park Ridge Rd.
Lake Boone Trail
North Carolina Museum of Art
1
Six Forks Rd.
Cary-Macedonia Rd.
Franklin Rd.
54
Western Blvd.
440
Athens Dr.
Jones
Lake Johnson
Macedonia
Dillard Dr.
Holly Springs Rd.
Avent Ferry Rd.
North Carolina State University
Pullen Park
Lake Raleigh
Wade Ave.
Glenwood Ave.
70
St. Marys St.
Lassiter Mill Rd.
Oberlin Rd.
50
440
Wake Forest Rd.
To Henderson & Norlina
40
64
Walnut Creek
Capital Blvd.
Crabtree Creek
1
401
Lake Trojan
Lake Wheeler Rd.
Old Tryon Rd.
S. Saunders St.
South St.
Wilmington St.
Hammond Rd.
State Capitol
Edenton St.
New Bern Ave.
Lenoir St.
RALEIGH
To Fayetteville
50
70
401
Fayetteville Hwy.
70
50
Garner Rd.
Poole Rd.
440
Rock Quarry Rd.
64
401
40
To Rocky Mount
To Goldsboro

ANDREW JOHNSON'S BIRTHPLACE (Mordecai Historic Park and Mordecai House), 1 Mimosa St., Tel. 834-4844.

One of three North Carolina native sons who became president, Andrew Johnson was born in a small cabin about a block from the capitol building. The 17th president's birthplace has been moved to Mordecai Historic Park and is open to visitors. Be sure to see the restored Mordecai House with the original furnishings. Five generations of one of North Carolina's oldest families lived here (until 1964). Other historic buildings have also been relocated to the park to create a 19th-century village, including a kitchen, law office, and post office.

Admission: $3 adults, $1 children 7 to 17, free for children under 6; Mar–Nov, free every third Sun.

Open: Tues–Fri 10am–3pm, Sat–Sun 1:30–3:30pm. **Closed:** Mid-Dec to Mar.

NUCLEAR-REACTOR BUILDING, North Carolina State University Campus, Hillsborough St. Tel. 737-2191.

In direct contrast to all that history, the "age of the atom" is very much a part of the Raleigh scene, and you can visit the first college-owned reactor in the country on the North Carolina State University campus. Emphasis here is on peaceful utilization of atom-splitting. Once on campus, ask for directions to the nuclear-reactor building.

Open: Hours vary, call in advance.

SPORTS & RECREATION

Besides sightseeing, recreational possibilities include camping or picnicking in the Triangle area at ✪ **William B. Umstead State Park,** halfway between Raleigh and Durham on U.S. 70 (Rte. 8, Box 130, Raleigh, NC 27612; tel. 919/787-3033); and fishing and boating at the municipally owned and operated **Lake Wheeler,** five miles southwest of Raleigh on Rhamkatte Road.

Sports fans will want to check locally to see if the North Carolina State University championship basketball team, the Wolfpack, is playing.

WHERE TO STAY
EXPENSIVE

RALEIGH MARRIOTT CRABTREE VALLEY, 4500 Mariott Dr., Raleigh, NC 27612. Tel. 919/781-7000. Fax 919/781-3059. 375 rms and suites. A/C TV TEL **Directions:** U.S. 70 opposite Crabtree Valley Mall.

$ Rates: $100–$110 single or double. Extra person $10. Children under 18 stay free with parents. Weekend rates available. AE, CB, DC, MC, V.

✪ One of Raleigh's prettiest hotels boasts attractive public areas and guest rooms. There's a pool (with poolside beverage and lunch service), an exercise room, a games room, a gift shop, an intimate restaurant, and a cozy bar/lounge. The concierge level has minibars in suites and a private lounge; rates for the concierge level are slightly more and include continental breakfast. There's nightly entertainment with dancing, and there are golf privileges at a local course.

MODERATE

THE BROWNESTONE HOTEL, 1707 Hillsborough St., Raleigh, NC 27605. Tel. 919/828-0811; or toll free 800/237-0772, 800/331-7919 in N.C. Fax 919/828-0811. 210 rms. A/C TV TEL

$ Rates: $60 single; $70 double. Extra person $10. Luxury level (including continental breakfast), $70 single; $75 double. AE, DC, MC, V.

⑤ The Brownestone represents luxury at moderate prices, with beautiful rooms, a lovely restaurant and lounge, laundry service, and limousine service to the airport. They can also provide babysitters. Most rooms have balconies, and studios have a kitchen. On the luxury level, there's a private lounge and a concierge. Repeat guests will notice the recent renovations.

COURTYARD BY MARRIOTT, 1041 Wake Town Rd., Raleigh, NC 27609. Tel. 919/821-3400. Fax 919/821-1209. 153 rms, 14 suites. A/C TV TEL
$ Rates: Sun–Thurs $60–$65 single; $70–$75 double. Lower rates Fri–Sat and for stays of seven nights or more. Children under 12 stay free with parents. AE, DC, MC, V.

⭐ This attractive complex is built around a courtyard area with pool. The rooms are tastefully decorated and comfortably furnished; some have a poolside balcony or patio, and some have refrigerators. There's a whirlpool and exercise room, as well as a heated pool, and the dining room serves breakfast buffets at moderate prices.

HOLIDAY INN NORTH, 2815 Capitol Blvd., Raleigh, NC 27604. Tel. 919/872-7666, or toll free 800/HOLIDAY. Fax 919/872-3915. 269 rms, 3 suites. A/C TV TEL
$ Rates: $55–$73 single or double. Children under 19 stay free with parents. AE, CB, DC, DISC, MC, V.

On U.S. 1 and Rte. 401, this is an exceptionally nice member of the Holiday Inn chain. They added a tower two years ago, renovated all older guest rooms, and built the Holidome, which encloses an indoor pool, a Jacuzzi, a minigolf course, and an exercise room. Brandy's Holidome Restaurant serves all three meals, and there's dancing in Stars Lounge Monday through Saturday. The complex is filled with an abundance of plants and trees and fountains.

RESIDENCE INN BY MARRIOTT, 1000 Navaho Dr., Raleigh, NC 27609. Tel. 919/878-6100, or toll free 800/331-3131. Fax 919/876-4117. 144 one- and two-bedroom units. A/C TV TEL
$ Rates: $90 studio single or double, $45 on weekends. AE, DC, DISC, MC, V.

The inn has one- and two-bedroom units with fully equipped kitchens, some with fireplaces and some for nonsmokers and the physically handicapped. In addition to the complimentary wine-and-cheese reception every evening and the weekly cocktail party, guests can enjoy the heated swimming pool, whirlpools, sports court and fitness center, and barbecue and picnic facilities.

VELVET CLOAK INN, 1505 Hillsborough St., Raleigh, NC 27605. Tel. 919/828-0333; or toll free 800/334-4372, 800/662-8829 in N.C. 172 rms and suites. A/C TV TEL
$ Rates: $59–$89 single or double. Children under 12 stay free with parents. Weekend rates available. AE, DC, MC, V.

This inn is slightly reminiscent of New Orleans in style, with lots of exposed brick and wrought-iron touches. Rooms are attractive and frequently renovated, and amenities include complimentary coffee and morning newspapers in the lobby. There's also an enclosed pool and tropical garden, health club privileges (right next door), and free airport transportation. Baron's Restaurant and Nightclub provides entertainment. For more elegant dining, there's the Charter Room, which also often has live music.

BUDGET

FAIRFIELD INN BY MARRIOTT, 2641 Appliance Court, Raleigh, NC 27604. Tel. 919/856-9800, or toll free 800/228-2800. Fax 919/856-9800, ext. 709. 132 rms. A/C TV TEL
$ Rates: $36–$40 single; $42–$47 double. Weekend rates and senior discounts available. Children under 18 stay free with parents. AE, CB, DISC, MC, V.

The Fairfield Inn sits high on a hill and is just a short drive from downtown Raleigh. The rooms all have an attractive decor, pleasing furnishings, a seating area, and a work area with desk. There are nonsmoking rooms and rooms equipped for the handicapped. All are good-size, but those on the third floor are more spacious. There's complimentary coffee in the lobby, and several good restaurants are in the immediate vicinity.

WHERE TO DINE

I've eaten barbecued pork in a lot of places, but nowhere on earth does it taste quite like it does in Piedmont North Carolina. Slow-cooked in an open pit over hickory chips and basted all the while with a highly seasoned sauce, then finely chopped (no slabs of pork slathered with sauce, such as you get in New York, for instance), it is truly food fit for a king. But you really have to know your cook, even in North Carolina, and almost every locality has a favorite. The word in Raleigh is that Cooper's Barbecue is *the* place. So *go!* One final word: Don't expect anything elegant by way of decor—part of the mystique of North Carolina barbecue is that it's always served in plain surroundings, with lots of hush puppies and coleslaw.

EXPENSIVE

ANGUS BARN, U.S. 70 W at Airport Rd. Tel. 787-3505.
  Cuisine: STEAK. **Reservations:** Recommended. **Directions:** Go northwest on U.S. 70 W., about 12½ miles from downtown.
$ **Prices:** Appetizers $3.50–$8.95; main courses $14–$35; children's special $8.95. AE, MC, V.
  Open: Dinner Mon–Sat 5–11pm, Sun 5–10pm; Wild Turkey Lounge 4–11pm.
  Closed: Major holidays.

This is one of the best places in these parts for charcoal-broiled steak or choice ribs of beef; there's also an excellent selection of fresh seafoods. The setting in a restored 19th-century barn is rustic, but fireplaces add a graceful note. The food is superior, and beer, wine (ask to see the impressive Grand Wine Cellar), and cocktails are available. It's well worth the drive.

CASA CARBONE RISTORANTE, 6019-A Glenwood Ave. Tel. 781-8750.
  Cuisine: ITALIAN. **Reservations:** Recommended.
$ **Prices:** Dinner $7–$15. AE, DC, DISC, MC, V.
  Open: Dinner Mon–Sat 5–10pm, Sun 4–9pm.
Traditional southern Italian cuisine—pasta, veal, and chicken dishes—is featured here, and the homemade breads and desserts furnish the finishing touches. It's in the Oak Park Shopping Center.

42ND STREET OYSTER BAR AND SEAFOOD GRILL, 508 W. Jones St. Tel. 831-2811.
  Cuisine: SEAFOOD/GRILL. **Reservations:** Not required. **Directions:** Four blocks west and two blocks north of the Capitol.
$ **Prices:** Appetizers $5–$6; main courses $10–$16. AE, DC, MC, V.
  Open: Mon–Fri 11am–11pm, Sat 5–11pm, Sun 5–10pm. **Closed:** Holidays.
This large, lively restaurant is housed in a restored warehouse that dates from the 1930s. Oysters on the half shell share menu honors with platters of fried or steamed fish and lobster, prime rib, and fried chicken. Servings are plentiful, and there's also a children's menu.

GREENSHIELDS BREWERY & PUB, 214 E. Martin. Tel. 829-0214.
  Cuisine: AMERICAN. **Reservations:** Accepted on weekdays.
$ **Prices:** Appetizers $2.25–$5.95; main courses $4.75–$6.75; dinner for two $18–$30. AE, DISC, MC, V.

Open: Lunch daily 11:30am–2:30pm; dinner Mon–Sat 5:30–10pm, Sun 5–9pm. This upscale yet casual place is known for its beer brewed on the premises—there are four kinds, in fact. The restaurant portion is quiet and comfortable. On the bar/pub side is a wide-screen TV, a fireplace, and bookshelves. You can order a sandwich in the pub or more hearty fare in the main dining room.

MODERATE

BIG ED'S CITY MARKET RESTAURANT, 220 Wolfe St. Tel. 836-9909, or 836-9912.

Cuisine: REGIONAL/AMERICAN. **Reservations:** Not required.

$ **Prices:** Breakfast $4–$6; lunch $5–$8.50. No credit cards.

Open: Mon–Fri 6:30am–2pm, Sat 7am–noon.

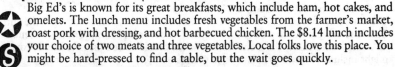

Big Ed's is known for its great breakfasts, which include ham, hot cakes, and omelets. The lunch menu includes fresh vegetables from the farmer's market, roast pork with dressing, and hot barbecued chicken. The $8.14 lunch includes your choice of two meats and three vegetables. Local folks love this place. You might be hard-pressed to find a table, but the wait goes quickly.

BLACK DOG CAFE, 208 E. Martin St. Tel. 828-1994.

Cuisine: CAFE/LIGHT. **Reservations:** Not required.

$ **Prices:** Appetizers $3–$6.29; lunch main courses $4.75–$7.50; dinner for two $21–$30. MC, V.

Open: Lunch Tues–Sat 11am–2:30pm; dinner Wed–Sat 5–10pm.

The Black Dog sits at the corner in the City Market—a prime location for people-watching. The decor is over the top, fun, and flavorful. I like the white and teal tile designs, and the adjoining gift shop, and I had to laugh at the fire hydrant indicating the bathroom. Clever. The dog theme is played out well. On your menu are savory grilled meats and pastas. Salads are a big attention-getter, too.

COOPER'S BARBECUE, 109 E. Davis St. No tel.

Cuisine: BARBECUE. **Reservations:** Not accepted.

$ **Prices:** Barbecue plates $4–$10. No credit cards.

Open: Mon–Sat 11am–9:30pm (hours may vary).

The word in Raleigh is that this is *the* place for barbecue. Even if you're a fan of that Texas stuff, you'll leave Cooper's a convert. Prices are reasonable and portions are generous. Don't expect a fancy decor, but do expect lots of hush puppies and coleslaw. You'll find a convenient parking lot just across the street. Bravo!

IRREGARDLESS CAFE, Morgan St. Tel. 833-8898.

Cuisine: VEGETARIAN (no red meat). **Reservations:** Not required.

$ **Prices:** Appetizers $4; main courses $5–$13; dinner for two $25. AE, DISC, MC, V.

Open: Lunch Mon–Fri 11:30am–2:15pm, Sun 10am–2pm; dinner Mon–Sat 5:30–9:30 or 10pm.

Despite being in a state that earns much of its income from tobacco production, this café has a no-smoking policy in force (perhaps that's why they call it the Irregardless Cafe!). The plants, knotty pine, and table candles create a woodsy effect. On the menu is salsa chicken, catfish, vegetarian dishes, salads, and sandwiches. The menu changes daily, and you can hear about it over the phone by calling 833-9920.

MOUNTAIN JACKS, 2711 Capitol Blvd. Tel. 872-2300.

Cuisine: STEAKS. **Reservations:** Not required. **Directions:** Go one block off I-40 (entry via Howard Johnson's).

$ **Prices:** Appetizers $4.25–$7.95; main courses $12.95–$17.95. AE, DC, MC, V.

Open: Lunch Mon–Fri 11:30am–2pm; dinner Mon–Thurs 5–10pm, Fri 5–11pm, Sat 4:30–11pm, Sun 4–9pm.

A large, rustic eatery, Mountain Jacks features prime rib and choice steaks as well as a large selection of seafood, plus chicken and a lovely rack of lamb with a rosemary-mint glaze. Among steaks, look for the top-grade filet mignon and whisky peppercorn steak. Prices in this popular place are good value for the money; the portions are hefty. Combination orders (prime ribs and seafood, perhaps—you choose two menu items) are specials at $17.95. There's also a cocktail lounge with occasional entertainment.

THUNDERBIRD BAR & GRILLE, 329 S. Blount St. Tel. 821-2662.
    Cuisine: AMERICAN/DINER. **Reservations:** Not required.
$ Prices: Appetizers $4–$4.55; main courses $4–$9.95. AE, CB, DC, DISC, MC, V.
    Open: Mon–Fri 11:15am–3:15pm.

You can't miss this place: There's a teal-colored 1956 Thunderbird sitting at the entry. This is Hard Rock Café on a strict budget. The decor is plainish. The menu items are all named after cars—the Delta 88 is chicken créole served on rice. Ethnic touches might include something Italian or Mexican.

BUDGET

K & W CAFETERIA, North Hills Mall. Tel. 782-0353.
    Cuisine: CAFETERIA. **Reservations:** Not accepted. **Directions:** Take the U.S. 1/64 Bypass for five miles.
$ Prices: Meals $4–$7. No credit cards.
    Open: Daily 11am–8pm.

For good food at truly budget prices, the K & W chain is dependable throughout the state. Food is above average for cafeteria service; specialties are fried chicken and roast beef. Baking is done on the premises.

EVENING ENTERTAINMENT

Check local newspapers for the current disco scene, which tends to change frequently. Productions of the **Raleigh Little Theatre** and concerts by the **North Carolina Symphony** are also publicized in local newspapers. Many of the larger hotels have lounge entertainment and dancing.

CHARLIE GOODNIGHT'S, 861 W. Morgan St. Tel. 828-5233.

Charlie's is an entertainment complex with a comedy nightclub, an original bar, the New Bar, and two food outlets. The "old bar" has no cover charge and features live bands with rock-and-roll music. The comedy club features name entertainers, and the New Bar is an upscale dance place with a cover charge, usually $5. One restaurant offers a Mexican menu and the other is a grill and seafood spot. If there's anything going on in Raleigh, its probably going on at Charlie's. It's open Tuesday through Saturday from 5pm to 2:30am.

RESEARCH TRIANGLE PARK

Located on 5,200 acres in the center of a rough triangle formed by Raleigh, Durham, and Chapel Hill, Research Triangle Park doesn't qualify as a true "sightseeing" destination. Still, it's worthwhile to drive through it, for this is one of the largest research centers in the country. Over 50 institutions (including the Environmental Protection Agency, General Electric, DuPont, the National Institute for Environmental Health Sciences, the Burroughs-Wellcome Foundation, and IBM) have invested millions here in projects under way, completed, or projected.

To reach the park, turn off the East-West Expressway from Raleigh to Durham onto N.C. 54. There are lots of signs.

WHERE TO STAY

GUEST QUARTERS SUITE HOTEL, 2515 Meridian Pkwy., Durham, NC 27713. Tel. 919/361-4660, or toll free 800/424-2900. Fax 919/361-2256. 203 rms. A/C TV TEL

$ Rates: $114 single; $134 double. AE, CB, DC, DISC, MC, V.

Here is a fine example of how wonderful a hotel can be. It's a seven-story, sloped building sitting in a park setting on the shore of a small man-made lake. RTP (Research Triangle Park) is a business environment, but this hotel is more like a resort. The jogging trail, paddle boats, volleyball court, outdoor pool, dock, lighted tennis court, and sundeck make you want to be outside. You can even rent a bicycle. No wonder it's so popular. Inside is a pool, whirlpool, workout stations, and video games. The restaurant features a seafood and grill menu, and there is a lounge, too. All the accommodations are suites, with wet bars, refrigerators, two TVs, sleeping and living areas, and dining tables. You can request a video player and a coffeemaker as well.

MARRIOTT AT RESEARCH TRIANGLE PARK, 4700 Guardian Dr., Morrisville, NC 27560. Tel. 919/941-6200, or toll free 800/228-9290. Fax 919/941-6229. 224 rms. A/C TV TEL

$ Rates: $109–$114 single; $119–$124 double; $59 weekends. AE, CB, DC, DISC, ER, MC, V.

Just look above to see how much the weekend rates are slashed to attract business. That's wonderful. During the week, when commercial folk come here to conduct business, the place is often packed. That gives the rest of us an opportunity to slip on on weekends and keep things going—it's sort of like being subsidized by someone else. The slick, six-story hotel really does impress. Sun streams through the skylights in the lobby, and you can see the courtyard from the restaurant. White lights twinkle in the trees of the bar. Recoup from a late night out at the sunny terrace or take a swim, sauna, whirlpool, or workout. Like other Marriott hotels, accommodations are quite fine with remote-control TVs, dining tables, double or king-size beds, ample baths, and room service.

SHERATON IMPERIAL HOTEL & TOWERS, 4700 Emperor Blvd., Morrisville, NC 27560. Tel. 919/941-5050, or toll free 800/325-3535. Fax 919/941-5156. 331 rms. A/C TV TEL **Directions:** Take exit 282 off I-40.

$ Rates: $98–$108 single or double. AE, CB, DC, DISC, MC, V.

This is a surprise entry in the RTP neighborhood, and it lives up to its lofty name. Again, during the week, it's a haven for executives, but weekends, it's quiet and offers appealing rates. There's a lot here for your money: a restaurant with excellent prices and guaranteed fast service, a be-bop Bill Haley atmosphere in the lounge, and an outdoor pool and whirlpool. For a fee, you can use the executive health club next door. Within its 10 floors are lovely guest rooms, three floors of which are executive or club-level accommodations with upgraded appointments and facilities.

2. DURHAM

23 miles W of Raleigh; 12 miles NE of Chapel Hill; 54 miles E of Greensboro; 81 miles E of Winston-Salem; 140 miles NE of Charlotte

GETTING THERE By Plane For service to Raleigh/Durham International Airport, see "Raleigh," above.

By Train Amtrak (tel. toll free 800/USA-RAIL) has a station in Durham on Pettegrew Street (no street number).

By Bus   The **Greyhound/Trailways** bus station is at 820 Morgan St. (tel. 919/687-4800).

By Car   Reached from the east via N.C. 98 and U.S. 40 joining N.C. 147, from the north and west via U.S. 85, and from the south via U.S. 15/501 joining U.S. 40 to N.C. 147. The AAA office in Durham is **Carolina Motor Club,** 3909 University Dr., Durham, NC 27717 (tel. 919/489-3306).

ESSENTIALS   The **area code** is 919. Visitor information is available from the **Durham Convention & Visitors Bureau,** 101 E. Morgan St., Durham, NC 27701 (tel. 919/687-0288, or toll free 800/446-8604). They can supply local bus route information.

In the late 1860s, when Washington Duke walked 137 miles back to his farm in Durham after being mustered out of the Confederate forces at the end of the Civil War, he took up life again as a tobacco farmer. That first year, he started grinding and packaging the crop to sell in small packets. Then, in 1880, he decided there was a future in cigarettes—then a new idea—and set to work with his three sons to manufacture them on a small scale. By 1890 they had formed the American Tobacco Company, and a legendary American manufacturing empire was under way. Durham, which was a small village when Duke came home from the war, blossomed into an industrial city, taking its commercial life from the "golden weed." And it still does. From September until the end of December, tobacco warehouses ring with the chants of auctioneers moving from one batch of the cured tobacco to the next, followed by buyers who indicate their bids with nods or hand signals.

Even Duke University, the cultural heart of Durham, owes its life's breath to tobacco, for it was little noticed as Trinity College until national and international prominence came with a Duke family endowment of $40 million in 1924. Along with a change in name, the university gained a new West Campus, complete with massive Gothic structures of stone, flagstone walks, and box hedges. Its medical center has become one of the most highly respected in the world.

WHAT TO SEE & DO

IN DURHAM

DUKE HOMESTEAD STATE HISTORIC SITE, 2828 Duke Homestead Rd. Tel. 477-5498.

Duke Homestead is a national historical landmark, and you can visit the home, the original factory building, and the farm. Take time to go through the **Tobacco Museum,** which traces the history of tobacco from Native American days to the present. A color film, *Carolina Bright,* serves as an orientation to the site.

Admission: Free.

Open: Apr–Oct Mon–Sat 9am–5pm, Sun 1–5pm; Nov–Mar Tues–Sat 10am–4pm. Sun 1–5pm. **Directions:** Half a mile north of I-85; take the Guess Road exit.

MUSEUM OF LIFE AND SCIENCE, 433 Murray Ave. Tel. 220-5429.

This museum is especially planned for children, but no matter what your age, you'll love the new exhibits on the human body, weather, geology, and physics. The large diorama is of the *Apollo 15* lunar landing, complete with a sample of moon rock, and the exciting hands-on exhibits in the Science Arcade and in the Nature Center's Discovery Room. Other exhibits include communications and small science for young children. The 78 acres also hold the Farmyard Loblolly Park and a mile-long narrow-gauge railroad. It's north of I-85 off Duke Street.

Admission: $5 adults, $3.50 children 3 to 12 and senior citizens, free for children under 3.

Open: Labor Day–Memorial Day, Mon–Sat 10am–5pm, Sun 1–5pm. Memorial Day–Labor Day, Mon–Sat 10am–6pm, Sun 1–6pm.

AT DUKE UNIVERSITY

The campuses of Duke University cover more than 1,000 acres on the west side of the city. The **East Campus,** which was the old Trinity College, features Georgian architecture, and its red-brick and limestone buildings border a half-mile-long grassy mall. There's an excellent ✪ **Museum of Art** on this campus, just off West Main Street, that's free (open Tuesday through Friday 9am to 5pm, Saturday 11am to 2pm, and Sunday 2 to 5pm) and holds marvelous collections of classical, pre-Columbian, African, medieval, European, American, and Asian art, in addition to changing special exhibitions.

It's the **West Campus** (a short drive away on winding, wooded Campus Drive), however, that really steals the show. Its Gothic-style buildings and beautifully landscaped grounds are nothing short of breathtaking.

The highlight of this showplace is the ✪ **Duke Chapel,** reminiscent of England's Canterbury Cathedral. The bell tower of the majestic cruciform chapel rises 210 feet and houses a 50-bell carillon that rings out at the end of each workday and on Sunday. There's a half-million-dollar Flentrop organ with more than 5,000 pipes (said to be one of the finest in the western hemisphere) in a special oak gallery, its case 40 feet high. Renowned organists perform at the console in public recitals on the first Sunday of each month. Seventy-seven stained-glass windows light the long nave with soft shades of reds, blues, greens, and yellows, and highlight an ornate screen and carved-oak choir stalls. Visiting hours are 8am to 5pm daily, and there are interdenominational services every Sunday at 11am.

The university's **Botany Department Greenhouses** (some 13 rooms of plants, both native and rare) are open to the public from 10am to 4:30pm and hold the most diverse collection of plants in the Carolinas. The West Campus is also the setting of **Duke Medical Center,** which has gained worldwide fame for its extensive treatment facilities and varied research programs.

Basketball fans will want to check to see if the Duke Blue Devils, 1991 and 1992 NCAA champions, are playing at home during their stay.

To find out more about Duke, call the Admissions Office (tel. 684-3214). They'll be glad to arrange special guided tours. I especially recommend a tour of the **Sarah P. Duke Gardens,** 55 acres of gardens on the West Campus that draw more than 200,000 visitors each year. In a valley bordered by a pine forest, the garden features a lily pond, stone terraces, a rose garden, a native-plant garden, an Asiatic arboretum, a wisteria-draped pergola, and colorful seasonal plantings. It's open every day from 8am until dark—a good place to have a picnic lunch or to end a day of campus sightseeing.

WHERE TO STAY

If Durham is your choice as a Piedmont base, you should know that rates sometimes go up during Duke University graduation periods and for major sporting events.

BROWNSTONE MEDCENTER INN, 2424 Erwin Rd., Durham, NC 27705. Tel. 919/286-7761; or toll free 800/367-0293, 800/872-9009 in N.C. 140 rms. A/C TV TEL

$ Rates (including continental breakfast): $48 single; $56–$130 double. Extra person $8. AE, MC, V.

✪ This is a conveniently located inn with tastefully furnished guest rooms, an indoor pool, whirlpool, sauna, coin laundry, beauty shop, and a dining room. There are health club privileges nearby, and free transportation to the airport and to Duke University Medical Center. The inn is wheelchair-accessible. The Sunday brunch is excellent.

FAIRFIELD INN BY MARRIOTT, 3710 Hillsborough Rd., Durham, NC 27705. Tel. 919/382-3388, or toll free 800/228-2800. 135 rms. A/C TV TEL
Directions: Take exit 173 from I-85.
$ Rates (including continental breakfast): $40 single; $46 double. Extra person $3. Children under 18 stay free with parents. Senior discount available. AE, DC, DISC, MC, V.

This member of Marriott's budget motel chain has especially stylish guest rooms, a pool, and a restaurant right next door. For full details of the many special features offered by Fairfield Inns, see Chapter 1, "Where to Stay and Dine."

OMNI DURHAM HOTEL & CONVENTION CENTER, 201 Foster St., Durham, NC 27701. Tel. 919/683-6664, or toll free 800/THE-OMNI. Fax 919/683-2046. 187 rms. A/C TV TEL
$ Rates: $59–$79 single or double. AE, CB, DC, DISC, MC, V.
If you want to be close to the Ninth Street cafés and shops, stay in this downtown hotel. From some rooms, you can see the Duke University Chapel. Downtown Durham often clears out during the weekends, so the hotel offers excellent weekend rates. A restaurant is in part of the open lobby. There are no health facilities, but the hotel van will take you to a club nearby. Many folks go to Chapel Hill for entertainment. You can expect full first-class treatment in rooms with all the expected amenities and comforts.

WHERE TO DINE

Brightleaf Square is a complex of former warehouses built between 1900 and 1904 and once used to store tobacco. Its name is taken from the flue-cured local tobacco. A host of restaurants and shops are located here, where tobacco was aged until 1970 when the warehouses closed down. You can enjoy a stroll and ice cream in the courtyards. The **Satisfaction Restaurant and Bar,** 19-J Brightleaf Square (tel. 682-7397), is popular with the student crowd. It's open Monday through Saturday 11am–1am and is decorated with exposed brick, ice cream–parlor chairs, knotty pine, a wide-screen TV, and the back end of a VW. Pizza is a specialty. Brightleaf is located downtown at West Main Street.

MODERATE

ANOTHERTHYME, 109 N. Gregson St. Tel. 682-5225.
Cuisine: VEGETARIAN/SEAFOOD. **Reservations:** Recommended.
$ Prices: Lunch $4–$8; dinner $7–$15. AE, MC, V.
Open: Lunch Mon–Fri 11:30am–2:30pm; dinner Mon–Thurs 6–10pm, Fri–Sat 6–11pm. Sun 6–9pm; late-night meals daily 10pm–1am. **Closed:** Major holidays.
The atmosphere here is casual and the menu is creative, crossing ethnic culinary borders with innovative dishes that emphasize vegetarian courses and seafood. Charcoal-grilled swordfish steaks and seafood kebabs are popular with locals. This fashionable place is one of the few in the region with a late-night menu. On Thursday and Saturday there's live jazz from 10:30pm to 2am.

CLAIRE'S, 2701 Chapel Hill Rd. Tel. 493-5721.
Cuisine: CONTINENTAL. **Reservations:** Recommended.
$ Prices: Dinner $13–$20. AE, DC, MC, V.
Open: Mon–Sat 4pm–midnight.

⭐ You'll find Claire's in a lovely 1909 house, recently placed on the register of National Historic Places. There are five dining rooms, with outdoor dining during warm months. The menu now includes a selection of Southern foods. One new item is Summer Seafood Gumbo—a hearty stew with oysters, shrimp, garlic sausage, and a lobster claw, served over rice. Other entrées might include sautéed snapper, poached salmon, or rack of lamb. For such quality, the prices are moderate. There's a large and varied wine list, and the comfortable Claire's Lounge serves beer and cocktails.

FRENCH QUARTER, 115 N. Duke St. Tel. 688-4586.

Cuisine: CAJUN. **Reservations:** Accepted.

$ Prices: Appetizers $3.50–$5.25; main courses $6.95–$11.95; dinner for two $21. AE, CB, MC, V.

Open: Dinner Mon–Thurs 5–10pm, Fri–Sat 5–11pm, Sun 5–9:30pm.

The French Quarter is both a night spot and a restaurant. Both sides are immensely popular. They brew their own amber, golden, and dark beer. One of the specialties is crayfish étoufée (sautéed crayfish with a spicy sauce over rice). Live bands perform Tuesday and Thursday through Saturday (with a $2 to $4 cover).

BUDGET

FRANCESCA'S DESSERT CAFFE, 706 Ninth St. Tel. 286-4177.

Cuisine: CAFE. **Reservations:** Not required.

$ Prices: $1.50–$3 desserts, coffees, and teas. No credit cards.

Open: Sun–Thurs 11:30am–11:30pm, Fri–Sat 11:30am–midnight.

⭐ Make a stop at Francesca's for flavored coffees or maybe ice cream waffle cones. The decor is rather mod looking, and there's wooden benches outside for you to watch the passersby. Inside, the decor is streamlined with contemporary art hanging on brick walls. Try the pecan turtle tart or white chocolate cheesecake.

NINTH STREET BAKERY, 776 Ninth St. Tel. 286-0303.

Cuisine: CAFE. **Reservations:** Not required.

$ Prices: Lunch $3–$7. MC, V.

Open: Mon–Thurs 7am–7pm, Fri 7am–11:30pm, Sat 8am–11:30pm, Sun 8am–5pm.

⭐ Stop at the bakery for a cup of tea and something sweet. There are munchies, soups, salads, coffees, and teas. The crowd is youthful, and the atmosphere is very relaxing.

RAVENA'S RESTAURANT, CAFE & BOOKSTORE, 716 Ninth St. Tel. 286-3170.

Cuisine: CAFE. **Reservations:** Not required.

$ Prices: Appetizers $3.95; sandwiches $2.95–$4.95; salads $2.50–$6.95. DISC, MC, V.

Open: Sun–Thurs 10am–10pm, Fri–Sat 11am–11pm.

Ⓢ The sign outside invites you to come in and study. And the students do. Amid 25,000 used paperback books, the bookstore and café delight readers and coffee lovers. Each table has fresh flowers stuck in a wine bottle. It's cute, country, and casual. Just what students appreciate. On the menu are sandwiches, salads, soups, submarines, wine, beer, and of course, espresso and cappuccino.

TALK OF THE TOWN, 108 E. Main St. Tel. 682-7747.

Cuisine: AMERICAN. **Reservations:** Not required.

$ Prices: Soups and salads $1.50–$3.25; burgers $2.25–$3.50; sandwiches $2.50–$4.50. MC, V.

Open: Tues–Wed 11am–3pm, Thurs 11am–midnight, Fri 11am–2am, Sat 8pm–2am

Every other Friday, Talk of the Town comes alive with amateurs at the microphone. Other times live bands play ($4 cover). The students enjoy coming here because it's a hoot and a half and it's cheap.

EVENING ENTERTAINMENT

DEVINES RESTAURANT & SPORTS BAR, 904 W. Main St. Tel. 682-0228.

The jocks from Duke and UNC come here to watch their favorite teams battle. Several monitors, including one theater size, keep patrons abreast of the action. On the bar menu are sandwiches, burgers, salads, and soups. The rivalry and revelry are healthy here. It's open daily from 11:30am to 2am.
Admission: $1. Wed.

3. CHAPEL HILL

28 miles W of Raleigh; 12 miles SW of Durham; 48 miles SE of Greensboro; 74 miles E of Winston-Salem; and 127 miles NE of Charlotte

GETTING THERE By Plane   Nearest service is to Raleigh (see above).

By Train   Nearest service is to Raleigh (see above).

By Bus   The **Greyhound/Trailways** depot is at 311 W. Franklin St. (tel. 919/942-3356).

By Car   Chapel Hill is reached from the east by U.S. 40 and I-85, from the west by I-85, from the north by N.C. 57, and from the south by N.C. 54.

ESSENTIALS   The **area code** is 919. For sightseeing information contact the **Chapel Hill–Carrboro Chamber of Commerce,** 104 S. Estes Drive (P.O. Box 2897), Chapel Hill, NC 27514 (tel. 919/967-7075).

The third point of the Research Triangle area is Chapel Hill, a small city that has managed to hold on to its "village" atmosphere in spite of a university that annually enrolls over 22,000 students. Chapel Hill *is* the University of North Carolina, and has been in existence since 1795, when it was the first state university in the country. The 2,000-acre campus holds 125 buildings, ranging from Old East, the oldest state university building in the country (its cornerstone was laid in 1793), to Morehead Planetarium, which was an astronaut-training center in the early days of the space program.

When the Civil War erupted, the student body here was the second largest in the country, after Yale's.

Then the fighting started and most of UNC's undergraduates and faculty left for battlefields. After the war and reconstruction, the school closed down from 1868 to 1875. Since its reopening, it has consistently been a leader in American education and a center of liberal intellectualism in a generally conservative state. So strong is the attachment and affection of those connected with the university that more than once it and Chapel Hill have been described as "the southern part of heaven."

WHAT TO SEE & DO

Your best introduction to the university is a free one-hour campus tour that leaves from Morehead Planetarium (the west entrance) on East Franklin Street (for details, contact the University News Bureau, 210 Pittsboro St., tel. 962-0045).

With the tour or on your own, look for the **Old Well,** once the only source of drinking water for Chapel Hill. It stands in the center of the campus on Cameron Avenue, in a small templelike enclosure with a dome supported by classic columns. Just east of it is **Old East,** begun in 1793 and the country's oldest state university building. Across the way stands the "newcomer," **Old West,** built in 1824. **South Main Building,** nearby, was begun in 1798 and not finished until 1814; in the interim, students lived inside the empty shell in rude huts. At the **Coker Arboretum** at Cameron Avenue and Raleigh Street, five acres are planted with a wide variety of plants. As you walk the campus you'll hear popular tunes coming from the 167-foot **Morehead-Patterson Bell Tower,** an Italian Renaissance–style campanile.

You won't want to miss ✪ **Morehead Planetarium,** on East Franklin Street (tel. 549-6863). The "star" of the permanent scientific exhibits here is a large orrery showing the simultaneous action of planets revolving around the suns, moons revolving around planets, and planets rotating on their axes. There's also a stargazing theater with a 68-foot dome. Show times vary considerably, so call for the current schedule. Admission to the planetarium is free; for the show, it's $3 for adults, $2.50 for seniors and students, $2 for children 12 and under.

Try to catch a PlayMakers Repertory Company production at the **Paul Green Theatre.** The company offers professional productions of classical or contemporary drama, as well as new works.

Basketball fans will want to see the University of North Carolina–Chapel Hill Tarheels, the 1993 NCAA champions.

Off campus, the ✪ **North Carolina Botanical Garden,** on Laurel Hill Road and U.S. 15-501 Bypass (tel. 962-0522), is open mid-March to mid-November weekdays from 8am to 5pm, Saturday 10am to 5pm, and Sunday 2 to 5pm. It boasts 330 acres of nature trails, as well as herb gardens, a collection of carnivorous plants, and native plants in habitat settings. Admission is free.

WHERE TO STAY

IN CHAPEL HILL

CAROLINA INN, 105 W. Cameron Ave. (P.O. Box 1110), Chapel Hill, NC 27514. Tel. 919/933-2001. 140 rms. A/C TV TEL

$ Rates: $44–$82 single; $54–$92 double. AE, MC, V.

This historic old inn is owned and operated by the university. The colonial decor creates a warm atmosphere, and rooms vary in size and style. There's a moderately priced restaurant and an inexpensive cafeteria, as well as an attractive lounge. Reserve as far in advance as possible at this popular hostelry. There are some single (twin) rooms available at special rates.

OMNI EUROPA, 1 Europa Dr., Chapel Hill, NC 27514. Tel. 919/968-4900. Fax 919/968-3520. 171 rms. A/C TV TEL

$ Rates: $104 single; $114 double. Extra person $12. Children under 16 stay free with parents. AE, DC, DISC, MC, V.

Ground-floor rooms have private patios and upper floors have private balconies at this tastefully decorated and furnished hotel. Centrally located, it has a pool, gift shop, lighted tennis courts, and golf privileges nearby. There's entertainment and dancing in the attractive lounge. The health club nearby is free to guests.

SIENA HOTEL, 1505 E. Franklin St., Chapel Hill, NC 27514. Tel. 919/929-4000, or toll free 800/223-7379. Fax 919/968-8527. 80 rms. A/C TV TEL

$ Rates (including continental breakfast): $99–$105 single; $109–$115 double. AE, CB, DC, MC, V.

I stumbled onto the Siena when I was looking for the Omni Europa and fell for this place over its neighbor. The four-story stucco hotel is designed in a Mediterranean look with the accent on upscale to attract the UNC parents.

The restaurant enjoys an excellent reputation. There might be a wait to be seated for Sunday brunch here ($14.95), but it's worth it. Other times, the menu is northern Italian. Rooms look European, warm, and inviting, with remote-control TVs in armoires, upholstered reading chairs, and various bed arrangements. This is also close to Chapel Hill nightlife.

NEARBY

FEARRINGTON HOUSE INN, 2000 Fearrington Village Center, Pittsboro, NC 27312. Tel. 919/542-2121. Fax 919/542-4202. 23 rms. A/C TV TEL **Directions:** 10 minutes south of Chapel Hill via U.S. 15/501.
$ **Rates** (including breakfast): $150–$230 double. MC, V.

The Fearrington House will tug at your heart . . . and your purse, but you won't be disappointed. This isn't the kind of place that lends itself to children, so come solo. The 60 acres of grounds are meticulously kept; the rose gardens are quite a sight. And I can't say enough about the restaurant. It's in a separate white clapboard building with an elegant decor, ranging from sunny French country to Laura Ashley styling. Little alcoves make dining an intimate experience. The food is expertly prepared and served. Another, more traditional restaurant is also available. Rooms are just as inviting with lots of little details: silk or dried flowers, antiques mixed with high quality reproductions, double ottomans, stereos, cable TVs, cathedral ceilings, some seating areas, marble tables, various bed arrangements, and luxuriously appointed baths. You won't find comparable accommodations anywhere in North Carolina.

WHERE TO DINE

CROOK'S CORNER, 610 W. Franklin St. Tel. 929-7643.
   Cuisine: REGIONAL. **Reservations:** Recommended on weekends.
$ **Prices:** Appetizers $3.50–$5; main courses $8–$17. MC, V.
   Open: Dinner daily 6–10:30pm; Sun brunch 10:30am–2pm.

Behind the rather quirky facade of Crook's Corner lurks one of the South's superb restaurants. The seasonal menu may include such delights as shrimp and grits or cajun ribeye or vegetarian pasta. Among the side dishes are such down-home delicacies as fresh collard greens and hoppin' John—blackeyed peas and rice with scallions, tomato, and cheddar. Their wine-by-the-glass list is excellent.
The walls of the dining room are a continuously changing exhibition of works by local artists. Seating capacity is limited to 70; there's seating for about 50 more outside in nice weather. You may have to wait for a table—but it's worth it.

PYEWACKET RESTAURANT, 431 W. Franklin St. Tel. 929-0297.
   Cuisine: SEASONAL AMERICAN. **Reservations:** Not required. **Directions:** The Courtyard, ½ mile west of Columbia St.
$ **Prices:** Lunch under $10; dinner $11–$20. AE, DC, MC, V.
   Open: Lunch Mon–Thurs 11:30am–2:30pm; dinner Mon–Thurs 6–10pm, Fri–Sat 6–10:30pm, Sun 5:30–9:30pm.
The decor is "elegant eclectic" here. There's a cozy lounge with comfortable couches, two high-ceilinged rooms done in soft reddish browns, and a greenhouse dining room with windows all around (no smokers allowed in this area). Lunch choices include a selection of pasta, soups, sandwiches, omelets, salads, and desserts; at dinner, seafood, vegetarian, and chicken specialties are featured.

RESTAURANT LA RESIDENCE, 220 W. Rosemary St. Tel. 967-2506.
   Cuisine: CONTINENTAL. **Reservations:** Recommended.

$ Prices: Dinner $15–$25. AE, DC, MC, V.
Open: Dinner Tues–Sat 6–9:30pm, Sun 6–8:30pm.

Housed in a half-century-old residence surrounded by a patio and gardens, this restaurant has several small dining rooms, each with its own decor. A bistro and bar are also available for more casual dining. New chef Devon Mills has moved away from the classical French cooking for which Restaurant la Residence was long known, but you won't be disappointed with the exciting new menu of eclectic and traditional dishes prepared with the freshest seasonal ingredients. For dessert, try the homemade ice creams or sorbets, or the chocolate soufflé cake. There's an exceptionally fine (but limited) wine list.

---

4. GREENSBORO

78 miles W of Raleigh, 54 miles W of Durham, 48 miles W of Chapel Hill, 27 miles E of Winston-Salem, and 91 miles NE of Charlotte

GETTING THERE By Plane Greensboro is served by **American** (tel. toll free 800/433-7300), **Continental** (tel. toll free 800/525-0280), **Delta** (tel. toll free 800/221-1212), **United** (tel. toll free 800/241-6522), and **USAir** (tel. toll free 800/428-4322).

By Train Amtrak has one northbound and one southbound train through Greensboro daily (tel. toll free 800/USA-RAIL).

By Bus The **Greyhound/Trailways** depot is at 501 W. Lee St. (tel. 919/379-9086).

By Car Reach Greensboro from the east and southwest via I-85, from the west via U.S. 40, and from the south via U.S. 220. For AAA services, contact the **Carolina Motor Club,** 14-A Oak Branch Dr., Greensboro, NC 27419 (tel. 919/852-0506).

ESSENTIALS The **area code** for Greensboro is 919; for Spencer, it's 704. For tourist information on Greensboro and vicinity, contact the **Greensboro Area Convention and Visitors Bureau,** 317 S. Greene St., Greensboro, NC 27401 (tel. 919/274-2282, or toll free 800/344-2282). Ask also for information on city bus routes and schedules.

Greensboro was settled by freedom-loving Scotch-Irish, Germans, and Quakers, and the Scotch-Irish and the Germans and their descendants fought valiantly in the Revolution and the War of 1812. When North Carolina seceded from the Union in 1861, Greensboro became an important Confederate supply depot, and when the rebel cause was lost, Jefferson Davis met with Union General Johnston in Greensboro to arrange surrender terms. Today, the thriving city is a leader in higher education and the manufacture of textiles, cigarettes, and electronic equipment, as well as home to a large insurance industry.

WHAT TO SEE & DO

Aside from the sightseeing attractions listed below, bargain hunters will want to visit two nearby towns, both overflowing with factory outlet shops. High Point, 17 miles south of Greensboro (so named because it was the highest point along the 1853 North Carolina and Midland Railroad from Salem to Fayetteville), is notable for its furniture and hosiery shops. Burlington, 21 miles east of Greensboro, is a major textile center, with scores of factory outlets for clothing, fabrics, sheets, towels, blankets, and the like.

IN TOWN

GREENSBORO HISTORICAL MUSEUM, 130 Summit Ave. Tel. 373-2043.

Greensboro was O. Henry's hometown and the birthplace of Dolley Madison. The short-story writer was known as William Sidney Porter in these parts. Here you'll find an exhibit illustrating his life and work, plus a fine collection from Dolley Madison's life as the only native-born North Carolina First Lady. Other exhibits include early modes of transportation, furnishings, pottery, textiles, and military artifacts. Another exhibit of note recognizes the civil rights lunch counter sit-ins at Woolworth's.

Admission: Free.
Open: Tues–Sat 10am–5pm, Sun 2–5pm.

NEARBY

GUILFORD COURTHOUSE NATIONAL MILITARY PARK, 2332 New Garden Rd. Tel. 288-1776.

This 220-acre park marks one of the closing battles of the Revolution, the Battle of Guilford Courthouse on March 15, 1781. Gen. Nathanael Greene (Greensboro was named for him) led a group of inexperienced troops against Lord Cornwallis. Although he was defeated, he inflicted severe losses on the British. Cornwallis hotfooted it out of this part of the country and headed for Yorktown, Virginia, where he surrendered his depleted forces just seven months later, on October 19. The visitor center has films, brochures, and displays about the historic battle. There are also wayside exhibits along the two-mile road that connects some of the many monuments. The tour road closes at 4:30pm.

Admission: Free.
Open: Visitors' center daily 8:30am–5pm. **Closed:** Christmas Day and New Year's Day. **Directions:** Go six miles northwest of Greensboro on U.S. 220.

ALAMANCE BATTLEGROUND STATE HISTORIC SITE, N.C. 62., Burlington. Tel. 227-4785.

This is where those upstart farmers marched against Royal Governor Tryon in 1771 to protest corrupt government practices. Ill-trained and poorly equipped, they were soundly defeated—the battle lasted only two hours—but the stout-hearted "Regulators" were among the first Southern colonists to demonstrate their objection to royal rule. The visitor center has an audiovisual presentation. The John Allen House is a restored log dwelling typical of North Carolina backwoods homes at the time of the battle.

Admission: Free.
Open: Visitors' center, Apr–Oct, Mon–Sat 9am–5pm, Sun 1–5pm; Nov–Mar, Tues–Sat 10am–4pm, Sun 1–4pm. **Directions:** Take I-85/40 exit 143 to N.C. 62, then go six miles to site.

IN SPENCER

Just about halfway between Greensboro and Charlotte, a little off I-85 (near historic Salisbury), the little town of Spencer is a mecca for dyed-in-the-wool railway buffs.

SPENCER SHOPS AND NORTH CAROLINA TRANSPORTATION MUSEUM, 411 S. Salisbury Ave., Spencer. Tel. 704/636-2889.

The shops were established in 1896 as a major repair facility for the Southern Railway. Opened as a museum in 1983, the Master Mechanics Building is the focal point in the 57-acre site. Visitors are free to wander and inspect the growing collection of transportation memorabilia. Once, in the 1930s, this facility built a locomotive in one day. It's a friendly, informal place. Staff members are likely to jump in with anecdotes about the shops' history at your first show of enthusiasm. Rail rides are sometimes available, and a large museum shop offers unusual railroad items ranging from 15¢ maps to *Orient Express* crystal.

Note: Just across the street, stop in at Krider's Restaurant (tel. 704/633-5219), where Evelyn Krider loves to recall the days when railroading was the hub of activity in Spencer. She also serves up *very* good home-cooked meals at unbelievably low prices.

Admission: Free, but donations accepted. Train rides $2–$3.50 per person.

Open: Apr–Oct, Mon–Sat 9am–5pm, Sun 1–5pm. Nov–Mar, Tues–Sat 10am–4pm, Sun 1–4pm. Hours subject to change. **Directions:** Take exit 79 off I-85.

WHERE TO STAY

IN GREENSBORO

BILTMORE GREENSBORO HOTEL, 111 W. Washington St., Greensboro, NC 27401. Tel. 919/272-3474. 29 rms. A/C MINIBAR TV TEL **Directions:** Take exit 125 off I-85.
$ Rates (including continental breakfast): $75–$105 single or double. AE, CB, DC, DISC, MC, V.

New ownership has turned this hotel around. Heavily renovated, it boasts excellent rooms—better than the Sheraton and more homey to boot. The rooms have hardwood floors, canopy four-poster beds, armoires, remote-control TVs, residential furnishings, and fine baths. Other extras include a business center and lobby lounge area with a fireplace. This is small and intimate.

GREENSBORO–HIGH POINT MARRIOTT, 1 Marriott Dr., Greensboro, NC 27409. Tel. 919/852-6450, or toll free 800/228-9290. Fax 919/665-0900. 299 rms. A/C TV TEL **Directions:** Follow signs to Piedmont Triad Airport.
$ Rates: $70–$115 single or double. AE, DC, DISC, ER, MC, V.

The Marriott is the first and last thing you'll see coming or going from the airport in Greensboro. It's a spacious, well thought out operation with an indoor pool, an outdoor pool, tennis courts, and laundry facilities. Marriott has a way of keeping everything fresh, including the flowers, the starched linens, and the nicely groomed staff. You have a choice of two restaurants: casual and not-so-casual. Service is good in both. The tartan fabrics look smart in the lounge. Signature room amenities include the remote-control TV and mirrored closet doors along with reading chairs, dining tables, and pleasing colors.

PARK LANE HOTEL–FOUR SEASONS, 3005 High Point Rd., Greensboro, NC 27403. Tel. 919/294-4565, or toll free 800/942-6556. Fax 919/294-0572. 161 rms. A/C TV TEL **Directions:** Take exit 217-B off I-40.
$ Rates: $60 single; $65 double. Extra person $5. Children under 18 stay free with parents. Senior discount available. AE, DC, MC, V.

The rooms at this hotel are nicely furnished, some with refrigerators, and some with whirlpool baths. Some rooms are especially designed for the handicapped. Facilities include a heated pool, a sauna, an exercise room, a coin laundry, and no-smoking rooms. A restaurant serves moderately priced meals, and there's a cocktail lounge. This was formerly the Best Western Executive Center.

RESIDENCE INN BY MARRIOTT, 2000 Veasley St., Greensboro, NC 27407. Tel. 919/294-8600, or toll free 800/331-3131. Fax 919/294-2201. 128 suites. A/C TV TEL **Directions:** Take exit 217A off I-40, then go one block south, then one block west.
$ Rates (including breakfast and wine-and-cheese happy hour): $92 studio suite; $97 double suite; $119 penthouse suite. Discount for stays beyond 6 nights. AE, DC, DISC, MC, V.

Here you'll find the suites typical of this chain. Other amenities include health-club privileges, barbecue facilities, complimentary hospitality hour Monday through Thursday, and free airport transportation. The Four Seasons Mall, less than half a mile away, has good shopping and restaurants.

SHERATON GREENSBORO, 303 N. Elm St., Greensboro, NC 27401. Tel. 919/379-8000, or toll free 800/325-3535. Fax 919/275-2810. 280 rms. A/C TV TEL
$ Rates: $80–$90 single or double. AE, DC, DISC, MC, V.
One of the Sheraton's claims to fame is an excellent health club joined to the hotel. It's got everything—indoor pool, whirlpool, weight machines, and fitness staff. This mid-rise hotel also sports a restaurant with a firehouse theme. Some of the maintenance has slipped, but staying here on weekends can be a good value.

IN HIGH POINT

RADISSON HOTEL, 135 S. Main St., High Point, NC 27260. Tel. 919/889-8888, or toll free 800/333-3333. Fax 919/889-8888, ext. 7988. 249 rms. A/C TV TEL
$ Rates: $88–$103 single; $98–$113 double. AE, CB, DC, DISC, ER, MC, V.
The Radisson is a manageable hotel with only eight floors, an attentive staff, an indoor pool, a whirlpool, a sauna, and a fitness area. Good values are offered on weekends. Many of the areas in the hotel have recently been redone. Many carpets are new in rooms, and standard fittings include desks, dining tables, remote-control cable TV, and room service.

WHERE TO DINE

CELLAR ANTON'S, 1628 Battleground Ave. Tel. 273-1386.
   Cuisine: SEAFOOD/PASTA. **Reservations:** Not required.
   $ Prices: Salads, sandwiches $4–$6; main courses $6–$12. AE, MC, V.
   Open: Mon–Sat 11am–10pm, later on weekend, **Closed:** Sun and major holidays.
This charming restaurant has a loyal local clientele, drawn by the beautifully prepared fresh seafood and Italian dishes, including homemade pastas. Cellar Anton's also offers a children's menu, and children eat free on Monday and Tuesday.

GIOVANNI'S, 3938 Market St. Tel. 855-8000.
   Cuisine: ITALIAN. **Reservations:** Recommended.
   $ Prices: Dinner $10–$24. AE, MC, V.
   Open: Dinner Sun–Fri 5–10pm, Sat 5–11:30pm. **Closed:** Major holidays.
It's southern Italian cuisine in this chef-owned and -operated restaurant. All pasta and baked goods are made on the premises. There's also periodic entertainment.

5. WINSTON-SALEM

104 miles W of Raleigh, 81 miles W of Durham, 27 miles W of Greensboro, 81 miles NW of Charlotte, and 144 miles E of Asheville

GETTING THERE   By Plane   Winston-Salem is served by **American** (tel. toll free 800/433-7300), **Delta** (tel. toll free 800/221-1212), **Continental** (tel. toll free

800/525-0280), **United** (tel. toll free 800/241-6522), and **USAir** (tel. toll free 800/428-4322).

By Train The nearest **Amtrak** station is in Greensboro (see above).

By Bus The **Greyhound/Trailways** depot is at 250 Greyhound Court (tel. 919/724-1429).

By Car U.S. 40 is the main approach to Winston-Salem, running east to west; from the north, it's U.S. 311 and U.S. 52; from the south, U.S. 52.

ESSENTIALS The **area code** is 919. The **Convention and Visitors Bureau,** Chamber of Commerce, P.O. Box 1408, Winston-Salem, NC 27102 (tel. 919/725-2361, or toll free 800/331-7018), can tell you about attractions, accommodations, dining, and local bus transportation. Also, stop by the **visitors' center,** 601 N. Cherry St., Suite 100, Winston-Salem, NC 27102 (tel. 919/777-3796).

Before 1913, the twin communities of Winston and Salem coexisted in perfect harmony; their incorporation that year into a single city has proved a happy, productive union. Winston, founded in 1849, contributed an industry-based economy, while Salem added the crafts, emphasis on education, and sense of order that its Moravian settlers brought from Pennsylvania in 1766.

Salem (the name comes from the Hebrew word *shalom,* meaning "peace") was the last of three settlements established in the Piedmont by Moravian clergy and laymen in the early 1750s; the little towns of Bethabara and Bethania came first. In Salem, the hardworking newcomers laid out a pleasant community. They were devout people who had fled persecution in Europe and brought to the New World their artisans' skills, a deep love of music and education, and an absolute rejection of violence in any form.

Eventually, "progress" encroached on the boundaries of the beautiful old congregational town. In 1949, an organized effort was begun to restore those homes and shops that were in a state of deterioration and to reconstruct others that had disappeared. Today there are more than 30 buildings restored with meticulous attention to authenticity and still others in the process of renovation. Devout the Moravians were, glum they were not: The bright, cheerful reds and blues and soft greens and yellows in the restored interiors and exteriors replicate the colors with which they surrounded themselves in those early days. Their love of good food is also preserved in today's Old Salem, especially at the Old Salem Tavern (see below), serving meals in an authentic colonial Moravian setting.

Surrounding Old Salem, the vigorous new city goes about its business of commerce and industry with a minimum of environmental blight. Maybe that's because its citizens have retained a sense of aesthetic values handed down from the early inhabitants. There is a genteel air about the place that almost convinces you progress doesn't *have* to be abrasive.

WHAT TO SEE & DO
SIGHTS

HISTORIC OLD SALEM, Old Salem Rd. Tel. 721-7300.

Near the very center of the city, Old Salem has *got* to be the place you head for first in Winston-Salem. The visitor center, on Old Salem Road, has exhibits that trace the Moravians' journey from Europe to America and finally to North Carolina, and sells admission tickets. Costumed hosts and hostesses will show you around, and you'll see craftspeople in Moravian dress practicing the trades of the original settlement.

When Moravian boys reached the age of 14, they moved into the **Single**

Brothers House—the half-timbered section was built in 1769, and the brick wing in 1786—where they began an apprenticeship to a master artisan for seven years. Academic studies continued as they learned to be gunsmiths, tailors, potters, and shoemakers. Adolescent girls lived in the **Single Sisters House,** diagonally across the town square, where they learned the domestic arts they would need when marrying time arrived. Young single women *still* live in this building: It's a dormitory for Salem College.

Be sure to go into the **Tavern,** built in 1784 to replace an earlier one that burned. George Washington spent two nights here in 1791 and commented in his diary on the industriousness of the Moravians. The dining room, sleeping rooms, barns, and grounds are not much different now from when he stopped by; the cooking utensils in the stone-floored kitchen with its twin fireplaces are genuine period artifacts.

The **Wachovia Museum** (the Moravians called this region Wachovia after a district in Saxony that had offered refuge to the sect) was once the boys' school. Period musical instruments are displayed here, along with a host of other historical items. You can also visit the **Market-Firehouse** and the **Winkler Bakery,** where bread and cookies are still baked in the big wood-burning ovens. Many homes have distinctive signs hanging outside to identify the shops inside. One of my favorites is the tobacco shop of Matthew Miksch, a yellow weather-boarded log cottage with a miniature man hanging at the door clutching tobacco leaves and a snuff box.

Like the historic district of Williamsburg, Virginia, Old Salem still functions as a living community. Many of the homes you see restored on the outside are private residences, and the young people walking the old streets with such familiarity are no doubt students at Salem College, living a 20th-century campus life in an 18th-century setting.

On the square, the **Home Moravian Church,** which dates from 1800, is the center of the denomination in the South. Visitors are always welcome at services; hundreds show up for the Easter Sunrise Service, the Christmas Lovefeast (on December 24), and the New Year's Eve Watch Night Service. One block north of the square, the graveyard named "God's Acre" contains more than 4,000 graves, all marked with nearly identical stones. Prince and pauper are shown the same respect.

Admission: Admission to Old Salem $10 for adults, $5 for children 6 to 14; combination ticket to restored buildings plus entry to Museum of Early Southern Decorative Arts $13 adults, $6 students.

Open: Mon–Sat 9:30am–4:30pm, Sun 1:30–4:30pm.

HISTORIC BETHABARA PARK, 2147 Bethabara Rd. Tel. 924-8191.

Three miles northwest of downtown Winston-Salem is the 1753 site of the first Moravian settlement in North Carolina. There are two 18th-century homes, a 200-year-old Moravian church, the excavated foundations of the town of Bethabara, a rebuilt French and Indian War fort, nature trails, and picnic tables. There's also a visitors center, with a slide presentation about Bethabara and the beginnings of Winston-Salem. Guided tours of the buildings are free.

Admission: Free.

Open: Apr–Nov, Mon–Fri 9:30am–4:30pm, Sat–Sun and holidays 1:30–4:30pm.

REYNOLDA HOUSE AND GARDENS, Reynolda Rd. Tel. 725-5325.

Reynolda House, Museum of American Art, reopened in 1992 after being closed for almost a year for renovation. R. J. Reynolds, the tobacco tycoon, built this mansion, which now holds an excellent collection of furnishings and American art. The lake porch has been enclosed to provide an additional 2,000 square feet of space for programs and exhibits. A much-expanded costume collection is on display as part of Reynolda House's 25th anniversary celebration.

Admission: House $6 adults, $5 senior citizens, $3 students and children; gardens free.

Open: House Tues–Sat 9:30am–4:30pm, Sun 1:30–4:30pm; gardens daily 7:30am–5pm.

INDUSTRIAL TOURS

You can also tour two sites that play key roles in the region's economy. **Stroh Brewery** (tel. 788-6710) has a 30-minute guided tour of the plant and a first-rate explanation of the brewing process. Take the South Main Street exit 5½ miles south on U.S. 52. Admission is free and tours begin on the hour, Monday through Friday from 11am to 4pm; closed on holidays.

R. J. Reynolds Tobacco Company, Whitaker Park Cigarette Plant, Reynolds Blvd. (tel. 741-5718), is where 300 million cigarettes are produced every day. After viewing murals showing the various stages of tobacco production, you'll be given a tour of the plant. Admission is free and it's open Monday through Friday from 8:15am to 6pm. Drive three miles north on U.S. 52, west on Akron Drive, and east on Reynolds Boulevard. Hours are extended to 8pm from late May to early September.

WHERE TO STAY

BROOKSTOWN INN, 200 Brookstown Ave., Winston-Salem, NC 27101. Tel. 919/725-1120, or toll free 800/845-4262. 71 rms and suites. A/C TV TEL
   Directions: Take the Cherry Street exit from I-40.
$ Rates (including afternoon wine and cheese and continental breakfast): $85–$105 single; $101–$121 double. Extra person $10. Children under 12 stay free with parents. Senior discount available. AE, MC, V.

Housed in an 1837 cotton mill that supplied material for Confederate uniforms, this jewel offers spacious rooms with two double beds, a chest of drawers, armoire, love seat, desk, chairs, tables, and a live palm tree. Suites have a separate sitting room and hot tub. Silk flowers, quilts, baskets, and wooden decoys adorn the parlor areas, decorated in lovely Wedgwood blue, burgundy, gold, and olive. The inn, on the National Register of Historic Places, is conveniently near the Old Salem restoration. Another area of the mill, its former boiler, is the site of one of the popular Darryl's restaurants.

HOLIDAY INN NORTH, 3050 University Pkwy., Winston-Salem, NC 27105. Tel. 919/723-2911, or toll free 800/HOLIDAY. Fax 919/777-1003. 191 rms. A/C TV TEL
$ Rates: $48–$80 single or double. AE, CB, DC, DISC, MC, V.

Here is a suburban operation in a U-shaped building that's close to the Coliseum and only about three miles from the center of town. Besides the outdoor pool surrounded by carpet, you'll find a fitness spot to work out your tensions. Little extras, such as tea and coffee at the registration desk, are helpful. You might try the entertainment in the lounge or enjoy a good meal in the restaurant. The accommodations are standard, clean, and comfortable.

MARQUE OF WINSTON-SALEM, 300 W. 5th St., Winston-Salem, NC 27101. Tel. 919/725-1234, or toll free 800/527-2341. Fax 919/722-9182. 293 rms. A/C TV TEL
$ Rates: $75–$110 single or double. AE, CB, DC, DISC, ER, MC, V.

Probably rated the number two hotel in town, behind the Stouffer across the street, this first-class highrise was once a Hyatt. It still pleases the largely business clientele who stay here. I like the atrium lobby—it's not too big and the adjoining restaurant and lounge, the latter with a wide-screen TV, invite you to linger. A garage with a moderate fee is adjacent. The whirlpool swirls in the fitness area. All the rooms are comfortable, and you can pay a little more for the two top floors, which have added amenities.

RESIDENCE INN BY MARRIOTT, 7835 North Point Blvd., Winston-Salem, NC 27106. Tel. 919/759-0777, or toll free 800/331-3131. Fax 919/759-7671. 88 suites. A/C TV TEL **Directions:** Take the Cherry Street exit from I-40.

$ Rates (including breakfast and social hour): $86 studio suite; $106 penthouse suite. Weekend and extended-stay rates available. AE, DC, DISC, MC, V.

In addition to the upscale suites, each with fully equipped kitchen, most with fireplaces, this outstanding all-suite inn offers fitness-center privileges, golf-club membership, barbecue and picnic facilities, and a weekly cocktail hour. It is especially well located for sightseeing in this area, only one mile southwest of Wake Forest University. The hotel is wheelchair-accessible.

WHERE TO DINE

IN OLD SALEM

OLD SALEM TAVERN DINING ROOM, 736 S. Main St. Tel. 748-8585.
   Cuisine: AMERICAN/CONTINENTAL. **Reservations:** Recommended for dinner, and for lunch for six or more.
$ Prices: Lunch $5–$8; dinner $10–$22. AE, MC, V.
   Open: Lunch daily 11:30am–2pm; dinner Mon–Sat 5–9pm.

Here, as everywhere else in the restored village, authenticity is the keynote. The dining rooms were built in 1816 as an annex to the 1784 Tavern next door, and the simply furnished rooms and colonial-costumed staff provide an appropriate 18th-century ambience. During summer months you can eat in the outdoor arbor, which, like the indoor rooms, is candlelit at night. Favorite dishes include Tavern chicken pie (at lunch) and rack of lamb and roast duckling (dinner only). The pumpkin-and-raisin muffins are a specialty, and a wonderful dessert is the Moravian gingerbread topped with homemade lemon ice cream.

IN WINSTON-SALEM

K & W CAFETERIA, 720 Coliseum Dr. Tel. 724-1568.
   Cuisine: CAFETERIA/SOUTHERN. **Reservations:** Not accepted. **Directions:** Take the Cherry Street exit from I-40.
$ Prices: Lunch $3–$5; dinner $5. No credit cards.
   Open: 11am–8:30pm. **Closed:** Christmas Day.

This branch of the reliable cafeteria chain specializes in home baking, Southern fried chicken, roast beef, and seafood. Very good value for dollar.

LA CHAUDIERE, 120 Reynolda Village. Tel. 748-0269.
   Cuisine: FRENCH. **Reservations:** Recommended. **Directions:** Take the Silas Creek exit from I-40 to Reynolda Road.
$ Prices: Appetizers $7.25–$9.75; main courses $17.95–$30. AE, DC, MC, V.
   Open: Dinner Tues–Sun 6–9:30pm. **Closed:** Mon and major holidays.
In a lovely French country setting, this charming restaurant specializes in the modern and classical cuisines of France. In season, it also presents regional game dishes. There's an excellent wine list and, in good weather, patio dining.

LEON'S CAFE, 924 S. Marshall St. Tel. 725-9593.
   Cuisine: AMERICAN. **Reservations:** Accepted. **Directions:** Take the Cherry Street exit from I-40, one block west and south of Old Salem.
$ Prices: Appetizers $3–$5; main courses $6–$18. MC, V.
   Open: Dinner daily 6–10pm. **Closed:** Holidays.

Locals flock to this low-key neighborhood eatery with a surprisingly sophisticated menu. Main courses vary from week to week; some beef and chicken dishes are quite innovative.

RAINBOW NEWS & CAFE, 712 Brookstown Ave. Tel. 723-0858.
   Cuisine: CAFE. **Reservations:** Not required.
$ Prices: Appetizers $3.75–$3.95; main courses $6.95–$8.95. MC, V.
   Open: Mon–Thurs 9am–9pm, Fri 9am–10pm, Sat 10am–10pm.

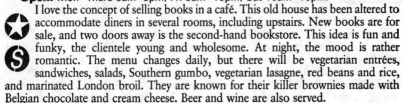

I love the concept of selling books in a café. This old house has been altered to accommodate diners in several rooms, including upstairs. New books are for sale, and two doors away is the second-hand bookstore. This idea is fun and funky, the clientele young and wholesome. At night, the mood is rather romantic. The menu changes daily, but there will be vegetarian entrées, sandwiches, salads, Southern gumbo, vegetarian lasagne, red beans and rice, and marinated London broil. They are known for their killer brownies made with Belgian chocolate and cream cheese. Beer and wine are also served.

RYAN'S, 719 Coliseum Dr. Tel. 724-6132.
   Cuisine: CONTINENTAL. **Reservations:** Recommended. **Directions:** Take the Cherry Street exit from I-40.
$ Prices: Lunch $5–$10; dinner $15–$30. AE, DC, MC, V.
   Open: Lunch Mon–Fri 11:30am–2pm; dinner Mon–Thurs 5:30–10pm, Fri–Sat 5:30–10:30pm. **Closed:** Major holidays.

In a wooded setting overlooking a stream, Ryan's is rustic in decor but has a truly sophisticated continental menu. Beef dishes are specialties, as are some excellent seafood creations. Homemade soups are exceptional, and there's a good wine list. Valet parking is available.

6. CHARLOTTE

143 miles SW of Raleigh; 140 miles SW of Durham; 127 miles SW of Chapel Hill; 91 miles SW of Greensboro; and 81 miles S of Winston-Salem

GETTING THERE **By Plane** Charlotte-Douglas International Airport is served by **American** (tel. toll free 800/433-7300), **Delta** (tel. toll free 800/221-1212), **TWA** (tel. toll free 800/221-2000), **United** (tel. toll free 800/241-6522), **USAir** (tel. toll free 800/428-4322), and **USAir Express,** and there are plans for international flights in the near future.

By Train **Amtrak's** daily service to Washington, D.C., and Atlanta through Charlotte both depart in the early morning hours (tel. toll free 800/USA-RAIL).

By Bus The **Greyhound/Trailways** depot is at 601 W. Trade St. (tel. 704/372-9536, or 704/527-9393).

By Car North-south routes through Charlotte are I-85 and I-77; I-40, a major east-west highway, joins I-77 some 40 miles to the north. Contact AAA through the **Carolina Motor Club,** 7421 Carmel Executive Park, Suite 110, Charlotte, NC 28226 (tel. 704/541-7409).

ESSENTIALS The **area code** is 704. For sightseeing, accommodation, dining, and shopping, contact: **Charlotte Convention & Visitors Bureau,** 122 E. Stonewall St., Charlotte, NC 28202 (tel. 704/334-2282, or toll free 800/231-4636). **Charlotte Transit** (tel. 704/336-3366) can furnish local bus routes and schedule information.

SPECIAL EVENTS **Springfest,** in late April, is a three-day festival held in uptown Charlotte. The streets come alive with music and other entertainment, while street vendors dispense a wide variety of foods. For six full days in mid-September, the **Festival in the Park** in Freedom Park celebrates native arts and crafts.

One of the largest cities in the Piedmont, Charlotte was named for King George III's wife, Queen Charlotte. Evidently, however, its residents didn't take their royal affiliation too seriously: When Lord Cornwallis occupied the town briefly in 1780, he was so annoyed by patriot activities that he called the town a "hornet's nest," a name proudly incorporated into the city seal.

Indeed, more than a year before the Declaration of Independence was signed in Philadelphia, the Mecklenburg Declaration, proclaiming independence from Britain, was signed in Charlotte on May 20, 1775. At 211 W. Trade Street, the Captain James Jack monument is a memorial to the man who carried the document on horseback to Philadelphia and the Continental Congress. According to Charlotte citizens, Thomas Jefferson used their declaration as a model for the one he wrote.

In 1865, Confederate President Jefferson Davis convened his last full cabinet meeting here. After the Confederacy fell and the local boys came home from war, the city set out on a course that freed it of dependence on slave labor and eventually led it to a position of industrial leadership in the South. The Catawba River provided water power for industrialization, and development of manufacturing plants and textile mills was rapid. There are now more than 600 textile plants within a 100-mile radius.

For years, the Charlotte region was also the major gold producer for the United States. A branch of the U.S. mint was located here from 1837 to 1913. This exquisite 1835 William Strickland structure is now part of the Mint Museum, which houses one of the southern Atlantic region's major art collections.

In the last decade or so, Charlotte has been sprouting skyscrapers, including the 40-story, trapezoidal steel-and-glass tower of the Nations Bank Plaza. Suburban areas have also mushroomed, with landscaped housing developments and enormous shopping malls springing up in every direction. This is the "new" South, built squarely on the foundation of the Old South.

WHAT TO SEE & DO

If you're in Charlotte during April and May, drive north on N.C. 49 to the **University of North Carolina at Charlotte** campus to see their spectacular **botanical gardens.** It's a wonderland of rhododendrons, azaleas, and native Carolina trees, shrubs, wildflowers, and ferns. There's also a tropical rain forest conservatory in the gardens' McMillan Greenhouse.

ATTRACTIONS IN TOWN

MINT MUSEUM OF ART, 2730 Randolph Rd. Tel. 337-2000.

 With the recently added Dalton wing, this stately museum displays a fine survey of European and American art, as well as the internationally recognized Delhom Collection of porcelain and pottery. Also featured are pre-Columbian art, contemporary American prints, African objects, vast collections of costumes and antique maps, and gold coins originally minted at the facility.

Admission: $4 adults, $2 students, $3 senior citizens, free for children 12 and under.

Open: Tues 10am–10pm, Wed–Sat 10am–5pm, Sun 1–6pm. **Closed:** Holidays.

CHARLOTTE NATURE MUSEUM, 1658 Sterling Rd. Tel. 372-6261, ext. 38.

If you're traveling with children, don't miss this one. The exhibits and displays are designed to develop an awareness and appreciation of nature, especially for young children.

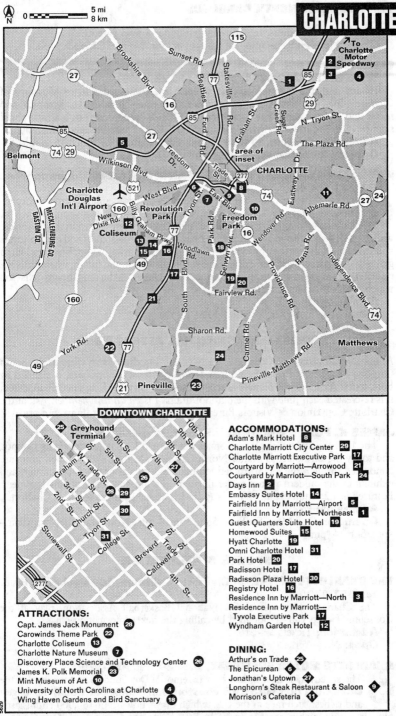

CHARLOTTE

5 mi
8 km

To Charlotte Motor Speedway

Belmont

CHARLOTTE

Charlotte Douglas Int'l Airport

Coliseum

Revolution Park

Freedom Park

Matthews

Pineville

DOWNTOWN CHARLOTTE

Greyhound Terminal

ACCOMMODATIONS:
Adam's Mark Hotel **8**
Charlotte Marriott City Center **29**
Charlotte Marriott Executive Park **17**
Courtyard by Marriott—Arrowood **21**
Courtyard by Marriott—South Park **24**
Days Inn **2**
Embassy Suites Hotel **14**
Fairfield Inn by Marriott—Airport **5**
Fairfield Inn by Marriott—Northeast **1**
Guest Quarters Suite Hotel **19**
Homewood Suites **15**
Hyatt Charlotte **19**
Omni Charlotte Hotel **31**
Park Hotel **20**
Radisson Hotel **17**
Radisson Plaza Hotel **30**
Registry Hotel **16**
Residence Inn by Marriott—North **3**
Residence Inn by Marriott—Tyvola Executive Park **17**
Wyndham Garden Hotel **12**

ATTRACTIONS:
Capt. James Jack Monument **28**
Carowinds Theme Park **22**
Charlotte Coliseum **13**
Charlotte Nature Museum **7**
Discovery Place Science and Technology Center **26**
James K. Polk Memorial **23**
Mint Museum of Art **10**
University of North Carolina at Charlotte **4**
Wing Haven Gardens and Bird Sanctuary **18**

DINING:
Arthur's on Trade **25**
The Epicurean **6**
Jonathan's Uptown **27**
Longhorn's Steak Restaurant & Saloon **9**
Morrison's Cafeteria **11**

5629

Admission: $1 adults, free for children under 3 with parents.
Open: Mon–Fri 9am–5pm, Sat 9am–6pm, Sun 1–6pm. **Closed:** Holidays.

DISCOVERY PLACE SCIENCE AND TECHNOLOGY CENTER, 301 N. Tryon St. Tel. 372-6261, or toll free 800/935-0553.

Joining with the Nature Museum to form the combined Science Museums of Charlotte, Inc., this uptown center features such permanent exhibits as a tropical rain forest and an aquarium. The focus here is a hands-on approach to learning about science. There is an OMNIMAX theater, and a Kelly Space Voyager Planetarium.
Admission: $5 adults, $4 students and senior citizens, $3 for children 3 to 5.
Open: Mon–Sat 9am–6pm, Sun 1–6pm.

WING HAVEN GARDENS AND BIRD SANCTUARY, 248 Ridgewood Ave. Tel. 331-0664.

One of Charlotte's most delightful attractions, these gardens were the inspiration and longtime labor of love of Mrs. Elizabeth Clarkson, known as Charlotte's "bird lady"; 142 winged species have been sighted in the three-acre walled garden she created from a once-bare clay field. Birdwatchers and garden-lovers will have a field day, as they browse through the Upper, Lower, Main, Wild, and Herb gardens. The gardens are perhaps at their most splendid in the spring, when birds are returning from their winter sojourn in warmer climes. A bulletin board tells you which birds are around at the moment.
Admission: Free.
Open: Sun, Tues–Wed 3–5pm. Hours may vary.

NEARBY PRESIDENTIAL ATTRACTIONS

About 20 miles south of Charlotte, via N.C. 16, **Waxhaw** is so close to the South Carolina border that President Andrew Jackson, who was born here, is claimed by both states. Although the pioneer aspect of the little town has long since disappeared, it is re-created each June with the outdoor drama *Listen and Remember*. Ask at the Charlotte Convention & Visitors Bureau (see above) for current hours and prices.

JAMES K. POLK MEMORIAL, U.S. 521, Pineville. Tel. 889-9191.

The 11th president of the United States was born in 1795 in Mecklenburg County, and today the birthplace is one of North Carolina's historic sites. Guided tours are conducted through the reconstructed log buildings typical of the 19th century, and exhibits in the modern visitor center illustrate the life and times of this President. Featured is a 25-minute film, *Who Is Polk?* It's about 12 miles south of Charlotte.
Admission: Free.
Open: Apr–Oct, Mon–Sat 9am–5pm, Sun 1–5pm. Nov–Mar, Tues–Sat 10am–4pm, Sun 1–4pm.

SPORTS & RECREATION

THE CHARLOTTE HORNETS, Charlotte Coliseum, 100 Paul Buck Blvd. Tel. 357-4700.

The Charlotte Hornets, of the National Basketball Association, play at the Coliseum. Tickets can be obtained by calling the ticket information office.
Admission: Tickets $7–$16.
Open: Nov–Apr.

CHARLOTTE MOTOR SPEEDWAY, U.S. 29. Tel. 455-3200.

The speedway is host in late May (Memorial Day Sunday) of each year to the **Coca-Cola 600 NASCAR Winston Cup Stock Car Race,** the longest and richest such race in the U.S., which draws upward of 160,000 enthusiastic fans. In early October, the **Mello Yello 500 Winston Cup Stock Car Race** is run. You can get exact dates and full details of both events by writing Charlotte Motor Speedway, P.O. Box 600, Concord, NC 28026, or by calling the above telephone number.

Admission: Varies with event.

Open: Memorial Day Sunday and early October. **Directions:** Go 12 miles northeast of Charlotte on U.S. 29 (just off I-85).

PARAMOUNT CAROWINDS THEME PARK, I-77 South, Charlotte. Tel. 588-2600, or toll free 800/822-4428.

If you're taking children along on your Charlotte trip, you undoubtedly already know about Carowinds. Even without the kids, it's worth a day just for fun. The $40-million park straddles the North and South Carolina state line. The rides are entertaining and inventive, especially the flume and mine train rides; my romantic favorite is the sternwheeler, which set me thinking of slower days. The Thunder Road and Carolina Cyclone rollercoasters may beckon the more adventurous. For sightseeing, look for Pirate Island and a re-creation of the Old Charleston waterfront. Fast-paced revues are on view at Paramount and Troubador's Roost Theatre. In Blue Ridge Junction, you'll enjoy the shops and crafts at Queen's Colony; and you can tap your toes to bluegrass music in Harmony Hall. *Note:* They won't let you bring pets in, but there is a kennel for stashing them.

Admission (including all rides and most entertainment): $23 for those 7 and over, $11.50 for those 4 to 6 and over 60; free for children 3 and under. **Parking:** $3.

Open: Second week in June to mid-Aug, Sat–Thurs 10am–8pm. Mid-Mar to early June and Sept to early Oct, Sat–Sun 10am–8pm. **Closed:** Mid-Oct to mid-Mar. **Directions:** Go 10 miles south on I-77 to the N.C.–S.C. border.

WHERE TO STAY

EXPENSIVE

ADAM'S MARK HOTEL, 555 S. McDowell St., Charlotte, NC 28204. Tel. 704/372-4100, or toll free 800/444-2326. Fax 704/372-2599. 599 rms. A/C TV TEL

$ Rates: $65–$95 single or double. AE, CB, DC, DISC, MC, V.

Less than six blocks from the center of town, the Adam's Mark is a staple in the Charlotte skyline and hotel scene. With easy access, it's a favorite of convention planners who also get good rates—and that translates into almost equal offerings for the general public. The entire complex is spacious. Dark woods are used in the efficient lobby, and there are two restaurants: one for dinner only and the other in a casual setting for all meals. On weekends, the lounge hops with local young folks. Besides the two pools, there are racquetball courts, a sauna, fitness room, and whirlpool. The hotel's shuttle van will take you to the airport or the shops downtown.

CHARLOTTE MARRIOTT CITY CENTER, 100 W. Trade St., Charlotte, NC 28202. Tel. 704/333-9000, or toll free 800/228-9290. Fax 704/342-3419. 431 rms. A/C TV TEL

$ Rates: $90–$115 single; $105–$130 double. AE, CB, DC, DISC, ER, MC, V.

The constant movement of guests coming and going keeps this place alive. The main restaurant with a buffet table and the more formal continental dining room are popular. Then there is the lounge, where office staffs come after work and sports crowds gather at game time. You also have at your disposal a health club with sauna, whirlpool, indoor pool, and fitness machines. Accommodations are first rate.

CHARLOTTE MARRIOTT EXECUTIVE PARK, 5700 Westpark Dr. Charlotte, NC 28217. Tel. 704/527-9650, or toll free 800/228-9290. Fax 704/527-6918. 298 rms. A/C TV TEL

$ Rates: $99–$117 single or double. AE, DC, DISC, MC, V.

During the week, the Marriott caters to the business crowd, but on weekends, the trade is leisure and motor travelers. Great rates are as attractive as the three food outlets, the lounge where a pianist is presented, and even the lounge with a stage and entertainment. You can swim outdoors from the indoor pool, enjoy a hot sauna, swirl in the whirlpool, and make a match point at the two lighted tennis courts. You won't be disappointed with the fine first-class rooms here, either.

EMBASSY SUITES HOTEL, 4800 S. Tryon St., Charlotte, NC 28217. Tel. 704/527-8400, or toll free 800/362-2779. Fax 704/527-7035. 274 suites. A/C TV TEL **Directions:** Take exit 6B off I-77.

$ Rates (including breakfast): $134–$144 single or double. AE, CB, DC, DISC, MC, V.

Embassy Suites always beckons its guests to stretch out, unpack, and enjoy their private space. Who can resist with all the extra room, two TVs, separate living and sleeping areas, a wet bar, microwave oven, and refrigerator? The ingredients work. And these rooms are wrapped around an atrium where full complimentary breakfasts are served in the morning and afternoon drinks are provided during happy hours. There's also an indoor pool, sauna, whirlpool, sundeck, and exercise room.

GUEST QUARTERS SUITE HOTEL, 6300 Morrison Blvd., Charlotte, NC 28211. Tel. 704/364-0203, or toll free 800/424-2900. 208 suites. A/C TV TEL

$ Rates: $89–$149 single or double. AE, CB, DC, DISC, MC, V.

I've stayed in a dozen Guest Quarters hotels around the United States, and this is one of my favorites. It has a country-club atmosphere—quiet and soothing—where everyone seems to whisper. The courtyard has neatly tended shrubs and hidden speakers radiating soft music. All day long, the silver service is set out in the registration lobby, so you can grab a fast cup of coffee or linger by the piano. The café is more formal than you might expect, and the antiques are a welcome touch. You can dine inside or out. For those with energy left, try the sauna, whirlpool, outdoor pool, or fitness room.

HYATT CHARLOTTE, 5501 Carnegie Blvd., Charlotte, NC 28209. Tel. 704/554-1234, or toll free 800/228-9000. Fax 704/554-8319. 262 rms. A/C TV TEL

$ Rates: $99–$125 single or double. AE, DC, DISC, MC, V.

There aren't enough superlatives to describe the Hyatt. It could be my favorite in town. The fountain is a departure from Hyatt's mold, and the Italian overtones are rich and inviting. Perhaps the pressure was on during construction with the upscale mall across the way, or maybe they were merely trying to knock our socks off. The slant in the restaurant is to northern Italian. Hop over to the health club to expend some energy on the bicycles and workout stations or in the indoor pool, sauna, and whirlpool. Unlike some of this hotel's siblings, there's no commercialism—only understated elegance. On the weekend, you can get some good buys (on the rooms and at the mall).

OMNI CHARLOTTE HOTEL, 222 E. Third St., Charlotte, NC 29202. Tel. 704/377-6664, or toll free 800/THE-OMNI. Fax 704/377-4143. A/C MINIBAR TV TEL

$ Rates: $129–$144 single or double. AE, CB, DC, DISC, MC, V.

If the Marriott or Radisson wanted competition, they got it from the Omni. Shooting up 21 stories, the Omni offers a bistro café; a quiet bar; use of the YMCA nearby; self-parking; and great rooms with at least two phones, minibars, attractive color schemes, and excellent bathrooms. The plaza around the Omni is often filled with office workers at lunch enjoying the sun.

PARK HOTEL, 2200 Rexford Rd., Charlotte, NC 28211. Tel. 704/364-8220, or toll free 800/334-0331. Fax 704/365-4712. 194 rms. A/C TV TEL
$ Rates: $105–$135 single or double. AE, CB, DC, DISC, MC, V.
Near the Hyatt and a Guest Quarters, this is one of a trio of deluxe hotels that will certainly satisfy you. The styling is classic with fluted columns, green marble, and comfortable appointments. The restaurant is elegant and service attentive and unobtrusive. The lounge is quiet and sophisticated. Amenities include 24-hour room service, an outdoor pool and whirlpool, an indoor whirlpool, sauna, and fitness room. I particularly love the courtyard. Rooms are furnished with armoires, two-line phones, four-poster beds, remote-control TV, and partly marbled baths.

RADISSON PLAZA HOTEL, Nations Bank Plaza, Charlotte, NC 28280. Tel. 704/377-0400. Fax: 704/347-0649. 365 rms and suites. A/C TV TEL
Directions: Take the Trade Street East exit from I-77.
$ Rates: $99–$109 single or double; $250–$400 suites. Children under 18 stay free with parents. Weekend rates available. AE, CB, DC, MC, V. **Parking:** Free.
At the corner of Trade and Tryon Streets, it's part of the trapezoidal North Carolina Nations Bank Plaza building. It's connected by a covered walkway above the street to Charlotte's new convention center. Rooms are the ultimate in comfort and contemporary design. There's concierge service, a pool, a health club, and free covered parking. The hotel has a bright, airy coffee shop and an elegant upscale restaurant, Reflections, where dinners range from $11 to $22. It also offers one of the city's most popular Sunday brunches from 11:30am to 2pm, in the $12 to $15 range. This is one of the most convenient locations in town.

RESIDENCE INN BY MARRIOTT, 8503 U.S. 29, Charlotte, NC 28262. Tel. 704/547-1122, or toll free 800/331-3131. 91 suites. A/C TV TEL
Directions: Take the Harris Boulevard exit from I-85 N; turn right at top of ramp, then right at second traffic light.
$ Rates: $89 one bedroom; $99 two bedrooms; $64–$84 weekends. Senior discounts and discounts for extended stays available. AE, DC, MC, V.
One of the two upscale Marriott facilities in the area, it's located on the north side of town. Guests enjoy the barbecue and picnic facilities. Good restaurants are within easy reach. All units have full kitchens, complete with microwave ovens; most have fireplaces. There's a guest laundry, and each unit has a private entrance with parking just outside. The hotel is wheelchair-accessible.

RESIDENCE INN BY MARRIOTT, TYVOLA EXECUTIVE PARK, 5800 West Park Dr., Charlotte, NC 28217. Tel. 704/527-8110, or toll free 800/331-3131. 80 suites. A/C TV TEL **Directions:** Take the Tyvola Road exit from I-77.
$ Rates: $95 studio suite; $110 penthouse suite. Discounts for extended stays, senior discounts, and weekend rates available. AE, DC, DISC, MC, V.
This is the other upscale Marriott establishment in town, and is located in the Tyvola Executive Park area. Facilities are basically the same as those described in the previous entry.

MODERATE

COURTYARD BY MARRIOTT, 6023 Park Rd., Charlotte, NC 28210. Tel. 704/552-7333, or toll free 800/321-2211. 146 rms. A/C TV TEL
$ Rates: $72 single; $82 double; $55 weekends. Senior discounts and discounts for extended stays (six nights or longer available). AE, DC, MC, V.
Built in the attractive courtyard style, it has a swimming pool. As with all branches of this chain, the rooms are especially spacious, with a separate seating area, an oversize work desk, a boiling-water faucet, and instant coffee. The hotel is wheel-chair accessible.

COURTYARD BY MARRIOTT, 800 Arrowood Rd., Charlotte, NC 28217. Tel. 704/527-5055, or toll free 800/321-2211. 146 rms. A/C TV TEL
Directions: Take the Arrowood exit from I-77.
$ Rates: $66 sing;e $76 double. Senior discounts and discounts for extended stays (six nights or longer) available. AE, DC, DISC, MC, V.
See above listing for details about this chain property.

DAYS INN, 122 W. Woodlawn Rd., Charlotte, NC 28217. Tel. 704/527-1620, or toll free 800/325-2525. Fax 704/527-1615. 142 rms. A/C TV TEL
Directions: Take exit 6B or 7 from I-77.
$ Rates: $42 single; $48 double; $50 suite. AE, DC, MC, V.
The dependable Days Inn people have three motels in Charlotte, but I especially like this one, which is convenient to the airport and Carowinds. Rooms are comfortable, and the decor is adequate. This one has a pool, a restaurant, and one unit especially fitted for the handicapped.

HOMEWOOD SUITES, 4920 S. Tryon St., Charlotte, NC 28217. Tel. 704/525-2600, or toll free 800/225-5466. Fax 704/521-9932. 144 rms. A/C TV TEL
$ Rates (including continental breakfast Mon–Thurs): $79–$150 single or double. AE, CB, DC, DISC, MC, V.
While the Homewood Suites may not have a restaurant, it seems to have everything else. Monday to Thursday afternoons, you can slip into the lobby for a happy hour drink. For leisure time, consider the outdoor whirlpool or swimming pool. There's a fitness room too. All the suites have living and sleeping areas with either king-size or two double beds plus a full kitchen. These are excellent for families at a moderate price.

RADISSON HOTEL, 5624 Westpark Dr., Charlotte, NC 28217. Tel. 704/527-8000, or toll free 800/333-3333. Fax 704/527-4278. 178 rms. A/C TV TEL
$ Rates: $79–$99 single or double. AE, CB, DC, DISC, MC, V.
The Radisson is a bit quieter than its neighbor, the Marriott, but that's okay. Maybe it's the rates that keep everyone calm here—they're good during the week and are even better on the weekends. Sit in the piano lounge and look out to the fountained courtyard or relax in the sauna or whirlpool; pump up your heart in the exercise room, take a swim and calm down again in the whirlpool. It's all here.

REGISTRY HOTEL, 321 W. Woodlawn Rd., Charlotte, NC 28217. Tel. 704/525-4441. 180 rms. Fax 704/523-3601. A/C TV TEL
$ Rates: $80–$100 single or double. Weekend rates available. AE, CB, DC, DISC, MC, V.
This hotel doesn't have the glitz or fancy overtones that some Registry hotels enjoy. Instead, it's quiet, civilized, and low key. To start your day off right, you'll find coffee and tea service in the lobby each morning. And the last thing at night you'll remember is the turndown service with a chocolate mint on your pillow. Try the continental restaurant and the bar, or work out in the fitness area, sauna, steam room, whirlpool, or swimming pool. Appointments in the accommodations are more residential here than the traditional hotel furnishings and include wingback chairs, armoires, marble tables, desks, and attractive window treatments.

WYNDHAM GARDEN HOTEL, 4200 Wilmount Rd., Charlotte, NC 28208. Tel. 704/357-9100, or toll free 800/822-4200. Fax 704/357-9159. 174 rms. A/C TV TEL
$ Rates: $89 single; $99 double. AE, CB, DC, DISC, MC, V.
You'll be impressed with the Wyndham Garden Hotel. Extras, such as marble in two colors, fireplaces, and soothing lighting, make this a sophisticated atmosphere. In the

upbeat café, you can choose from a wide variety on the American menu; a bar adjoins. In guest rooms, the dark woods, armoires, deep carpets, double or king-size beds, and coffeemakers contribute to a comfortable stay. If you like, visit the indoor whirlpool, fitness room, or outdoor swimming pool.

BUDGET

FAIRFIELD INN BY MARRIOTT—AIRPORT, 3400 S. I-85 Service Rd., Charlotte, NC 28208. Tel. 704/392-0600, or toll free 800/228-2800. 135 rms. A/C TV TEL **Directions:** Take I-85 exit 33.

$ Rates: $41–$45 single; $41–$51 double. Children under 6 stay free with parents. Family rates available. AE, DC, MC, V.

This attractive budget-priced inn is near the airport, and amenities include a pool and free coffee and tea in the lobby. For a full description of this chain's special features, see Chapter 1, "Where to Stay and Dine."

FAIRFIELD INN BY MARRIOTT—NORTHEAST, 5415 N. I-85 Service Rd., Charlotte, NC 28206. Tel. 704/596-2999, or toll free 800/228-2800. 133 rms. A/C TV TEL **Directions:** Take exit 41 from I-85.

$ Rates: $39.95–$42.95 single; $45.95–$48.95 double. Family rates available. AE, DC, MC, V.

Located on the northeast side of town, and identical in style to the listing above.

WHERE TO DINE

EXPENSIVE

THE EPICUREAN, 1324 East Blvd. Tel. 377-4529.
   Cuisine: STEAK/SEAFOOD. **Reservations:** Recommended at dinner.
$ Prices: Dinner $12–$20; children's plates $10. AE, DC, MC, V.
   Open: Dinner Mon–Sat 6–10pm. **Closed:** Major holidays and first two weeks in July.

For broiled live lobster or prime rib, you probably can't do better in the Charlotte area. In business for more than a quarter of a century, this chef-owned establishment is popular for the excellence of its food. It boasts one of the city's most extensive wine lists. Everything (except the wine!) is made from scratch.

JONATHAN'S UPTOWN, 330 N. Tryon St. Tel. 332-3663.
   Cuisine: AMERICAN. **Reservations:** Recommended. **Directions:** Take the Trade Street exit from I-77.
$ Prices: Appetizers $4–$8; main courses $14–$20. AE, DC, MC, V.
   Open: Dinner Mon–Sat 5:30–10:30pm, Sun 6–9:30pm.

For a special late-night treat, try this popular rendezvous spot where upwardly mobile young Charlotteans drop in for live jazz and fresh American cuisine. It's a sophisticated "big city" room with a dramatic black-and-white decor; service is deft and friendly. The menu features innovative creations that change weekly. Jonathan's boasts an exceptional wine cellar. Dress may be casual, but this definitely doesn't mean jeans or sneakers. If you're staying in the uptown Radisson or Marriott, it's a short stroll.

The Jazz Lounge (with a small cover charge) is open 9pm to 1am Wednesday through Saturday. A limited menu is also served in the bar adjoining the dining room from 5pm to 1:30am Monday through Saturday.

MODERATE

LONGHORN'S STEAK RESTAURANT & SALOON, 700 E. Morehead. Tel. 332-2300.

Cuisine: AMERICAN/STEAKS. **Reservations:** Not required.
$ **Prices:** Burgers $4.50–$5.70; steaks $13.95–$17.95. AE, MC, V.
Open: Mon–Thurs 11am–11:30pm, Fri 11am–11pm, Sat 4–11pm, Sun 5–10pm.

⭐ When you are good and hungry for something from the grill, head to Longhorns. The wait is worth it for those 22-ounce Porterhouse steaks, New York–strip steaks, and ribeye steaks. For fish lovers, there is the 10-ounce salmon. All the meals include a salad, rolls, and Texas taters or rice. The one-story clapboard building packs them in. While you are waiting, order your favorite libation in the cozy bar and throw your peanut shells on the floor.

BUDGET

ARTHUR'S ON TRADE, 129 W. Trade St., Tel. 333-4867.
Cuisine: SANDWICHES. **Reservations:** Not accepted.
$ **Prices:** Meals $3–$5. No credit cards.
Open: Mon–Fri 10:30am–2:30pm.

⭐ Arthur's, with five convenient locations, offers freshly made sandwiches, hoagies, quiches, soups, and salads in a comfortable café atmosphere. Each includes a wine shop, and the last three listed below (open until 9:30pm Monday through Friday) also have a deli, a bakery, and an array of fancy foods. Other locations are: Arthur's First Union, 1 First Union Center (tel. 343-2835); Arthur's at Belk Southpark, 4400 Sharon Rd. (tel. 366-6456); Arthur's at Belk Eastland, 5501 Central Ave. (tel. 568-4251); and Arthur's at Belk Carolina Place Mall, 11009 Carolina Place Pkwy., Pineville (tel. 541-7372).

MORRISON'S CAFETERIA, in the Eastland Mall, 5633 Central Ave. Tel. 568-7136.
Cuisine: CAFETERIA. **Reservations:** Not accepted.
$ **Prices:** Meals $3–$7. No credit cards.
Open: Daily (including major holidays) 11am–8:30pm.
This is a reliable cafeteria. You can have breakfast for about $3, and there are daily $4 specials (Monday it's baked, chopped steak, Tuesday it's one-quarter broiled or fried chicken). Sunday dinner, served all day, is turkey and dressing, salad, vegetable, bread, and dessert, for $7. They have another cafeteria at Southland Park Mall (tel. 364-7522).

EVENING ENTERTAINMENT

The superb **Charlotte Symphony Orchestra** season runs from September through May; check local newspapers, or call 332-6136 for performance dates. **Carolina Opera** (tel. 332-7177) presents performances from October through April, and the **Charlotte Pops** gives outdoor concerts (small fee) in Freedom Park on Sunday evenings in the summer. Classic plays are often performed by **Theatre Charlotte,** 501 Queens Rd. (tel. 376-3777), usually from Thursday through Sunday. The **Blumenthal Performing Arts Center** (tel. 372-1000) is the newest facility to join the performance venues; it features three theaters for various productions—from rock concerts to intimate stage performances.

Charlotte usually has two or three good nightclubs and discos in full swing, but they come and go with such regularity that your best bet is to check local newspapers.

CHAPTER 4

THE SANDHILLS OF NORTH CAROLINA

1. PINEHURST & SOUTHERN PINES

The Sandhill's porous, sandy soil is a reminder that in prehistoric times Atlantic Ocean waves rolled over the land. It also provides the ideal drainage that is crucial to the area's standing as Golf Capital of the World, for no matter what the rainfall, no puddles accumulate on the rolling green golf courses (there are more than 30 within a 15-mile radius). And with mean temperatures ranging between 44° and 78° Fahrenheit, the game is played year round.

But golf hasn't always been king here. When Boston philanthropist James Walker Tufts bought up 5,000 acres of land in 1895 at $1 per acre, his plan was to build the little resort village of Pinehurst as a retreat from harsher climes for wealthy Northerners. Recreation then consisted mainly of croquet on the grassy lawns, outdoor concerts, hayrides, or just quiet walks through the pines. Tufts's attention first turned to golf—which had only recently arrived from Great Britain—when one of his dairy employees complained that guests were "hitting the cows with a little white ball." By 1900, Tufts had enlisted Donald Ross (who had honed his skills at Scotland's St. Andrews) to come to Pinehurst and introduce golf. Ross designed courses here that drew some of the most distinguished golfers in the world: Ben Hogan, Walter Travis, Bobby Jones, Walter Hagen, Patty Berg, Sam Snead, Arnold Palmer, Gary Player, Jack Nicklaus—just to name a few.

For years, golfing on the superb courses of the Pinehurst Country Club was by invitation only. Today, however, although the golf world's top players consider Pinehurst their own turf, you don't have to wait for an invitation, or be a millionaire, to play. Prices are certainly high enough at Pinehurst, but they're not exorbitant by comparison with other luxury resorts around the country. And there is a profusion of others hotels and motels—something in almost any price range—and, expert or duffer, guests can always play the Pinehurst courses.

In 1973, the first World Open Championship was played in Pinehurst; the event was replaced in 1977 by the Colgate Hall of Fame Classic. In September 1974, President Gerald Ford presided at the opening of the World Golf Hall of Fame, overlooking Ross's famous Number Two Course (one of the top 10 in the country).

Pinehurst, built by Frederick Law Olmsted (the architect-landscaper who planned New York's Central Park), has retained its New England–village air, with a village green and shaded residential streets. Year-round greenery is provided by pines (some with needles 15 inches long), stately magnolias, and hollies. Moderate temperatures account for color through all seasons—camellias, azaleas, wisteria, peach trees, dogwoods, and summer-blooming yard flowers. Shops, restaurants, hotels, and other business enterprises make this a self-sufficient community. For those whose idea of a good time is not chasing after that little white ball, there's a tennis club with lots of excellent courts, over 200 miles of riding trails and stables with good mounts for hire, boating on a 200-acre lake, trap-and-skeet ranges, archery, over 9,000 acres of woods to explore via meandering pathways, and shopping in the little boutiques.

Over the years, this region has become an internationally renowned mecca for artists, craftspeople, and potters. Scattered around the vicinity in rustic, pine-sheltered workshops, the potters welcome visitors, and most are quite happy to have you watch them at their work. The short drive from Pinehurst to Southern Pines (about five miles) on Midland Road (N.C. 2), a highway divided by a strip of pines and bordered by lovely homes and lavish gardens, goes right past Midland Crafters. You'll see it on your right. The rambling white building is a virtual gallery of American crafts, ranging from beanbags to paintings to furniture to candles to pottery to glassware to . . . well, almost any handcraft you can think of.

1. PINEHURST & SOUTHERN PINES

71 miles SW of Raleigh; 77 miles SE of Greensboro

GETTING THERE By Plane Raleigh/Durham is the nearest commercial airport (see Chapter 3, "Raleigh"). Moore County has a small, private airport (tel. 919/692-3212).

By Train Amtrak (tel. toll free 800/USA-RAIL). has one northbound and one southbound train daily through Southern Pines.

By Bus For local **Greyhound/Trailways** information, call 919/944-1983.

By Car U.S. 1 runs north and south through Southern Pines; N.C. 211 runs east and west; U.S. 15/501 reaches Pinehurst from the north; there's direct area access to I-95, I-85, and I-40. You'll really need a car to get around this entire area.

ESSENTIALS The **area code** is 919. I strongly recommend that you write ahead for details on sightseeing, golfing and other sports, accommodations, and dining, to the **Pinehurst Area Convention and Visitors Bureau,** P.O. Box 2270, Southern Pines, NC 28388 (tel. 919/692-3330, or toll free 800/346-5362).

Golf, golf, and more golf—that's why most people come to Pinehurst. If there's a hotel or motel that doesn't arrange play for its guests, I didn't find it. Most can also set you up for tennis, cycling, horseback riding, or boat rentals on one of the many lakes around. For a complete list of golf courses, ask the visitors bureau (see "Essentials," above) for their "Accommodations/Golfing" brochure.

PINEHURST
WHAT TO SEE & DO

Horseback riders can arrange for mounts by calling the **Pinehurst Stables** (tel. 295-6811), where expert instruction is available for novices and superb mounts for experienced riders. They also offer carriage rides, an especially nice way to see the village, as well as pony rides for children. **Tennis** buffs will find nearly 100 public courts in the area (tel. 947-2504 for locations, hours, and fees); and the **Pinehurst Gun Club** (tel. 295-6811) provides everything you need for trap and skeet shooting.

Aside from recreation facilities, the Pinehurst area also offers the **❂ World Golf Hall of Fame,** PGA Blvd., P.O. Box 1908, Pinehurst, NC 28374 (tel. 295-6651, or toll free 800/334-0178 outside North Carolina). Even nongolfers will be impressed by the white-columned porticoes and sparkling fountains of the Entrance Pavilion, which overlooks Pinehurst Country Club's Number Two course. The north and south wings tell the story of the development of golf and people associated with it, like Henry VIII's first wife, Katherine, who loved it as much as Scotland's three kings James (II, III, and IV) hated it. Hundreds of golf items are displayed, including balls used from 1750 to 1850 made of tanned animal hides stuffed with leather. The Ryder Cup Room, Old Clubmakers Shop, and new Walter Hagen exhibit offer more fascinating insights into the grand old game.

The theater is the only one in the world devoted exclusively to golf, and it features films of major tournaments as well as instructional films. Behind the museum is the actual Hall of Fame with bronzes of the inductees, a shrine completely surrounded by water, approached by a covered walkway. It is open daily from 9am to 5pm; admission is $3 for adults, $2.50 for seniors, $2 for those 10 to 18, and free for children under 10. Closed mid-December to mid-February.

WHERE TO STAY

Although the Pinehurst Hotel and Country Club is still the place to stay in Pinehurst, as it has been from the beginning, there are several other hotels in the village that offer luxury on a smaller scale, and graciousness on the same level, at somewhat more moderate prices.

CAMPING For those who like to camp, the **Heritage,** Whispering Pines, NC 28327 (tel. 919/949-3433), a 200-acre country estate five miles north of Pinehurst off U.S. 1, is a peaceful and relaxing place. With a spring-fed, 14-acre lake and sandy beach, it offers swimming, canoeing, pedal boats and fishing, a playground, shuffleboard, volleyball, basketball, croquet, a putting green, hayrides, a barnyard petting farm, and horseshoes. A meeting room with a large deck overlooks the lake. This beautiful wooded setting is only a few minutes away from restaurants and shopping. There are 50 sites with water and electric, 22 with full hookups, flush toilets, hot showers, laundry, ice, picnic tables, and firewood. Rates start at $18.

HOLLY INN, Pinehurst, NC 28374. Tel. 919/295-2300, or toll free 800/ 533-0041. 77 rms. A/C TV TEL
$ Rates: $80–$120 single or double. AE, DC, MC, V.

When I drove up to the Holly Inn and parked at the shady sidewalk out front, I wanted to dig out a book from my trunk and head for one of the green rockers on the front porch. A fireplace burns in the lobby, antiques adorn the bar, and elegance surrounds you in the continental restaurant. The dining room has an exceedingly marvelous reputation. Golf, biking, tennis, and more are all nearby. Most of the rooms have two double beds, and a few have king-size beds.

MAGNOLIA INN, 65 Magnolia Rd., Pinehurst, NC 28374. Tel. 919/295-6900, or toll free 800/526-5562. 12 rms. A/C TV
$ Rates: (including breakfast and dinner): $55–$75 per person. AE, MC, V.

Reportedly, the owner of the Pinehurst Hotel first built this dormered inn with lots of Victorian detail. Later, he built the now famous Pinehurst. After the Pinehurst was constructed, the owner couldn't see past this inn, so two floors were chopped off. Sadly, a lot of the Victorian detail was sacrificed in the carnage, but I think you'll agree that it's still warm and delightful. In fact, I prefer it to the bigger places because it's more romantic. Casablanca fans twirl overhead on the front porch, and a little pool is in back. Inside, the rooms are sunny and flowery. A tavern was added with a pub menu. Breakfast and dinner are served in the pink-and-white dining room. Two of the guest rooms have wood-burning fireplaces. Step forward to be charmed.

MANOR INN, Community Rd., Pinehurst, NC 28374. Tel. 919/295-4500, or toll free 800/487-4653. 46 rms. A/C TV TEL
$ Rates: $122 double. AE, CB, DC, DISC, MC, V. **Closed:** Jan–Mar.
The staff here at the Manor isn't as plentiful as at its big brother, the famous Pinehurst Hotel and Country Club, but at least the flags over the portico will be waving at you upon arrival. For a small place overshadowed by history and service nearby, it does a

good job. Some improvements include redesigning the sports bar with a greenhouse effect, fireplace, and wide-screen TV. You will have to go out to eat, unless you want to order something from the light menu offered in the bar. Rooms have remote-control TVs, armoires, and other reasonable appointments. Overall, the value is rather good.

PINE CREST INN, 200 Pine Crest Lane, Pinehurst, NC 28374. Tel. 919/295-6121. 40 rms. AC TV TEL

$ Rates (including breakfast and dinner): Seasonal, $45–$72 per person single or double. Golf and sports packages available. AE, DC, MC, V.

⭐ Right in the heart of the village, the Pine Crest Inn was described by an English visitor as having "all the flavor and courtesies of our countryside inns." It draws people back year after year. Bob Barrett (proprietor since 1961) tells me that ⑤ some 80% of his guests are returnees—and small wonder, for the two-story, white-columned building radiates warmth from the moment you enter the lobby with its comfortable armchairs, fireplace, and informal dining room and bar to one side. Meals in the three dining rooms (with fireplaces and pretty wallpaper) are of such quality that they draw people from as far away as Raleigh and Charlotte (see "Where to Dine," below). Pinehurst golf privileges are extended to guests here; Mr. Barrett will even arrange starting times. Tennis and horseback riding can be arranged at nearby facilities.

PINEHURST HOTEL AND COUNTRY CLUB, Carolina Vista (P.O. Box 4000), Pinehurst, NC 28374. Tel. 919/295-6811, or toll free 800/487-4653. Fax 919/295-6546. 223 rms, 50 villas, 170 condominiums. A/C TV TEL

$ Rates (MAP): $92–$137 per person. Golf and tennis packages available. AE, DC, MC, V.

⭐ The white, four-story main building, with columned porches lined with comfortable rocking chairs, was called the Carolina for years, and you'll still hear residents refer to it by that name. Whatever you call it, when you drive up to the portico and walk through the huge lobby furnished with a pleasing mixture of antique and contemporary fittings, you'll know this is a place where the art of gracious living is still practiced. Public spaces and guest rooms have undergone extensive renovation; while bright, cheerful colors predominate in the spacious accommodations, there's an air of subdued elegance that newer establishments never seem quite able to achieve. Besides the main building, there are spacious villas and one-, two-, and three-bedroom condominiums.

The major attraction is the seven 18-hole golf courses, especially the world-famous Number Two. Five courses begin and end at the elegant original clubhouse, while courses Six and Seven have their own clubhouses. Greens fees for all courses vary seasonally, and there's always a surcharge for courses Two and Seven.

The tennis complex, with some 26 courts (18 are clay, 4 lighted for night play), is presided over by a highly professional staff. Clinics and individual instruction are available to all guests. There are nine trap-and-skeet fields (two of which are lighted), and croquet and bowling lawns.

To all this add bicycles, a huge L-shaped pool and deck area, and 200 acres of fishing, boating, and swimming at Lake Pinehurst, and you have a resort with facilities second to none. In the evenings the hotel's sophisticated dinner dancing and entertainment offerings draw large crowds. Rates include breakfast and dinner.

WHERE TO DINE

Expensive

CAROLINA DINING ROOM, Pinehurst Hotel, Carolina Vista, Pinehurst. Tel. 295-6811.

Cuisine: AMERICAN/CONTINENTAL. **Reservations:** Required.
$ Prices: Fixed-price five-course dinner, $28. AE, DC, DISC, MC, V.
Open: Daily 6:30–9:30pm.

This formal dining room serves dinner in candlelit elegance. The menu is extensive and, needless to say, the service is impeccable. Beef, veal, chicken, and seafood fresh from Carolina coastal waters are presented in classic American style, or with rich sauces and in less traditional combinations. During the high season, there's top-flight entertainment and dinner dancing.

THE COVES, Market Square. Tel. 295-3400.
Cuisine: AMERICAN. **Reservations:** Recommended on weekends.
$ Prices: Appetizers $3–$6; main courses $13–$18; dinner for two $30. AE, MC, V.
Open: Mon–Sat 11:30am–10:30pm, Sun noon–9:30pm.

The main dining room is a pleasant affair with natural woods. Downstairs is the pub done up in knotty pine. Sandwiches and salads are popular, as are the pies, ice cream, and cakes. The downstairs bar may stay open later, depending on their mood and business.

Moderate

GREENHOUSE RESTAURANT, Pinehurst Place, 905 Linden Rd.
Pinehurst. Tel. 295-1761.
Cuisine: LIGHT MEALS. **Reservations:** Not required.
$ Prices: Lunch under $8.
Open: Lunch daily 11:30am–3pm. **Closed:** Holidays.

The Greenhouse is a light, airy place with blond bentwood chairs and, as you might expect, lots of hanging plants. The menu has such specialties as crab and seafood on a toasted English muffin topped with cheddar cheese sauce, and specialty meatballs and provolone cheese in a zesty tomato sauce on toasted loaf bread. Soups are memorable, as are desserts, such as the Greenhouse mud pie and strawberry shortcake. There is a wide selection of beer and mixed drinks, as well as wine by the glass.

Combine lunch with a delightful shopping experience at the shops in this interesting complex. They're open Monday through Saturday from 9:30am to 5:30pm and Sunday from 11:30am to 4pm, and offer a wide variety of brass, arts and crafts, baskets, sportsware, and candles.

PINE CREST INN, Dogwood Rd., Pinehurst. Tel. 295-6121.
Cuisine: CONTINENTAL. **Reservations:** Required.
$ Prices: Dinner $7–$20. AE, CB, DC, DISC, MC, V.
Open: Daily 6–9pm.

Although small, the Pine Crest Inn's restaurant has made such a name for itself that reservations are called in from towns all over the state. The prime beef, homemade pastries, and super-freshest vegetables account for this reputation. People also come back for the warm hospitality. There's dancing in Mr. B's Lounge. There's a piano bar, too.

Budget

PINEHURST PLAYHOUSE RESTAURANT & YOGURT, 100 West Village
Green. Tel. 295-8873.
Cuisine: DELI. **Reservations:** Not required.
$ Prices: Menu items 50¢–$4. No credit cards.
Open: Mon–Fri 8am–4pm, Sat 11am–4pm.

The former theater houses a number of retail establishments, including this casual eatery and yogurt shop. The sandwiches are named after Broadway shows. If you're looking for a quick, light bite, stop in.

VILLAGER DELI & RESTAURANT, Market Square, Tel. 295-1005.
  Cuisine: DELI. **Reservations:** Not required.
  $ Prices: Salads and sandwiches $4–$6. AE, MC, V.
  Open: Mon–Sat 8am–4pm.
At the Villager Deli, you can order up a hearty sandwich or a smooth slice of cheesecake with blackberries. There are specials every day, and all the tables have fresh flowers. The open kitchen arrangement and Windsor chairs are a nice touch.

YESTERDAY'S, 140 Chinquapin Rd. Tel. 295-0780.
  Cuisine: AMERICAN. **Reservations:** Recommended on weekends.
  $ Prices: Appetizers $4–$7; sandwiches and salads $5; main courses $5–$6. MC, V.
  Open: Mon–Sat 11:30am–9:30pm.
Yesterday's is a gathering hole for locals who like something lively in their evening out. Thursday is karaoke night. On Friday and Saturday, live bands play everything from pop to rock to country. There's a cover charge on weekends ranging from $2 to $6, depending on who's playing. This inviting restaurant and bar has a charming brick courtyard; the bar has tartan fabrics and a cozy fireplace. The menu includes vegetable lasagne, fish and chips, and spaghetti.

EVENING ENTERTAINMENT

Evening entertainment is mostly found at the golf resorts. Check, though, to see what's going on at **Sandhills Community College,** Airport Road (tel. 692-6185), which often stages jazz and other variety shows.

AN EXCURSION TO SEAGROVE & ASHEBORO

About an hour's drive to the northwest is the little town of ✪ **Seagrove** on U.S. 220, which has been turning out pottery for over 200 years. The red and gray clays of this region were first used by settlers from Staffordshire, England; the first items they produced were jugs for transporting whisky. The art is practiced today just as it was then: Clays are ground and mixed by machines turned by mules, simple designs are fashioned on kick wheels, and glazing is done in wood-burning kilns. Many of the potters work in or behind their homes, with only a small sign outside to identify their trade; if you have difficulty finding them, stop and ask—everybody does, so don't be shy. There are some sales rooms in town, but the real fun is seeing the pottery actually being made. And while you're asking, inquire about **Jugtown,** a group of rustic, log-hewn buildings in a grove of pines where potters demonstrate their art Monday through Saturday. Be sure to stop by the **Potter's Museum,** one mile north of Seagrove on U.S. 220, to browse through items of long-ago vintage and a gift shop displaying today's wares. It's free; open Tuesday through Saturday from 10am to 4pm, closed on major holidays and for the month of January.
    Of some 28 potters operating in the Seagrove area, two have caught my fancy. At **Walton's Pottery,** Rte. 2, Seagrove (just off N.C. 705 on Chrisco Road; tel. 879-3270), Susan and Don Walton's potter's wheel turns out delicate cutout candleholders as well as a full line of more traditional bowls, vases, teapots, and casseroles. It's open 10am to 5pm, Monday through Saturday (open 1 to 5pm on Sunday in November). **M. L. Owens Pottery,** Rte. 2, Seagrove (tel. 462-3553), is where Melvin Owens has been turning the wheel since 1937, following in the tradition begun by his grandfather in 1895.
    A little north of Seagrove (still on U.S. 220), you'll come to Asheboro, where you should turn east on U.S. 64, then head south on N.C. 159 to reach the **North**

Carolina Zoological Park, Rte. 4, Asheboro (tel. 879-7000). The 300-acre Africa region, the first of seven continental regions planned for the 1,448-acre park, features 700 animals in unbarred natural habitats. In this still-developing, world-class zoo, gorillas and 200 rare animals (like meerkats) inhabit the African Pavilion, while lions, elephants, and chimpanzees dwell in spacious outdoor habitats. A 37-acre African Plains exhibit is home to a dozen species of antelope, gazelles, and oryx. The R. J. Reynolds Forest Aviary holds 150 exotic birds flying free amid lush tropical trees and plants. There's a tram ride, a picnic area, restaurants, and gift shops. The zoo is open April through October 15, Monday through Friday from 9am to 5pm, and Saturday, Sunday, and holidays from 10am to 6pm; October 16 through March, hours are daily from 9am to 4pm. Adults pay $5; seniors and children 2 to 12, $3.

AN EXCURSION TO MT. GILEAD

West of Pinehurst, just off N.C. 731 or N.C. 73, the ✪ **Town Creek Indian Mound,** Rte. 3, Mt. Gilead (tel. 439-6802), gives you a fascinating glimpse into the lives of the Native Americans who established the religious, ceremonial, and burial center some 300 years ago on this bluff overlooking the junction of Little River and Town Creek. The remnants have now been excavated and/or reconstructed: a major temple, the dwelling place of priests, ceremonial grounds, and many, many artifacts. There's no charge, but hours vary with the season and day of the week, so call before stopping by.

SOUTHERN PINES

WHAT TO SEE & DO

SIGHTS & EVENTS   The **Campbell House,** a handsome Georgian structure on East Connecticut Avenue that was once a family residence, now houses the Arts Council of Moore County, and its art galleries display the works of local artists.

On the Fort Bragg–Aberdeen Road, 1½ miles southeast of Southern Pines, you'll come to ✪ **Weymouth Woods–Sandhills Nature Preserve,** a beautiful nature spot with foot and bridle paths and some 600 acres of pine-covered "sandridges." There's also a natural history museum, free, that's open Monday through Saturday from 9am to 6pm and Sunday from noon to 5pm.

There are a lot of fine horse farms in the Sandhills. Steeplechasers trained here show up regularly at tracks around the country, and trotters and pacers are also trained in the area. The late Del Cameron, renowned three-time winner of the Hambletonian, kept a winter training stable in the Sandhills for more than 30 years.

The **Mid-South Horse Show Association** holds schooling shows every Sunday afternoon from January to April; in early March there's the **Moore County Hounds Hunter Trials** at Hobby Field, Southern Pines, with reserved parking spaces overlooking the course for spectators; and the **Stoneybrook Steeplechase Races** are held on the second Saturday in April on a farm near Southern Pines where race horses are bred and trained the rest of the year by owner Michael G. Walsh, an Irishman from County Cork. The **Pinehurst Area Convention and Visitors Bureau,** P.O. Box 2270, Southern Pines, NC 28387, can furnish exact dates and full details on all these events as well as others throughout the year.

SHOPPING   Like those in Pinehurst, shops here are small, charming, and filled with interesting, often exquisite items. Outstanding among the offbeat shops is **Something Special,** on Pennsylvania Avenue (tel. 692-9602). Inside are collectors' dolls and dollhouses, miniature grandfather clocks that keep actual time, all kinds of materials to make your own dollhouse, and such special items as miniature dentures. Look for **Downtown Southern Pines,** U.S. 1 in the Broad Street area, a charming collection of shops and restaurants in the historic district.

WHERE TO STAY

DAYS INN, 1420 U.S. 1, Southern Pines, NC 28387. Tel. 919/692-7581, or toll free 800/325-2525. Fax 919/692-9689. 120 rms. A/C TV TEL
$ **Rates** (including breakfast): $45 single; $47–$52 double. Children under 13 stay free with parents. Golf packages available. AE, MC, V.
The Days Inn has comfortably furnished guest rooms. Most rooms have either a private patio or balcony. There's a wading pool, a full-size pool, Jacuzzi, restaurant, and lounge with entertainment. The hotel is wheelchair-accessible.

ECONO LODGE, U.S. 1, P.O. Box 150, Southern Pines, NC 28387. Tel. 919/944-2324, or toll free 800/424-4777. Fax 919/944-7155. 91 rms. A/C TV TEL
$ **Rates:** $37 single; $43 double. Golf packages available. AE, CB, DC, DISC, MC, V.
There are picnic areas on the grounds of the Econo Lodge, and some of the comfortable rooms have king-size beds. Other amenities include a restaurant and pool. The hotel is wheelchair-accessible.

HYLAND HILLS RESORT, 41110 U.S. 1, Southern Pines, NC 28387. Tel. 919/692-7615, or toll free 800/841-0638. 50 rms. A/C TV TEL
$ **Rates:** $34 single; $44 double; $47 efficiency. Golf packages available. DISC, MC, V.
In an attractive wooded setting, all the efficiencies and spacious rooms here have patios. Efficiencies are well equipped, and there's a pool. There's a $20 to $29 fee for play on the 18-hole golf course right on the premises.

MID PINES, a Clarion Resort, 1010 Midland Rd., Southern Pines, NC 28387. Tel. 919/692-2114, or toll free 800/323-2114. Fax 919/692-4615. 118 rms. 7 cottages, 10 lakeside villas. A/C TV TEL
$ **Rates:** $50–$90 single; $52–$110 double; $198 cottage or villa. Children under 12 stay free with parents. Lower rates off-season. AE, DC, DISC, MC, V.

⭐ This leading resort boasts a graceful, colonial-style main building with wings flanking the main entrance, and a beautiful lobby rotunda with twin white staircases. Rooms in the three-story hotel are decorated with style; there are also cottages on the grounds, some with fireplaces, as well as tastefully decorated and furnished lakeside villas. There's an 18-hole golf course, a putting green, a landscaped pool, four lighted tennis courts, and a recreation room. Both the lovely formal dining room and the more informal terrace (overlooking the fairways of the championship golf course) serve excellent meals—I especially liked the buffet lunch on the terrace—at moderate to expensive prices. Call for villa and cottage rates.

WHERE TO DINE

ANTOINE'S, 270 S.W. Broad St. Tel. 692-5622.
  Cuisine: FRENCH. **Reservations:** Recommended.
$ **Prices:** Lunch $6–$8; dinner $17–$20. MC, V.
  Open: Lunch 11:30am–2pm; dinner 5:30–10pm.
You'll find superb French cuisine in a charming and intimate setting.

LOB STEER INN, U.S. 1 North. Tel. 692-3503.
  Cuisine: STEAK/SEAFOOD. **Reservations:** Recommended.
$ **Prices:** Appetizers $3–$5; main courses $10–$29. AE, DC, MC, V.

Open: Dinner daily 5–10:30pm.

⭐ For prime steaks, lobster and other fresh seafood, and an excellent salad bar, this eatery is one of the best and most popular places in the area. The menu includes steak-and-lobster combination plates, and children's plates in a wider variety than usual.

MORRIE'S DELI AND BAKERY, 120 S. W. Broad St. Tel. 692-5759.

Cuisine: DELI/BAKERY. **Reservations:** Not accepted.
$ Prices: Menu items $3–$5. No credit cards.
Open: Mon–Sat 9:30am–3pm.

Ⓢ Morrie's is a great place for a midday snack. Everything is homemade, and the menu includes large sandwiches (including such filler-uppers as hot meatball sandwiches), quiche, pasta, burgers, and hot dogs. Salads are fresh, and homemade desserts are terrific. If you get the itch to do a bit of entertaining in your hotel room, Morrie's caters smashing lazy Susan trays.

WHISKEY McNEILL'S, 181 N.E. Broad St. Tel. 692-5440.

Cuisine: SANDWICHES/SALADS. **Reservations:** Not accepted.
$ Prices: Salad plates and sandwiches $5–$8. MC, V.
Open: Sun–Thurs 11:30am–9pm, Fri–Sat 11:30am–10pm.

Ⓢ This whimsical place was once a service station, and leftover gas pumps now adorn the interior. The menu offers a nice mixture of gourmet-quality sandwiches (many made with croissants), burgers, salads (including a standout seafood salad of whitefish, shrimp, and crabmeat), tasty homemade soups (don't miss the traditional Southern-style Brunswick stew), and homemade desserts.

EVENING ENTERTAINMENT

Most area golf resorts have dancing and occasional evening entertainment. In addition, check the following for current goings-on.

MANNIE'S DINNER THEATRE, 210 W. Pennsylvania Ave. Tel. 692-8400.

Professional troupes appear in Broadway shows here in a relaxed atmosphere. Every Saturday doors open at 6:30pm, dinner is served at 7pm, and performances begin at 8:30pm. The $22 price includes dinner and show but not tax, tip, or dessert. They serve lunch daily from 11am to 2:30pm.

PERFORMING ARTS CENTER, N.W. Broad St. Tel. 692-4356.

Home to the Sandhills Little Theater and a number of other local concert and entertainment groups, and the site of periodic travelogue and arts council shows.
Admission: Varies with event.

AN EXCURSION TO CAMERON & SANFORD

The entire little town of **Cameron,** about 10 miles north of Southern Pines (off U.S. 1), has been designated a historic district, with some 19 historical sites and buildings. More than 60 antiques dealers have shops here, and there's an annual antiques street fair the first Saturday in May and again in October. Among things to look for are the **Greenwood Inn** (1874), the **Muse Brothers' store** (1880), and the fine Queen Anne–style **Rodwell House** (1890). Most shops open Wednesday through Saturday from 10am to 5pm. After a morning of delightful sightseeing and shopping, have lunch at **Miss Bell's Antique and Tea Room** (served from 11am to 2pm).

About 35 miles north of Southern Pines via U.S. 15/501 and N.C. 42, North Carolina's frontier days spring to life at the **Alston House,** also known as the House in the Horseshoe (for the horseshoe bend of the Deep River, which the house overlooks), Rte. 3, Sanford (tel. 947-2051). Built in the late 1770s, the two-story frame house, with its central hall plan, is typical of plantation houses of that era; the bullet holes were made in 1781 when Whigs and Tories battled it out on the grounds. "Miss Ruby" Newton, who takes visitors through the house, will fill you in with other anecdotes about the house and its owners down through the years. The first weekend of every August, a Revolutionary War battle is reenacted here, and in early December there's a cheery open house and candlelighting celebration. Admission is free. From April to October, hours are Monday through Saturday from 9am to 5pm and Sunday from 1 to 5pm; November to March, hours are Tuesday through Saturday from 10am to 4pm, Sunday from 1 to 4pm.

CHAPTER 5

THE NORTH CAROLINA MOUNTAINS

1. BOONE
2. ASHEVILLE
3. CHEROKEE
4. THE GREAT SMOKY MOUNTAINS NATIONAL PARK

There's something about mountains! "Majestic" is much overworked, but it applies. In North Carolina's incredibly beautiful Blue Ridge Mountains, although men and women have made their homes here since the first push westward, it is *nature* that endures. Their peaks and valleys now hold a variety of posh and not-so-posh resorts and other holiday attractions, but they seem only to enhance what was here in the beginning.

To come in late spring is to see green creeping up the peaks as trees leaf out. In summer, wildflowers blossom to make a carpet of colorful blooms. Fall brings vivid reds and yellows and oranges to give a flamelike hue to every mountainside. Wildlife still flourishes, streams are clear, and forests of birch, poplar, beech, hickory, and oak are undisturbed. This is one of those rare places where "civilization" has been smart enough to protect nature as well as enjoy it.

THE BLUE RIDGE PARKWAY

South of Waynesboro, Virginia, the Blue Ridge Parkway takes up where Virginia's Skyline Drive leaves off at Rockfish Gap, between Charlottesville and Waynesboro, and continues winding and twisting along the mountain crests for some 470 miles, passing through most of western North Carolina before it reaches the Great Smoky Mountains National Park near the Tennessee border.

You'll drive at elevations ranging from 649 to 6,053 feet above sea level. There's no toll on the parkway, and there are frequent exits to nearby towns. There are 11 visitor contact stations, nine campgrounds (open May through October only; no reservations) with drinking water and comfort stations, but no shower or utility hookups; restaurants and gas stations; and three lodges, plus one location featuring rustic cabins for overnight accommodations (reservations are recommended). Opening and closing dates for campgrounds and cabins are flexible, so be sure to check in advance. Before you set out, write ahead for maps and detailed information to: Superintendent, Blue Ridge Parkway, 200 BB&T Building, One Pack Square, Asheville, NC 28801 (tel. 704/259-0701).

At many overlooks you'll see a rifle-and-powderhorn symbol and the word "Trail," which means that there are marked walking trails through the woods. Some take only 10 or 20 minutes and provide a delightful, leg-stretching break from the confines of the car; others are longer and steeper and may take an hour or more if you go the entire way.

There are a few simple rules laid down by the National Park Service, which administers the parkway: No commercial vehicles are permitted; no swimming in lakes and ponds; no hunting; pets must be kept on a leash; and above all else, no fire except in campground or picnic area fireplaces. Another good rule to follow is to keep your gas tank half filled at all times—it's no place to be stranded! Oh, yes, the speed limit is 45 miles an hour—and they're quite serious about that.

Don't plan to hurry down the Blue Ridge: If you don't have time to amble and drink in the beauty, you'll only be frustrated. If you want to drive the entire length of the parkway, allow at least two or three days. On the first day, drive the Virginia half, then stop for the night at Boone, North Carolina, not far from the state border. The final two legs of the trip—from Boone to Asheville and from there to Fontana Village—can be easily accomplished in another day's drive.

A HOSTEL ALONG THE PARKWAY The only licensed **American Youth Hostel** along the Blue Ridge Parkway is about 10 miles southeast of Galax, Virginia, 2 miles north of the North Carolina border and 100 feet off the parkway (milepost 214.5). The hostel building is a faithful copy of an ancient Yorktown house, and there's a 19th-century log cabin adjacent. Accommodations are dormitory-style with a kitchen where hostelers do their own cooking, and a common room for relaxing and socializing. There's a mountain stream flowing through the 25 acres on which the hostel sits, and the views are stunning. The overnight fee is $10. American Youth Hostels membership is a requirement (for applications, contact American Youth Hostels, Dept. 854, P.O. Box 37613, Washington, DC 20013-7613, tel. 202/783-6161). Book by contacting: **Blue Ridge Country-AYH Hostel,** R.R. 2, Box 449, Galax, VA 24333 (tel. 703/236-4962 after 5pm).

---

1. BOONE

189 miles W of Raleigh; 95 miles NE of Asheville; 10 miles W of the parkway

GETTING THERE By Plane The nearest airport is at Asheville (see below).

By Bus For local **Greyhound/Trailways** information, call 704/253-5353. The nearest stop is Asheville, 50 miles away (see below).

By Car U.S. 321 reaches Boone from the west and intersects U.S. 421 running west from the parkway.

ESSENTIALS The **area code** is 704. The **Boone Area Chamber of Commerce,** is at 112 W. Howard St., Boone, NC 28607 (tel. 704/264-2225).

Boone (named for Daniel, of course—he had a cabin here in the 1760s) draws hunters and fishermen to the abundantly stocked streams and forests. For summer visitors, there's a beautifully produced outdoor drama, Kermit Hunter's *Horn in the West,* as well as the Appalachian Summer festival of concerts, drama, and art exhibits.

WHAT TO SEE & DO

The Boone/Banner Elk/Blowing Rock area, sometimes called "the High Country," has been a summer resort retreat for Southerners since the 1800s. In recent years, skiers have been attracted to the high slopes during winter months as well. There are five excellent skiing facilities and a wealth of winter accommodations, restaurants, and entertainment spots such as **Ski Beech Ski Resort,** P.O. Box 1118, Banner Elk, NC 28604 (tel. 387-2011). Friends who head for the hills every winter weekend tell me this is the best skiing in the South. Lift rates, subject to change, are in the $25-per-day range, and increase on weekends and holidays. Skis can be rented, and a professional ski school offers classes as well as private lessons. There's also a children's ski program, and nonskiing tykes can stay and play in the Land of Oz nursery.

Kermit Hunter's ✪ ***Horn in the West,*** is presented in the Daniel Boone Theatre, P.O. Box 295, Boone, NC 28607 (tel. 264-2120), every night except Monday from late June through mid-August. It tells a vivid story of pioneer efforts to win freedom during the American Revolution. Performances begin at 8:30pm and admission is $8 to $9 (half price for children 13 and under).

Located adjacent to the theater is the **Hickory Ridge Homestead Museum** (tel. 264-2120), an 18th-century living-history museum in a re-created log cabin. It's open during late June through mid-August, Tuesday through Sunday from 1 to 8:30pm; May to late June and mid-August through October weekends only. Traditional craftspeople demonstrate their skills, and there's a homestead store. An apple festival is held on the grounds in late October, and Christmas events lighten mid-December.

In the immediate vicinity, don't miss **Blowing Rock,** two miles southeast of the town of the same name on U.S. 321 (tel. 295-7111), where you can stand on "the Rock," as it's affectionately called, throw a handkerchief or some other light object off the edge, and have it sent right back up to you by strong updraft. In addition, the observation tower, gazebos, and gardens offer really splendid views of the John's River Gorge and nearby Blue Ridge peaks. The observation tower is open daily in April and May 8:30am to 6pm; June through August, 8am to 8pm; September through November 8am to 6pm (as long as weather permits). Adults pay $4; children 6 to 11, $1. Another natural phenomenon at Blowing Rock is **Mystery Hill,** where balls roll and water runs uphill. Its pioneer museum is interesting, and you'll get a kick out of the mock grave marked simply "HE WUZ A REVENOOR"—a pile of dirt with boots sticking out one end!

Don't think the **Tweetsie Railroad Theme Park** (tel. 264-9061, or toll free 800/526-5740), halfway between Boone and Blowing Rock, is for the kiddies only; the whole family will enjoy it. An old narrow-gauge train winds along a three-mile route here, suffering mock attacks by "Indians" and "outlaws." It runs daily from late May through October, from 9am to 6pm, and the fare is $12.95 for adults, $10.95 for children 4 to 12 and seniors over 60. There's mountain music and other entertainment, restaurants, Western shops, country fair rides, a petting zoo, and a crafts area.

✪ **Grandfather Mountain** (one mile off the parkway on U.S. 221 near Linville) is the highest peak in the Blue Ridge. You can see as far as 100 miles from the **Mile High Swinging Bridge,** and the **Environmental Habitat** is home to Mildred the Bear and her black bear friends. In spacious separate sections you can also view native deer, cougars, and bald and golden eagles (which have been injured and cannot live in the wild on their own). Kilt-clad Scots (from Scotland as well as all parts of North America) gather here early in July for the annual **Highland Games and Gathering of the Clans.** Bagpipe music, dancing, wrestling, and tossing the caber (a telephone-pole-like shaft)—as well as the colorful mix of people bent on two days of fun—make it a spectacle not to be missed.

WHERE TO STAY

HOLIDAY INN, 710 Blowing Rock Rd., Boone, NC 28607. Tel. 704/264-2451. Fax 704/264-2451. 138 rms. A/C TV TEL

$ Rates: $49–$69 single; $59–$79 double. AE, DC, MC, V.

Facilities here include a heated pool, health-exercise club, and running track, as well as a restaurant that serves moderately priced meals. Rooms are nicely done up to the standard of this dependable motel chain.

HOUND EARS LODGE, P.O. Box 188, Blowing Rock, NC 28605. Tel. 704/963-4321. 27 rms and suites. A/C TV TEL

$ Rates (including breakfast and dinner): Mid-June to Oct. $150 single; $244 double. Rates vary in other months. AE, MC, V.

★ One of the most exclusive resort lodges in this part of the country. If "deluxe" is your travel style, this will be a mountain visit par excellence. The unusual name comes from a nearby rock formation. The setting is gorgeous, the rooms and suites are the ultimate in luxury, and it's surrounded by beautifully landscaped grounds. Facilities include a swimming pool, golf course, tennis courts, fishing, and skiing in winter months. It's seven miles west of Boone, half a mile off N.C. 105.

WHERE TO DINE

DAN'L BOONE INN, 105 Hardin St. Tel. 264-8657.
 Cuisine: SOUTHERN. **Reservations:** Not accepted.
$ **Prices:** Sat–Sun $6 breakfast; daily $10 lunch or dinner; children's plates $2.50. No credit cards.
 Open: June–Oct, Sat–Sun 8am–9pm, Mon–Fri 11am–9pm. Nov–May Mon–Fri 5–9pm, Sat–Sun 8am–9pm.

For family-style meals that are really something special—and at prices that won't hurt—you can't go wrong here. Everything is home-cooked, and the fare is definitely Southern; country ham and biscuits, fried chicken, and the like. Lunch or dinner comes with soup or salad, a choice of three meats, five vegetables, homemade biscuits, dessert, and beverage.

---

2. ASHEVILLE

241 miles W of Raleigh; 95 miles SW of Boone; 90 miles NE of Fontana; 48 miles NE of Cherokee

GETTING THERE By Plane Asheville's airport is served by **American Eagle** (tel. toll free 800/433-7300), **Delta** (tel. toll free 800/221-1212, **USAIR** (tel. toll free 800/428-4322), and **United Express** (tel. toll free 800/241-6522).

By Bus For local **Greyhound/Trailways** information, call 704/253-5353.

By Car I-40 passes through Asheville from the east and west; I-26 runs southeast (as far as Charleston); U.S. 23/19A runs north and west; and I-240 is a perimeter highway circumventing the city. For AAA services, contact **Carolina Motor Club,** 660 Merrimon Ave., Suite 1, Asheville, NC (tel. 704/253-5376).

ESSENTIALS The **area code** is 704. Write or visit the **Asheville Convention and Visitors Bureau,** 151 Haywood St. (P.O. Box 1011), Asheville, NC 28802 (tel. 704/258-6109, or toll free 800/257-1300.

SPECIAL EVENTS Special happenings at Biltmore House include a spring **Festival of Flowers, September International Exposition,** and **Christmas at Biltmore**—inquire ahead for specific dates.
 Special events at the Folk Art Center include **Fiber Day** in May, the **World Gee Haw Whimmy Diddle Competition** in August, **Celebrate Folk Art** in September, and **Christmas with the Guild** in December. In July and October, try not to miss *Mountain Sweet Talk,* a two-part, two-act play presented by Barbara Freeman and Connie Regan-Blake, among this country's best mountain storytellers. Call ahead for dates and times.
 If you are here the first weekend of August, don't miss the **Annual Mountain Dance and Folk Festival,** held at the Civic Center on Haywood Street, where the fiddlers, banjo pickers, ballad singers, dulcimer players, and clog dancers don't call it quits until there's nobody interested in one more square dance. This is the oldest such festival in the country, and you're encouraged to join in even if you don't know a "do-si-do" from a "swing-your-partner." And every Saturday night from early July

through August (except for the first Saturday in August), there's a ✪ **Shindig-on-the-Green** at the City County Plaza (College and Spruce Streets), where you'll find many of those same mountain musicians and dancers having an old-fashioned wingding. It's free, and lots of fun; if sitting on the ground isn't your thing, take along a blanket or chair.

In Brevard, 27 miles southwest of Asheville, there's a music festival held from late June through mid-August at the **Brevard Music Center.** Nationally and internationally famous artists perform daily in symphony, chamber music, band, and choral concerts, as well as musical comedy and opera. Write P.O. Box 592, Brevard, NC 28712, or call 704/884-2019 for schedules and reservations. Some events are free, others cost up to $16.

Since 1797, Asheville has grown from a tiny mountain trading village at the confluence of the French Broad and Swannanoa rivers, into a year-round resort. It boasts architectural gems from several eras, and cultural features that give it a special flavor.

WHAT TO SEE & DO

IN ASHEVILLE

In recent years there's been a vigorous effort to preserve and restore remnants of the city's colorful past, and a concise "Asheville Heritage Tour" brochure, available from the Asheville Chamber of Commerce, will guide you through such points as the historic downtown district. Don't miss **Biltmore Village** (a cluster of some 24 cottages housing interesting boutiques, craft shops, and restaurants), and the **Montford historic district,** with its more than 200 turn-of-the-century residences. In the downtown area, amid marvelous art deco buildings, you'll see the **Lexington Park** area, a center for artists and artisans whose workshops are tucked away down a little alleyway, and **Pack Place,** a developing center for all sorts of cultural activities.

An overwhelmingly magnificent structure is the ✪ **Biltmore Estate,** 1 North Pack Square, Asheville, NC 28801 (tel. 255-1700, or toll free 800/543-2961), on U.S. 25, two blocks north of I-40. The French Renaissance château, built by George W. Vanderbilt, has 250 rooms! There isn't an ordinary spot in the place, not even the kitchen. Vanderbilt gathered furnishings and art treasures from all over the world for this palace (for instance, Napoleon's chess set and table from St. Helena are here), and then went further, creating one of the most lavish formal gardens you'll ever see. There are more than 200 varieties of azaleas, plus thousands of other plants and shrubs. Admission to the house and gardens is $22 for adults, $16.50 for children 10 to 17 (9 and under free with parents). You should allow a minimum of two hours for the self-guided tour. If you plan to make a day of it, there's a charming restaurant in a renovated barn, as well as an interesting winery. Biltmore is closed Thanksgiving, Christmas Day, and New Year's Day.

There's no charge to visit the **Grove Wood Gallery** (a pet project of Mrs. Vanderbilt's), two miles north of town on Macon Street via Charlotte Street, on the grounds of the Grove Park Inn (tel. 253-7651). Mrs. Vanderbilt wanted to preserve the traditional wool-manufacturing skills of the mountain people and help the weavers turn those skills into a paying industry, so she set up the cluster of old-world buildings and found local orders for the beautiful handwoven fabrics; eventually a mail-order business evolved that still thrives. You can visit the complex and the two free museums, the **Antique Automobile Museum** and the **gallery** which are free and open Monday through Saturday from 9am to 5pm, Sunday from 1pm to 5pm. Shops occupying the charming, ivy-covered buildings display a wide range of goods, from crafts to books to antiques.

Thomas Wolfe grew up in Asheville and immortalized the town and its citizens (much to their dismay) in his *Look Homeward, Angel.* The boarding house Dixieland, which figures so prominently in the book, is at 48 Spruce St. and is maintained as a literary shrine, with hours that vary seasonally (call 253-8304 for details). Adults pay $1; children through high school, 50¢. Both Wolfe and William Sydney Porter (O. Henry) are buried in Riverside Cemetery (entrance on Birch Street off Pearson Drive).

NEARBY

Some five miles east of downtown Asheville, at milepost 382 on the Blue Ridge Parkway, the ✪ **Folk Art Center,** P.O. Box 9545, Asheville, NC 28815 (tel. 704/298-7928), is operated by the Southern Highland Handicraft Guild, a nonprofit organization of craftspeople of the nine-state Southern Appalachian region. The contemporary wood-and-stone structure houses the finest in both traditional and contemporary handcrafts of the region, the **Allanstand Craft Shop** (one of the oldest craft shops in the country, established in 1895), and exhibition and museum areas.

✪ **Chimney Rock Park** is 25 miles southeast of Asheville on U.S. 74/64. The granite monolith rises to a height of 315 feet, and you can reach its top by a stairway, a trail, or (as in my case) an elevator. There's an observation lounge open daily (weather permitting), and the charge is $8 for adults, $4 for children 6 to 15. Trails lead to Needle's Eye, Moonshiner's Cave, and Devil's Head (on the way to Hickory Nut Falls, twice the height of Niagara). Food service is available for $6 and under, and there are picnic facilities. For full details and a free vacation brochure and map, contact: Chimney Rock Park, P.O. Box 39, Chimney Rock, NC 28720 (tel. 625-9611, or toll free 800/277-9611).

Stately **Mount Mitchell** (highest point in the east) is in the state park that bears its name, some 33 miles northeast on the parkway, then five miles north on N.C. 128. There are a museum, a tower, and an observation lodge at Mount Mitchell; camping and picnicking facilities are available in the park.

About 30 miles southeast of Asheville on U.S. 25 is the little town of ✪ **Flat Rock,** home to the North Carolina State Theater's **Flat Rock Playhouse,** which stages performances from late June through August. It is better known, however, as the last home of two-time Pulitzer prize–winning writer-poet-historian ✪ **Carl Sandburg,** who lived at Connemara Farm (on Little River Road, just west of U.S. 25) for some 22 years, longer than he'd ever lived in any other place. His home and the farm are preserved just as they were in his lifetime—the typewriter sitting on an orange crate in his top-floor hideaway and his guitar propped against a chair in the living room—and there's no charge to visit and stroll around the grounds.

BLACK MOUNTAIN   About eight miles east of Asheville on U.S. 70, you'll find Black Mountain, a small mountain community with 75 antique shops that seems suspended in time. Stop by the **Old Depot,** which has been turned into a center for the work of local craftspeople and where you'll often hear the sweet music of oldtime dulcimers played by local musicians who also sing traditional ballads of these hills. If you're in the area the first weekend in December, don't miss the lighting of a Christmas tree. In mid-October, there's the three-day **Black Mountain Festival,** when traditional music and dance make for an ideal family event.

MAGGIE VALLEY   A little west of Asheville on the Blue Ridge Parkway, a turn east at Wagon Road Gap will take you down a steep, winding road to the first forestry school in the United States. There's an interesting museum for visitors. Along the way, you go past **Sliding Rock,** where children often delight in sliding down the glass-slick surface, and **Looking Glass Falls.**

Nearer the end of the parkway, at Maggie Valley on U.S. 19, an entertainment center, the **Ghost Town in the Sky** (tel. 926-1140) is great fun. Separate Western, mining, and mountaineer towns have been re-created on different levels of the mountaintop, and there's something going on in each one all the time. Shows are staged in the saloons, there are street gunfights, and all sorts of Western and mountaineer types wander about. You reach the park (3,364 feet up) by means of twin inclined railways, a shuttle bus, or a chair lift. Kids will enjoy the ride. It's open from 9am to 6pm daily from early May through October (weather permitting). Admission is $15 for adults, $12 for children 3 to 9.

From the middle of December until mid-March, there's very good skiing at the **Cataloochee Ski Area at Maggie Valley** (Rte. 1, Box 502, Maggie Valley, NC 28751; tel. 704/926-0285, or toll free 800/768-0285). A base lodge serves three hearty meals daily in ski season.

WHERE TO STAY

IN ASHEVILLE

DAYS INN, 1500 Tunnel Rd., Asheville, NC 28805. Tel. 704/298-5140, or toll free 800/325-2525. 125 rms, 22 efficiencies (no utensils). A/C TV TEL **Directions:** Take exit 55 from I-40.

$ Rates: Seasonal, $33–$65 single or double; $43–$75 efficiency. AE, DC, MC, V. The hillside location provides spectacular mountain views, especially when autumn foliage begins to turn. There's a pool, kiddie playground, restaurant, gift shop, and laundry service, and it's only 5 miles from Biltmore House.

FOREST MANOR MOTOR LODGE, 866 Hendersonville Rd., Asheville, NC 28803. Tel. 704/274-3531. 21 rms, 3 kitchenettes. A/C TV TEL **Directions:** Take exit 50 on U.S. 25.

$ Rates (including continental breakfast): $39–$89 single; $49–$99 double. **Closed:** Early Jan–late Feb.

Four miles from the city center, in a scenic, wooded setting, Lloyd and Leone Kirk's lodge offers bungalow-style rooms, pine-paneled and attractively furnished, each with an inviting porch entrance bordered by well-tended flower beds. The Kirks so pride themselves on cleanliness that if you find any evidence of dirt, there's no charge! It's a relaxed, friendly place to stay. Guests enjoy the heated pool in summer.

GREAT SMOKIES HILTON, 1 Hilton Dr., Asheville, NC 28806. Tel. 704/254-3211, or toll free 800/445-8667. Fax 704/254-1603. 280 rms. A/C TV TEL

$ Rates: $70–$132 double. AE, DC, DISC, MC, V.
In addition to the high-quality guest rooms (some with wet bars) typical of Hilton hotels, there is a heated pool and sauna, as well as tennis courts and an 18-hole golf course. Meals in the excellent dining room run under $25.

GROVE PARK INN AND COUNTRY CLUB, 290 Macon Ave., Asheville, NC 28804. Tel. 704/252-2711, or toll free 800/438-5800. 510 rms A/C TV TEL

$ Rates: $90–$240 single or double. AE, DC, MC, V.

For mountain vacationing that is rustic and at the same time luxurious, reserve at this favorite of the southern gentry since 1913. It has hosted such notables as F. Scott Fitzgerald, FDR, Woodrow Wilson, Thomas Edison, and Henry Ford, and is listed in the National Register of Historic Places. The inn is built on the side of Sunset Mountain at an elevation of 3,100 feet. In its "great hall" lobby, flanked on each end by 14-foot fireplaces, comfortably padded chairs and sofas create a feeling of coziness despite the 120-foot-long dimensions of the room. Package plans are offered for sports enthusiasts and honeymooning couples and on holidays. Notable among the numerous fine restaurants and lounges are the Horizons

Restaurant, featuring innovative classic cuisine; the Blue Ridge Dining Room and legendary outdoor dining veranda for moderately priced meals; and the Carolina Café, overlooking the mountains, for light meals and continuous service. (See "Where to Dine," below.) After dark, Elaine's Nightclub swings into action with variety shows and dancing on weekends.

Also, the shopping arcade, nine tennis courts, indoor and outdoor swimming pools, the sports center, and the 18-hole golf course keep guests busy.

HAYWOOD PARK HOTEL, 1 Battery Park Ave., Asheville, NC 28801. Tel. 704/252-2522 or toll free 800/228-2252. 33 suites. A/C TV TEL **Directions:** Take the Civic Center exit off I-240.

$ Rates (including continental breakfast): $110–$250 single or double. Children under 12 stay free with parents. AE, DC, MC, V.

A sophisticated setting in the heart of downtown Asheville. Suites are a nice blend of luxury (with marble baths, oversize tubs, Jacuzzis, minibars, and fridges in some) and practicality (computer hookups in all). Brenna's Restaurant and Lounge provides both casual and more formal dining.

THE RED ROOF INN–WEST, 16 Crowell Rd., Asheville, NC 28806. Tel. 704/667-9803, or toll free 800/843-7663. 109 rms. A/C TV TEL **Directions:** Take exit 44 off I-40, and go one block north on U.S. 19 to Crowell Road.

$ Rates: $35–$38 single; $42–$45 double. Children under 18 stay free with parents. AE, DC, DISC, MC, V.

As is usual with this chain, rooms are comfortably furnished. There's cable TV in all, and many have oversize beds. Free coffee is served in the lobby, and there's a restaurant nearby.

A Bed-and-Breakfast

CEDAR CREST VICTORIAN INN, 674 Biltmore Ave., Asheville, NC 28803. Tel. 704/252-1389. 10 rms, 2 suites. A/C TV

$ Rates (including continental breakfast): $65–$115 single; $70–$120 double; $85–$150 suite. AE, MC, V.

A stay here is like a lovely trip back to the Victorian era. Built in 1894, this grand mansion is a fantasy of leaded glass, ornately carved fireplaces, antique furnishings, and a massive oak staircase. Owners Barbara and Jack McEwan have indulged their romantic and whimsical imaginations in furnishing the guest rooms—all have period antiques and the decor in each is unique, with a canopied ceiling in one, a marvelous carved walnut bed in another, and brass bedsteads in a third. All have private or semiprivate baths. Several have working fireplaces. Evening coffee and chocolate are served in the parlor. A cottage with two suites is adjacent to the main house. Cedar Crest does not accept children under 12 or pets, and smoking is permitted only in designated areas. You might elect the option of breakfast in bed.

NEARBY

THE GREYSTONE INN, Greystone Lane (P.O. Box 6), Lake Toxaway, NC 28747. Tel. 704/966-4700, or toll free 800/824-5766. 33 rms and suites. A/C TV TEL

$ Rates (including breakfast and dinner): $109–$165 per person double. AE, MC, V.

This is the sort of getaway spot for which you may begin to yearn as the scenery of the Blue Ridge Mountains unfolds around you. Set on a wooded peninsula on Lake Toxaway, this restored 1915 mansion welcomes guests with an engaging mix of antique furnishings and modern comforts (including Jacuzzis in all rooms). Each room has its own unique character, and many have working fireplaces. The stone fireplace is also a focal point in the oak-paneled living room; the library is a beautifully appointed oasis; and the terrace is the perfect setting for before-dinner drinks.

For dedicated do-nothings, there are wicker rocking chairs on the glassed-in sun porch overlooking the lake. Complimentary midafternoon tea is served with cakes. In addition to main-house guest rooms, there are six lovely two- and three-bedroom cottages that come equipped with full kitchens.

Meals in the Hearthsides dining room (for guests only) feature gourmet selections such as veal française Scandi and rainbow mountain trout amandine. Dinner is a six-course affair. Tennis courts, fishing, waterskiing, swimming, sailboating, and golf are available on the property or nearby.

WHERE TO DINE

Some of the best eating in Asheville is to be found at the ✪ **Grove Park Inn,** 290 Macon Ave. (tel. 252-2711). Even if you stay elsewhere, you really should plan at least one meal at this great old hostelry. Sunday brunch in the inn's **Blue Ridge Dining Room** is an Asheville tradition, with a sumptuous international buffet table laden with so many plantation "extras" (omelets and waffles made to order, etc.) that any thought of sticking to a diet will evaporate at once. Priced at $21, it is extremely popular with locals, so reserve as early as possible. Equally popular is the Friday-night seafood buffet for $24. If an elegant, gourmet meal is what you're after, reserve at the inn's **Horizons Restaurant,** where professional service compliments such specialties as bouillabaisse and medaillons of venison. It's open for dinner only (6:30 to 10pm); prices are $40 and under. For more casual meals, there's the lovely **Carolina Café** looking out to the mountains, with light lunches (salads, sandwiches, quiches, burgers) for under $12 and a very good dinner menu featuring sautéed scampi, fresh mountain trout, and the like for $20 and under.

BILL STANLEY'S SMOKY MOUNTAIN BARBEQUE AND BLUE GRASS, 20 S. Spruce St. Tel. 253-4871.

Cuisine: BARBECUE. **Reservations:** Recommended on weekend nights.
$ Prices: Barbecue sandwiches and plates under $10. AE, DC, MC.
Open: Daily 5:30–whenever.

If it's real Southern mountain food you're after, you'll find yourself coming back here again and again. The large dining room has an authentic "mountain rustic" decor, and the friendly staff brings a real "down-home" welcome along with some of the most mouthwatering barbecue (beef, pork, and chicken) you're likely to encounter in the entire state. Plates come piled high with that scrumptious barbecue or smoked chicken, catfish, sliced ham, or sliced turkey. Side orders include such Southern favorites as corn on the cob and potato salad, and it goes without saying that hush puppies are the highlight of any meal. After 8pm Monday to Saturday, be prepared to shake a leg or two to some of the best foot-stomping mountain music in the South (see "Evening Entertainment," below).

DEPOT RESTAURANT, 30 Lodge St. Tel. 277-7651.

Cuisine: AMERICAN. **Reservations:** Not required.
$ Prices: Lunch $5–$8; dinner $7–$14. AE, MC, V.
Open: Mon–Thurs 11:30am–10pm, Fri–Sat 11:30am–11pm, Sun 11:30am–7:30pm.

The charming Depot Restaurant is housed in the 1896 railway station. It's a relaxed place, with a large menu that includes chicken, seafood, pork, veal, and beef dishes. Locals, however, come for the prime rib (at the remarkable price of $9 in a six-course special on weekends!).

THE MARKET PLACE, 20 Wall St. Tel. 252-4162.

Cuisine: CONTINENTAL. **Reservations:** Recommended.

$ Prices: Dinner $25–$30. AE, DC, MC, V.
Open: Mon–Sat 6–9:30pm.

⭐ Dress can be casual in this relaxed restaurant, although a second, candlelit dining area is more formal. The chef here uses nothing but the freshest ingredients—all herbs and vegetables are locally grown, and the pasta, pastries, and bread are made right on the premises. Innovative dishes featuring veal, chicken, and beef lean toward the nouvelle style in preparation and presentation, and the highly professional staff is knowledgeable about their award-winning wine list.

STEVEN'S RESTAURANT, 159 Charlotte St. Tel. 253-5348.
   Cuisine: INTERNATIONAL. **Reservations:** Recommended.
$ Prices: Lunch $5–$7; dinner $17–$24. AE, MC, V. Discounts to seniors and children.
   Open: Lunch Mon–Fri 11:30am–2pm; dinner daily 5–10pm. **Closed:** Holidays.
This second-floor restaurant has created a marvelous Victorian decor that adds an informal elegance to any meal. Heading the list of specialties here is the rack of lamb. Freshly baked bread and homemade desserts also star, and there's an extensive and very good wine list. Early bird specials are offered from 5 to 6:30pm.

EVENING ENTERTAINMENT

Lovers of mountain "hoedown" sessions should head for ❂ **Bill Stanley's,** 20 S. Spruce St. (tel. 253-4871), any night, where local clog dancers often go through their spirited paces to the music of honest-to-goodness mountain musicians, and patrons are lured to join the ranks of square dancers. Residents from miles around congregate here for the kind of traditional free-spirited fun that is a hallmark of the Blue Ridge Mountains. Call ahead to find out just when the music begins. This is definitely a "don't miss"! (It's also a mecca for barbecue lovers—see "Where to Dine," above.) Music starts about 7pm and a $3 cover charge usually applies.

3. CHEROKEE

298 miles SW of Raleigh; 48 miles SW of Asheville

GETTING THERE   By Plane   The nearest airport is Asheville (see above).

By Bus   For local **Greyhound/Trailways** information call 704/253-5353. The closest stop is Sylva, 18 miles away.

By Car   From the southern end of the Blue Ridge Parkway and points south, U.S. 441 leads to Cherokee; U.S. 19 runs east and west through the town.

ESSENTIALS   The **area code** is 704. The **Cherokee Visitor Center,** Main St., Cherokee, NC 28719 (tel. 704/497-9195, or toll free 800/438-1601) can fill you in on attractions and special events in the area. For advance information, contact: **Cherokee Travel and Promotion,** P.O. Box 460, Cherokee, NC 28719 (same telephone numbers as above).

SPECIAL EVENTS   A powerful drama, *Unto These Hills,* now tells the moving story of those tragic days when so many Native Americans traveled the "Trail of Tears." It is presented at the outdoor Mountainside Theater (P.O. Box 398, Cherokee, NC 28719; tel. 704/497-2111), off U.S. 441, from mid-June through late August at 8:30pm Monday through Saturday. Many of the actors are portraying their own ancestors. Tickets are $8 for adults, $5 for children 12 and under; $10 for reserved seating for all ages.

The Blue Ridge Parkway comes to an end at Cherokee, right at the entrance to the **Qualla Boundary Cherokee Indian Reservations,** where Native American life has moved into the 20th century but has held on to age-old traditions. You can see competitions in archery and blowguns, for example, or watch a game of Cherokee stickball, one of the roughest games anywhere. Periodically (but not according to schedule), you can also see traditional dances. The 8,000 or so Cherokee who live on the reservation are descendants of a proud tribe, many of whom hid out in the Great Smokies in 1838 to escape that blot on American history, the removal of all Eastern tribes to the West. A government Indian agent, one William H. Thomas (part Indian himself), bought part of the land that is now the reservations and gave it to the Cherokee who'd managed to stay. Later a total of 50,000 acres was handed over to the tribe by the U.S. government.

WHAT TO SEE & DO

The **Museum of the Cherokee Indian,** on U.S. 441 at Drama Road (tel. 497-3481), tells the story of the Cherokee through exhibits of such items as spear points several centuries old and multimedia theater shows. It's open from mid-June through August, Monday through Saturday 9am to 8pm, Sunday 9am to 5:30pm; other months, hours are 9am to 5pm daily except major holidays. Admission is $3.50 for adults, $1.75 children 6 to 12.

For a glimpse of Cherokee life 250 years ago, you should visit ✪ **Oconaluftee Indian Village,** off U.S. 441 (Cherokee, NC 28719; tel. 497-2111, or 497-2315). It's an authentic Cherokee community whose residents wear the tribal dress and practice the same crafts as their ancestors. You'll see dart guns being made or a log canoe being shaped by fire, and beautiful beadwork taking shape under skilled fingers. The seven-sided **Council House** conjures up images of the leaders of seven tribes gathered to thrash out problems or to worship their gods together. It's a kind of living museum of a way of life and a period of our country's history that is all too often distorted by fiction writers and Hollywood movies. You can visit the village any day from mid-May through late October; there are guided tours daily from 9am to 5:30pm for $8 for adults, $4 for children 6 to 12 (MasterCard and VISA credit cards are accepted).

Youngsters will find Christmas alive and well, even in summer, at **Santa's Land Park and Zoo** (tel. 497-9191), about 2½ miles east of Cherokee on U.S. 19. Santa and his helpers are busy getting ready for December 25 in a charming Christmas village, and there's a zoo with (what else?) reindeer and other domestic and exotic animals. Just for fun, there are some amusement rides. It's open for visitors from early May through October; adults pay $9 (children 2 through 12, $8).

WHERE TO STAY

BEST WESTERN GREAT SMOKIES INN, P.O. Box 1809, Cherokee, NC 28719. Tel. 704/497-2020. 152 rms. A/C TV TEL
$ Rates: April–Nov $50–$65 single or double. Children under 12 stay free with parents. Seniors discounts available. AE, MC, V. **Closed:** Dec–Mar.
This attractive member of the Best Western chain has spacious rooms with a nice decor and comfortable furnishings. The coin laundry is a bonus for travelers. In addition to the full-size pool, there's a wading pool. Forty guest rooms were added and represent the best value. It's located one mile north of town on U.S. 441 at Acquoni Road.

PIONEER MOTEL, P.O. Box 397, Cherokee, NC 28719. Tel. 704/497-2435. 21 rms, 6 cottages. A/C TV TEL
$ Rates: $38–$55 single or double; $60–$150 cottage for six to eight people. AE, DC, MC, V. **Closed:** Dec to early Apr.

S The Pioneer represents very good value, especially for families who book into the cottages. All cottages have fully equipped kitchens, and three are by the river. Guest rooms are modestly, but comfortably furnished. Amenities include lawn games, fishing privileges, and a heated pool. A restaurant is just across the road. Cottages are open all year. It's on U.S. 19 South.

WHERE TO DINE

While there are numerous fast food shops and cafés in Cherokee, your best dining bet is in one of the better motels in the vicinity. The **Best Western Great Smokies Inn** (see above), for example, serves all three meals (7am to 9pm) at modest prices (under $15 for dinner). You will find the food and service more than adequate—and prices comparable—at all motels.

AN EASY EXCURSION

Gem-quality blood-red rubies are found in only two places in the world—the Magok Valley in Burma and the **Cowee Valley** north of Franklin, N.C. To get to the mining area, take U.S. 23 from Asheville or U.S. 441 from Cherokee, to Franklin, then N.C. 28 north for about six miles. After passing the Cower Creek Road, keep right at the next two intersections and you will be on Ruby Mine Road. The mines are about three miles beyond Cowee Baptist Church.

While these ruby and sapphire mines are played out for commercial purposes, rockhounds still find thousands of dollar's worth of gem-quality stones every year. For an admission charge of about $7 a day (8am to 5pm seven days a week, April through October) and about 25¢ a gallon, you can sort through the gem-bearing gravel—and keep anything you find. The **Shuler Ruby Mine** (tel. 524-3551), has only native stones and provides assistance to novice gem-seekers. Then stop in at **Ruth and Bud's Cowee Gem Shop** (tel. 369-8233), where Bud Schmidt, a former hobbyist rockhound himself, will examine your finds and offer expert faceting and mounting services. If you want to stay for more than a day, bunk in at **Miner's Rest** (within walking distance of the mines), where Ruth and Bud Schmidt provide three completely furnished efficiency apartments, each fully heated and air-conditioned, at $45 a day for three and $55 for four people (weekly and monthly rates available). For reservations, call 704/524-3902 or write to Miner's Rest, 23 Matlock Creek Rd., Franklin, NC 28734.

4. THE GREAT SMOKY MOUNTAINS NATIONAL PARK

50 miles W of Asheville via U.S. 19; 4 miles N of Cherokee via U.S. 441;
U.S. 441 (Newfound Gap Road inside the Park) bisects the park from
Cherokee to Gatlinburg, Tennessee

GETTING THERE By Plane The nearest airport is at Asheville (see above).

By Bus For local **Greyhound/Trailways** information, call 704/253-5353. The closest service is Asheville.

By Car Visitors (other than hikers) will want a car in order to see the park properly. For pertinent highways, see above.

ESSENTIALS The **area code** is 704. Contact: Superintendent, Great Smoky Mountains National Park, Gatlinburg, TN 37739 (tel. 615/436-1200). The North Carolina entrance to the park is the **Oconaluftee Center,** two miles north of

Cherokee on U.S. 441, open daily except Christmas Day (tel. 704/497-9146). Admission to the park is free.

The Great Smoky Mountains, named for the smoky blue haze that crowns their tops, run for more than 70 miles, picking up where the Blue Ridge Parkway ends. The 520,000-acre park lies half in North Carolina, half in Tennessee.

The Great Smoky Mountains are one of nature's most impressive extravaganzas—16 of their majestic peaks soar to 6,000 and more feet, and for a 36-mile stretch none is lower than 5,000 feet. They shelter bears, deer, wild turkeys, and grouse, among other forms of wildlife; summer brings an ever-changing kaleidoscope of color from flowering plants; and within the park boundaries there are no less than 130 native species of tree in 180,000 acres of virgin forest. Magnificent!

WHAT TO SEE & DO

The **visitor center** at Cherokee (see above) can furnish a detailed map of the park and other information booklets; an excellent audio tape is available in Cherokee shops and motels for about $12. The best views are undoubtedly those from **Newfound Gap** and **Clingman's Dome** (in the Tennessee half). Also in Tennessee, some 25 miles west of the Sugarlands entrance, is **Cade's Cove,** an outdoor museum of log cabins, a gristmill, and barns typical of those used by original mountain settlers.

Hiking and camping are best along the 70 miles of Appalachian Trail, following the ridge that forms the North Carolina–Tennessee border. Any of the entrance visitors' centers can furnish details about campsites and shelters spaced a day's walk apart along the way. Be warned, however, that reservations are required between mid-May and October—contact MIXTIX, P.O. Box 85705 San Diego, CA 92186 (tel. toll free 800/365-2267). Shorter nature trails make ideal walking stops to break the drive through the park.

Clear, rushing mountain streams abound with trout (inquire in Cherokee about the required state license for fishing). Horseback riding is also popular, with more than 900 miles of marked horse and foot trails to explore, and saddle horses are available within the park—inquire at the visitors' centers.

WHERE TO STAY & DINE

Cherokee (see above), with its proximity to the park entrance, is the ideal base. A pleasant alternative is the mountain resort at Fontana Dam, just outside park boundaries.

FONTANA VILLAGE RESORT, Fontana Dam, NC 28733. Tel. 704/498-2211, or toll free 800/849-2258. 93 rms, 257 cottages. A/C TV TEL

$ Rates: Seasonal, $29–$125 single or double in inn; $40–$125 one-, two-, or three-bedroom cottage. AE, MC, V.

Built near a 30-mile-long lake formed by the construction of Fontana Dam, the resort has an inn, cottages, and a campground. The "cottages" include several luxurious two-bedroom houseboats. Sports-minded people will be in their element here, with stocked trout ponds, tennis courts, riding horses, and miniature golf (plus a par-three course) right at hand. In addition, there are all sorts of crafts workshops, and square dances from March through November. If you don't cook your own meals in the fully equipped cottage kitchens, the resort has a cafeteria and the Peppercorn Dining Room, where the whole family can eat reasonably (breakfast $3 to $5, lunch $3 to $7, dinner $5 to $17). Meals at the Village Grill run about the same or slightly lower in price. It's 42 miles west of Cherokee via U.S. 19 S and N.C. 28.

CHAPTER 6

PLANNING A TRIP TO SOUTH CAROLINA

The smallest Southern state, South Carolina is also probably the most romantic. Through centuries of change, South Carolinians have managed to hold on to vestiges of their Revolutionary, Civil War, and modern past, preserving virtually *unchanged* the inherent courtesies of the Old South. Modern entrepreneurs conduct business in the same courtly fashion as did the inhabitants of those gracious antebellum houses you'll see everywhere.

The state is a cornucopia of holiday treats. Along more than 280 miles of South Carolina seashore, there are lovely white-sand beaches shaded by palms, resort islands like Hilton Head that are a world apart, and Charleston, with its Old South charm still intact. Inland, the Columbia area reflects both the New South and some of the Old in the university campus, which has served, with its great old oaks and early 1800s buildings, as the background for several movies about antebellum life. Sports enthusiasts are drawn by coastal and inland fishing, as well as by the unusually long hunting season (Thanksgiving to March 1, more or less) for such game as deer, wild turkey, quail, fox, and more. Equestrians come for horse shows, polo, the Carolina Cup Steeplechase (in late March) and Colonial Cup Steeplechase (in mid-November) at Camden, and harness racing and other horse events in Aiken (beginning about the middle of March). The Darlington Raceway features the Southern 500 (Labor Day) late-model stock-car races. And history buffs, of course, can retrace all those colonial, Revolutionary, and Civil War events.

WHAT'S SPECIAL ABOUT SOUTH CAROLINA

Beaches

☐ Myrtle Beach and its satellite beaches, known collectively as the Grand Strand, stretch for 55 sunny, resort-filled miles.

Sea Islands

☐ Hilton Head, a golf and tennis mecca between the Intracoastal Waterway and the Atlantic Ocean south of Charleston.

☐ Daufuskie Island, adjacent to Hilton Head, but still largely undeveloped.

Historic Cities and Towns

☐ Charleston, the gracious lady of the Old South.

☐ Beaufort, the small port city north of Hilton Head, whose 18th-century streets are still lined with residences of that era.

☐ Columbia, capital of the state, whose turbulent history includes its occupation in 1865 by Union General William T. Sherman, who burned some 84 city blocks.

1. GETTING TO KNOW SOUTH CAROLINA

GEOGRAPHY & HISTORY

There are really two South Carolinas, with differences between the coastal "low country" and the "up country" (including the rolling midlands) so distinct I sometimes feel there should be a state line between the two. South Carolinians, however, seem able to accept those geographical divisions at home and at the same time take great pride in presenting a united front to the rest of the world. The lay of the land produces a subtropical coastal resort area in the low country, while the cool mountain breezes of the up country offer a respite from summer heat—all of which makes South Carolina attractive to visitors year-round.

It isn't only the topography of the state that makes for the distinctiveness of each section. The differences really spring from a history of settlement and development that saw aristocratic rice and indigo planters build one lifestyle along the coast, while German, Scots-Irish, and Welsh immigrants gravitated farther inland to build another.

The first attempts to settle along the coast were as early as 1526 and 1562, but nothing came of them. It wasn't until Charles II of England granted both the Carolinas to eight noblemen, the "lords proprietors," that colonists arrived to stay. Charles Towne was established at Albemarle Point in 1670, then moved 10 years later to the peninsula at the mouths of the Ashley and Cooper rivers. That low, marshy country proved ideal for large rice and indigo plantations,

DATELINE

● **1526** First temporary European settlement in South Carolina.

● **1670** First permanent European settlement at Charles Towne.

● **1721** South Carolina becomes a royal colony.

● **1740** Nearly half of Charles Towne destroyed by fire.

● **1780** Battle of Kings Mountain, an American victory that was a turning point in the Revolution.

● **1786** State capital is moved from Charleston to Columbia.

(continues)

DATELINE

- **1860** South Carolina is first state to secede from the Union.
- **1861** The rebel firing on Fort Sumter opens Civil War hostilities.
- **1865** Union forces, under Gen. William T. Sherman, burn Columbia.
- **1868** South Carolina is readmitted to the Union.
- **1895** Present state constitution adopted.
- **1947** State primary elections are opened to African-Americans.
- **1950** Savannah River Plant of the Atomic Energy Commission constructed near Aiken.
- **1964** Expansion in industry, especially in textiles, sets an all-time record.

and Charles Towne's harbor was perfect for shipping these crops around the world. Successful planters maintained huge homes on outlying farms, and most built mansions in town as well. A life of formal ease and graciousness developed that has never entirely disappeared.

Away from the coast, hardy frontiersmen set up small farms, built up a brisk trade in pelts, and fought Native Americans, often with no help from their British landlords—they had little time or inclination for the social goings-on in Charles Towne. A sore point was the issue of taxation—although everyone paid taxes, only the low country had any say in how things were run. (That remained the case until 1770, even though there was popular representation in the colonial government as early as 1693.) This rift was exacerbated during the Revolution, when British troops in South Carolina were frequently aided by local loyalists—mostly from the low country.

The first decisive American victory of the war was won here at Fort Moultrie in June 1776. Nevertheless, Charles Towne was occupied by the British in 1780. It was supposed to be the jumping-off point for a British drive to join forces in the north and crush Washington's troops. But thanks to the efforts of Continental troops under Gen. Nathanael Greene—and South Carolina natives who followed "the Swamp Fox" (Frances Marion) and "the Gamecock" (Thomas Sumter) in a very effective sort of guerrilla warfare—the royal soldiers were more or less confined to Charles Towne (renamed Charleston in 1783). There are some historians who contend that the battles of Kings Mountain (in 1780) and Cowpens (1781) were *the* decisive encounters of the Revolution. When independence was finally achieved, South Carolina was the eighth state to ratify the federal constitution, in 1788.

By 1790, cantankerous up-country citizens were making such a fuss about the state's capital remaining in low-country Charleston, while four-fifths of the white population lived inland, that the state government was moved to neutral ground, in centrally located Columbia. The low-country population (which controlled four-fifths of the wealth) continued to maintain state offices, however, and the state supreme court actually met in both cities to hear appeals until 1865.

In December 1860, when tensions between the North and South reached the breaking point, the state legislature passed an Ordinance of Secession that made South Carolina the first state to secede from the Union. In *that* step, citizens seemed united. Their first military action was to take Fort Sumter from the federal troops garrisoned there, and they continued to hold it until 1865. Altogether, the state lost 22% of its population in the bitter Civil War; General Sherman, in his "march to the sea," saw to it that just about the entire state was left in shambles.

If there's one thing all South Carolinians—low-country or up-country—have in abundance, it's pride. That pride suffered greatly, along with the economy, as carpetbaggers and scalawags moved in during the period following the war. "Yankee" and "Rebel" distinctions seem to be more alive here today than in any other single place in the South. That's not really surprising, since it was not until World War II that

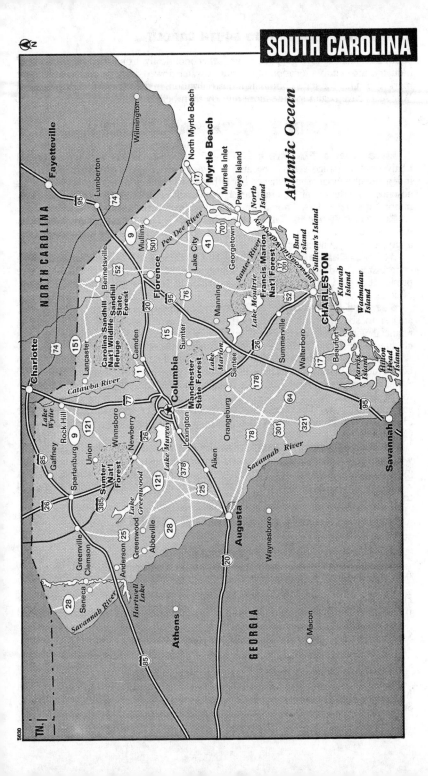

SOUTH CAROLINA

South Carolina began to get back on its feet economically. Ironically, it was "Yankee" industry, moving to a location of enormous water-powered energy and a ready labor market, that led the state's booming industrialization. In the last few decades, the Civil War scars have begun to fade more quickly than before.

FAMOUS SOUTH CAROLINIANS

Eliza Lucas Pinckney (1716–1793) Most famous for her successful cultivation of indigo, which became a major cash crop in the state. A strong, independent woman, she managed her father's two plantations near Charleston in his absence from the age of 16. Her marriage to Charles Pinckney in 1744 produced two important state leaders, Thomas and Charles Cotesworth Pinckney.

General Thomas Sumter (1734–1855) This Revolutionary War hero, who played a key role in driving the British from South Carolina, has given his name to a city, a county, and a fort.

John C. Calhoun (1782–1850) This prominent South Carolinian was both a congressman and senator from his home state before his two elections as vice president of the United States in 1824 and 1828. In 1845, he was appointed secretary of state.

Bernard M. Baruch (1870–1965) Best known as confidant and economic adviser to six American presidents through two world wars, this South Carolina financial wizard had accumulated millions at the age of 30, and his expertise is credited with many developments in the American economy.

James F. Byrnes (1879–1972) President Franklin D. Roosevelt had such confidence in Byrnes that he was affectionately known as the "assistant president." A member of the Supreme Court, he resigned during World War II to serve as director of economic stability and director of war mobilization and went on to become secretary of state. His long, brilliant political career included service in the House of Representatives and the Senate and one term as governor of South Carolina.

Dr. Anne Austin Young (1892–1966) An outstanding physician, Dr. Young was one of the first American women to earn distinction as an obstetrician and gynecologist. Among her achievements are the construction of a medical clinic in Zaire, and financing the building of three churches and three schools. She is reported to have delivered no less than 9,500 infants.

RECOMMENDED BOOKS

GENERAL

Able, Gene, and Jack Horan. *Paddling South Carolina: A Guide to Palmetto State River Trails.*

Fraser, Walter J., Jr. *Charleston! Charleston!*

Junior League of Charleston. *Charleston Receipts.* Cookbook with local color and history notes.

Smith, Clyde H. *South Carolina: A Scenic Discovery.* Photo book.

ARCHITECTURE & HISTORY

Milling, Chapman J. *Red Carolinians: Indians of North and South Carolina.*

Smith, Alice R. Huger, and D. E. Huger. *The Dwelling Houses of Charleston, South Carolina.*

Wallace, David Duncan. *South Carolina: A Short History.*

2. INFORMATION & MONEY

Before leaving home, write or call ahead for specific information on sports (fishing, hunting, beaches, etc.) and sightseeing to: **South Carolina Division of Tourism,** 1205 Pendleton St., P.O. Box 71, Columbia, SC 29202 (tel. 803/734-0122; fax 803/734-0138). They can also furnish *South Carolina: Smiling Faces, Beautiful Places,* a detailed booklet with photos that covers each region of the state.

When you come to South Carolina, look for one of the ten **travel information centers** located on virtually every major highway near borders with neighboring states. Information sources for specific destinations in the state are listed in the South Carolina chapters that follow.

WHAT THINGS COST IN SOUTH CAROLINA	U.S. $
Taxi from Charleston airport to city center	$17.00
Bus fares in Charleston (exact change)	.75
Local telephone call	.25
Double at John Rutledge House Inn in Charleston (deluxe)	150.00
Double at Hawthorne Suites Hotel in Charleston (moderate)	110.00
Double at Hampton Inn in Charleston (budget)	65.00
Lunch for one at Magnolia's in Charleston (moderate)	10.00
Lunch for one at Reuben's Downtown Delicatessen in Charleston (budget)	5.50
Dinner for one without wine at Robert's in Charleston (deluxe)	70.00
Dinner for one without wine at Colony House in Charleston (moderate)	15.00
Dinner for one at Frannie's Diner in Charleston (budget)	6.95
Bottle of beer	1.75
Coca-Cola	1.00
Cup of coffee	1.00
Roll of ASA 100 Kodachrome film, 36 exposures	5.50
Admission to Charleston Museum	5.00
Movie ticket	6.00
Ticket to Charleston Symphony concert	15.00

3. WHEN TO GO — CLIMATE & EVENTS

CLIMATE

Although parts of South Carolina can be very hot and steamy in summer, temperatures are never extreme, as is shown in the average highs and lows noted below.

SOUTH CAROLINA AVERAGE TEMPERATURES (IN FAHRENHEIT)

	High	Low
Charleston	88	44
Columbia	93	35
Greenville/Spartanburg	77	43

SOUTH CAROLINA
CALENDAR OF EVENTS

FEBRUARY

☐ **Low-country Oyster Festival.** Charleston. Held at historic Boone Hall Plantation, featuring the honored bivalve, music, and exhibits. Early February.

☐ **Southeastern Wildlife Exposition.** Charleston. Wildlife art show featuring paintings, sculpture, carvings, and other art in historic buildings. Mid-February.

MARCH

☐ **Springfest.** Hilton Head Island. Month-long celebration, with music, art, a seafood festival, and entertainment.

☐ **Steeplechase and Hunt Meet.** Aiken. One of three horseracing events known as the Aiken Triple Crown. Mid-March.

☐ **Carolina Cup.** Steeplechase and flat-racing event for thoroughbreds. Late March.

☐ **Darlington 200.** Darlington. Busch Series Grand National stock-car race. Late March.

☐ **Family Circle Magazine Cup Tennis Tournament.** Hilton Head Island. Top women tennis players compete for $500,000 in prizes. Late March to early April.

APRIL

☐ **Seafood Festival.** Murrells Inlet. Low-country food, arts and crafts, educational exhibits, and entertainment. Mid-April.

☐ **South Carolina Festival of Roses.** Orangeburg. A canoe race, beauty contest, arts and crafts, sports tournaments, and entertainment are held in Edisto Gardens. Late April.

MAY

☐ **A(ugusta) Baker's Dozen.** Columbia. One of the country's leading storytellers tells stories for children and conducts workshops and lectures for storytellers. Early May.

☐ **Spring Fling/Jazz in the Park.** Spartanburg. Around-the-clock entertainment, as well as arts and crafts. Early May.

☐ **Greek Spring Festival.** Charleston. Ethnic music and dancing, food, and even a Greek Orthodox religious service. Early May.

☐ **Riverplace Festival.** Greenville. A spring arts festival in the South Main Street area. Third week of May.

☐ **Gullah Festival.** Beaufort. The African-oriented culture of the low-country sea islands celebrates its fine arts and customs. Late May.

☐ **Spoleto Festival USA.** Charleston. International arts festival with more than 100 events, including opera, chamber music and symphonic concerts, theater, dance, and art. Late May to early June.

JUNE

☐ **Edisto Summer Festival.** A family affair, with carnival rides, children's bingo, a shrimp boil, barbecue dinners, street dances, and arts and crafts. Mid-June.

JULY

☐ **Freedom Weekend Aloft.** Greenville. More than 100 hot air balloons take to the skies. Great picture taking and rides offered. July 4th week.

☐ **Beaufort County Water Festival.** Beaufort. The "Blessing of the Fleet" is a highlight of this celebration, which also includes dances, concerts, talent shows, a sailing regatta, a parade, and a low-country supper. Mid-July.

AUGUST

☐ **Carolina Craftsmen's Summer Classic.** Myrtle Beach. Arts and craftspeople from all over the United States exhibit at the Convention Center. Early August.

SEPTEMBER

☐ **Mountain Dew Southern 500.** Darlington. NASCAR'S oldest Winston Cup series for stock-car racing. Early September.

OCTOBER

☐ **Anniversary of the Battle of King's Mountain.** King's Mountain. Reenactment of the battle often called the turning point of the Revolution. Early October.

☐ **Fall for Greenville.** Greenville. Main Street is closed down to accommodate food booths. A bicycle race is also a tradition. Second week of October.

☐ **South Carolina State Fair.** Columbia. Agricultural exhibits, carnival rides, and grandstand entertainment are featured in this 122-year-old event. Mid-October.

NOVEMBER

☐ **Plantation Days.** Charleston. Colonial harvest time is created with authentic cider- and syrup-making, candle dipping, spinning, milking, and the like at Middleton Place Gardens. Mid-November.

☐ **Colonial Cup.** Camden. Championship international steeplechase racing. Mid-November.

DECEMBER

☐ **Christmas in Charleston and at Middleton Place.** Charleston. Special events of the season held throughout the holiday month.

☐ **Christmas in Olde York.** York. A tour of historic homes with 18th- and 19th-century holiday decorations. Mid-December.

4. TIPS FOR THE DISABLED, SENIORS, SINGLES, FAMILIES & STUDENTS

The Columbia telephone directory contains a special section of "Community Service Numbers" that is quite comprehensive and includes services for most of these groups.

FOR THE DISABLED   The State of South Carolina provides numerous agencies to assist those with disabilities. For specific information, call the **South Carolina Handicapped Services Information System** (tel. 803/777-5732). Two other agencies that may prove helpful are: **South Carolina Protection & Advocacy System for the Handicapped** (tel. 803/782-0639); and the **Commission for the Blind** (tel. 803/734-7520). See Chapter 1 for more information.

FOR SENIORS   Seniors may want to contact the **South Carolina Commission on Aging** (tel. 803/735-0210) or the **Retired Senior Volunteer Program** (tel. 803/252-7734). When sightseeing or attending entertainment events, always inquire about discounts for seniors—they're plentiful. Also see Chapter 1 for general tips.

FOR SINGLES   See Chapter 1 for general information.

FOR FAMILIES   See Chapter 1 for general information.

FOR STUDENTS   See Chapter 1 for general information. To contact leading South Carolina universities and colleges, call the **Information Service Office** at: University of South Carolina, Columbia (tel. 803/777-8161; inquire about their campuses in Orangeburg, Aiken, Conway, and Spartanburg); Clemson University, Clemson (tel. 803/656-3413, ext. 2061); The Citadel, Charleston (tel. 803/792-5006); and Furman University, Greenville (tel. 803/294-2000, ext. 2185).

5. ALTERNATIVE/ADVENTURE TRAVEL

See Chapter 1 for general information on bicycle touring, camping, and hiking. Contact the **South Carolina Division of Tourism** (see "Information," above) for sports, fishing, and hunting holidays. For information on educational vacations, contact the information service offices listed under "For Students," above.

6. GETTING THERE

BY PLANE   Myrtle Beach has scheduled air service via **American Eagle** (an American Airlines affiliate; tel. toll free 800/433-7300), as well as **Delta Connection** (tel. toll free 800/221-1212) and **USAir** (tel. toll free 800/428-4322). You can fly into Charleston on American, American Eagle, Delta, USAir, USAir Express, **United** (tel. toll free 800/241-6522), and **United Express** (call United). Columbia is served by American Eagle, Delta, Delta Connection, United, United Express, and USAir. Greenville–Spartanburg is served by American, American Eagle, Delta, Delta Connection, **Northwest Airlink** (tel. toll free 800/225-2525), USAir, and USAir

Express. Many travelers prefer to fly into the Savannah, Georgia, International Airport via American, American Eagle, Delta, Delta Connection, United, United Express, USAir, or USAir Express and drive or take a limousine to Hilton Head, one hour away.

BY TRAIN   **Amtrak** (tel. toll free 800/USA-RAIL) reaches Camden, Charleston, Clemson, Columbia, Denmark, Dillon, Florence, Greenville, Kingstree, Spartanburg, and Yemassee. Amtrak also has tour packages that include hotel, breakfasts, and historic-site tours in Charleston at bargain rates.

BY BUS   **Greyhound/Trailways** buses reach almost any destination in South Carolina. For schedule and route information, call the Greyhound Travel Information Center in Columbia (tel. 803/779-0650) or the Greyhound/Trailways depot nearest you.

BY CAR   Interstate 95 enters South Carolina from the north near Dillon and runs straight through the state to Hardeeville on the Georgia border. The major east-west artery is I-26, running from Charleston northwest through Columbia and on up to Hendersonville, North Carolina. U.S. 17 runs along the coast, and I-85 crosses the northwestern region of the state. South Carolina furnishes excellent travel information to motorists, and there are well-equipped, efficiently staffed visitor centers at the state border on most major highways.

7. GETTING AROUND

BY PLANE   **Delta** and **USAir** (see "Getting There," above) both have flights within South Carolina, although schedules are sometimes awkward for connections.

BY TRAIN   See "Getting There," above, for **Amtrak** destinations.

BY BUS   **Greyhound/Trailways** (see "Getting There," above) operates intrastate routes to most South Carolina towns.

BY CAR   The marvelous interstate and U.S. highways (see "Getting There," above) give South Carolina a network of exceptionally good roads. Even when you leave the highways for the state-maintained byways, driving is easy on well-maintained roads. AAA services are available through the **Carolina Motor Club** in Charleston (tel. 803/766-2394), Columbia (tel. 803/798-9205), Greenville (tel. 803/297-9988), Myrtle Beach (tel. 803/272-1141), and Spartanburg (tel. 803/583-2766).

8. SUGGESTED ITINERARIES

These are driving itineraries and should be modified to allow more time if you're traveling by bus.

IF YOU HAVE ONE WEEK

Day 1   Arrive in Myrtle Beach. Settle in, do a little beachcombing, and end the day with a low-country seafood dinner at one of this area's fine restaurants.

Days 2 and 3   Spend the day at the beach and use Day 3 for a day trip to Murrell's Inlet, Georgetown, or Little River or for a charter-boat fishing trip.

Day 4   Myrtle Beach to Charleston. Make the 98-mile drive an all-day affair, with stops at the Brookfield Gardens or Georgetown.

Days 5 and 6 One day is for sightseeing in this lovely old city with its picturesque and historic buildings, the other for a day trip to Edisto Island or to Middleton Gardens.

Day 7 Depart Charleston.

IF YOU HAVE TWO WEEKS

Days 1 through 6 Same as above.

Day 7 Charleston to Columbia. This is a 120-mile drive, with plenty of time to stop by Orangeburg's beautiful Edisto Gardens.

Day 8 Sightseeing in Columbia, including a visit to the outstanding Riverbank Zoo.

Days 9 through 13 Make day trips south to Aiken, east to Camden and Florence, and north to Rock Hill, York, and King's Mountain National Military Park.

Day 14 Depart Columbia.

IF YOU HAVE THREE WEEKS

Days 1 through 13 Same as above.

Day 14 Columbia to Spartanburg. Make this just-under-200-mile drive a leisurely one, keeping an eye out for a rural or small-town lunch break at one of the several eateries specializing in down-home cooking.

Day 15 Sightseeing in Spartanburg and Greenville.

Day 16 Visit nearby Walnut Grove Plantation and the Thomas Price House.

Day 17 Day trip to Cowpens National Battlefield.

Days 18 and 19 The Cherokee Foothills Scenic Highway. This 130-mile drive deserves a minimum of two days to soak in glorious mountain scenery from numerous overlooks and visit the Cherokee Indian Museum at Keowee-Toxaway State Park. Make your overnight stop in one of the state or county parks or in motel accommodations en route, which are plentiful. End your drive on day 19 at the southern end of the highway, Lake Hartwell State Park.

Day 20 Swimming, fishing, boating, and other lake activities, or a day trip to historic Pendleton and the Ninety-Six National Historic Site.

Day 21 Depart Lake Hartwell.

9. WHERE TO STAY & DINE

While South Carolina boasts just about every imaginable type of accommodations, there's not always a wide range of choice in a specific location. Coastal resorts offer everything from posh luxury hotels to modest, inexpensive motels, and Charleston has several small inns that offer unequaled hospitality of the Old South style. In between, almost every town and city has representatives of the major chains and independently owned modern motels, which more than adequately meet the traveler's needs. As everywhere else, it pays to reserve ahead. The travel information centers at major points of entry to the state operate a free reservation service, but it's risky to rely on this, especially if you come during spring or summer: Rooms can be scarce even as late as October along the coast.

An alternative to hotel or motel vacationing—and one that works particularly well for families—is the rental of a cottage or apartment. South Carolina's resort areas have literally hundreds available on a weekly basis, and it's a fairly simple matter to engage one if you plan far enough in advance.

There are also cabin accommodations available all year in 12 of South Carolina's state parks. All are heated and air-conditioned and fully equipped with cooking utensils, tableware, and linens. Rates range from $35 to $165 per night, $135 to $500 per week, and cabins accommodate anywhere from 4 to 12 people. Here again, however, advance reservations are absolutely necessary for summer. For full details on these cabins, and on accommodations at the 31 other state parks, write: **South Carolina State Parks,** 1205 Pendleton St., Columbia, SC 29201 (tel. 803/734-0156).

See "Where to Stay & Dine" in Chapter 1 for general tips on bargain dining.

FAST FACTS   SOUTH CAROLINA

American Express Services in South Carolina are through: Palmetto Travel Service, 4 Liberty St., Charleston (tel. 803/577-5053); B&A Travel Service, 2001 Greene St., Columbia (tel. 803/256-0547); Long's Travel Agency, 33 Office Park Rd., Hilton Head Island (tel. 803/842-4700); and Woodside World-Wide Travel Service, 108 W. McBee Ave., Greenville (tel. 803/233-4118).

Area Code It's 803 for the entire state.

Business Hours Banks and offices are open Monday to Friday from 9am to 5pm; shops Monday to Saturday 10am to 6pm (until 10pm and on Sunday in some large shopping malls).

Climate See "When to Go—Climate & Events," earlier in this chapter.

Emergencies Dial "911" for police, ambulance, paramedics, and fire department.

Hitchhiking It's illegal on all state, U.S., and interstate highways.

Liquor Laws The minimum drinking age is 21. Some restaurants are licensed to serve only beer and wine, but a great many serve those plus liquor in minibottles, which can be added to cocktail mixers. If you think you'll want a drink on Sunday, stock up: There's no alcohol sold after midnight Saturday and all day Sunday, except in establishments with special permits in Charleston, Columbia, Hilton Head, and North Myrtle Beach.

Maps Without question, the best map is the official South Carolina Highway Map, available through travel information centers or the Division of Tourism (see "Information and Money," above).

Newspapers and Magazines The major papers are *The State* (Columbia), *Greenville News,* and *Charleston Post and Courier.* The *Sandlapper* is a local quarterly magazine.

Police See "Emergencies," above.

Taxes The state sales tax is 5%.

Telephone Local calls from pay telephones cost 25¢.

Weather Call 822-8135.

CHAPTER 7

COASTAL SOUTH CAROLINA

**1. MYRTLE BEACH &
THE GRAND STRAND**
2. HILTON HEAD ISLAND

All the romance, beauty, and graciousness of the Old South manage to survive along South Carolina's coast. Perhaps the Grand Strand up around Myrtle Beach looks like most other beach resort areas—but a little farther south, at Georgetown and all the way down the coastline to Beaufort (near Hilton Head), automobiles and modern dress seem almost out of place on the old, cobblestone streets and amid the grand old homes.

Scenically, the coastline is breathtaking. Its broad, white-sand beaches are warmed by the Gulf Stream and fringed with palm trees and rolling dunes. Palms mingle with live oaks, dogwood, and pines, and everywhere you'll see the silver-gray something called Spanish moss draped airily from tree branches. I call it "something" because even scientists can't quite figure out what it is—it isn't really a moss, because that grows on the ground; it isn't a parasite, because it doesn't feed on sap from the trees; and it has no roots—it seems to extract nourishment somehow from the air. They call it an epiphyte (air plant), but as yet they aren't sure just how it manages to keep alive and grow. My favorite quotation about Spanish moss is the answer given in a South Carolina publication to the questions about the lovely mystery: "Yes, it does grow on trees; no, it isn't a parasite; no, they *don't* take it in at night and put it out in the morning."

Speaking of native plants: Whatever you do, *don't* pull the graceful sea oats that grow on sand-dune stretches along the beaches; it's against the law, and an infraction carries a stiff fine. The hardy plant (it grows from Cape Charles, Virginia, to the Gulf Coast of Mexico and is officially named *Uniola paniculato*) not only acts as a natural anchor for the dunes, since it catches and holds blowing sands, but also serves as a plentiful food supply for shore birds.

The subtropical climate of low-country South Carolina, where spring arrives early and summer lingers until late October, is ideal for golf, tennis, fishing, or just sitting on an uncrowded beach. There are islands that don't even require a boat for a visit (South Carolina has provided marvelous double-laned causeways)—such as Pawleys, Seabrook, Edisto, and Hilton Head islands. Besides golf courses and beaches, there are amusement parks, stock-car races, nightspots with top entertainment, an internationally known sculpture garden, and some of the best seafood restaurants on the Atlantic coast.

---

1. MYRTLE BEACH &
THE GRAND STRAND

131 miles E of Columbia; 98 miles N of Charleston;
156 miles N of Hilton Head

GETTING THERE   By Plane   See "Getting There," in Chapter 6.

By Train **Amtrak's** nearest stop is in Florence, 69 miles west of Myrtle Beach (tel. toll free 800/USA-RAIL).

By Bus For **Greyhound/Trailways** information, call 803/779-0650.

By Car U.S. 17 runs north and south through Myrtle Beach; U.S. 501 runs east from Florence.

ESSENTIALS The **area code** is 803. The **Myrtle Beach Area Chamber of Commerce,** is at 1301 N. Kings Hwy. (P.O. Box 2115), Myrtle Beach, SC 29578 (tel. 803/626-7444). One publication jam-packed with specific area information is *See & Do* (available from the Myrtle Beach Area Chamber of Commerce).

———————

Myrtle Beach, with a permanent population of about 25,000, is at the center of the Grand Strand, a 60-mile string of beaches that includes Little River, Cherry Grove, Crescent Beach, Ocean Drive, Atlantic Beach, Surfside Beach, Garden City, Murrells Inlet, Litchfield Beach, and Pawleys Island. Named for the abundance of myrtle trees in this area, Myrtle Beach itself is an ideal base for a Grand Strand vacation. If you're looking for a wild, swinging kind of beach resort, this isn't it. It certainly isn't dull, but the tone here is that of a family resort, with almost as much attention paid to children's needs as to those of adults. Many hotels and motels provide activity programs and playgrounds with supervision, and nearly all have babysitter lists for parents who like a little nightlife.

WHAT TO SEE & DO

The big attraction is the beach—and sunbathing, swimming, boating, and all the other water sports rank first among things to do. Fishing is right up there with them; whether you cast your line from the surf, a public pier, or a charter boat, you'll probably wind up with a pretty good catch. Surf fishing is permitted all along the beach, and there are fishing piers at Garden City, Surfside, Second Avenue, State Park, Windy Hill, Kits, Crescent Beach, Tilghman Beach, Cherry Grove, and Springmaid. Charter boats ("head boats," as the locals say) are available at marinas up and down the Strand, and even at the height of the season you'll be able to book a trip without much difficulty. Depending on the season, your catch may include croaker, bluefish, flounder, spot, pompano, black sea bass, or whiting.

If you're not swimming or fishing, chances are you'll be out on the links swinging a golf club on one of the more than 78 public courses; some three dozen or so are of championship caliber. Most motels and hotels hold memberships in more than one club and will issue guest cards that will entitle you to reduced greens fees. Fees run anywhere from $8 to $30, depending on the club and the time of year. All area courses are well laid-out and maintained, and the "season" extends from February through November. Play is heaviest, however, from early February until late April. There are also more than 200 public and private tennis courts in the Grand Strand area.

When you get tired of all that sports activity, there's the boardwalk, lined with all sorts of amusements and good for a window-shopping stroll. Or spend a day at the **Myrtle Waves Water Park,** 10th Avenue at U.S. 17N Bypass, Myrtle Beach, SC 29577 (tel. 448-1026). Its 20 acres hold a variety of water slides as well as a wave pool, children's playpool, video arcade, and tanning deck. Admission is $13.95 for those 4 through 54, $8.95 for those over 54. Hours vary considerably, so it's best to call ahead. Open May to mid-September.

WHERE TO STAY

The Grand Strand is lined with hotels, motels, condominiums, and cottages. The Myrtle Beach Area Chamber of Commerce (see "Essentials," above) publishes a free accommodations directory. Highest rates are June 15 through Labor Day.

EXPENSIVE

THE BREAKERS RESORT HOTEL, 2006 N. Ocean Blvd., P.O. Box 485, Myrtle Beach, SC 29578-0485. Tel. 803/626-5000, or toll free 800/845-0688. Fax 803/626-5001. 250 rms and kitchen units. A/C TV TEL

$ Rates: $25–$260 single or double. Children under 16 stay free with parents. Senior discounts and golf, honeymoon, and family packages available. AE, DC, MC, V.

In addition to its glorious north beachfront location, the Breakers offers a wide range of amenities, such as indoor and outdoor pools, whirlpools, saunas, fitness rooms, free tennis, golf privileges, a restaurant, and a lounge with entertainment and dancing. Guest rooms are nicely decorated in beach colors, and most have balconies and refrigerators. In summer, there's a children's program.

MYRTLE BEACH HILTON OCEANFRONT GOLF RESORT, 10000 Beach Club Dr., Myrtle Beach, SC 29577. Tel. 803/449-5000. Fax 803/497-0168. 392 rms. A/C TV TEL **Directions:** Take Highway 17 nine miles north of Myrtle Beach to Arcadian Shores.

$ Rates: $50–$165 single or double. AE, DC, DISC, MC, V.

This hotel goes by a collection of names: Myrtle Beach Hilton and Arcadian Shores Golf Club as well as the Myrtle Beach Hilton and Golf Club, not to mention the name above. The imposing highrise is shaped in a Y with accommodations radiating from the central core, where a huge tapestry hangs down 10 floors. Entertainment is featured in the rooftop lounge, or you can sip something in the mezzanine level bar. All meals are served in an upscale restaurant, and light snacks are offered at the poolside café in good weather. Besides the outdoor pool and wading pool, there are lighted tennis courts and a playground for the kids. The hotel's affiliated golf club is next door.

OCEAN CREEK PLANTATION, 10600 N. Kings Highway, Myrtle Beach, SC 29572. Tel. 803/272-7724, or toll free 800/845-0353. Fax 803/272-9627. 385 rms. A/C TV TEL **Directions:** Take Highway 17 north, almost to North Myrtle Beach.

$ Rates: $35–$200 single or double. AE, CB, DC, MC, V.

Guests at the Ocean Creek Plantation enjoy many recreational amenities situated around the clusters of accommodations located on almost 60 acres. Seven tennis courts accept your serve, while a health center welcomes guests with its indoor pool, whirlpool, sauna, and fitness facility. The Beach Club on the ocean operates in summer. Besides the health center pool, several other outdoor pools are located at the various buildings, which rise as high as 15 floors. Condominiums may be categorized as studios, one-bedrooms, two-bedrooms, lodge units, beachside towers, or tennis villas. A restaurant is always open for breakfast but sometimes closes for lunch and dinner off-season.

THE PALACE, 1605 S. Ocean Blvd., Myrtle Beach, SC 29577. Tel. 803/448-4300, or toll free 800/334-1397. 300 suites. A/C TV TEL

$ Rates: $50–$260 single or double. AE, CB, DC, DISC, MC, V.

Known as an all-suite hotel, The Palace rises a striking 23 floors on the beachfront and opens on one side to a waterfall in a courtyard. Unwind at the bar, five whirlpools, indoor/outdoor pool, steam room, fitness rooms, sauna, or game room. Parking is

MYRTLE BEACH & THE GRAND STRAND

SOUTH CAROLINA
★ Columbia Myrtle Beach

Atlantic Beach ⑤
Brookgreen Gardens ⑭
Cherry Grove Beach ②
Crescent Beach ④
Garden City ⑫
Georgetown ⑰
Litchfield Beach ⑮
Little River ①
Murrells Inlet ⑬
Myrtle Beach National
  Golf Course ⑨
Myrtle Beach
  State Park ⑩
Mrytle Waves
  Water Park ⑧
Ocean Drive Beach ③
Ocean Plaza Pier ⑦
Pawleys Island ⑯
Surfside Beach ⑪
Windy Hill Beach ⑥

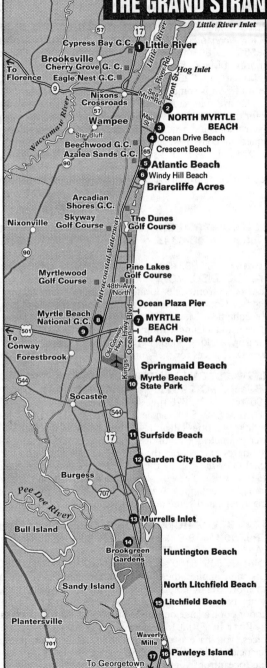

Airport

handy in the five-story garage. Each suite has one or two bedrooms, a kitchen, tropical patterns and colors, furnished balconies, two double beds, and other homey extras.

RADISSON RESORT HOTEL AT KINGSTON PLANTATION, 9800 Lake Dr., Myrtle Beach, SC 29577. Tel. 803/449-0006, or toll free 800/333-3333. Fax 803/497-1017. 270 rms. A/C TV TEL **Directions:** Take Highway 17 north of Myrtle Beach.
$ Rates: $80–$260 single or double. AE, CB, DC, DISC, MC, V.
The Radisson is something of a loner, away from the central beach area in its own little enclave. The short drive through a residential area keeps the pace slow. Watch out for the ducks. Sports-minded guests will pass right by the busy plush lobby of this 20-story hotel and head for the beach; indoor and outdoor pools; tennis, squash, and racquetball courts; weight and fitness rooms; sauna; and whirlpool. Besides the standard units with king-size or double beds, kitchenettes, sofabeds, and balconies, the Radisson offers almost 200 privately-owned condominiums ranging in size from one to three bedrooms. The hotel gets a lot of the conference trade too.

MODERATE

THE BEACHCOMBER, 1705 S. Ocean Blvd., Myrtle Beach, SC 29577. Tel. 803/448-4345, or toll free 800/262-2113. 45 rms and apartments. A/C TV TEL
$ Rates: $32–$98 single or double. Weekly, monthly, and golf packages available. AE, DC, DISC, MC, V.
These oceanfront units located two miles south of the town center have private balconies. Connecting units are available, as are deluxe rooms (with refrigerators) and fully equipped one- or two-bedroom efficiencies. There are two pools (one for children) and a laundry room on the premises. Golf and tennis privileges are available at nearby facilities. Shopping, amusement centers, and restaurants are not far. After Labor Day, prices for the same accommodations drop considerably.

BEST WESTERN LANDMARK RESORT, 1501 S. Ocean Blvd., Myrtle Beach, SC 29577. Tel. 803/448-9441, or toll free 800/845-0658. Fax 803/626-1501. 325 rms. A/C TV TEL
$ Rates: $40–$130 single or double. AE, DC, DISC, MC, V.
Standing 14 stories tall amid the beach action, the Best Western is one of this chain's better examples of mid-priced accommodations. Its pink-and-green lobby makes a nice impression, as does the garden-like restaurant and bar. For more action, try the nightclub or the grill by the outdoor pool. In winter, the same pool is enclosed for year-round use. There is also a sauna. Almost half a dozen floors have balconies. Rooms are equipped with one king-size or two double beds, tropical colors, refrigerators, and some ocean vistas.

CORAL BEACH HOTEL, 1105 S. Ocean Blvd., Myrtle Beach, SC 29577. Tel. 803/448-8421, or toll free 800/843-2684. Fax 803/626-0156. 300 rms. A/C MINIBAR TV TEL
$ Rates: $35–$160 single or double. AE, CB, DC, DISC, ER, MC, V.
As its name implies, the Coral Beach Hotel is decked out in fresh coral-colored paint with more trendy colors inside. In case the sun doesn't shine, you can hop in the tanning bed, use the indoor pool, fitness room, or game room. There is also an outdoor pool, a large outdoor whirlpool, children's pool, sauna, steam room, and fun Lazy River Tube Ride to keep you busy. This is a great place to take the kids. For food choices, you have a snack bar and a full-service restaurant. All the rooms are efficiencies with sofabeds or Murphy beds, living rooms, kitchens with microwave ovens (oceanfront), one or two TVs, and balconies. Rooms without full kitchens have refrigerators.

HOLIDAY INN OCEANFRONT, 6th Ave. S. at S. Ocean Blvd., Myrtle Beach, SC 29577. Tel. 803/448-4481, or toll free 800/845-0313. Fax 803/448-0086. 311 rms. A/C TV TEL

$ Rates: $40–$125 single or double. AE, CB, DC, DISC, MC, V.

When Hurricane Hugo blew through the area a couple of years ago, the Holiday Inn took a direct hit. It closed for nine months and invested millions of dollars in appointments and reconstruction. Today the hotel features a lobby bar, a lounge with neon lighting, a café, and sports facilities, including an indoor pool, outdoor pool, indoor whirlpool, fitness area, sauna, and sundeck. All the rooms have VCRs, beach colors, and armoires.

MYRTLE BEACH MARTINIQUE RESORT AND CONFERENCE CENTER, 71st Ave. N. and N. Ocean Blvd., Myrtle Beach, SC 29578. Tel. 803/449-4441, or toll free 800/542-0048. Fax 803/497-3041. 204 rms. A/C TV TEL

$ Rates: $40–$150 single or double. AE, CB, DC, DISC, MC, V.

With a name like Martinique Resort, this hotel is bound to have a tropical ambience, and that's just what it has. The bar is tropically flavored and appointed with bamboo and plum decor and offers views of the ocean. The restaurant, too, has tall windows and ocean views. All the rooms and efficiency units are oceanfront and tropically inspired. Most have two double beds, good-sized baths, and balconies. The hotel is north of the town center.

SHERATON MYRTLE BEACH RESORT, 2701 S. Ocean Blvd., Myrtle Beach, SC 29577. Tel. 803/448-2518, or toll free 800/845-6701. Fax 803/448-1506. 220 rms. A/C TV TEL

$ Rates: $50–$120 single or double. AE, DC, DISC, MC, V.

Sporting a fresh coat of paint, the Sheraton sits attractively on the southern end of the beach scene quietly and efficiently doing its own thing. This resort offers a smart-looking restaurant, a fancy lounge, an exercise room, an outdoor whirlpool, and an outdoor pool. You can book a room here with one or two double beds, or a king-size bed, or you can choose an efficiency unit. All have refrigerators. Nautical colors and modern appointments make this a moderately priced, first-class operation.

YACHTSMAN, 1400 N. Ocean Blvd., Myrtle Beach, SC 29577. Tel. 803/448-1441, or toll free 800/868-8886. Fax 803/626-6261. 344 units. A/C MINIBAR TV TEL

$ Rates: $50–$160 single or double. AE, CB, DC, DISC, MC, V.

If you need a room with a kitchen, consider this first-class establishment. Two short-stacked towers flank the taller mirror-faced central tower. The rooms range from studios and efficiencies to one- and two-bedroom apartments. Spend your time at the two outdoor pools and two outdoor whirlpools, the indoor pool and whirlpool, sauna, or weight room, or playing shuffleboard or minigolf.

BUDGET

COMFORT INN, 2801 S. Kings Hwy., Myrtle Beach, SC 29577. Tel. 803/626-4444, or toll free 800/221-2222. 152 rms. A/C TV TEL **Directions:** Go four miles south of the town center on U.S. 17 Business.

$ Rates: $31–$77 single; $39–$79 double. Children under 18 stay free with parents. Senior discounts available. AE, CB, DC, DISC, MC, V.

Nonsmokers will find smoke-free rooms here. In addition to exceptionally nice guest rooms, there are suites and efficiencies, a few with in-room whirlpools. Amenities include a pool, whirlpool, health club, and sauna, and there's a restaurant close by.

DAYS INN CENTRAL, 601 S. Ocean Blvd., Myrtle Beach, SC 29577. Tel. 803/448-1491, or toll free 800/325-2525. 156 units. A/C TV TEL

$ Rates: $24–$104 single, double, or suite. Weekly, monthly, and golf packages available. AE, DC, DISC, MC, V.

As its name implies, this Days Inn is centrally located. One-room efficiencies, two-room apartments, suites, and penthouses all have cooking facilities, including a microwave; some have in-room whirlpools. There are two outdoor pools and an Olympic-size indoor pool in addition to a whirlpool; a pool and a playground for the kids; and a coin laundry. A good restaurant is within walking distance, and guests enjoy golf privileges at nearby courses.

DRIFTWOOD ON THE OCEANFRONT, 1600 N. Ocean Blvd., Myrtle Beach, SC 29577. Tel. 803/448-1544, or toll free 800/942-3456. Fax 803/448-2917. 90 rms. A/C TV TEL
$ Rates: $20–$92 single or double. AE, CB, DC, DISC, MC, V.

For three generations, guests have come to expect a good value from this oceanfront family-owned motel. There are no food and beverage outlets—only accommodations, a charcoal grill, laundry room, two outdoor pools, and a lawn game or two. That's all. Come to the Driftwood if you want the beach setting and can't afford to spend too much for unneeded extras, such as hotel lobbies, weight rooms, or conference centers. All the rooms have kitchens or refrigerators, and some have ocean views and balconies.

JAMAICAN, 3006 N. Ocean Blvd., Myrtle Beach, SC 29577. Tel. 803/448-4321, or toll free 800/258-1164. 45 rms and suites. A/C TV TEL
$ Rates: $25–$87 single or double; $54–$100 one- or two-bedroom suite. Weekly and monthly rates available. AE, MC, V.

Ⓢ North of the town center, the Jamaican has bright, airy rooms and efficiencies, each with a private balcony and ocean view. The staff is exceptionally pleasant and helpful. The beach is less crowded here, and right next door is one of the area's top restaurants, the Sea Captain's House (see "Where to Dine," below). The boardwalk, Pavilion, and amusement area are 20 short blocks south (a very long stroll or a short drive). There are oceanfront pools for kids and adults, and golf and tennis facilities are close by. Efficiency units now have microwave ovens.

MYRTLE SHORES, 1902–1904 N. Ocean Blvd. (P.O. Box 335), Myrtle Beach, SC 29578. Tel. 803/448-1434. 12 two-bedroom suites, 26 efficiencies. A/C TV TEL
$ Rates: Seasonal $65–$85 single or double. Long-term winter rates available. MC, V.

This oceanfront apartment motel near the town center is very popular with families. It has spacious and attractive guest quarters with refrigerators, and most rooms have private balconies. There's a heated pool, and golf and tennis privileges are available. Daily maid service is offered, and there are coin-operated washers and dryers.

OCEAN DUNES/OCEAN SANDS RESORT AND VILLAS, 74th Ave. N., Myrtle Beach, SC 29578. Tel. 803/449-7441, or toll free 800/845-6701. Fax 803/449-1879. 608 units. A/C TV TEL
$ Rates: $40–$170 single or double. AE, DC, DISC, MC, V.

★ This combination of two hotels has much to see and do. Facilities include a health club with whirlpools, weight machines, saunas, steam room, indoor pool, sun room, and health bar. You can also check out the outdoor pool, kiddies' pool, and sunning deck. The gourmet pizza shop is new but pricey, and there's even a grocery store. Besides standard guest rooms in the towers, you may choose from the suites, apartments, and town houses. Standard equipment in rooms includes balconies and refrigerators.

ST. JOHN'S INN, 6801 N. Ocean Blvd., Myrtle Beach, SC 29577. Tel. 803/449-5251, or toll free 800/845-0624. 87 rms, 21 efficiencies. A/C TV TEL

$ Rates: $25–$90 single or double; $35–$85 efficiency. Golf and tennis packages available. AE, DISC, MC, V.

This three-story motel, north of the town center and across the street from the beach, is more than just a motel. The fine landscaped grounds and Mediterranean-style building lend themselves to a pleasant stay. Some of the decor is right out of the 1970s Caribbean; the lounge is yellow and green, and sometimes in the busy season music is played. Your evening meal may be enjoyed in the steak and seafood restaurant, while day meals are provided in the coffee shop. Soak up the rays in the courtyard, with its outdoor pool and whirlpool. On the side are lawn games. About one unit in three is an efficiency, and rooms have one king-size bed or two double beds.

SERENDIPITY INN, 407 71st Ave. N., Myrtle Beach, SC 29577. Tel. 803/449-5268. 12 rms, 3 suites. A/C TV TEL **Directions:** Take Kings Highway (U.S. 17N) to 71st Avenue North, then turn east toward the ocean.

$ Rates (including breakfast): $50–$85 single or double; $65–$82 suite. AE, MC, V.

This is a Spanish-style inn located on a quiet side street, a block and a half from the beach. All of the rooms are decorated and furnished individually, and there are lovely suites ideal for honeymooners, or for anyone who just wants a little pampering. A marvelous breakfast buffet includes fresh fruit, hard-boiled eggs, hot breads, and more. The outdoor heated pool and whirlpool are good diversions. You can cook your own steaks and chicken on the grill provided for and shared by all guests. The hospitality extended by Cos and Ellen Ficarra, owners of the Serendipity, is as warm as the climate.

TEAKWOOD MOTEL, 7201 N. Ocean Blvd., Myrtle Beach, SC 29572. Tel. 803/449-5653, or toll free 800/868-0046. 25 rms and efficiencies. A/C TV TEL

$ Rates: $30–$59 single or double. Weekly rates available. No credit cards.

Rooms and efficiencies at the Teakwood are attractively furnished, some in Polynesian decor. There's free coffee in the lobby, a heated pool, a playground, and a pleasant cookout area. Airport transportation is offered, along with golf privileges. The motel is five miles north of the town center.

CAMPING

There are lots of campsites along the Grand Strand, many on the oceanfront, and rates drop considerably after Labor Day. Most will accept families only—no singles. On the ocean, about halfway between Myrtle Beach and North Myrtle Beach, there are 760 sites at the **Apache Family Campground,** 9700 Kings Rd., Myrtle Beach, SC 29572 (tel. 803/449-7323). Amenities include a free swimming pool and recreation pavilion, water, electricity, shade shelters, modern bathhouses with hot water, sewer hookups, carpet golf, a laundry, trading post, playground, public telephones, ice, beach umbrellas, floats for rent, and golf privileges. You can reserve here year-round, except for the week of July 4th. Rates are $15 to $25.

WHERE TO DINE

Prices are no measure of quality here; they are unexpectedly moderate at even the best of the restaurants.

MODERATE

PLANTERS BACK PORCH, U.S. 17 South and Wachesaw Rd., Murrells Inlet. Tel. 651-5263 or 651-5544.
Cuisine: SEAFOOD/LOW COUNTRY. **Reservations:** Recommended.
$ Prices: Appetizers $1–$5.50; main courses $8–$18. AE, MC, V.

Open: Dinner daily 5–10pm. **Closed:** Jan–Feb.

Way back when, low-country families used to entertain and dine on the wide porches that ran between the main house and the summer kitchen out back. This fine restaurant, in an old farmhouse built 15 miles south of Myrtle Beach before the turn of the century, takes its name from that custom, offering good eating in a garden atmosphere that re-creates the graciousness of the old days. The new interior is bright and cheerful. You can dine on enclosed porches that run along each side, but my favorite is the main room with its cathedral ceiling and fireplace at one end. Since this eatery is operated by the Rice Planter's people, the food is superb, and similarly priced. Try the Back Porch Inlet Dinner, a seafood feast that goes on and on and on. Low-country specialties include Carolina cured ham and Southern fried chicken, and the homemade biscuits are out of this world.

RICE PLANTER'S, 6707 N. Kings Hwy. Tel. 449-3456, or 449-3457.
Cuisine: SEAFOOD. **Reservations:** Recommended.
$ Prices: Appetizers $2.50–$5; main courses $8.50–$18; fixed-price dinner $18. AE, DISC, MC, V.
Open: Dinner daily 5–10pm. **Closed:** Dec 24–25.

Treat yourself to at least one dinner here. The present building has replaced the original, which burned in 1975, resulting in a loss of irreplaceable artifacts and antiques from rice plantations in the area. Not lost, however, was the charm. Manager David Gilbert seems to be everywhere with a warm welcome and a watchful eye on the service, which matches the food in excellence. A favorite is the Rice Planter's Dinner, which begins with shrimp, followed by clam chowder, fried shrimp, filet of fish, oysters, baked crabmeat, and deep-sea scallops. It comes with a crisp salad of greens, potato, tartar sauce, and home-baked bread. For those who are not a seafood lover, other specialties include steak and low-country dishes—Carolina cured ham or Southern fried chicken. Incidentally, there's an excellent gift shop adjoining the restaurant, which is four miles north of the town center.

SEA CAPTAIN'S HOUSE, 3000 N. Ocean Blvd. Tel. 448-8082.
Cuisine: SEAFOOD. **Reservations:** Recommended.
$ Prices: Appetizers $4.50–$4.90; main courses $8–$18; children's menu under $8. AE, DISC, MC, V.
Open: Breakfast daily 7–10am; lunch daily 11:30am–2:30pm; dinner daily 5–10pm.

Presided over by David Brittain in an old beachfront home 1½ miles north of the town center, this restaurant, family-run since 1963, is loved by a host of South Carolinians, as well as by "outsider" regulars who vacation at Myrtle Beach year after year. In the paneled inner dining room, a fireplace adds to the informal, friendly atmosphere on cool nights. A glassed-in patio affords a superb ocean view. She-crab soup is a specialty; the seafood platter includes five different fish, served with slaw, potatoes, and hush puppies; and there's a selection of charcoal-broiled steaks, pork chops, and Southern fried chicken.

TONY'S ITALIAN RESTAURANT, 1407 U.S. 17, North Myrtle Beach. Tel. 249-1314.
Cuisine: ITALIAN. **Reservations:** Recommended.
$ Prices: Appetizers $2.25–$6; complete dinner $7.50–$19; children's menu under $6. AE, DISC, MC, V.
Open: Mid-Feb to Labor Day, dinner daily 5–10pm; Sept–Nov, Mon–Sat 5–10pm. **Closed:** Dec–Jan.

Located across from Robber's Roost golf course, 10 miles north of Myrtle Beach, this restaurant offers a change from all that wonderful fresh seafood. It's a casual, cozy, welcoming place offering such specialties as fresh veal dishes and homemade pastas.

There'll usually be fresh clams on the menu, too. The oldest Italian restaurant on the Grand Strand, Tony's is about a 20-minute drive north from the heart of Myrtle Beach.

BUDGET

In addition to the Morrison's listed below, there's a branch of the wonderful **Bojangles Famous Chicken & Biscuits** chain at 2301 S. Kings Hwy. (tel. 626-9051). It serves breakfast from 6 to 9:30am, and lunch and dinner to 10pm. Specialties are (guess what?) chicken, homemade biscuits, and sandwiches. A meal here will run well below $5.

MORRISON'S CAFETERIA, Myrtle Square Mall, 2501 N. Kings Highway. Tel. 448-4302.
   Cuisine: AMERICAN. **Reservations:** Not accepted.
$ Prices: Lunch averages $4.50; dinner $5.25. MC, V.
   Open: Daily 11am–8:30pm. **Closed:** Dec 25.
This dependable and convenient cafeteria dishes up wholesome home-cooked meals. They do their own baking, and the hot-table selections include many low-country specialties. It's one mile north of the town center.

EVENING ENTERTAINMENT

Most of the nightlife along the Grand Strand is centered in hotel or motel lounges, some in leading restaurants. Music may vary from country-and-western to jazz to nostalgia to rock-and-roll to disco. Check out dinner-theater offerings in a romantic rooftop setting at the Hilton; the Breakers' bar, which has entertainment and dancing Monday through Saturday nights; and the bar at St. John's Inn (closed Sunday and Monday), which also has entertainment and dancing.

EASY EXCURSIONS FROM MYRTLE BEACH

Myrtle Beach is a good touring center. Historic old Georgetown makes an easy day trip, with stops at Murrells Inlet, Pawleys Island, and Brookgreen Gardens.

MURRELLS INLET, PAWLEYS ISLAND & LITCHFIELD

En route to Georgetown, you'll pass the charming old fishing village of **Murrells Inlet** (home of terrific seafood restaurants) and ✪ **Pawleys Island,** which has been a resort for over 200 years and is a great place to shop for handcrafts, such as the famous Pawleys Island rope hammock. Look for the Hammock Shop, in a cluster of handcraft shops called Plantation Stores, where you'll find wicker, pewter, miniature doll furniture, brass, and china. **North Litchfield** and **Litchfield Beach** lie between Murrells Inlet and Pawleys Island.

Where to Stay

LITCHFIELD INN, 1 Norris Dr., Litchfield, SC 29585. Tel. 803/237-4211, or toll free 800/637-4211. 142 rms. A/C TV TEL **Directions:** Go east off U.S. 17, south of Myrtle Beach.
$ Rates: $36–$125 single or double; efficiencies slightly higher. AE, MC, V.
The Litchfield Inn is for sports-minded travelers who appreciate the two golf courses, 19 tennis courts, walkways over the dunes to the ocean, adults' and children's pools, boating, and fishing. Multiple buildings are built up two or three stories with a main

inn rising seven floors. Accommodations vary from standard hotel rooms to efficiencies to suites and villas.

BROOKGREEN GARDENS

Halfway between Myrtle Beach and Georgetown on U.S. 17 (near Litchfield Beach), Brookgreen Gardens (tel. 237-4218) is a unique sculpture garden and wildlife park on the grounds of a colonial rice plantation. The garden was laid out in 1931 as a setting for American garden sculpture from the mid-19th century to the present. Archer Milton and Anna Hyatt Huntington planned the garden walks in the shape of a butterfly with outspread wings, all leading back to the central space, which was the site of the plantation house. On opposite sides of this space are the Small Sculpture Gallery and the original plantation kitchen. In the wildlife park, an outstanding feature is the Cypress Bird Sanctuary, a 90-foot-tall aviary housing species of wading birds within half an acre of cypress swamp. Tape tours are available for $1. Admission is $5 adults, $2 children ages 6 to 12, children under 6 free. Open daily 9:30am to 4:45pm. Closed on Christmas Day. To write for information, contact Brookgreen Gardens, 1931 Brookgreen Gardens Dr., Murrells Inlet, SC 29576.

GEORGETOWN

A short drive (about 35 miles) south on U.S. 17, ✪ **Georgetown** is an incredibly long step back in time. The pre-Revolutionary houses, churches, and public buildings are best seen on a train tour that runs daily at 10 and 11am and 1, 2, and 3pm, with an excellent commentary. For reservations and fare information, contact the **Georgetown Chamber of Commerce,** 600 Front St. (P.O. Box 1776), Georgetown, SC 29440 (tel. 546-8436, or toll free 800/777-7705). They will also set you out on self-guided tours armed with maps and brochures.

This small enclave of only 11,000 people boasts more than 50 historic homes and buildings dating back as far as 1737. The lifestyles of pre-Revolutionary days comes alive in these homes and museums. You can take a leisurely stroll along the Harbor Walk, tour the antebellum homes, or grab a bite to eat at some of my favorite spots along the main street. Georgetown is wonderful because it rarely is crowded with tourists.

What to See and Do

HAROLD KAMINSKI HOUSE, 1003 Front St. Tel. 546-7706.
A pre-Revolutionary home (ca. 1760), the Kaminski House is furnished with antiques from the 18th and mid-19th centuries. Tours are offered on the hour except at 1pm.
Admission: $4 adults, $2 children under 12.
Open: Mon–Fri 10am–5pm. **Closed:** Holidays.

PRINCE GEORGE WINYAH CHURCH, Broad and Highmarket Sts. Tel. 546-4358.
Services in this church, which dates to about 1750, have been interrupted only by the Revolution and the Civil War. That stained-glass window behind the altar was once part of the slaves' chapel on a nearby plantation.
Admission: Free.
Open: Daily 8am–4pm.

RICE MUSEUM, 1842 Market Building, Front and Screven Sts. Tel. 546-7423.

The Rice Museum is the repository of maps, artifacts, dioramas, and other exhibits that trace the development of rice cultivation—which was for so long Georgetown's primary economic base—from 1700 to 1900. There's also a scale model of a rice mill.

Admission: $2 adults, free for students.
Open: Mon–Sat 9:30am–4:30pm.

Where to Dine

DANIEL'S WATERFRONT EATERY, 713 Front St. Tel. 546-4377.

Cuisine: AMERICAN. **Reservations:** Not required.
$ Prices: Appetizers $2.75–$4.40; main courses $10–$15. AE, MC, V.
Open: Lunch Mon–Sat 11am–2:30pm; dinner Tues–Sat 5–10pm.

A boat hangs from the ceiling of this restaurant and the rest of the decor is just as interesting: lots of wood and brick. Upstairs is a lounge with water views and an outdoor deck. Specialties include cajun shrimp, shrimp-and-crab-salad platters, grilled chicken, and steaks.

KUDZU BAKERY, 714 Front St. Tel. 546-1847.

Cuisine: BAKERY. **Reservations:** Not accepted.
$ Prices: Sandwiches $3, pastries from 75¢. No credit cards.
Open: Dec–Feb, daily 8am–4pm; Mar–Nov, daily 8am–6pm.

Owners Joey and Stacy Rabon have a winner with this old-time looking bakery in the center of town. The exposed brick and skylight make a nice impression, and with just seven stools it feels like it's your own special place. They always have a variety of about 10 cakes and 5 pies, besides the cookies and muffins. Try the red velvet cake or the carrot cake. If you want something more substantial, they'll make a fresh sandwich for you. The name Kudzu comes from a vine that grows in the South.

PINK MAGNOLIA, 719 Front St. Tel. 527-6506.

Cuisine: SOUTHERN REGIONAL. **Reservations:** Not required.
$ Prices: Salads $5–$6.50; chowder $2.50–$3.50; main courses $4.95–$6.95. MC, V.
Open: Sept–Feb, lunch Mon–Sat 11:30am–2pm; Mar–Aug, dinner daily 5:30–9pm.

The Pink Magnolia opens for lunch or dinner only, but it serves some breakfast favorites, such as eggs Benedict. On the menu in this country-inspired restaurant is chicken pie, crabcakes, crab quiche, fried-chicken salad, and shrimp chowder. The atmosphere is cheerful, and the staff is friendly.

RIVER ROOM, 8012 Front St. Tel. 527-4110.

Cuisine: REGIONAL. **Reservations:** Not required.
$ Prices: Appetizers $5.75–$6.50; main courses $11–$17. AE, MC, V.
Open: Lunch Mon–Sat 11am–2:30pm; dinner Mon–Sat 5–10pm.

The River Room rewards its guests with views of the water from its cozy dining room and features an adjacent bar equally inviting, with lots of wood and brick. The guests are smartly dressed in a casual way. Specials might be shrimp créole, black bean soup, cajun fried squid, yellow grits with sautéed shrimp and sausage, plantation crab casserole, or blackened grouper or tuna with basil cream sauce. At noon, sandwiches cost $4.75 to $5.95.

THOMAS CAFE, 703 Front St. Tel. 546-7776.

Cuisine: AMERICAN REGIONAL. **Reservations:** Not accepted.

$ Prices: Appetizers $1.99; main courses $3.99; lunch for two $10. No credit cards.
Open: Daily 5:30am–2pm.

The Thomas Café is the kind of place where Charles Kuralt might come to talk to the people. With only three tables, a few booths, and a handful of counter stools, it is real Americana and caters to locals. Your waitress might be a spry 80 years old. The lunch special may cost a mere $3.99 and include pork chops or fried chicken, carrot salad, green beans, buttered potatoes, corn bread, and coffee or tea. Wow! What a price. This is the Old South with no nonsense hospitality, y'all.

---

2. HILTON HEAD ISLAND

156 miles S of Myrtle Beach; 186 miles SE of Columbia;
65 miles S of Charleston; 52 miles NE of Savannah, Georgia.

GETTING THERE   By Plane   See "Getting There," in Chapter 6.

By Train   The nearest **Amtrak** stop is Savannah, Georgia, about 52 miles south of Hilton Head Island (tel. 800/USA-RAIL).

By Bus   Greyhound/Trailways serves Savannah, Georgia, one hour south.

By Car   You get to Hilton Head via a bridge, about 40 miles east of I-95 South (exit 28), 52 miles north of Savannah, Georgia (exit 5, I-95 North).

By Boat   For boat owners, getting there is simple, since Hilton Head is located directly on the Intracoastal Waterway.

GETTING AROUND   By Car   U.S. 278 is the divided highway that runs the length of the island.

By Taxi   Yellow Cab (tel. 686-6666) has flat two-passenger rates determined by zone, with an additional $2 per extra person.

ESSENTIALS   The **area code** is 803. The **Hilton Head Visitors and Convention Bureau,** P.O. Box 5647, Hilton Head Island, SC 29938 (tel. 803/785-3673), will help you either before or after your arrival. Their 10-minute VHS video "Hilton Head Island: Simply Better" ($22.50 check or money order includes postage and handling) gives a great rundown on activities, dining, and shopping. The **Hilton Head Island Visitor Information Center** (open Monday to Friday 8:30am to 5:30pm, Saturday 10am to 4pm, and Sunday noon to 4pm) is on U.S. 278. Ask for their free guide booklet, "Hilton Head Island Vacation Planner."

SPECIAL EVENTS   Spring blossoms at Hilton Head with a variety of special events, the earliest of which is **Springfest,** a March festival featuring seafood feasts, music, concerts, stage shows, and tennis and golf tournaments. In early or mid-April, top tennis players congregate for the **Family Circle Magazine Cup Tennis Tournament,** held at the Sea Pines Racquet Club. Outstanding PGA golfers also descend on the island in mid-April for the **MCI Heritage Classic** at Harbour Town Golf Links. To herald the approach of fall, there's the **Hilton Head Celebrity Golf Tournament** on Labor Day weekend at Palmetto Dunes and Sea Pines Plantation.

Spain, France, and England squabbled over ownership of Hilton Head—the largest sea island between New Jersey and Florida—from the early 1600s until the mid-1700s. Native Americans, certain of their claim to the land, harassed them all. By the end of the 18th century, however, things had quieted down enough for large plantations to flourish here, and a leisurely island lifestyle evolved. Today's "plantations" (as most resort areas here call themselves) hold on to that leisure, and offer it to all comers. The "crop" cultivated here now is tourism, not rice. About 450,000 to 500,000 resort guests annually visit the island, whose permanent population is about 25,000.

Although it covers only 42 square miles (it's 12 miles long, and 5 miles wide at its widest point), Hilton Head has a feeling of spaciousness, thanks to judicious planning from the start of its development in 1952. The broad beaches on its ocean side, beautiful sea marshes over on the sound, and natural wooded areas of live and water oak, pine, bay, and palmetto trees have all been carefully preserved amid the explosion of commercial enterprise. It's an environmental paradise that attracts artists, writers, musicians (jazz, classical, and even rock), theater groups, and artisans. The only "city" (of sorts) is Harbour Town, at Sea Pines Plantation, a charming Mediterranean-style cluster of shops and restaurants.

WHAT TO SEE & DO

RECREATION Hilton Head's economic base is recreation, and it goes on year-round here in a subtropical climate that ranges in temperature from the low 50s in winter to mid-80s in summer. For additional information on suppliers for recreational activities, stop by the information center (see "Essentials," above) for an island directory.

With more than 25 golf courses (18 of championship caliber) and over 300 tennis courts, golf and tennis compete with miles and miles of beach for first place on the "what to do" list. Access to all three come with most hotel accommodations, and many are open to the public for a small fee. Boaters, as well as sailing and fishing devotees, have only to hie themselves down to the **Harbour Town Yacht Basin and Marina** (tel. 671-4534, or 671-2704) or one of the seven other marinas that can dock yachts up to 100 feet long, where they'll find a sailing club, all sorts of rental boats, and charter fishing boats for hire (there's an annual billfishing tournament).

Cycling is a popular way to explore the island, and rental bikes are readily available at many hotels and shopping centers, as well as **Harbour Town Bicycles,** Graves Plaza, U.S. 278 (tel. 671-5386). More than 25 miles of rambling bike paths crisscross major points. There are five horseback riding stables, with boarding facilities for those who bring their own mounts. You'll find them at Sea Pines, Moss Creek, Hilton Head, and Rose Hill plantations, and at **Sandy Creek Stables** (tel. 689-3423). Birdwatchers will have a field day, since more than 250 species of birds have been counted here by the Audubon Society.

TOURS To explore Hilton Head's surrounding waters, contact **۞ Adventure Cruises, Inc.,** Shelter Cove Harbour, Suite G, Harbourside III, Hilton Head Island, SC 29928 (tel. 803/785-4558), for a brochure outlining their sightseeing and dinner cruises. Sightseeing on the ground level is a specialty with **Low Country Adventures, Ltd.** (tel. 681-8212), which can arrange special-interest tours, as well as furnish airport transportation on the island and from Savannah.

SHOPPING Hilton Head is browsing heaven, with more than 30 shopping centers spread around the island, stocked with everything from designer clothing to island and low-country crafts. Chief shopping sites include Pinelawn Mall (Matthews Drive and U.S. 278), with over 30 shops and half a dozen restaurants; and Coligny Plaza (Coligny Circle), with more than 60 shops, a movie theater, foodstands, and several good restaurants.

WHERE TO STAY

There is really no such thing as "budget" on Hilton Head Island. It is possible these days, however, to spend time here for a reasonable cost. Of course, the older resort establishments (called "plantations") are the very embodiment of luxury, with prices to match. When booking, be sure to ask about golf, tennis, or family package rates. Also, the following listings are either priced according to the season indicated, or are listed for the high season rate; *count on off-season rates to be much lower.*

The oldest and most comprehensive central reservation service on the island, **Hilton Head Central Reservation Service,** P.O. Box 5312, Hilton Head Island, SC 29938 (tel. toll free 800/845-7018 in the U.S. and Canada), can book you into all hotel rooms and villas anywhere on the island, and there's no booking fee.

Another option is the rental of private homes. For up-to-date availability, rates, and bookings, contact **Island Rentals and Real Estate,** P.O. Box 5915, Hilton Head Island, SC 29938 (tel. 803/785-3813, or toll free 800/845-6134).

EXPENSIVE

HOLIDAY INN CROWNE PLAZA RESORT, 130 Shipyard Dr., Hilton Head, SC 29928. Tel. 803/842-2400, or toll free 800/HOLIDAY. Fax 803/785-8463. 363 units. A/C TV TEL

$ Rates (introductory): $169 double.

After being closed for renovation for several months, this resort finally reopened in the spring of 1993 as one of Holiday Inn's Crowne Plaza gems, in Shipyard Plantation, off U.S. 278. Much renovation has been done to the property: the landscaping has been changed; the accommodations have been redone; the public areas, such as its restaurants, have been revamped; and the recreational amenities have been improved. There are indoor and outdoor pools, lighted tennis courts, a putting green, a golf course, and a fitness center for your enjoyment. As we go to press, the rates offered are introductory, but a tariff schedule for each season will be established. Holiday Inn hopes to make this property a contender for top billing on the island—though, for the time being, The Westin Resort remains head and shoulders above all competition.

HYATT REGENCY HILTON HEAD, P.O. Box 6167, 1 Hyatt Circle, Hilton Head Island, SC 29938. Tel. 803/785-1234. Fax 803/842-4695. 505 rms. 31 suites. A/C MINIBAR TV TEL

$ Rates: $95–$275 single or double. Children under 18 stay free with parents. Tennis and golf packages available. AE, DC, MC, V.

This is a deluxe oceanfront hotel on the grounds of the Palmetto Dunes Resort, on U.S. 278, with complete resort facilities. There are three restaurants, a pool bar, two lounges with entertainment, an outdoor pool and whirlpool, and health-club facilities complete with saunas, whirlpool, indoor pool, and exercise/weight room. In addition, there are three 18-hole golf courses, 25 tennis courts, and sailboats. In the summer months, a good children's program is available. Luxuriously appointed guest rooms all have private balconies.

PALMETTO DUNES RESORT, P.O. Box 5606, Hilton Head Island, SC 29938. Tel. 803/785-1161, or toll free 800/845-6130. 500 villas. A/C TV TEL

$ Rates: $100–$235 villa. Weekly and monthly rates available. AE, DC, MC, V.

Located midway along the island's coastline, off U.S. 278, seven miles south of the bridge, this is one of Hilton Head's finest resorts. It's a family-oriented vacation spot, with 3 miles of beach, 5 golf courses, 28 pools, wading pools, an excellent tennis center with 25 courts, rental bikes, sailboats, canoes, a playground, supervised children's programs, a multitude of shops, and 20 restaurants. The 500 one- to four-bedroom villas vary in size and style; some feature fireplaces and balconies. Call or write for full details.

THE WESTIN RESORT, 2 Grasslawn Ave., Hilton Head Island, SC 29928. Tel. 803/681-4000, or toll free 800/228-3000. 410 rms. A/C MINIBAR TV TEL

Rates: $205–$295 single or double. Children under 18 stay free with parents. Golf and tennis packages available. AE, DC, MC, V.

The Westin, located one mile off U.S. 278, overlooks miles of superb sandy beach and has garnered many awards for its truly luxurious accommodations and facilities set on 27 acres. You'll be impressed with the spectacular entry loaded with thousands of blossoms. Everything is refined and elegant, and throughout the hotel, you'll find a Southern atmosphere and classic styling. Facilities include one indoor and two outdoor pools, tennis courts, golf courses, an excellent health club, a games room, lawn games, a barber shop, a beauty shop, and recreational programs. The rooms are deluxe with thick carpets, expensive appointments, and many special extras. Two- and three-bedroom villas have Jacuzzis.

MODERATE

SEA CREST MOTEL, Avocet St. (P.O. Box 5818), Hilton Head Island, SC 29938. Tel. 803/785-2121, or toll free 800/845-7014. 90 units. A/C TV TEL
Rates: $49–$99 single or double; $299–$575 efficiency per week; $375–$760 apartment per week. Significant discounts available off-season. AE, MC, V.

The exceptionally large and attractive rooms here all have two double beds, and two-bedroom apartments and rooms with kitchenettes are also available. All units overlook the pool or the ocean, and golf and tennis privileges can be arranged. This is the prettiest of the reasonably priced motels, and it's located north of Coligny Circle.

SEA PINES PLANTATION, P.O. Box 7000, Hilton Head Island, SC 29938. Tel. 803/785-3333, or toll free 800/845-6131. 500 villas. A/C TV TEL **Directions:** Take U.S. 278 to Sea Pines Circle.
Rates: High season, $85–$250 villa. Golf, tennis, weekly, and honeymoon packages available. AE, MC, V.

Hilton Head's first resort has a faithful following who would not stay anywhere else. Its clientele includes hordes of golfers, since it's the home of the MCI Heritage Classic, a major stop on the PGA tour. Spread over more than 5,000 acres, it has 4 miles of ocean beach, 14 miles of bike trails, 3 championship golf courses, 50 tennis courts, 25 pools, marinas, an outstanding children's summer recreation program, and more than 12 restaurants and entertainment spots within its boundaries. If you're not a Sea Pines guest, you can eat, shop, or enjoy the nightlife here, but there's a small fee to enter the grounds. For full details, write for a free "Sea Pines Vacation Guide" and package brochure. All of the one- to four-bedroom accommodations are privately owned, so the decor in each varies.

BUDGET

FAIRFIELD INN BY MARRIOTT, 9 Marina Side Drive, Hilton Head Island, SC 29928. Tel. 803/842-4800, or toll free 800/228-2800. 120 rms, 14 suites. A/C TV TEL **Directions:** Take U.S. 278, nine miles south of the bridge.
Rates: $30–$57 single or double; $48–$85 suite. Senior discounts and golf package available. AE, DC, MC, V.

Set in Shelter Cove, this motel has all the special features of Marriott's budget chain: complimentary coffee and tea, no-smoking rooms, same-day dry cleaning, etc., plus easy access to the beach, golf, tennis, marinas, and shopping. This establishment is wheelchair-accessible.

MOTEL 6, 830 William Hilton Pkwy., Hilton Head Island, SC 29928. Tel. 803/785-2700. 117 rms. A/C TV TEL **Directions:** Take U.S. 278 to Shelter Cove.
Rates: $26–$32 single; $26–$38 double. AE, CB, DC, DISC, MC, V.

Motel 6 was formerly a Knights Inn, but it changed hands a couple of years ago. It still offers good budget accommodations. There are no longer efficiencies, but the area has grown up some, and now three restaurants are situated next door. There's an outdoor pool, and free coffee is offered in the reception area. Public beaches and golf and tennis facilities are not far away.

RED ROOF INN, 5 Regency Pkwy., Hilton Head Island, SC 29928. Tel. 803/686-6808. Fax 803/842-3352. 108 rms, 4 suites. A/C TV TEL
$ Rates: $35 single; $41–$53 double; $65–$80 suite. AE, CB, DC, DISC, MC, V.
This wheelchair-accessible hotel, on U.S. 278 between Palmetto Dunes and Shipyard Plantation, offers rooms with over-size beds, free coffee for guests, free local telephone calls, Showtime on TV, and an outdoor pool. A restaurant, public beaches, and sports facilities are all close by.

CAMPING

Outdoor Resorts RV Resort & Yacht Club, 43 Jenkins Rd., Hilton Head Island, SC 29926 (tel. 803/681-3256, or toll free 800/845-9560), has some 200 RV sites situated on the Intracoastal Waterway. Amenities on the premises include two pools, saunas and whirlpools, lighted tennis courts, charter-fishing arrangements, marina and ramp, grocery shop, coin laundry, and restaurant. Rates for up to four people range from $24 to $28, depending on the season.

WHERE TO DINE

I counted close to 100 eating spots on Hilton Head—and I may have missed a few. Rest assured that a good restaurant will never be far away. Many offer daily "happy hour" or "early bird" specials; make it a practice to ask when the menu is presented.

ALEXANDER'S, Palmetto Dunes Resort, Area 2, Queen's Folly Rd. Tel. 785-4999, or 842-1444.
  Cuisine: CONTINENTAL/SEAFOOD. **Reservations:** Recommended.
$ Prices: Appetizers $5–$8; main courses $10.95–$19.95. AE, DC, MC, V.
  Open: Dinner daily 5–10pm. **Closed:** Dec to mid-Feb.
  Alexander's features high ceilings and lots of windows overlooking a pictur-esque lagoon. The chef-owner specializes in shrimp, crab, and fresh fish dishes, with salmon Oscar a standout. Among nonseafood offerings, the rack of lamb is outstanding. It's located seven miles south of the bridge.

DAMON'S RESTAURANT, Village at Wexford. Tel. 785-6677.
  Cuisine: AMERICAN/BARBECUE. **Reservations:** Not accepted. **Directions:** Take U.S. 278, one mile north of Sea Pines Circle.
$ Prices: Appetizers $3.50–$5.25; main courses $3–$6 at lunch, $8–$16 at dinner. AE, DISC, MC, V.
  Open: Daily 11:30am–10pm.
  When you've begun to feel a little "finny" from all that seafood, try the barbecue ribs, chicken, shrimp, steaks, or prime rib at Damon's. They also do a terrific onion loaf. There's a full bar and good wine list.

FUDDRUCKERS, 32 Shelter Cove Lane. Tel. 686-5161.
  Cuisine: AMERICAN. **Reservations:** Not accepted. **Directions:** Take U.S. 278 to Shelter Cove Plaza, just north of the Palmetto Dunes entrance.
$ Prices: Appetizers $2.95–$4.50; burgers, sandwiches, salads $3.90–$5.95. AE, DISC, MC, V.
  Open: Daily 11am–10pm.
For dependable budget meals, this restaurant dishes up burgers, hot dogs, steaks, chicken, salads, and a long list of snacks. Their brownies are held in high esteem hereabouts.

GASLIGHT RESTAURANT, 303 Market Place. Tel. 785-5814.
  Cuisine: FRENCH. **Reservations:** Recommended.
  $ Prices: Appetizers $5–$8; main courses $17–$24. AE, MC, V.
  Open: Lunch Mon–Fri noon–2pm; dinner Mon–Sat 6–10pm.
Most often you'll find Serge Prat, owner of this popular spot near Sea Pines Circle, in the kitchen, since he's also the chef. Specialties include rack of lamb, salmon, Dover sole, and beef Wellington. There's a fine wine list, and service is as good as the food. Jackets are suggested at dinner.

HUDSON'S SEAFOOD HOUSE ON THE DOCKS, 1 Hudson Rd. Tel. 681-2772.
  Cuisine: SEAFOOD. **Reservations:** Not accepted. **Directions:** Go to Skull Creek, just off Squire Pope Road (signposted from U.S. 278); for boaters, go to Intracoastal Waterway markers 13 and 14.
  $ Prices: Appetizers $2.95–$4.95; main courses $11.95–$15.95. AE, MC, V.
  Open: Lunch daily 11am–2:30pm; winter, dinner daily 6–10pm, summer 5–10pm.
Built as a seafood processing factory in 1912, this restaurant still processes fish, clams, and oysters for local distribution—so there's no need to mention freshness. If you're seated in the north dining room, you'll be eating in the original oyster factory. A few "drydock" courses show up on the menu, but I strongly recommend the seafood, such as stuffed prawns or blackened catch of the day. Local oysters are also a specialty, breaded and deep fried. Before and after dinner, stroll on the docks past shrimp boats and enjoy the view of the mainland and nearby Parris Island. Sunsets here are always spectacular. Lunch is served in the Oyster Bar.

THE LITTLE VENICE RISTORANTE, Harbourside II, Shelter Cove. Tel. 785-3300.
  Cuisine: ITALIAN. **Reservations:** Recommended.
  $ Prices: Appetizers $5.95–$6.50; main courses $11.95–$19.95; early dining special 20% off for cash (5–6pm). AE, DC, DISC, MC, V.
  Open: Lunch daily noon–2:30pm; dinner daily 5–10pm.
This charming restaurant near the Palmetto Dunes entrance overlooks Shelter Cove Harbour, and in fine weather you can dine outside under an awning. Pasta is homemade (try the linguine with clams), and veal comes in several incarnations. Local seafood is prepared Italian-style; the shrimp fra diavolo is superb.

EVENING ENTERTAINMENT

Nightlife is found chiefly in hotel or shopping-center lounges, which can be quiet, intimate rendezvous spots or lively entertainment centers with top performers. **The Island Playhouse** presents polished, professional theater throughout the year—call 785-4878 for dates and prices. Live music for easy listening is a feature at the Westin Resort's **Gazebo Lounge** (tel. 681-4000); **Café Europa** at the Lighthouse in Harbour Town (tel. 671-3399); and **Hemingway's Lounge** at the Hyatt Regency in Palmetto Dunes (tel. 785-1234).

EASY EXCURSIONS
DAUFUSKIE ISLAND

If you're hungry for a taste of an earlier age, before the arrival of all these sophisticated "plantations" and holiday resorts, make arrangements for a day trip to Daufuskie Island. Inhabited now by only a few hundred residents, Daufuskie is hauntingly alive with the rhythms of history. As early as 2000 B.C., this was the province of the Muskogee Indians. In the 1500s, the Spanish appeared; in the 1600s, English settlers established thriving indigo plantations. During the Revolution, the settlers here remained loyal Tories; by the time of the Civil War, cotton was king here, only to be toppled by the boll weevil. The present-day population consists almost entirely of descendants of slaves; their Gullah culture comes to the fore as they greet and pass the time of day with visitors in accents left over from 17th- and 18th-century West African dialects.

There are a handful of points of embarkation from Hilton Head, and you will arrive by ferry at Haig Point or possibly the public landing. Nearby, the **Strachan Mansion** (which was brought by barge from St. Simon's Island, Georgia), offers a general store and delicatessen. Take a look at the 1872 lighthouse, the ruins of a Haig Point plantation house, and its group of slave cabins. Cars have not as yet invaded Daufuskie (residents use a few), so sightseeing consists mainly of rambling down dirt roads shaded by live oak, with occasional stops to chat with residents. It makes for a relaxing, oddly comforting sort of day that puts the stresses of our modern life into proper perspective. Since there are now three developments under way on the island—a community of private holiday homes and private country clubs—who knows how much longer you'll have the privilege?

To arrange transportation to Daufuskie by private ferry, contact **Adventure Cruises** (tel. 785-4558); **Haig Point,** usually in conjunction with residents (tel. toll free 800/992-3635); or the **Melrose Company** (tel. 681-6173).

BEAUFORT

Just a few miles away on S.C. 170, Beaufort (low-country pronunciation is "Bewfort") is a picturesque old seaport with narrow streets shaded by huge old live oaks and homes that have survived from the 1700s (the oldest was built in 1717 and is at Port Republic and New Streets). This was the second area in North America discovered by the Spanish (1520), the site of the first fort (1525) on the continent, and of the first attempted settlement (1562). Several forts have been excavated, dating from 1566 and 1577.

The **Beaufort Chamber of Commerce,** 1006 Bay St. (P.O. Box 910), Beaufort, SC 29901 (tel. 803/524-3163), has self-guided tours and lots of other information about this historic town. Visitors center hours are Monday through Saturday from 9:30am to 5:30pm, and Sunday from 10am to 5pm. If your trip plans are for early to mid-October, write the **Historic Beaufort Foundation,** P.O. Box 11, Beaufort, SC 29901, for specific dates and detailed information on their two days of antebellum house and garden tours. Highlights to look for are the 1844 Greek Revival–style **George Parsons Elliott House,** 1001 Bay St., a Union hospital during the Civil War; the **John Mark Verdier House,** 801 Bay St., Union headquarters during that conflict; and the **Beaufort Museum,** which holds exhibits of the Revolutionary and Civil Wars, prehistoric relics, Indian pottery, and decorative arts. The Elliott House is open Monday through Friday from 11am to 3pm, and the Verdier House is open Tuesday through Saturday from 11am to 4pm. Both are closed in January.

CHAPTER 8
CHARLESTON

If the Old South still lives all through South Carolina's low country, it positively thrives in Charleston. All our romantic notions of antebellum days—stately homes, courtly manners, gracious hospitality, and, above all, gentle dignity—are facts of everyday life in the old city.

It all began when King Charles of England magnanimously gave eight of his loyal subjects the strip of land between the 29th and 36th parallels of latitude, all the way westward to the Pacific (somehow overlooking the fact that France and Spain already claimed much of that land). These "lord proprietors" sent out colonists, who first settled at Albemarle Point, then moved to the peninsula between the mouths of the Ashley and Cooper Rivers as a location more easily defensible against surprise attack.

By the mid-1770s, Charleston (originally named Charles Towne) was an important seaport. As desire for independence from Britain grew, Charlestonians threw out the last royal governor and built a palmetto-log and sand fort (Fort Moultrie, which stayed a working fort right on through World War II), on Sullivan's Island. They repulsed a British fleet on June 28, 1776, then sent couriers to Philadelphia to tell of the victory just in time to convince the Continental Congress that it could be done. The British returned in 1780, however, and took the city, holding it until December 1782. It took more than 300 ships to move them out—soldiers, Tory supporters, slaves, and tons of loot.

In 1860, the first Ordinance of Secession, passed in Columbia, was actually signed here in Charleston when an epidemic caused the legislature to move. Soon thereafter, South Carolinians opened fire from Fort Johnson against the Union-held Fort Sumter, and the Civil War was off and running. Although it was attacked again and again during the war, the city remained a Confederate stronghold until February 1865.

During all those tumultuous years, Charleston was essentially a center of gentility and culture, of wealthy rice and indigo planters who pleasured themselves with imported luxuries, built magnificent town houses (to which they regularly repaired for the summer to escape backcountry mosquitoes and malaria), supported the first theater in America, held glittering "socials," and originated the Planter's punch cocktail. Many of those families still own and live in the homes their planter ancestors built, and they still take pride in their beautiful walled gardens and offer a gracious welcome to visitors. Despite the ups and downs of family fortunes, Charlestonians

WHAT'S SPECIAL ABOUT CHARLESTON

Historic Homes and Museums
- [ ] The Edmondston-Alston House, a wealthy merchant's mansion that dates from 1828.
- [ ] The Nathaniel Russell House, with its unique "free-flying" staircase.
- [ ] The Joseph Manigault House, an 1803 Adams-style mansion.
- [ ] The Old Slave Market Museum, which chronicles the history and achievements of African Americans in the United States.
- [ ] The Charleston Museum, the oldest museum in the country.

Churches, Gardens, and Plantations
- [ ] St. Michael's Episcopal Church, where George Washington worshiped during his tour of the South.

- [ ] Congregation Beth Elohim, a splendid example of Greek Revival architecture.
- [ ] Middleton Place, a working plantation with gardens that date from 1741.
- [ ] Cypress Gardens, an enchanted, moss-draped woodland with boat rides among the knobby trees.
- [ ] Boone Hall Plantation, approached by way of a romantic avenue bordered by moss-draped oaks.
- [ ] Drayton Hall, with its interesting Georgian-Palladian home.

manage to maintain a way of life that, in many respects, has little to do with wealth. The simplest encounter with Charleston natives seems invested with a "social" air, as though the visitor were a valued guest to be pleased. There are those who detect a certain snobbishness in Charlestonians, and, in truth, you'd have to live here a few hundred years to be considered an "insider"—but I'll settle for this kind of "outsider" acceptance anytime!

1. ORIENTATION

ARRIVING

BY PLANE   See "Getting There," in Chapter 6. Charleston International Airport is in North Charleston on I-26, about 12 miles west of the city. Taxi fare into the city runs about $17; the airport limousine has a $9 fare (tel. 767-7111).

BY TRAIN   **Amtrak** arrives at 4565 Gaynor Ave., North Charleston (tel. toll free 800/USA-RAIL).

BY BUS   The **Greyhound/Trailways** station is located at 3610 Dorchester Rd. (tel. 803/744-4247).

BY CAR   The main north-south coastal route, U.S. 17, passes through Charleston; I-26 runs northwest to southeast, and ends in Charleston. Charleston is 120 miles southeast of Columbia via I-26 and 98 miles south of Myrtle Beach via U.S. 17.

DID YOU KNOW . . . ?

- The first indigo crop in the United States was grown here in 1690 and proved the basis, along with rice, for many a Charleston family fortune.
- America's first fire insurance company, the Friendly Society for the Mutual Insurance of Houses Against Fire, was established in 1736 in Charleston (but was wiped out financially when a disastrous fire in 1740 burned down half the city).
- The first "weather man" in America, Dr. John Lening of Charleston, began recording daily temperatures in 1738 to study the effect of weather on the human body.
- The first shipment of American cotton abroad (seven bags exported to England, at a value of about $873) was from Charleston in 1748.
- A British flag was pulled down in Charleston and replaced by the Stars and Stripes in 1775, the first time it happened in the colonies.
- The country's first "fireproof" building was constructed here in 1826, designed by Robert Mills (the architect of the Washington Monument).
- The first steam locomotive hauling passengers in America ran from Charleston to Hamberg, S.C., in 1831—as one newspaper reported, "on the wings of the wind, annihilating space and leaving all the world behind at the fantastic speed of 15 m.p.h."
- The first shot in the "War for Southern Independence" was fired here in 1861.

TOURIST INFORMATION

The **Visitor Reception & Transportation Center (VRTC),** 375 Meeting St., Charleston, SC 29402 (tel. 803/853-8000), just across from the Charleston Museum, provides maps, brochures, tour information, and access to South Carolina Automated Ticketing. The helpful staff will assist you in finding accommodations and planning your stay. Numerous tours depart hourly from the VRTC, and restroom facilities, as well as parking, are available. Be sure to allow time to view the 24-minute multi-image presentation "Forever Charleston." To obtain an advance copy of the comprehensive "Visitors Guide," call 803/853-8000 or write P.O. Box 975, Charleston, SC 29402. The center is open from April to October on Monday to Friday from 8:30am to 5:30pm and on Saturday and Sunday from 8am to 5pm, and from November to March daily from 8:30am to 5:30pm.

FAST FACTS: CHARLESTON

Babysitters Most large hotels will supply a list of babysitters, but babysitters are generally unavailable in smaller establishments.

Currency Exchange Try Carolina Foreign Exchange at the main terminal in the Charleston International Airport (tel. 767-7474).

Dentist Try Orthodontic Associates of Charleston, 86 Rutledge Ave. (tel. 723-7242).

Doctor For physician referral or 24-hour emergency room service, contact Charleston Memorial Hospital, 326 Calhoun St. (tel. 577-0600); or Roper Hospital, 316 Calhoun St. (tel. 724-2970). Call Doctor's Care (tel. 556-5585) for names of walk-in clinics.

Emergencies Call 911.

Newspapers Charleston's daily is the *News & Courier.*

Radio/TV Both AM and FM frequencies carry major radio networks in addition to several South Carolina local stations. Major TV channels are 2 (ABC), 4 (NBC), 5 (CBS), 7 (PBS), and 24 (FOX).

Restrooms Public restrooms are located at Broad and Meeting Streets, Queen and Church Streets, Market Street between Meeting and Church Streets, and other clearly marked strategic points in the historic and downtown districts.

Weather Call 744-3207.

CITY LAYOUT

Charleston's streets are laid out in an easy-to-follow grid pattern. Main north/south thoroughfares are King, Meeting, and East Bay Streets; Trad, Broad, Queen, and Calhoun Streets bisect the city from east to west. South of Broad Street, East Bay becomes East Battery.

NEIGHBORHOODS IN BRIEF

The Historic District   In 1860, according to one Charlestonian, "South Carolina seceded from the Union, Charleston seceded from South Carolina, and south of Broad Street seceded from Charleston." The city preserves its early years here at its southernmost point, the conjunction of the Cooper and Ashley Rivers. The lovely White Point Gardens, right in the "elbow" of the two rivers, provide a sort of gateway into this area where virtually every home is of historic or architectural interest. Between Broad Street and Murray Boulevard (which runs along the south waterfront), you'll find such sightseeing highlights as St. Michael's Episcopal Church, the Calhoun Mansion, the Edmonston-Alston House, the Old Exchange/Provost Dungeon, the Heyward-Washington House, Catfish Row, and the Nathaniel Russell House.

Downtown   Extending north from Broad Street to Marion Square at the intersection of Calhoun and Meeting Streets, this area encloses noteworthy points of historical interest, good shopping, and a gaggle of historic churches. Just a few of its highlights are the Old City Market, the Dock Street Theatre, Market Hall, the Old Powder Magazine, the Thomas Elfe Workshop, Congregation Beth Elohim, the French Huguenot Church, St. John's Church, and the Unitarian Church.

Above Marion Square   The visitor center is located on Meeting Street north of Calhoun. The Charleston Museum is just across the street, and the Aiken-Rhett Mansion, Joseph Manigault Mansion, and Old Citadel are all within easy walking distance of each other in the area bounded by Calhoun Street to the south and Mary Street to the north.

Outlying Areas   Bordering its inner core, Charleston has lots to entice sightseers. East of the Cooper River, visit the aircraft carrier *Yorktown* at Patriot's Point; Boone Hall Plantation; Fort Moultrie; and public beaches at Sullivan's Island and Isle of Palms. Head west across the Ashley River Bridge to pay tribute to Charleston's birth at Charles Towne Landing and visit such sightseeing highlights as Drayton Hall, Magnolia Gardens, and Middleton Place. One of the area's most popular beaches, Folly Beach County Park, is also west of the Ashley River.

2. GETTING AROUND

BY BUS   City bus fares are 75¢, and there's service from 5:35am to 10pm (until 1am to North Charleston). Between 9:30am and 3:30pm, senior citizens and the handicapped pay 25¢. Exact change is required. For route and schedule information, call 722-2226.

BY TROLLEY   The **Downtown Area Shuttle (DASH)** is the quickest way to get around the main downtown area daily. Fare is 75¢, and you'll need exact change. A pass good for the whole day costs $1. For hours and routes, call 724-7368.

BY TAXI   Leading taxi companies are **Yellow Cab** (tel. 767-6565) and **Safety**

Cab (tel. 722-4066); each company has its own fare structure. Within the city, however, fares seldom exceed $3 or $4. You must call for a taxi—there are no pickups on the street.

BY CAR   If you're staying in the city proper, park the car and leave it for day trips to outlying areas. You'll find parking facilities scattered about the city, with some of the most convenient at Hutson Street and Calhoun Street, both near Marion Square; on King Street between Queen and Broad; and on George Street between King and Meeting. Leading car-rental companies are: **Avis Rent-a-Car** (tel. 767-7038, or toll free 800/331-1212); **Budget Car and Truck Rentals** (tel. 577-5194, or toll free 800/527-0700); and **National Car Rental** (tel. 723-8266, or toll free 800/328-4567).

3. WHERE TO STAY

Charleston has many of the best inns in America. The hotels and motels are priced in direct ratio to their proximity to the 789-acre historic district; if prices in the center are too high for your budget, find a place west of the Ashley and drive in to town for sightseeing.

Bed-and-breakfast accommodations range from historic homes to carriage houses to simple cottages, and they're found in virtually every section of the city. For full details and booking, contact: **Historic Charleston Bed and Breakfast,** 43 Legare St., Charleston, SC 29402 (tel. 803/722-6606).

EXPENSIVE

CHARLESTON MARRIOTT, 4770 Marriott Dr., Charleston, SC 29418. Tel. 803/747-1900, or toll free 800/228-9290. Fax 803/744-2530. 294 rms. A/C TV TEL

$ Rates: $115 single or double. AE, CB, DC, DISC, ER, MC, V.
Here's a big name hotel with all the amenities and services you'll appreciate, such as room service, a whirlpool, an indoor/outdoor pool, and a fitness room. True, it lacks the individuality of the charming historic district inns, but it's convenient, upscale, and offers particularly good rates from time to time. I like the parquet floor in the lobby, the fluted columns, and the knotty pine appointments. They serve buffets with themes in the garden-style restaurant. It's off I-26, five miles from the airport, and a 10- to 15-minute drive north of the town center.

JASMINE HOUSE, 64 Hasell St., Charleston, SC 29401. Tel. 803/577-5900, or toll free 800/845-7639. Fax 803/577-0378. 10 rms. A/C TV TEL

$ Rates (including continental breakfast): $110–$135 single; $140–$175 double. AE, DISC, MC, V.
This is a pretty sister act to the Indigo Inn across the street. With less than a dozen rooms, this old mansion is a delight as it has no public rooms and only a private outdoor whirlpool in back. The entrance, which has a high ceiling and a lovely staircase, is where breakfast is served each morning and where wine is offered later in the day. All the guest rooms have fireplaces—but for now they don't work. The ceilings rise 14 feet, and you may find floral drapes and bedspreads, wicker, pineapple four-poster beds, crown molding, and whirlpool tubs.

JOHN RUTLEDGE HOUSE INN, 116 Broad St., Charleston, SC 29401. Tel. 803/723-7999, or toll free 800/476-9741. Fax 803/720-2615. 19 rms and suites. A/C MINIBAR TV TEL

$ Rates (including continental breakfast): $110–$180 single; $110–$200 double. AE, MC, V.

Come to the John Rutledge House in the historic district, off King Street, if you deserve some pampering in a romantic setting. It is my favorite inn in Charleston. When the fathers of the United States Constitution needed an idea man, they went to John Rutledge, and today you can stay in the room where he worked on that historic document. The inn dates to 1762, though the third floor was added in the 1850s. The place exudes Southern hospitality and charm. The private, brick courtyard has wrought-iron pieces and neat landscaping. Your room or suite will either be in the main house or in the carriage house and may have brick floors, striped English fabrics, brass appointments in the bathroom, and a fireplace. In fact, all the rooms in the main house have gas-burning fireplaces that burn 24 hours. There are stocked refrigerators, draped canopy beds, and attentive service. A super continental breakfast is served in your room, or a more complete breakfast may be ordered for a moderate fee. You're in for a treat.

MILLS HOUSE HOTEL, 115 Meeting St., Charleston, SC 29401. Tel. 803/577-2400, or toll free 800/874-9600. Fax 803/722-2112. 214 rms. A/C TV TEL

$ Rates: $105–$150 single; $125–$165 double. Children under 19 stay free with parents. AE, CB, DC, DISC, MC, V. **Parking:** Valet, $8–$9.

The Mills House, between Queen and Broad Streets, was widely heralded as one of the city's finest reconstructions when it opened on the site of an earlier historic hostelry. With its period decor and ambience amid 20th-century amenities, it's a heartening example of how past and present can blend. It's more formal than some inns around here and is affiliated with Holiday Inn. Afternoon tea is served in the landscaped courtyard with a fountain. Take a ride on one of the hotel's bicycles, then relax in the heated courtyard Jacuzzi. There's also a small outdoor pool.

OMNI HOTEL AT CHARLESTON PLACE, 130 Market St., Charleston, SC 29401. Tel. 803/722-4900, or toll free 800/843-6664. Fax 803/722-0728. 450 rms and suites. A/C MINIBAR TV TEL

$ Rates: $180 single, $200 double; $200–$860 suite. AE, DC, MC, V.

Charleston's first world-class hostelry opened late in 1986. Adjoining the Old City Market, between Meeting and King Streets, it mirrors the ambience of its 18th- and 19th-century surroundings. The lobby welcomes you with a pristine expanse of Italian marble; whitewashed Georgian pillars frame a stately double staircase. In guest rooms and suites, period furnishings include four-poster beds, an armoire, and a ceiling fan. The complete health club features a pool, gymnasium, sauna, steam bath, and Jacuzzi. The Palmetto Café and Louis's Charleston Grill offer a taste of regional and historic recipes. The top two floors are the Omni Club, with full concierge service and complimentary cocktails and continental breakfast. The $78-million Charleston Place revitalization, of which the hotel is part, is home to 25 upscale shops, such as Gucci, Godiva, Laura Ashley, and Banana Republic.

MODERATE

ANCHORAGE INN, 26 Vendue Range, Charleston, SC 29401. Tel. 803/723-8300, or toll free 800/421-2952. Fax 803/723-9543. 19 rms. A/C TV TEL

$ Rates (including continental breakfast): $95–$180 single or double. AE, DC, DISC, MC, V.

The Anchorage Inn, one block south of Market Street and five blocks to Battery, is fairly new to the Charleston inn scene but has come aboard to wow its guests. This small inn is intimate and delightful with many thoughtful details. The lobby has beautiful beams and wood, and the staircase is magnificent.

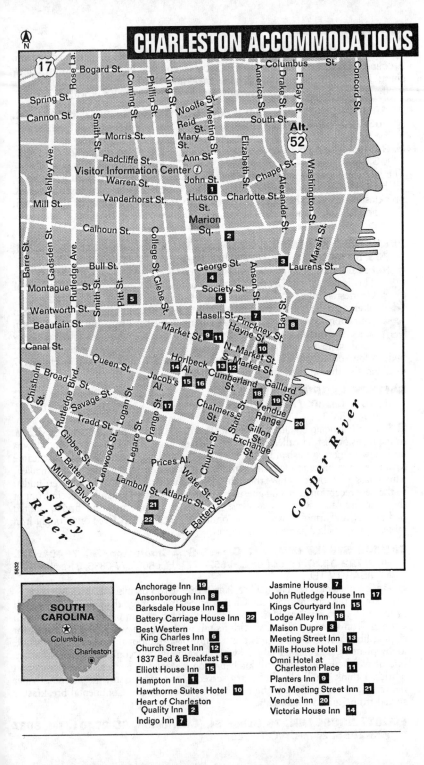

CHARLESTON ACCOMMODATIONS

Anchorage Inn **19**
Ansonborough Inn **8**
Barksdale House Inn **4**
Battery Carriage House Inn **22**
Best Western
  King Charles Inn **6**
Church Street Inn **12**
1837 Bed & Breakfast **5**
Elliott House Inn **15**
Hampton Inn **1**
Hawthorne Suites Hotel **10**
Heart of Charleston
  Quality Inn **2**
Indigo Inn **7**

Jasmine House **7**
John Rutledge House Inn **17**
Kings Courtyard Inn **15**
Lodge Alley Inn **18**
Maison Dupre **3**
Meeting Street Inn **13**
Mills House Hotel **16**
Omni Hotel at
  Charleston Place **11**
Planters Inn **9**
Two Meeting Street Inn **21**
Vendue Inn **20**
Victoria House Inn **14**

SOUTH
CAROLINA
★
Columbia
Charleston

5632

Each room is individually decorated in a style much like an old English coaching inn. A couple of parlor rooms provide nice spots to converse and to get to know fellow guests. Each morning a hot English buffet breakfast is served, and in the afternoon, tea is offered. Free newspapers and nightly turndown service is also provided.

ANSONBOROUGH INN, 21 Hasell St., Charleston, SC 29401. Tel. 803/723-1655, or toll free 800/522-2073. Fax 803/577-6888. 37 suites. A/C TV TEL

$ Rates (including continental breakfast): $90–$150 single or double. AE, DISC, MC, V.

The large and inviting suites have exposed beams, brick walls, sunken living areas, kitchens, and reproduction furnishings. A few rooms have glass-enclosed verandas. Breakfast is served in the lobby, decorated with 18th-century furniture, where you'll also find tea, coffee, and wine. The inn is larger than many in town but is still rather authentic and friendly.

BARKSDALE HOUSE INN, 27 George St., Charleston, SC 29401. Tel. 803/577-4800. Fax 803/853-0482. 10 rms. A/C TV TEL

$ Rates (including continental breakfast): $69–$150 single or double. MC, V.

This is one of my favorites. It's right across from the gym of the College of Charleston and only three blocks from the City Market. Sherry and tea are offered on the back porch, and a bottle of wine or champagne will be waiting in your room every night. There's a fountain in the back yard and a wrought-iron fence surrounding the front yard. Guests love the brass headboards, pretty floral wallpapers, ceiling fans, armoires with TVs, and queen-size four-poster beds. A few rooms have whirlpool tubs, and five have fireplaces. If you have children 7 or older, they too are welcome.

BATTERY CARRIAGE HOUSE INN, 20 S. Battery, Charleston, SC 29401. Tel. 803/727-3100, or toll free 800/775-5575. Fax 803/727-3130. 11 rms. A/C TV TEL

$ Rates (including continental breakfast): $70–$150 single or double. AE, MC, V.

In the mansion district called the Battery, this inn has had a history of ups and downs until new owners, a husband-and-wife team (he's a lawyer and she's an artist) came forward and stabilized its faltering reputation. Changes are still needed here to make it a first-class joint, but they have the right idea. A faux-stone floor and walls were added to the new reception area, and guests may receive afternoon tea and drinks in front of the new fireplace. Rooms may have four-poster beds, hardwood floors, quilted bedspreads, and armoires with TVs. Continental breakfast is served on wrought iron tables in the bricked garden or in rooms.

CHURCH STREET INN, 177 Church St., Charleston, SC 29401. Tel. 803/722-3420, or toll free 800/552-3777. Fax 803/577-0836. 31 suites. A/C MINIBAR TV TEL

$ Rates (including continental breakfast): $89–$185 double. AE, MC, V.

Adjacent to the City Market, the Church Street Inn is more than an inn. It's got all suites and a lovely breakfast room overlooking a fountained courtyard with wrought-iron furniture. The bar with its tall windows is new and is a great spot for sipping libations. The inn blends the warmth of a traditional inn (with brick work, lobby planters, and elegant fabrics) with contemporary accommodations. Suites are one or two bedrooms with full kitchens, some fireplaces, and attractive drapes and fabrics. I think you'll like the sherry served in the afternoons, the morning paper delivered to your room, and the evening turndown service. Continental breakfast is served from 7am to 10am daily.

ELLIOTT HOUSE INN, 78 Queen St., Charleston, SC 29401. Tel. 803/723-1855. 26 rms. A/C TV TEL

$ Rates (including continental breakfast): $89–$130 double. Seasonal packages and senior discounts available. AE, MC, V.

⭐ Come to the Elliott House, between King and Meeting Streets, if you enjoy breakfast on silver service delivered to your room or sipping champagne at sunset in the landscaped courtyard. This stalwart hotel has survived the Civil War, earthquakes, and hurricanes to become one of Charleston's most elegant small inns. The romance-filled inn has just a small lobby with a fireplace but fine rooms with floral fabrics and wide pine floors. They are often furnished with leather wingback chairs and armoires, which hide the TVs. Afternoon tea is also served. Take a ride on one of the hotel's bicycles, then relax in the heated Jacuzzi in the courtyard.

HAWTHORNE SUITES HOTEL, 181 Church St., Charleston, SC 29401. Tel. 803/577-2644, or toll free 800/527-1133. Fax 803/577-2697. 181 rms. A/C TV TEL

$ Rates: $85–$145 single or double. AE, DC, DISC, MC, V.

Ⓢ Now here is a four-story building that was built for today's functional standards and designed to fit into the motif of the City Market area with its granite-like exterior. Delicate yellow florals set off the dining room, where buffet breakfasts are served, and there's a courtyard with potted palms and tables and chairs. Other amenities include an outdoor whirlpool, a fitness room, and a laundry room. Hawthorne Suites is a growing name in the hospitality business and is noteworthy for its two-room suite arrangements featuring bedroom areas, small separate kitchens with two burner stoves, microwave ovens, refrigerators, and coffeemakers. You will also notice the cable TVs in armoires, one king-size or two double beds, and fine baths.

INDIGO INN, 1 Maiden Lane, Charleston, SC 29401. Tel. 803/577-5900 or toll free 800/845-7639. Fax 803/577-0378. 40 rms. A/C MINIBAR TV TEL

$ Rates (including continental breakfast): $70–$115 single; $80–$130 double. AE, MC, V.

I've been coming to the Indigo for more than six years and have never seen it look better. Oriental rugs cover parts of the flagstone floor in the lobby, and you can grab a cup of coffee or tea from the 18th-century sideboard. All the rooms face an interior courtyard where a new fountain sprinkler was added. The rooms have been upgraded with reproduction furniture, and some even have high cannonball four-poster beds. Little extras, such as remote-control TVs and small dressing areas, are helpful. It's at Meeting and Hasell Streets.

KINGS COURTYARD INN, 198 King St., Charleston, SC 29401. Tel. 803/723-7000, or toll free 800/845-6119. Fax 803/720-2608. 44 rms. A/C TV TEL

$ Rates (including continental breakfast): $85–$145 single; $100–$160 double. AE, MC, V.

⭐ The tiny entry to this inn in the historic district is deceiving because it opens inside to a charming brick courtyard with a fountain. The fireplace warms the small lobby, which has a brass chandelier. Besides the main courtyard, two other courts offer fine views from the breakfast room. The owners bought the building next door and blended 10 more rooms into the existing inn. Your room might be fitted with a canopy bed, Oriental rugs over hardwood floors, armoires, silk plants, and even a gas fireplace. Some rooms have refrigerators. Rates include evening chocolates and turndown service.

LODGE ALLEY INN, 195 E. Bay St., Charleston, SC 29401. Tel. 803/722-1611, or toll free 800/845-1004. Fax 803/722-1611, ext. 7777. 93 units. A/C MINIBAR TV TEL

$ Rates: $105–$150 single or double. Discounts available mid-Nov to early Feb. AE, MC, V. **Parking:** Complimentary valet parking.

The Lodge Alley Inn, between Queen and Cumberland Streets, offers fine first-class rooms, 34 of them with fireplaces. There are eight deluxe courtyard units and some larger suites with two bedrooms. All are decorated with period reproduction furnishings, pine floors, Windsor desks, butler's tables, and Oriental carpets. You'll find your refrigerator stocked with refreshments. The French Quarter, one of Charleston's most imaginative dining rooms, features a grand rotisserie where the chef prepares roast squab, saddle of lamb, and other house specialties. A la carte entrées are in the $13-to-$25 range. The Charleston Tea Party Lounge, with its ornate bar, is a favorite local watering spot.

MAISON DUPRE, 317 E. Bay St., Charleston, SC 29401. Tel. 803/723-8691, or toll free 800/844-4667. 15 rms. A/C TV TEL

$ Rates (including continental breakfast): $90–$150 single or double. AE, MC, V.

The Maison Dupre, a 10-minute walk from the City Market, at St. George Street, has been featured in country inn magazines because it is so photogenic. A French tailor built the annexes of the main house in 1803, while the original inn is Federal-style. Guests come through an electronically-controlled gate to a lovely courtyard. Reception is in the former kitchen where two fireplaces burn. In fact, all the public rooms have fireplaces. The paintings by the owner's wife are somewhat distracting and appear out of focus with the rest of the inn. Some of the rooms have queen-size canopied beds, and most have Oriental rugs over wood floors. There is a beautiful sleigh bed in the honeymoon suite. Newspapers are delivered to rooms each morning, and chocolates are left at night with the turndown service. Continental breakfast is served every morning in the dining room.

MEETING STREET INN, 173 Meeting St., Charleston, SC 29401. Tel. 803/723-1882, or toll free 800/842-8022. Fax 803/577-0851. 54 rms. A/C TV TEL

$ Rates (including continental breakfast): $89–$139 single or double. AE, DISC, MC, V.

I can picture Michael Feinstein singing "Isn't It Romantic" whenever I walk through the courtyard here at night with its enticing lighting and the swirl of the outdoor whirlpool in the background. I've also enjoyed sipping a cool, summer drink at one of the wrought-iron tables. The interesting West Indies–like architecture bathed in pink stucco was artfully restored from the original 1870 days, when this was first constructed as a hotel. You won't even mind not having a restaurant, since so many special ones are within walking distance. The rooms are a mixture of traditional hotel appointments and reproductions, with some four-poster beds, armoires, wood shutters, and standard baths.

PLANTERS INN, Market at Meeting St., Charleston, SC 29401. Tel. 803/722-2345, or toll free 800/845-7082. Fax 803/577-2125. 36 rms, 5 suites. A/C TV TEL

$ Rates (including continental breakfast): $110–$125 single; $125–$140 double; $150–$165 suite. Lower rates available Dec–Feb and mid-June to mid-Sept. AE, DC, MC, V.

Years ago, Planters Inn enjoyed a grand reputation, but in the last few years, it has not been well maintained. When I visited, the wine and cheese display in the otherwise inviting parlor/reception area was lackluster. I didn't like the prominent price tags on the artwork either. Newspapers are provided in the morning and chocolates are left on your pillow at bedtime. This is no longer one of my top choices, but if you're in a pinch, you might stay here for the good location.

TWO MEETING STREET INN, 2 Meeting St., Charleston, SC 29401. Tel. 803/723-7322. 9 rms. A/C TV

$ Rates (including continental breakfast): $95–$155 double. No credit cards.

The two large porches of this gingerbread-style home provide views of the Battery. I find the fireplace, stained glass, and hardwood floors on the first floor as beautiful as the baby grand piano. The silver service is set out for afternoon tea. You might take breakfast at one of the small tables in the garden, on the porch, or in the splendid dining room. A refrigerator is located on each floor for use by everyone. All the rooms have fireplaces and Queen Anne Victorian appointments. Many rooms have four-poster canopy beds. One room even has a sunny balcony. Smoking is permitted on the porch outside, and children over 8 are welcome. Checks are accepted. The City Market is a 10-minute walk away.

VENDUE INN, 19 Vendue Range, Charleston, SC 29401. Tel. 803/577-7970, or toll free 800/845-7900. Fax 803/722-8381. 33 rms. TV TEL

$ Rates (including continental breakfast): $80–$135 single; $95–$145 double; $135–$220 suite for two. AE, DISC, MC, V.

The restaurant at the Vendue Inn is as well known as the inn itself. It's open for dinner only, but the same room is where the inn guests are served breakfast. When weather permits, drinks are taken on the roof with its panorama of the historic district. Complimentary sherry is served in the parlor room in the evenings. A few rooms have separate sitting rooms with wet bars and sofabeds. All the rooms have fine reproduction or authentic furniture, armoires, bed ruffles, and plenty of pillows, but the plumbing in the bathrooms must have been installed during the Nixon administration.

VICTORIA HOUSE INN, 208 King St., Charleston, SC 29401. Tel. 803/720-2944, or toll free 800/933-5464. Fax 803/720-2930. 16 rms. A/C MINIBAR TV TEL

$ Rates (including continental breakfast): $85–$125 single; $95–$140 double. MC, V.

You'd never think this inn was once a YMCA, but it was. And leave it to the owners of the John Rutledge House to make this a welcome addition to the inn crowd. The lobby is small and cheerful with ornamental detail work and a fireplace. Antique shops are out front on the ground level. There is an elevator, in case you're too tired to climb the stairs. Rooms have a country-inn decor with antique colors, wood shutters, king-size or double beds, high ceilings, and wallpapered bathrooms. If you can't afford the John Rutledge House, try this middle-priced alternative in the historic district.

BUDGET

BEST WESTERN KING CHARLES INN, 237 Meeting St., Charleston, SC 29401. Tel. 803/723-7451, or toll free 800/528-1234. Fax 803/723-2041. 91 rms. A/C TV TEL

$ Rates: $50–$130 single or double. Children under 18 stay free with parents; no charge for crib. AE, DC, DISC, MC, V.

One block from the historic district's market area, between Wentworth and Society Streets, this hotel has a small colonial-inspired restaurant where breakfast is served, a small pool, and a friendly staff. Rooms are better than you might expect from a motel. Some rooms have balconies, but views are limited. It's a good value and convenient to everything.

1837 BED AND BREAKFAST, 126 Wentworth St., Charleston, SC 29401. Tel. 803/723-7166. 8 rms. A/C TV

$ Rates (including full breakfast): $55–$95 single or double. AE, MC, V.

The design of the 1837 Bed and Breakfast is called a single house, because it is only a single-room wide—which makes for some interesting room arrangements. The porches are sloped, so water will run off easily. On one of the verandas you can sit under whirling ceiling fans and enjoy your breakfast or afternoon tea. The simple living room has a fireplace, while the so-called breakfast room is really part of the kitchen. My favorite room is number two in the Carriage House, which has authentic designs, exposed brick walls, a warm decor, a beamed ceiling, and three windows. All the rooms have separate entrances because of the layout. Three blocks off King Street, this is unpretentious and ideal for those who don't require too much creature comfort or historic significance in their accommodations. Rooms have refrigerators.

HAMPTON INN, 345 Meeting St., Charleston, SC 29401. Tel. 803/723-4000, or toll free 800/426-7866. Fax 803/722-3725. 171 rms. A/C TV TEL
$ Rates (including continental breakfast): $49–$69 single; $55–$75 double. AE, CB, DC, DISC, MC, V.

A 10-minute walk from the City Market, this is a wonderful new addition to the hotel scene in Charleston. Situated opposite the visitors' center (where many tours depart), it has some of the familiar Hampton Inn designs and features along with reproduction appointments. The colonial lobby is filled with natural woods and Oriental rugs. The fireplace is a warm addition, and coffee and tea are always available. You won't find much in the way of views here, but there is a fine outdoor pool with a pleasant deck, an exercise room, and ample parking. The accommodations are attractive with pretty florals and modern baths. This is a terrific offering for a great price. The value is excellent.

HEART OF CHARLESTON QUALITY INN, 125 Calhoun St., Charleston, SC 29401. Tel. 803/722-3391. 126 rms. A/C TV TEL
$ Rates: $45–$74 single; $45–$84 double. Senior discounts available. AE, DC, MC, V. **Parking:** Free.

Some rooms at this high-quality, conveniently located inn, at Calhoun and Meeting Streets, have balconies, and some have refrigerators. All are nicely decorated and comfortably furnished. The restaurant serves all three meals, with dinner entrées running a moderate $8 to $15. They have a courtesy van for local transportation.

NEARBY

MODERATE

HOLIDAY INN—RIVERVIEW, 301 Savannah Hwy. (U.S. 17), Charleston, SC 29407. Tel. 803/556-7100. Fax 803/556-6176. 181 rms. A/C TV TEL
$ Rates: $69–$76 single; $77–$84 double. Children under 19 stay free with parents. Senior discounts available. AE, DC, DISC, MC, V.
This circular 13-story hotel overlooks the Ashley River and the city on the opposite bank. It's just two miles from the center of town. Rooms have balconies. There's a pool, a rooftop dining room that serves all meals, and a lounge that features entertainment and dancing. Some rooms have been fitted for the handicapped.

RESIDENCE INN BY MARRIOTT, 7645 Northwoods Blvd., North Charleston, SC 29418. Tel. 803/572-5757, or toll free 800/331-3131. 96 suites. A/C TV TEL **Directions:** Exit 209 from I-26 at Ashley-Phosphate Road.
$ Rates (including continental breakfast): $90 single or double; $120 penthouse suite for two. Senior discounts available. AE, CB, DC, DISC, MC, V.

See "Where to Stay and Dine," in Chapter 1, for a recommendation of this attractive chain. Spacious studio rooms and two-story, two-bedroom penthouse suites are designed to create a "home away from home" ambience. All have full kitchen, and most have a fireplace. There's a small heated pool, a whirlpool, and a sports court, as well as a coin laundry on the wheelchair-accessible premises. They can also provide airport transportation.

BUDGET

ECONO LODGE, 2237 Savannah Hwy. (U.S. 17), Charleston, SC 29407. Tel. 803/571-1880. Fax 803/766-9351. 48 rms. A/C TV TEL
$ Rates: $32–$35 single; $35–$45 double. AE, DC, MC, V.
This hotel offers budget prices and a location close to Magnolia and Middleton Gardens and Charles Towne Landing. Several golf courses are also in the vicinity. There is no pool and no restaurant, but Perkins Pancake House is just down the road. Rooms are more than adequate, and rates are certainly a good value. It's just west of the Cooper River Bridge.

LA QUINTA MOTOR INN, 2499 La Quinta Lane, North Charleston, SC 29405. Tel. 803/797-8181. 122 rms. A/C TV TEL **Directions:** Take I-26 North to Ashley Phosphate Road (exit 209).
$ Rates (including continental breakfast): $42 single; $48 double. Children under 18 stay free with parents; cribs free. AE, DC, DISC, MC, V.
This is conveniently located near the new Charleston International Airport. You can call the inn direct from the airport baggage-claim area for free shuttle service to the hotel. Rooms in this clean, comfortable, well-run chain establishment are attractively furnished, and beds are extra-long. No-smoking rooms are available, and pets are welcome. There's also a pool. Shoney's restaurant next door will provide room service from 6am to 11pm

CAMPING

The **Charleston KOA** (Ladson, SC 29456; tel. 803/797-1045) is about 15 miles northwest of town on U.S. 78, one mile west of the junction with I-26. There are shaded, level sites, disposal station, laundry, store, propane gas, pool, recreation room, and playground. Sightseeing tours depart the campgrounds daily. You'll need to send a deposit to hold your reservation. Rates are $15 and up.

4. WHERE TO DINE

Little doubt Charleston has some of the best dining in America. The Southern way of cooking is an art form in Charleston, and you won't be disappointed with it. The only problem you'll have is deciding where to go. You'll see from my extensive list that I'm partial to fun spots, casual eateries, and restaurants where you can soak up as much atmosphere as calories. For more listings, pick up the "Official Dining Guide" from the visitors' center.

EXPENSIVE

JOHNNY'S SEAFOOD MARKET, 85 S. Market St. Tel. 722-5877.
Cuisine: SEAFOOD. **Reservations:** Recommended.
$ Prices: Appetizers $5–$7; main courses $13.50–$24.95; dinner for two from $35. AE, MC, V.
Open: Lunch Mon–Sat 11:30am–2:30pm; dinner Sun–Thurs 5:30–10pm, Fri–Sat 5:30–10:30pm. **Closed:** Sun in winter.
This casual place fills up fast so you might plan ahead to eat here. The bar is rather funky, with a plum and teal decor. Some of the restaurant's walls are painted brick.

Specialties on the largely seafood menu include pan-fried crabcakes, a seafood platter, and Norwegian salmon.

ROBERT'S OF CHARLESTON, 112 N. Market St. Tel. 577-7565, or toll free 800/729-0094.
   Cuisine: SOUTHERN. **Reservations:** Required, two weeks in advance for Fri–Sat in spring and fall.
$ Prices: Fixed-price dinner $70. AE, MC, V.
   Open: Dinner Tues–Sat 8pm seating.

For some time Robert's, in the Planters Inn, has enjoyed a fine reputation. The six-course dinner is always a masterpiece of perfection and includes scallop mousse, a seasonal salad, a poultry or game course, an intermezzo, an entrée of grilled tenderloin of beef, and dessert. A pianist provides a soothing backdrop to conversation. Robert or one of his vocalists introduces each course with songs from Broadway shows. The price includes dinner, wine, tax, and gratuities.

MODERATE

THE BAKER'S CAFE, 214 King St. Tel. 577-2694.
   Cuisine: CAFE. **Reservations:** Not required.
$ Prices: Main courses $6.25–$7.95. DC, MC, V.
   Open: Mon–Fri 8am–3pm, Sat–Sun 9am–3pm.

The menu selection at the Baker's Café is more complete than you'll find in a coffee shop. The rose-colored walls, ceiling fans, track lighting, local art, wood slatted chairs, and plum/brown tables create a cozy ambience. Egg dishes are wonderful, including eggs Florentine, eggs Copenhagen, and the local favorite—two poached eggs on a bed of Canadian snowcrab, Hollandaise, and rusks. Simple selections include croissants, muffins, Danish pastries, and scones. Sandwiches are also served. Brunch is popular on weekends.

BARBADOES ROOM, in the Mills House Hotel, 115 Meeting St. Tel. 577-2400.
   Cuisine: SEAFOOD/LOW COUNTRY. **Reservations:** Recommended for brunch and dinner.
$ Prices: Appetizers $4–$8; main courses $5.95–$10.95 at lunch, $11–$17 at dinner; Sun brunch $14.94. Children's menu under $8. AE, CB, DC, DISC, MC, V.
   Open: Breakfast and lunch daily 6:30am–2pm; dinner daily 5:30–10pm. Bar daily 11am–2am.

Specialties include filet mignon and shrimp andouille. Don't miss the famous Mills House mud pie—mocha ice cream in a chocolate-cookie crust, topped with fudge, whipped cream, and pecans. The lunch menu lists sandwiches, omelets, and seafood. Sunday brunch is a Charleston institution.

BLUE COYOTE GRILLE, 61 State St. Tel. 577-2583.
   Cuisine: AMERICAN/SOUTHWEST. **Reservations:** Not required.
$ Prices: Appetizers $2.50–$6.50; main courses $5.25–$14. AE, DC, DISC, MC, V.
   Open: Daily 11:30am–10 or 11pm.

You'll love this brand new eatery with a Southwest decor and Native American artifacts. Salsa and desserts are made fresh daily. Try the Tex-Mex specialties, fajitas, burgers, or sandwiches. You'll also find a full bar here.

COLONY HOUSE, 35 Prioleau St. Tel. 723-3424.
   Cuisine: AMERICAN/SEAFOOD. **Reservations:** Not required.
$ Prices: Appetizers $4–$6; main courses $12.50–$16.95. AE, DC, DISC, MC, V.
   Open: Lunch Mon–Fri 11:30am–2pm, Sat 11:30–3pm; dinner daily 5:30–10 or 11pm; Sun brunch 11am–2pm.

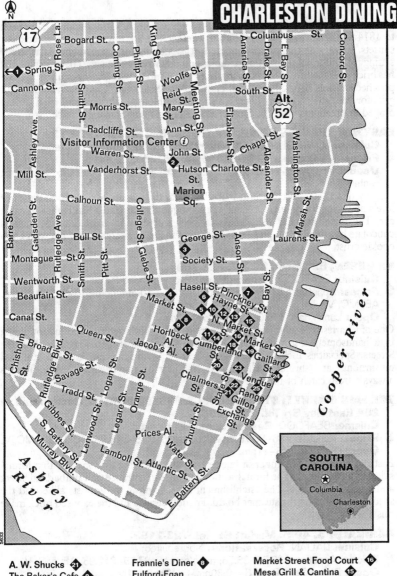

CHARLESTON DINING

A. W. Shucks ⬥21
The Baker's Cafe ⬥9
Barbadoes Room ⬥17
Blue Coyote Grille ⬥18
Bookstore Cafe ⬥2
Cafe Rainbow ⬥3
Colony House ⬥25
East Bay
   Trading Company ⬥22
82 Queen ⬥20
The Fish Market: Steam
   Room & Oyster Bar ⬥19

Frannie's Diner ⬥8
Fulford-Egan
   Coffees & Teas ⬥6
Garibaldi's ⬥16
Johnny Rockets ⬥16
Johnny's
   Seafood Market ⬥14
Kaminsky's
   Most Excellent Cafe ⬥12
Magnolia's ⬥23
Marina Variety Store ⬥1

Market Street Food Court ⬥16
Mesa Grill & Cantina ⬥15
Mistral ⬥11
Moultrie Tavern ⬥24
Olde Towne Restaurant ⬥4
Pinckney Cafe and Espresso ⬥7
Reuben's
   Downtown Delicatessen ⬥5
Robert's of Charleston ⬥10
Swensen's Cafe ⬥16
Wild Wing Cafe ⬥13

Situated in a former coffee warehouse at the waterfront park, this building dates back to 1814 and features a bar on the roof where guests are rewarded with spectacular sunsets. If you don't come for dinner, at least stop by for a sundowner. The inside setting is semiformal with intimate tables and fancy place settings. The adjoining bar has brickwork, ceiling fans, and a fireplace. The menu changes daily but might include poached mussels or fried soft-shell crabs for appetizers and Charleston shrimp and grits for your main course. There's also Colony House crabcakes and fried shrimp dipped in bread crumbs. The Sunday brunch features an à la carte price list.

EAST BAY TRADING COMPANY, 161 E. Bay St. Tel. 722-0722.
Cuisine: LOW COUNTRY/CONTINENTAL. **Reservations:** Not required.
$ Prices: Main courses $9.50–$16.95. AE, MC, V.
Open: Dinner Mon–Thurs 5:30–10:30pm, Fri–Sun 5:30–11pm. **Closed:** Sun in winter.

Stop by this 1880s warehouse to marvel at what the owners have done to the three levels now used for dining. On hand is an antique elevator and a San Francisco cable car. The menu includes seafood items, beef entrées, and great desserts, such as chocolate bourbon pecan pie, Cooper River mud pie, or peanut butter pie with Oreo cookie crust.

82 QUEEN, 82 Queen St. Tel. 723-7591.
Cuisine: SEAFOOD. **Reservations:** Recommended for dinner.
$ Prices: Appetizers $4–$6; main courses $5–$10 at lunch, $10–$19 at dinner. AE, MC, V.
Open: Lunch daily 11:30am–3pm; dinner daily 6–10pm.

One of Charleston's most popular restaurants offers both outdoor and indoor dining in a handsomely restored 19th-century town house, between King and Meeting Streets. Specialties include Carolina crabcakes; Daufuskie crab; sautéed veal and mushrooms; and shrimp, scallops, and crabmeat over spinach fettuccine. There's always a fresh catch of the day.

THE FISH MARKET: STEAM ROOM & OYSTER BAR, 12 Cumberland at 204 East Bay St. Tel. 723-1600.
Cuisine: SEAFOOD. **Reservations:** Not required.
$ Prices: Appetizers $3–$8.75; main courses $10.75–$16.95. DC, DISC, MC, V.
Open: Dinner daily 5–11pm.

East Bay Street has a number of fine restaurants, including this one—with a formal side and a casual side. The formal section has its own entrance on Cumberland Street and is more expensive. The establishment attracts locals and tourists alike, and the specials are listed on the steamer board. Friendly service and the exposed brick make this a winning setting.

GARIBALDI'S, 49 S. Market St. Tel. 723-7153.
Cuisine: ITALIAN. **Reservations:** Not required.
$ Prices: Appetizers $2.75–$5.75; main courses $7.75–$12.95. AE, MC, V.
Open: Dinner Sun–Thurs 6–10:30pm, Fri–Sat 6–11pm.

Garibaldi's is a successful Italian dining choice that also has branches in Columbia, S.C., and Savannah, Ga. The inside is decorated with wicker pieces, ladderback chairs, track lights, ceiling fans, and Italian memorabilia. You might start your meal with a salmon appetizer and continue with a pasta selection. The seafood specials are good, too, including the dolphin, stuffed grouper, and blackened tuna.

MAGNOLIA'S, 185 E. Bay St. Tel. 577-7771.
Cuisine: REGIONAL/NEW AMERICAN. **Reservations:** Recommended.
$ Prices: Appetizers and salads $4–$7; sandwiches $5.25–$7; main courses $7.25–$14.50.
Open: Daily 11:30am–11pm; bar 11:30am–midnight.

★ At a glance, you might think this immensely popular spot is an expensive, sophisticated establishment in New York. Well come inside for a taste of Southern hospitality and Southern charm. The service is as warm as the decor is trendy. Be sure to notice all the magnolia details used in the decor. At lunch, Magnolia's is filled with local office workers and museum-goers—all handsomely and attractively dressed. Sip a colorful drink with an umbrella in it at the bar while awaiting your table. I could go on and on about the food, but you might look twice at the crab stuffed pasilla pepper with yellow corn, tomato, and scallion salsa for an appetizer, and the grilled dolphin or the pork loin for an entrée. Be sure to leave room for dessert; in fact, if you can't get here for lunch or dinner, at least stop by for dessert. You might try banana cream pie with meringue, chocolate truffles with bourbon sauce, or mango tart tatin served warm with chantilly cream and orange custard sauce. Or, for something orgasmic, try the warm cream-cheese brownie with white-chocolate ice cream and chocolate sauce.

MARKET STREET FOOD COURT, S. Market and Church Sts.
Cuisine: VARIED.
$ Prices: $1.50–$6.
Open: Daily 8am–5pm.

Almost a dozen little establishments are contained in the food court area of the City Market. Some begin their day by serving breakfast, but most make their money at lunch, serving both the business community and tourists. The decor is inexpensive—mostly brick with canvas flags and cheap multicolored chairs. You can purchase Chinese, Japanese, Italian, Pizza, Greek, or American fare, in addition to subs, sandwiches, and cookies. Swensen's Ice Cream is here too.

MESA GRILL & CANTINA, 32½ N. Market St. Tel. 723-3770.
Cuisine: SOUTHWESTERN. **Reservations:** Not required.
$ Prices: Appetizers $3.50–$7.95; soups $5.95–$6.75; main courses $5.50–$14. AE, CB, DC, DISC, MC, V.
Open: Sun–Thurs 11am–midnight, Fri–Sat 11am–2am.

★ Who'd have thought that this Seaman's chapel with pastel-colored stained glass would ever become a Southwest restaurant? Seems like a perfect blending. The new owners have pulled the same colors used in the stained glass into the body of the restaurant, added a cactus here and there, some terra-cotta pots, and voilà—a neat new dining spot. Besides the main church, there is a courtyard for al fresco dining. The place was just getting started when I stopped in, but the potential is here, the service attentive, and the specialties tempting. The menu includes burgers, sandwiches, fajitas, or baby back ribs.

MISTRAL, 99 S. Market St. Tel. 722-5708.
Cuisine: FRENCH. **Reservations:** Recommended.
$ Prices: Appetizers $3.25–$6.95; dinner for two $30. AE, CB, DC, DISC, MC, V.
Open: Lunch Mon–Sat 11am–5pm; dinner Mon–Thurs 5–10pm, Fri–Sat 5pm–midnight.

Come to Mistral to add a bit of formality to your dining. The atmosphere is jazzy and sophisticated. In fact, you're likely to find jazz played on weekends between 9pm and midnight. On the menu are Caesar salad, crabcakes, and grilled swordfish.

MOULTRIE TAVERN, 18 Vendue Range Tel. 723-1862.
Cuisine: AMERICAN. **Reservations:** Not required.
$ Prices: Appetizers $2.62–$4.62; main courses $9.62–$17.62. AE, DC, DISC, MC, V.
Open: Lunch daily 11:30am–4pm; dinner daily 5:30–10pm.

Named after Gen. William Moultrie, a delegate to the Continental Congress of 1775, this authentic restaurant and tavern is filled with atmosphere to evoke the

American Revolution era. In addition to the small window panes, candlelight, ladderback chairs, and beamed ceiling, there are American Revolution appointments and artifacts, a British flag, and a lit fireplace. The building dates back to 1862 (that's why all the prices end in 62). To start, sample the boiled shrimp, then move on to the duck, quail, rabbit, lamb, chicken, or beef dishes.

OLDE TOWNE RESTAURANT, 229 King St. Tel. 723-8170.

Cuisine: GREEK/AMERICAN. **Reservations:** Not required.
$ Prices: Dinner for two $25. AE, DC, DISC, MC, V.
Open: Mon–Thurs 11am–10:30pm, Fri–Sat 11am–11pm, Sun 11am–10pm.

This moderately priced establishment features pork-kebobs, beef-kebobs, Greek hamburgers, steaks with Greek potatoes, soups, and salads. Its location, in the shadow of the Omni, makes it very popular, and the atmosphere is casual. The decor includes wood paneling and burgundy vinyl booths with an open kitchen. Chicken and pork spin on the rotisserie.

PINCKNEY CAFE AND ESPRESSO, 18 Pinckney St. (at Motley Lane). Tel. 577-0961.

Cuisine: AMERICAN/CAFE. **Reservations:** Not required.
$ Prices: Main courses $7.99–$12.99; sandwiches $5.95; dinner for two $25. No credit cards.
Open: Lunch Tues–Thurs 11:30am–3pm, Fri–Sat 11:30am–2:30pm; dinner Tues–Sat 6–10pm.

Now here is a fun spot. Located two blocks north of the City Market, it's casual, warm, and inviting. Picture an old home turned coffeehouse and restaurant. You'll find wide hardwood floors, comfortable slatted chairs, a fireplace, and a porch with ceiling fans for outdoor dining. The crowd is rather yuppie-ish. On the menu (written on a blackboard brought to your table) will be a creamy lemon broccoli soup with rosemary and thyme, sandwiches, omelets, and main courses. Specials may include a spinach quesadilla with seasoned spinach, and jack and feta cheese, all stuffed in a crisp flour tortilla and served with sour cream and salsa; turkey marsala; salmon cakes served with a shallot and dill cream sauce and stone ground grits; or Pinckney's pasta made with homemade cheese tortellini with shrimp and scallops in a tomato and scallion cream sauce. On the lighter side are specialty coffees ($1.50 to $2), including the Café Market Street, which is espresso with cocoa, sugar, cinnamon, nutmeg cream, and whipped cream; and the cappucino float. Wine and beer are available.

SWENSEN'S CAFE, 57 S. Market St. Tel. 722-1411.

Cuisine: AMERICAN/ICE CREAM. **Reservations:** Not accepted.
$ Prices: Salads $6.25; burgers $4.85–$5.45. No credit cards.
Open: Sun–Thurs 10:30am–11pm, Fri–Sat 10:30am–1am.

Anyone who's been to a Swensen's will recognize the familiar touches here, but it has a few changes perfect for Charleston—like the outdoor dining terrace that adjoins the plaza and fountain area. Inside are brick walls, Tiffany lamps, ice cream–parlor chairs, and marble tables. Beer and wine are now being served. Everyone comes here for a cold libation or ice cream favorite—there's a whole menu just for desserts. The deli selection is pretty good too.

WILD WING CAFE, 36 N. Market St. Tel. 722-WING.

Cuisine: AMERICAN/CAFE. **Reservations:** Not required.
$ Prices: Appetizers $1.95–$3.50; salads $5.95; 24 wings $8.25. AE, MC, V.
Open: Mon–Sat 11am–midnight, Sun noon–midnight.

Most locals can direct you to the Wild Wing—that's "Wild Wing" not "Wild Thing," though if you've been here when it's busy, you might imagine it's the latter. The bar is busy, really busy. The atmosphere is casual and the food great.

These are the basics—hot wings and cold beer. They also offer chicken quesadillas and salads, but folks come here for the hot and spicy wings. Your fingers will be sticky but tasty, but don't worry, the napkins are big terrycloth numbers. Come by and try it.

BUDGET

A. W. SHUCKS, 70 State St. Tel. 723-1151.
Cuisine: SEAFOOD. **Reservations:** Not required.
$ Prices: Lunch under $10, dinner $10–$15. AE, DC, DISC, MC, V.
Open: Restaurant daily 11am–10pm. Bar daily 11am–midnight.

In addition to its delectable low-country seafood dishes, A. W. Shucks specializes in steamed and raw oysters, steamed mussels, and clams. They also have a good selection of salads. The restaurant is located in the State Street Market.

BOOKSTORE CAFE, 412 King (at Hutson St.). Tel. 720-8843.
Cuisine: CAFE. **Reservations:** Not accepted.
$ Prices: Menu items $2.50–$4.95. No credit cards.
Open: Mon–Fri 7:30am–2:30pm, Sat–Sun 9am–2pm.

The Bookstore Café doesn't have a big selection of books, but it's fun anyway. The wallpaper looks like bookshelves, and the baskets, ceiling fans, and wood tables and chairs all make the artsy decor work. You'll find weekend specials on the blackboard. On hand will be potato casseroles with chili, cheddar, peppers, green onion, and sour cream, or maybe Kiawah sausage, gravy, onions, peppers, and cheddar served with two eggs on top and your choice of bread. The French toast is made with French bread. Three-egg omelets may come with poached salmon, ham and cheddar, or vegetarian ingredients. The basic eggs and grits with toast costs $2.50.

CAFE RAINBOW, 282 King St. Tel. 853-9777.
Cuisine: COFFEEHOUSE. **Reservations:** Not required.
$ Prices: Menu items 94¢–$3.99. AE, DISC, MC, V.
Open: Mon–Thurs 7am–11pm, Fri 7am–midnight, Sat 8am–midnight, Sun 10am–10pm.

What I enjoy most about Café Rainbow is its casual ambience and cheerful flavor—in both decor and menu. People are always playing chess on the large board in the front window, while others sit on sacks of coffee beans and watch. The crowd is rather granola-ish. The menu is light and flavorful with a soup of the day, a quiche, croissants with jam, homemade Belgian waffles with berries and nuts, muffins, and cookies. Or you can come just for coffee, caffè mocha, hot cocoa, or iced mochaccino.

FRANNIE'S DINER, 137 Market St. Tel. 723-7121.
Cuisine: DINER. **Reservations:** Not required.
$ Prices: Menu items 95¢–$6.95. DISC, MC, V.
Open: 24 hours.

Step back to the 1950s at Frannie's Diner, where you can order breakfast all day. The decor is right out of the old diner days—red, white, and black with chrome-trimmed red booths, pink and blue neon, 1950s photos, and a jukebox with "Happy Days" favorites. On the menu is French toast, blueberry pancakes, sausage and gravy with biscuits, and a number of sandwich standards, such as chicken breast with lettuce and tomato. Save room for a brownie with ice cream. Wine and beer are also available.

FULFORD-EGAN COFFEES & TEAS, 231 Meeting St. Tel. 577-4553.
Cuisine: COFFEEHOUSE. **Reservations:** Not required.
$ Prices: Soups $2.50; sandwiches $4.50–$4.95; quiche $4.50. MC, V.

Open: Daily 7am–midnight.

Fulford-Egan is not only a coffeehouse, but it's also an entertainment spot—many an evening you'll hear blues upstairs starting at 9pm. The cover charge might be $4 to $6, but the jazz is moving and sophisticated. Downstairs the aroma of the open coffee bags beckons folks off the street. Come in and sit at a table for two amid the exposed brick and coffee collectibles. There's a choice of 30 coffee blends and almost as many teas. Check out the mocha cappuccino, Kona cappuccino, or café au lait. On the munchie board are bagels, scones, and cinnamon toast. The delicious cakes and pies are a bit pricey at $3.95 a slice. Milkshakes and floats cost $3.50. The bar upstairs stays open later than midnight, usually as long as the crowd lasts.

JOHNNY ROCKETS, 41 S. Market St. (at State St.). Tel. 723-1700.
Cuisine: AMERICAN DINER. **Reservations:** Not accepted.
$ **Prices:** Menu items $3.50–$5.50.
Open: Mon–Thurs 11am–11pm, Fri–Sun 11am–2am.

One of my favorite places to go on Melrose Avenue in Los Angeles has opened a spot here in the historic district of Charleston. Johnny Rockets has earned the respect of diner fans and those who love a good time. The service is fun and attentive—you'll be charmed by the singing staff. It's super clean, and the food includes hamburgers, cheeseburgers, great fries, Cokes, root beer, pie, and ice cream. It's a part of our past that's a blast!

KAMINSKY'S MOST EXCELLENT CAFE, 78 N. Market St. Tel. 853-8270.
Cuisine: COFFEEHOUSE/WINE BAR. **Reservations:** Not accepted.
$ **Prices:** Specialty coffees and teas $1.95–$2.25; desserts $3.50–$4.25. AE, MC, V.
Open: Mon–Thurs 3pm–2am, Fri 2pm–2am, Sat–Sun noon–2am.

Following a morning of hearty sightseeing or diligent shopping, Kaminsky's is a perfect spot for resting your feet. The handsome bar, where a wide selection of wines is served, is out of the traffic flow and is a good spot for people-watching. The decor is relaxing and a bit granola-ish, in the nicest way. The desserts are delightfully sinful—the Italian cream cake or mountain chocolate cake might catch your fancy. This is just the power boost you need to make it through the afternoon.

MARINA VARIETY STORE, 17 Lockwood Blvd. Tel. 723-6325.
Cuisine: SEAFOOD/LOW COUNTRY. **Reservations:** Not accepted.
$ **Prices:** Appetizers $1.50–$3; main courses $4–$8. AE, MC, V.
Open: Daily 6am–9:30pm.

You can feed the entire family here without doing serious injury to your pocketbook. The restaurant occupies one side of a store that sells fishing supplies and souvenirs and overlooks the yacht basin. You can enjoy okra soup (it's delicious!) or chili, a variety of sandwiches, or fried fish dinners, all at budget prices. Breakfast is served to 11am: two eggs, bacon or sausage, toast, and grits cost about $4. Picture windows frame the comings and goings of all sorts of boats—I once saw a Chinese junk sail past. Orders are placed at the counter, and waitresses bring the food to comfortable booths. There's a relaxed atmosphere that I, for one, thoroughly enjoyed. Mike Altine, Jr., manager and son of the owner, tells me that the store has been serving locals and boat owners who put in to the adjacent dock for more than 25 years. It's on the Ashley River next to the municipal marina.

REUBEN'S DOWNTOWN DELICATESSEN, 251 Meeting St. Tel. 722-6883.
Cuisine: DELI. **Reservations:** Not accepted.

$ Prices: Menu items $5–$10. No credit cards.
   Open: Mon–Sat 9am–4pm, later in summer.
This New York–style deli is often packed at lunch with locals who come for the hearty sandwiches, salads, and other deli specialties. Homemade soups are a standout. It's at Meeting and Broad Streets.

5. WHAT TO SEE & DO

SUGGESTED ITINERARIES

IF YOU HAVE ONE DAY Don't stir outside the historic and downtown districts: spend the day visiting the historic homes and buildings there.

IF YOU HAVE TWO DAYS Devote **Day One** to the historic and downtown districts. On **Day Two,** choose between heading east across the Cooper River to Patriot's Point, Fort Moultrie, and Boone Hall Plantation, or turning west across the Ashley River to Charles Towne Landing, Middleton Place, Magnolia Gardens, and Drayton Hall.

IF YOU HAVE THREE DAYS Spend **Day One** as above. On **Days Two and Three,** explore the sights east of the Cooper River and west of the Ashley River (see above).

IF YOU HAVE FIVE DAYS OR MORE Spend **Days One through Three** as above. On **Day Four,** drive to Beaufort (see Chapter 7) and stay overnight. **Day Five,** drive to Hilton Head and stay at the beach as long as time permits.

THE TOP ATTRACTIONS

I always head for the **Battery** (if you want to be official about it, the **White Point Gardens**) to get back into the feel of this city. It's right on the end of the peninsula, facing the Cooper River and the harbor. There's a lovely park, shaded by palmettos and live oak and filled with walkways lined with old monuments and other war relics. The view toward the harbor looks out to Fort Sumter. I like to walk along the sea wall on East Battery and Murray Boulevard and sink slowly into the history of Charleston. You might venture into the neighborhood to see the architecture.

HISTORIC HOMES

EDMONDSTON-ALSTON HOUSE, 21 East Battery. Tel. 722-7171, or 556-6020.
   Built in 1828 as the home of a wealthy merchant, the house was later bought by a Colonel Alston, whose son redid it in the Greek Revival style. Overlooking the harbor, it contains some notable woodwork and holds family furnishings, paintings, and documents.
   Admission: General admission $5. Combination tickets with Nathaniel Russell House $8 (see below).
   Open: Guided tours Tues–Sat 10am–5pm, Sun–Mon 1:30–5pm.

CALHOUN MANSION, 16 Meeting St. Tel. 722-8205.
   This 1876 Victorian showplace, between Battery and Lamboll Streets, is complete with period furnishings (including a few original pieces), porcelain and etched-glass gas chandeliers, ornate plastering, and woodwork of cherry, oak, and walnut. The ballroom's 45-foot-high ceiling has a skylight.

Admission: $10 adults, $5 children 6 to 15.
Open: Wed–Sun 10am–4pm. **Closed:** Holidays.

NATHANIEL RUSSELL HOUSE, 51 Meeting St. Tel. 722-3405.

A fine example of the Federal style, this pre-1809 house has ornate interiors and period furnishings—and a lovely free-flying staircase that spirals three floors upward. It's between Tradd Street and Prices Alley.
Admission: General admission $5. Combination tickets with Edmondston-Alston House $8 (see above).
Open: Guided tours Mon–Sat 10am–5pm, Sun and holidays 2–5pm.

HEYWARD-WASHINGTON HOUSE, 87 Church St. Tel. 722-0354.

This lovely old house, between Tradd and Elliott Streets, built in 1772, was the home of Thomas Heyward, Jr., a signer of the Declaration of Independence. Furnishings are authentic to the period. Behind the main house is a garden, a kitchen, and servants' quarters.
Admission: $5 adults, $3.50 seniors, $3 children 3 to 12. Combination tickets (this house, Aiken-Rhett Mansion, Charleston Museum, and Joseph Manigault House) $15.
Open: Mon–Sat 10am–5pm, Sun 1–5pm.

THOMAS ELFE WORKSHOP, 54 Queen St. Tel. 722-2142.

Built before 1760 by Charleston's most famous cabinetmaker, this is a charming small version of a Charleston "single house," and its collections of cabinetmaking tools and artifacts add to its appeal. An adjoining gift shop showcases 18th-century reproductions and accessories. It's between Meeting and Church Streets.
Admission: $3.
Open: Tours hourly Mon–Fri 10am–noon.

JOSEPH MANIGAULT HOUSE, 350 Meeting St. Tel. 722-2996.

This 1803 Adams-style residence on the register as a National Historic Landmark was the home of a wealthy rice planter. The architecture of the house features a curving central staircase and an outstanding collection of Charleston, American, English, and French period furnishing. It's diagonally across from the visitors' center on the corner of John and Meeting Streets.
Admission: $5 adults, $3 children 3 to 12. Combination ticket (this house, Heyward-Washington House, Aiken-Rhett Mansion, and Charleston Museum) $15.
Open: Mon–Sat 10am–5pm, Sun 1–5pm.

AIKEN-RHETT MANSION, 48 Elizabeth St. Tel. 722-2996.

The home of Gov. William Aiken, built in 1817, displays some original furnishings, paint, and wallpaper. Enlarged in 1833 to 1836 in the Greek Revival style, it served as headquarters for Gen. P. G. T. Beauregard during the federal bombardment of 1864. It's between Judith and Mary Streets (one block east of Meeting Street, north of Charleston Museum).
Admission: Self-guided tours $5 adults, $3 children. Discounts for seniors and military personnel. Combination tickets (this house, Charleston Museum, Heyward-Washington House, and Joseph Manigault House) $15.
Open: Mon–Sat 10am–5pm, Sun 1–5pm.

MUSEUMS

CHARLESTON MUSEUM, 360 Meeting St. Tel. 722-2996.

The Charleston Museum, founded in 1773, is the first and oldest museum in America. The museum's collections preserve and interpret the social and natural history of Charleston and the South Carolina coastal region. The full

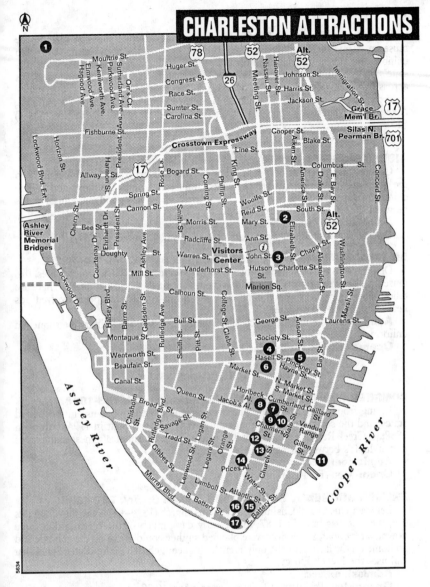

CHARLESTON ATTRACTIONS

N

78 · 52 · Alt. 52 · 26 · 17 · 701

Moultrie St. · Huger St. · Congress St. · Race St. · Sumter St. · Carolina St. · Fishburne · Johnson St. · Harris St. · Jackson St. · Immigration St. · Grace Mem'l Br. · Cooper St. · Blake St. · Silas N. Pearman Br. · Columbus St. · Concord St.

Sutherland Ave. · Ors Ct. · Orange Grove Rd. · Hanover St. · Nassau St. · Meeting St. · Aiken St. · Elizabeth St. · America St. · Drake St. · E. Bay St. · Washington St. · Marsh St. · Laurens St.

Elmwood Ave. · Kenilworth Ave. · Hagood Ave. · Parkwood Ave. · Bogard St. · Crosstown Expressway · Line St. · President St. · King St. · Alt. 52

Horizon St. · Lockwood Blvd. Ext. · Allway · Harmon St. · Spring St. · Phillip St. · Coming St. · Rose Ln. · Woolfe St. · Reid St. · South St. · Columbus St.

Ashley River Memorial Bridges · Cherry St. · Bee St. · President St. · Ehrhardt Dr. · Courtenay Dr. · Ashley Ave. · Doughty · Smith St. · Cannon St. · Morris St. · Radcliffe St. · Warren St. · Vanderhorst St. · Mary St. · Ann St. · John St. · Hutson St. · Chapel St. · Charlotte St. · Alexander St.

Visitors Center (i)

Lockwood Dr. · Halsey Blvd. · Barre St. · Gadsden St. · Rutledge Ave. · Smith St. · Pitt St. · Bull St. · College St. · Glebe St. · Mill St. · Calhoun St. · Marion Sq. · George St. · Society St. · Anson St. · Laurens St.

Montague St. · Wentworth St. · Beaufain St. · Canal St. · Chisholm St. · Broad St. · Queen St. · Hasell St. · Pinckney St. · Hayne St. · N. Market St. · S. Market St. · Cumberland · Gaillard

Ashley River · Rutledge Blvd. · Savage St. · Tradd St. · Logan St. · Legare St. · Orange St. · Church St. · Horlbeck Al. · Jacob's Al. · Chalmers St. · State St. · Vendue Range · Gillon St.

Murray Blvd. · Gibbes St. · Leinwood St. · Prices Al. · Water St. · Lamboll St. · Atlantic St. · S. Battery St. · E. Battery St. · White Point Gardens

Cooper River · Old Exchange & Provost Dungeon (11)

SOUTH CAROLINA
★ Columbia
Charleston ●

Aiken-Rhett Mansion (2)
American Military Museum (5)
Calhoun Mansion (16)
Charleston Museum (3)
The Citadel (1)
Congregation Beth Elohim (4)
Dock Street Theatre (9)
Edmondston-Alston House (15)
French Huguenot Church (10)
Gibbes Museum of Art (8)

Heyward-Washington House (13)
Joseph Manigault House (3)
Nathaniel Russell House (14)
Old Exchange & Provost Dungeon (11)
St. Mary's Roman Catholic Church (6)
St. Michael's Episcopal Church (12)
Thomas Elfe Workshop (7)
White Point Gardens (17)

scale replica of the famed Confederate submarine *Hunley* standing outside the museum is one of the most photographed subjects in the city. The museum also exhibits the largest Charleston silver collection, early crafts, historic relics, and the state's only children's "Discover Me" room with hands-on exhibits for youngsters. It's across from the visitors' center at Meeting and John Streets.

Admission: $5 adults, $3 children 3 to 12. Combination ticket (this museum, Aiken-Rhett Mansion, Joseph Manigault House, and Heyward-Washington House) $15.

Open: Mon–Sat 9am–5pm, Sun 1–5pm.

GIBBES MUSEUM OF ART, 135 Meeting St. Tel. 722-2706.

One of the country's finest collections of American art from the 18th century to the present—paintings, prints, drawings, miniature room interiors, and a fine collection of portraits—is on exhibit here. There's also a very good museum shop. It's between Queen and Horlbeck Streets.

Admission: $3 adults, $2 seniors and students.

Open: Tues–Sat 10am–5pm, Sun–Mon 1–5pm. **Closed:** Holidays.

AMERICAN MILITARY MUSEUM, 40 Pinckney St. Tel. 723-9620.

Dedicated to the men and women who have served in the U.S. armed forces, this museum displays uniforms and artifacts from all branches of the military. There are relics of virtually every armed conflict in which this country has been involved. It's near Church and Broad Streets.

Admission: $2 adults, $1 children under 12, free for military personnel in uniform.

Open: Mon–Sat 10am–6pm, Sun 1–6pm.

CHURCHES

CONGREGATION BETH ELOHIM, 90 Hassel St. Tel. 723-1090.

Dating from 1840, this is the oldest synagogue in continuous use in the United States, and the second oldest in the country. The original, built in 1794, burned in 1838; its Greek Revival replacement is considered one of America's finest examples of that style. It's between King and Meeting Streets.

Admission: Free.

Open: Mon–Fri 10am–noon.

FRENCH HUGUENOT CHURCH, 136 Church St. Tel. 722-4385.

Between Queen and Chalmers Streets, this church (1844–45) is the fourth on this site; the first was built in 1687. In the early days, much of the congregation came downriver by boat, so services were planned so they could arrive on the ebb tide and go home on the flood. It's the only French Huguenot church in the United States that still uses the French liturgy.

Admission: Free.

Open: Mon–Fri 10am–12:30pm; services Sun 10:30am.

ST. MARY'S ROMAN CATHOLIC CHURCH, 89 Hasell St. Tel. 722-7696.

This is the mother church (built in 1839) of the Roman Catholic dioceses of South Carolina, North Carolina, and Georgia. An earlier church (1789) burned on this site in 1838. It's between Meeting and King Streets.

Admission: Free.

Open: Daily 7am–4:30pm.

ST. MICHAEL'S EPISCOPAL CHURCH, 14 St. Michael's Alley. Tel. 723-0603.

⭐ This is the oldest church in the city, dating back to 1761. Its eight bells (imported in 1764) are well traveled: They were sent back to England as a British prize of war during the Revolution; back in the United States, they were burned during the Civil War, and had to cross the Atlantic again to be recast. The chandelier, installed in 1803, has been lighted by candles, gas, and electricity. Washington worshiped here during his 1791 southern tour. It's at Meeting and Broad Streets.

Admission: Free.

Open: Mon–Fri 9am–4:30pm (early closing Wed).

NEARBY SIGHTS

CHARLES TOWNE LANDING, 1500 Old Towne Rd. Tel. 556-4450.

⭐ This 663-acre park on S.C. 171 is located on the site of the first 1670 settlement. Underground exhibits show the colony's history, and there's a re-creation of a small village, a full-scale replica of a 17th-century trading ⓢ ship, and a tram tour for $1 (or you can rent a bike). There's no flashy "theme park" atmosphere: What you see as you walk under huge old oaks, past freshwater lagoons, and through the Animal Forest (which has animals of the same species that lived here in 1670) is what those early settlers saw. It's between U.S. 17 and I-126.

Admission: $5 adults, $2.50 seniors and children 6 to 14, free for the disabled.

Open: Daily 9am–5pm.

MIDDLETON PLACE, Ashley River Rd. (S.C. 61). Tel. 556-6020.

⭐ This was the home of Henry Middleton, president of the First Continental Congress, whose son, Arthur, was a signer of the Declaration of Independence. Today, the National Historic Landmark includes this country's oldest land-ⓢ scaped gardens, the Middleton Place House, and the Plantation Stableyards. The gardens, begun in 1741, reflect the elegant symmetry of European gardens of the period. Ornamental lakes, terraces, and plantings of camellias, azaleas, magnolias, and crape myrtle accent the grand design.

Fourteen miles northwest of Charleston, the Middleton Place House was built in 1755, and in 1865 all but the south flank was ransacked and burned by Union troops. It was restored in the 1870s as a family residence, and today it houses collections of fine silver, furniture, rare first editions by Catesby and Audubon, and portraits by Benjamin West and Thomas Sully. In the stableyards, craftspeople demonstrate life on the plantation of yesteryear. There are horses, mules, hogs, milk cows, sheep, and goats.

A plantation lunch is served at the **Middleton Place Restaurant,** open from 11am to 3pm, where dishes like okra gumbo, plantation chicken, and ham biscuits will cost between $5 and $10. Dinner is served on Friday and Saturday from 6 to 9pm.

Admission: Gardens and stableyards, $9 adults, $4.50 children 6 to 12 (plus $5 extra to tour the house), free for children under 5.

Open: Gardens and stableyard, daily 9am–5pm; house, Tues–Sun 10am–4:30pm, Mon 1:30–4:30pm.

CYPRESS GARDENS, U.S. 52, Moncks Corner. Tel. 552-0515.

⭐ This swamp garden was used as a freshwater reserve for Dean Hall, a huge Cooper River rice plantation, and was given to the city in 1963. Today, its giant cypress trees draped with Spanish moss provide an unforgettable setting for boats that glide among their knobby roots. Footpaths in the garden wind through a profusion of azaleas, camellias, daffodils, and other colorful blooms. The gardens are worth a visit at any time of year, but they're at their most colorful from March through April. It's 23 miles north of Charleston.

Admission: Mid-Feb to April (not including boat rides), $6 adults, $5 seniors, $2 children 6 to 16; $1 less (including boat rides) other months.
Open: Daily 9am–5pm.

MORE ATTRACTIONS

SIGHTS IN TOWN

THE CITADEL, Moultrie St. and Elmwood Ave. Tel. 792-5006, or toll free 800/868-3294.

The Citadel was established in 1842 as an arsenal, and to serve as a refuge for whites in case of a slave uprising. In 1922, it moved to its present location. The campus of this military college, with its buildings of Moorish design, including crenellated battlements and sentry towers, is especially interesting when the college is in session, when the public is invited to a precision drill parade on the quadrangle at 3:45pm almost every Friday. For a history of the Citadel, stop at the **Citadel Memorial Archives Museum** (tel. 792-6846).

Admission: Free.
Open: Daily 24 hours for drive-through visits; museum, Sun–Fri 2–5pm, Sat noon–5pm.

DOCK STREET THEATRE, 133 Church St. Tel. 723-5648.

The original Dock Street Theatre opened in 1736 as the first building in the colonies planned just for theater. In the early 1800s, after the theater burned down, the Planters Hotel was built around its ruins. The theater's back now (since 1936), remodeled and still doing business, with plays, ballet, concerts, and other events. It's the longtime home of the Footlight Players, Charleston's resident theater company, and opera and drama here are a part of the annual Spoleto Festival U.S.A. in May and June.

Admission: Free.
Open: Mon–Fri 9am–5pm. **Closed:** Holidays.

OLD EXCHANGE & PROVOST DUNGEON, 122 E. Bay St. Tel. 727-2165.

This is a stop many tourists overlook; in fact, sightseeing companies only stop here if requested. However, it's considered to be one of the three most important colonial buildings in the United States, because of the role it played in the American Revolution. In 1873, the building became the City Hall. The floor in the lobby is made of purbeck stone, and you'll find one of the largest collections of antique chairs—each of the Daughters of the American Revolution brought a chair here from home in 1921.

Admission: $3 adults, $2.50 seniors, $1.50 children 6 to 12.
Open: Daily 9am–5pm. **Closed:** Jan 1, Thanksgiving Day, Dec 24–25 and 31.

PLANTATIONS

BOONE HALL PLANTATION, Long Point Rd., Mount Pleasant. Tel. 884-4371.

This unique plantation is approached by a famous avenue of oaks, huge old moss-draped trees planted in 1743 by Capt. Thomas Boone. The first floor of the beautiful plantation house is elegantly furnished and open to the public. Outbuildings include the circular smokehouse and slave cabins constructed of bricks made on the plantation. It's on U.S. 17, nine miles north of Charleston.

Admission: $7.50 adults, $6 seniors 55 and over, $3 children 6 to 12.
Open: Apr–Labor Day, Mon–Sat 8:30am–6:30pm, Sun 1–5pm; Labor Day–Mar, Mon–Sat 9am–5pm, Sun 1–4pm.

DRAYTON HALL, Old Ashley River Rd. Tel. 766-0188.
This is one of the oldest surviving plantations. Built in 1738, it was owned by the Drayton family until 1974. Framed by majestic live oaks, the lovely Georgian-Palladian house is now a property of the National Trust for Historic Preservation (members of the Trust get in free). Its handcarved woodwork and plasterwork are nothing short of magnificent. Since such modern elements as electricity, plumbing, and central heating have never put in an appearance, the house is much as it was in its early years. It's on S.C. 61, nine miles north of Charleston.
   Admission: $7 adults, $4 school-age children.
   Open: Mar–Oct, daily 10am–4pm, with tours on the hour 10am–4pm; Nov–Feb, daily 10am–3pm. **Closed:** Thanksgiving Day, and Dec 25.

MAGNOLIA PLANTATION, Hwy. 61. Tel. 571-1266.
Ten generations of the Drayton family have lived here continuously since the 1670s. They haven't had much luck keeping a roof over their heads: The first mansion burned just after the Revolution, and the second was burned by Sherman. But you can't call its replacement "modern"—a simple, pre-Revolutionary house was barged down from Summerville and set on the basement foundations of its unfortunate predecessors. The magnificent gardens of camellias and azaleas among the most beautiful in America, reach their height of bloom in March and April, but are colorful year-round. You can tour the house, the gardens (which include an herb garden, horticultural maze, topiary garden, and biblical garden), and a petting zoo; climb the observation tower overlooking rice fields; ride canoes through a 125-acre waterfowl refuge; or walk or cycle through wildlife trails. New features on the grounds include an antebellum cabin that was restored and furnished, a plantation rice barge on display beside the Ashley River, and a "Nature Train" that carries guests on a 45-minute ride around the perimeter of the plantation. Low-country wildlife are visible in marsh, woodland, and swamp settings. The **Audubon Swamp Garden,** also on the grounds, is an independently operated 60-acre cypress swamp offering a close look at other Low-country wildlife, such as egrets, alligators, wood ducks, anhingas, otters, turtles, and herons. It's on S.C. 61, 10 miles northwest of Charleston.
   Admission: Garden, $8 adults, $7 seniors, $6 children 13 to 19, $4 children 4 to 12; plantation house tour $4 additional; add $1 Mar–May. Audubon Swamp Garden, $6 adults and seniors, $3 children; a combination ticket in conjunction with Magnolia Plantation makes the Audubon Swamp Garden admission only $4 adults and seniors, $2 children.
   Open: Plantation and gardens, daily 8am–5pm.

NEARBY SIGHTS

Both **Fort Moultrie,** on Sullivan's Island, West Middle Street, 10 miles east of the city (no phone), and **Fort Sumter** (in the harbor) are open to visitors. There's no charge at Fort Moultrie, which is open from 9am to 6pm in summer and 9am to 5pm in winter. To reach Fort Sumter, contact Fort Sumter Tours (see "Organized Tours," below).
   Edisto Beach State Park, on Edisto Island, is about 21 miles west on U.S. 17, then 29 miles south on S.C. 174. Its 1,255 acres are ideal for a day away from organized sightseeing. Swimming and fishing are good along two miles of beach, and there's a well-marked nature trail. Bring a picnic to lunch under one of the shelters, or pick up snacks at the store.

COOL FOR KIDS

Kids and navy vets will love the aircraft carrier **U.S.S. Yorktown** at Patriots Point (two miles east of the Cooper River Bridge). Its World War II, Korea, and Vietnam exploits are documented in exhibits, and general naval history is illustrated through models of ships, planes, and weapons. You can wander through the bridge, wheelhouse, flight and hangar decks, chapel, sick bay, and several other areas, and view the film "The Fighting Lady," depicting life aboard the carrier. The *Yorktown* is the nucleus of the world's largest naval and maritime museum. Also at Patriots Point, and welcoming visitors aboard, are the nuclear ship *Savannah,* the world's first nuclear-powered merchant ship; the World War II destroyer *Laffey;* the World War II submarine *Clamagore;* and the cutter *Ingham.* Patriots Point is open from 9am to 6pm daily April through October, 9am to 5pm November through March. Admission is $8 for adults, $7 for seniors over 62 and military personnel in uniform, and $4 for kids 6 to 11. Adjoining is the fine 18-hole public Patriots Point golf course. For further information, telephone 884-2727.

Among the attractions listed above, children will take special delight in **Charles Towne Landing** and **Middleton Place.**

WALKING TOUR — OLD CHARLESTON

Start: White Gardens at the Battery.
Finish: Aiken-Rhett Mansion, Elizabeth Street between Mary and Judith Streets.
Time: Six hours without touring historic attractions; add from ½ to 1 hour for each tour.
Best Times: Any time except midday, when the heat can be quite steamy, especially in summer months. Early evening can be quite pleasant if you don't plan to tour attractions.

The following is really a two-in-one walking tour, since I've made a distinction (as do Charlestonians) between "South of Broad Street" and "North Broad Street." If you have the luxury of two days to devote to this charming city, I strongly recommend that you explore each area in depth on successive days.

SOUTH OF BROAD STREET   Turning your back to the water, you'll face a row of large, graceful houses that line South Battery. When you walk away from the park, it's as though you're going through a sort of gateway into the rest of the town.

Once off South Battery, almost every home is of historic or architectural interest. You'll find detailed information about each house on the tour in the sections above. After a stroll through White Point Gardens, walk up Meeting Street to the:

1. **Calhoun Mansion,** at 16 Meeting Street, then return to South Battery Street and walk east two blocks alongside one gracious mansion after the other. Loiter a moment or two at East Battery Street to savor the harbor view, then turn north to the:
2. **Edmondston-Alston House,** at 21 East Battery. Take a few minutes to cross the street to the delightful new waterfront park. Continue north to the next intersection and turn left on Water Street for one block, then right on Church Street and continue north to the:
3. **Heyward-Washington House,** at 87 Church Street. Continuing north on Church, you'll pass:
4. **Catfish Row.** Its real name is Cabbage Row (after the vegetables that used to be sold on the sidewalk). It's a row of connected buildings from 89 to 91 Church Street. DuBose Heyward changed its name in his novel *Porgy,* and when he and George Gershwin collaborated on the opera *Porgy and Bess,* its fame spread all over the world. At Church and Elliot Streets, turn left to reach:

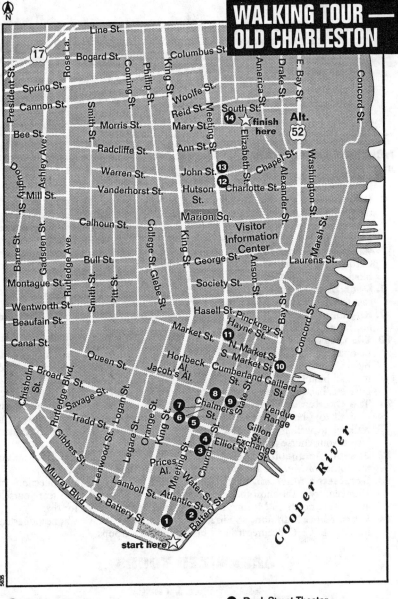

17

Line St.

Rose La.

Bogard St.

Columbus St.

Spring St.

Cannon St.

Bee St.

President St.

Ashley Ave.

Smith St.

Morris St.

Coming St.

Phillip St.

King St.

Woolfe St.

Reid St.

Mary St.

South St.

America St.

Drake St.

E. Bay St.

14 ⭐ finish here

Alt.
52
U.S.

Concord St.

Radcliffe St.

Ann St.

Elizabeth St.

Chapel St.

13

Warren St.

John St.

12

Vanderhorst St.

Hutson St.

Charlotte St.

Alexander St.

Washington St.

Marsh St.

Mill St.

Doughty St.

Calhoun St.

College St.

Glebe St.

Marion Sq.

Visitor
Information
Center

Barre St.

Gadsden St.

Rutledge Ave.

Bull St.

Smith St.

St. Philip St.

George St.

Anson St.

Laurens St.

Montague St.

Society St.

Wentworth St.

Bay St.

Concord St.

Beaufain St.

Hasell St.

Pinckney St.

Canal St.

Market St.

Hayne St.

11

N. Market St.

S. Market St.

10

Chisholm St.

Broad St.

Queen St.

Horlbeck Al.

Jacob's Al.

Cumberland St.

Gaillard St.

Rutledge Blvd.

Savage St.

Logan St.

Orange St.

King St.

8

7

Chalmers St.

9

State St.

Vendue
Range

Tradd St.

6 **5**

Gillon St.

Exchange St.

Gibbes St.

Lenwood St.

Legare St.

4

3

Elliot St.

Prices Al.

Meeting St.

Church St.

Water St.

E. Battery St.

Murray Blvd.

Lamboll St.

Atlantic St.

S. Battery St.

2

1

start here ⭐

Cooper River

N

Legend

1. Calhoun Mansion
2. Edmonston-Alston House
3. Heyward-Washington House
4. Catfish Row
5. St. Michael's Episcopal Church
6. City Hall
7. Washington Square
8. Dock Street Theater
9. Huguenot Church
10. Old City Market
11. The Charleston Carriage Company
12. Joseph Manigault Mansion
13. Charleston Museum
14. Aiken-Rhett Mansion

5. **St. Michael's Church,** at Meeting and Broad Streets. Look inside, then stroll through the adjoining graveyard, with headstones dating back over the centuries.

REFUELING STOPS   By now you may be ready for a bite to eat. **Reuben's Downtown Delicatessen,** at Broad and Meeting Streets (see "Where to Dine"), is a perfect place for snacks. You're in the perfect spot to choose any number of restaurants or coffeehouses. Check my favorites in the dining section for a few tips. If you spot something new, jot it down and let me know.

NORTH OF BROAD STREET   While you're in this vicinity, you may want to stop in at:

6. **City Hall,** at Broad and Meeting Streets, to have a look at the portrait gallery in the Council Chamber. The famous John Trumbull portrait of George Washington is there, along with Samuel F. B. Morse's painting of James Monroe. The adjacent park:
7. **Washington Square,** holds monuments to a whole slew of prominent South Carolinians, as well as the Fireproof Building, this country's first. Walk two blocks north to Queen Street and turn right to reach the:
8. **Dock Street Theatre,** on the corner of Queen and Church Streets. Continue east toward the waterfront and turn south at Church Street to visit the:
9. **Huguenot Church,** Church Street between Queen and Chalmers. Now turn north on Church Street and walk the few blocks to the:
10. **Old City Market,** at East Bay and Market Streets. It's a fascinating collection of open stalls under brick sheds with tile roofs that stretch for roughly three blocks. On either side of the open sheds, old market buildings have been leased to small boutiques filled with marvelous craft items, linens, cookware, clothing, gifts, etc. Back at the corner of Meeting and North Market, you'll find stands for:
11. **The Charleston Carriage Company.** This may be an ideal time to treat yourself to a horse carriage ride through many of the streets you've just been walking, as well as a few more (see "Organized Tours," below). From Market Street, your course is now along Meeting Street several blocks north to the:
12. **Joseph Manigault Mansion,** Meeting Street between John and Hutson. At the corner of Meeting and John, plan a leisurely interval at the:
13. **Charleston Museum,** this country's oldest, with several fine collections of 18th-century silver and other interesting exhibits. When you can tear yourself away, walk north on Meeting to Wragg Street and turn right for the:
14. **Aiken-Rhett Mansion,** 48 Elizabeth Street, which was Civil War headquarters for Gen. P. G. T. Beauregard and his Confederate troops.

ORGANIZED TOURS

SIGHTSEEING TOURS

★ **The Charleston Carriage Company,** 96 N. Market St. (tel. 577-0042), offers horse-drawn carriage tours (narrated) from 9am until dusk at $12 for adults, $4 for children 3 to 12. **Palmetto Carriage Tours,** 40 N. Market St. at Guignard (tel. 723-8145), uses mules and mule teams instead of the usual horse and carriage, and its guides are excellent; fares are $12 for adults, $4 for children 4 to 11. **Gray Line Bus Tours** offers coach tours of the city, as well as seasonal garden and plantation tours (tel. 722-4444 for schedules, fares, and pickup).

If you'd like a guided walking tour, contact Charleston Carriage Co., or try the **Charleston Tea Party Walking Tour** (tel. 577-5896), which includes tea in a private garden. Tours last two hours.

BOAT TOURS

Fort Sumter Tours, 205 King St., Suite 204 (tel. 722-1691), offers a "Harbor and Fort Sumter Tour" by boat, departing daily from the City Marina and from Patriots Point Maritime Museum. This is the only tour to stop at Fort Sumter, target of the opening shots of the Civil War. They also have an interesting "Charleston Harbor and Naval Base Tour," with daily departures from Patriots Point. The two-hour cruise passes the Battery, Charleston Port, Castle Pinckney, Drum Island, Fort Sumter, the aircraft carrier *Yorktown,* and sails under the Cooper River Bridge and on to the gigantic U.S. naval base. Call for schedules and fares.

6. SPORTS & RECREATION

SPECTATOR SPORTS

Baseball is just about it for spectator fans. Home games of the Texas Rangers' minor-league farm team, the **Charleston Rainbows,** are played at College Park Stadium, 701 Rutledge Ave. (tel. 723-7241). Any other sporting events will be reported in the "Database" sports column of the *News & Courier.*

North Charleston Coliseum is just what Charleston has been waiting for: a grand domed arena to host everything from figure skating to rock concerts. Its' unique glass wall panels let light stream in. It boasts the state's largest capacity: 13,600 seats for concerts and almost 12,000 for basketball. The new facility will host Charleston's even newer **East Coast Hocky League** team.

RECREATION

Water sports are very popular in the Charleston area, which has several fine public beaches for swimming and fishing. All are relatively unspoiled by the commercial jumble of fast-food and souvenir shops and amusement centers, although essential picnic and restroom facilities are found at most. You'll find public beaches at: **Folly Beach** and **Folly Beach County Park,** on Folly Island; **Beachwater Park,** on Kiawah Island; **Sullivan's Island; Isle of Palms;** and **Edisto Island,** a little longer drive from Charleston than the others. Charter-boat fishing can be arranged at the **City Marina** (tel. 724-7357). Those interested in windsurfing instruction should contact **Time Out Sailing** (tel. 577-5979) at the City Marina.

Cycling is easy and popular, given Charleston's flat landscape, and there are bike trails at many park areas in and around the city. **The Bicycle Shop,** 280 Meeting St. (tel. 722-8168) rents bikes. Couples or families can find pedal vehicles for up to four passengers at the **Pedal Carriage Co.,** 170 Church St. (tel. 722-3880), which also furnishes a historic district guide.

Public golf courses include **Charleston Municipal Golf Course,** 2110 Maybank St. (tel. 795-6517) and **Patriots Point Golf Course,** 100 Clubhouse Dr. (tel. 881-0042). Also, some resort developments offer play to nonresidents on a space-available basis; inquire at the visitors' center.

Tennis buffs will find courts open to the public at: **Charleston Tennis Center,**

19 Farmfield Ave. (tel. 724-7402) and **Kiawah Island,** 1 Kiawah Beach Dr. (tel. 768-2121).

---

7. SAVVY SHOPPING

GOOD BUYS Charleston is good shopping (as well as browsing) territory; keep an eye out for good buys in antiques and period reproductions, paintings and prints, low-country craft items, silverware, and designer clothes boutiques. High visibility antique shops usually have items offered at a premium.

MAJOR SHOPPING DISTRICTS **King Street** is lined with many specialty shops and boutiques; the **Old City Market,** East Bay and Market Streets, is a fascinating collection of stalls, specialty shops, and restaurants, with an intriguing flea market. The **Shops at Charleston Place,** 130 Market Street, is an upscale complex of top designer clothing shops (Gucci, Jaeger, Ralph Lauren, and the like). **State Street Market,** just down from the Old City Market, is another cluster of shops and restaurants.

---

8. EVENING ENTERTAINMENT

THE PERFORMING ARTS

The **Amazing Stage Company,** 133 Church St., Suite 7 (tel. 577-5967), produces a wide variety of plays and musicals at extremely moderate prices ($8 to $15) from October to May at the Dock Street Theatre. The **Charleston Symphony Orchestra,** 14 George St. (tel. 723-7528; 723-9693 for concert info; 577-4500 for Discover, MasterCard, or Visa bookings), presents classical music, chamber music, and pop concerts from September through May in Charleston's most historic theaters. During the same season, the **Charleston Civic Ballet** and **Charleston Opera Company** perform at Gaillard Municipal Auditorium, 77 Calhoun St. (tel. 577-4500, or 577-4502).

THE CLUB & BAR SCENE

Most of the larger hotels in Charleston have lounges with live music and/or entertainment, and there are several lively bars.

CHARLESTON SPORTS PUB & GRILLE, 4 Linguard Alley. Tel. 577-8887.
This popular sports bar is situated in the center of activity—at South Market Street. Inside you'll find two dozen TV monitors, so you won't miss a split second of any sports action, and lots of sports memorabilia. There are also tables outside, with some under cover. It's open daily from 11:30am to 2am.
Admission: Free.

FANNIGAN'S, 159 E. Bay St. Tel. 722-6916.
What a time you'll have here at Fannigan's when the DJ cranks up the sound! The decor features booths, a big bar, a fine dance floor with good lighting, and neon accents. They play oldies, dance music, and shag. On Tuesday through Friday a buffet is offered between 5 and 8pm. The crowd is mostly 25 to 35 years old. It's open Tuesday through Thursday 5pm to 2am, Friday 5pm to 4am, and Saturday 8pm to 2am.
Admission: $2 women, $3 men.

JUKEBOX, 4 Vendue Range. Tel. 723-3431.

Jukebox has two bars in one. The main bar is decked out in red-and-white-checked tile and blue and red neon. There's a wide-screen TV and a dance floor. The music ranges from oldies to pop—they play 1950s and 1960s music until 9pm. A light bar menu is also offered. The adjoining sports bar is just what you might expect. Jukebox is open daily from 4pm to 2am, but the sports bar stays open to 5am on Friday and Saturday.

Admission: $3–$5 Fri–Sat after 9pm.

A DINNER CRUISE

One of the most enjoyable ways I can think of to spend a Charleston evening is aboard the luxury yacht *Spirit of Charleston* for a three-hour cruise (with Gilligan, the Skipper too, er, sorry). Anyway, I think you'll have a good time for your $33 per person, not including drinks or gratuity. Cocktails are followed by a four-course prime rib dinner, and there's dancing to the music of a live band. For schedules, fares, and bookings, contact Fort Sumter Tours, 205 King St. (tel. 722-1691).

CHAPTER 9

COLUMBIA & CENTRAL SOUTH CAROLINA

1. COLUMBIA
2. EASY EXCURSIONS FROM COLUMBIA
3. AIKEN THOROUGHBRED COUNTRY

Moving inland from the coast, today's visitor comes face to face with vivid reminders of South Carolina's colorful past, as well as with the "New South," which is reflected all across this part of the state.

Industries, such as textiles, chemicals, precision-tool making, and metalworks, making full use of abundant water power, thrive alongside large farms producing dairy products, tobacco, soybeans, peaches, wheat, and cotton, plus large forests of pine trees for an ever-growing paper industry.

---

1. COLUMBIA

120 miles NW of Charleston; 131 miles W of Myrtle Beach; 75 miles NW of Aiken; 106 miles SE of Spartanburg

GETTING THERE   By Plane   See "Getting There" in Chapter 6.

By Train   For information on **Amtrak** service, call toll free 800/USA-RAIL.

By Bus   For **Greyhound/Trailways** information, call 803/779-0650.

By Car   I-20 reaches Columbia from the northeast and southwest, I-26 from the southeast and northwest, I-77 from the north.

ESSENTIALS   The **area code** is 803. The **Greater Columbia Convention and Visitors Bureau** is at 1012 Gervais St., Columbia, SC 29201 (tel. 803/254-0479).

Columbia, unlike many of our older cities, has the orderly look of a planned community, with streets laid out in an almost unbroken checkerboard pattern, and broad boulevards giving it a particularly graceful beauty. The city was created in 1786 as a compromise capital, located just three miles from the exact geographical center of the state in order to satisfy both low- and up-country factions. George Washington paid a visit to Columbia in 1791, just one year after the first general assembly convened in the brand-new city.

It was here, in the period leading up to the Civil War, that a convention held in the First Baptist Church passed the first Ordinance of Secession in the Southern states on December 17, 1860. (Because of a local smallpox epidemic, however, it was actually signed in Charleston.) Columbia itself was little touched by battle until General Sherman arrived with his Union troops on February 17, 1865, and virtually wiped out the town by fire: An 84-block area and some 1,386 buildings were left in ashes.

Although recovery during Reconstruction was slow, the city that emerged from almost complete devastation is one of stately homes and public buildings, with government and education (there are seven colleges located here) playing leading roles in its economy, followed closely by a wide diversity of industry. Fort Jackson, a U.S. Army basic training post on the southeast edge of town, adds another element to the economic mix.

WHAT TO SEE & DO

IN COLUMBIA

The ✪ **State House,** Main and Gervais Streets, begun in 1855, was only half-finished when General Sherman bombarded Columbia in 1865. The west and south walls are marked with bronze stars where shells struck. In the fire that wiped out so much of the city, the state house escaped destruction, but the architect's plans were burned, with the result that the dome is not the one originally envisioned. Despite that, the building, with its Corinthian granite columns, is considered one of the most beautiful state capitols in the country. The landscaped grounds hold memorial tablets and monuments, and inside are portraits and statues of South Carolina greats. The building is open every weekday from 9am to 5pm.

If the back of a commercial building can be called a "sightseeing" item, then the **Farm Credit Bank Building,** on Marion Street at Hampton, rates a mention. Painted by a local artist with the interesting name of Blue Sky, this 50-by-75-foot mural faces a parking lot behind the building. The painting pictures a highway tunnel opening onto a mountain sunrise, and it's so realistic that it looks as if you could drive right into it! If you're in this part of town, even at night (when it's floodlit), swing by and take a look.

Look for **Woodrow Wilson's boyhood home** at 1705 Hampton St., the restored 1820 **Hampton-Preston House** at 1615 Blanding St., and the **Robert Mills Historic House and Park** at 1616 Blanding St. Wilson you know; Wade Hampton was a South Carolina hero from a family of state leaders; and Robert Mills served seven presidents as the first federal architect, designing such landmarks as the Washington Monument, the U.S. Treasury Building, and the Old Patent Office in Washington, D.C. All three houses feature their original furniture, and the Mills House has some outstanding mantels and chandeliers of the Regency period. Another historic home is the **Mann-Simmons Cottage,** 1403 Richland St. Celia Mann was an African-American slave who bought her freedom and walked from Charleston to Columbia. Today, the home is a tribute to African-American history. The houses are open Tuesday through Saturday from 10:15am to 4:15pm and Sunday from 1:15 to 4:15pm; they're closed Thanksgiving Day and New Year's Day and the last two weeks of December. Admission to each is $3 for adults, $1.50 for ages 6 to 21, and free to senior citizens in March. A combination ticket may be purchased to view all four homes for $10.

COLUMBIA MUSEUM OF ART, 1112 Bull St. Tel. 799-2810.

✪ At Senate and Bull Streets, the museum building, built in 1902, was the private residence of the Thomas Taylor family. The permanent collection contains paintings, furniture, and sculpture of the baroque and Renaissance periods. It has an impressive permanent collection of more than 5,000 items. A focus of the collection is the work of native South Carolinians, including turn-of-the-century photos. The museum houses eight galleries and also hosts various musical presentations. The Gibbes Planetarium, located within the museum, is a sight-and-sound extravaganza the entire family will enjoy.

Admission: Museum, free. Planetarium, $2 adults; $1 seniors, military personnel, and children 6 to 12.

Open: Tues–Fri 10am–5pm, Sat–Sun 12:30–5pm. Planetarium show times vary.

GOVERNOR'S MANSION, 800 Richland St. Tel. 737-1710.

This was originally built in 1855 as officers' quarters for Arsenal Academy. When Sherman swept through the town, this was the only building on the academy grounds left standing. South Carolina governors have lived here since 1868. It's at Richland and Lincoln Streets.

Admission (including 30-minute guided tour): Free.

Open: Tues–Thurs by appointment only.

SOUTH CAROLINA STATE MUSEUM, 301 Gervais St. Tel. 803/737-4921.

The State Museum is housed in what was once the world's first all-electric textile mill. There are four floors, each dedicated to one of four important areas: art, history, natural history, and science and technology. Hands-on exhibits, realistic dioramas, and laser displays make for exciting browsing through South Carolina's past, from prehistory through the present and even into the future.

Admission: $4 adults; $3 seniors, military personnel, and college students; $1.50 children 6 to 17. Unaccompanied children under 13 are not admitted.

Open: Mon–Sat 10am–5pm, Sun 1–5pm. **Closed:** Thanksgiving Day, Dec 25.

UNIVERSITY OF SOUTH CAROLINA CAMPUS, Gregg, Pendleton, and Main Sts. Tel. 777-7700.

The 218-acre grounds are really lovely, lined with buildings dating from the early 1800s (the university was founded in 1801) and filled with ancient oaks and magnolias—so beautiful, in fact, that Hollywood regularly films on the historic Horseshoe, at the corner of Pendleton and Bull Streets. While you're here, it's worth half an hour or so to go by the **McKissick Museum,** located in a fine old building at the head of the Horseshoe. The museum features changing exhibitions on regional folk art, history, natural science, and fine art, as well as presentations based on the university's collection of historic 20th-Century-Fox Movietone newsreels.

Admission: Free.

Open (Museum): Mon–Fri 10am–4pm, Sat–Sun 1–5pm.

RIVERBANKS ZOOLOGICAL GARDENS, 500 Wildlife Pkwy. Tel. 779-8717, or 779-8730.

Be sure to save time to drive out to Riverbanks, a refuge for many endangered species (such as the American bald eagle). The animals and birds (more than 2,000!) here are the healthiest, liveliest I've ever seen in a zoo. Penguins are kept happy in an environment that duplicates the bacteria-free Antarctic ice shelf. Botanically significant trees and plants are labeled throughout the park. All kinds of domestic animals can be seen at the Farm, which also has an automated milking parlor in action for the education of city-bred folk. The **Aquarium Reptile Complex** is a spectacular facility that introduces the aquatic and reptilian creatures of South Carolina. The last tickets are sold one hour before closing. A 70-acre botanical garden opened in 1993. It's at the intersection of Greystone Boulevard and I-126.

Admission: $4 adults, $1.75 children 3 to 12, free for children under 3.

Open: Daily 9am–5pm. **Closed:** Thanksgiving Day, Dec 25.

NEARBY

When heading south from Columbia via S.C. 48, nature lovers may want to stop by the ✪ **Congaree Swamp National Monument,** 200 Caroline Sims Rd., Hopkins (tel. 803/776-4396). Located just 20 miles from the capital city, this

22,000-acre nature preserve is actually an alluvial floodplain. Its designation as a national monument assures the protection of perhaps the last significant old-growth riverbottom forest in the country. It is not rare to see ancient trees whose trunks measure more than 20 feet in circumference. There are some 20 miles of walking trails, 20 miles of self-guided canoe trails, and a spectacular 3,000-foot boardwalk opens up a cypress-tupelo forest to public view. On Saturdays there are guided nature walks beginning at 1:30pm. A boardwalk gives the handicapped access to the preserve. It's open daily from 8:30am to 5pm, and it's free. For more information, contact the superintendent at the address above.

To visit beautiful **Edisto Gardens,** drive 45 miles southeast from Columbia on U.S. 176 to Orangeburg. The 110-acre city park, located on U.S. 301 along the banks of the North Edisto River, is a wonderland of moss-draped oaks, camellias, and azaleas (which bloom from mid-March to mid-April), as well as flowering crabapple, day lilies, dogwoods, and over 9,500 roses that bloom from the middle of April until early October. It's one of the loveliest Southern gardens anywhere. There are also tennis courts and picnic areas, and the gardens are free (open every day from dawn to dusk).

If hunger pangs strike while you're in Orangeburg, stop at the **House of Pizza,** 910 Calhoun Dr. (U.S. 301) (tel. 531-4000), north of the Edisto Gardens entrance. Pizza, sandwiches, burgers, and salads are served here, but the real specialties in this superb eatery are Greek dishes, such as moussaka and the honey-sweet baklava. Their Greek salad is spectacular. And there's beer and wine. Prices are moderate. They have a take-out service if you should want to picnic in the gardens. Open Monday through Thursday 11am to 10:30pm, Friday and Saturday 11am to 11:30pm, Sunday 11am to 10:30pm.

From Orangeburg, it's a short drive on U.S. 301 to Lake Marion and Lake Moultrie, known collectively as the ❂ **Santee Cooper Lakes,** which cover more than 171,000 acres. Fishers note: Three world-record and eight state-record catches have been recorded here, and anglers flock to try their luck with the striped, largemouth, hybrid, and white bass, the catfish, and other assorted panfish that stock these waters. The lakes are ringed with fish camps, marinas, campgrounds, and modern motels. You don't have to be an angler to enjoy this beautiful region: There are numerous golf courses, tennis courts, and wildlife sanctuaries. The **Santee-Cooper Counties Promotion Commission,** Drawer 40, Santee, SC 29142 (tel. 803/854-2131, or toll free 800/227-8510 outside S.C.), can furnish full details on recreational facilities and accommodations. For details on camping and lakefront vacation cabins on Lake Marion, contact the Superintendent, Santee State Park, Rte. 1, Box 79, Santee, SC 29142 (tel. 803/854-2408). In all cases, be sure to inquire about fishing or golf package deals.

WHERE TO STAY

EXPENSIVE

COLUMBIA MARRIOTT, 1200 Hampton St., Columbia, SC 29201. Tel. 803/771-7000, or toll free 800/228-9290. Fax 803/254-8307. 301 rms. A/C MINIBAR TV TEL

$ Rates: $100–$120 single; $110–$120 double. AE, CB, DC, DISC, ER, MC, V.

This is one of the capital's leading deluxe hotels. The luxury guest rooms have cable TV and in-room movies; some have oversize beds, balconies, and refrigerators. Other facilities include an indoor pool, sauna, whirlpool, restaurant, and a lounge with entertainment. It's on U.S. 21 at Main Street.

WHITNEY HOTEL, 700 Woodrow St., Columbia, SC 29205. Tel. 803/252-0845, or toll free 800/637-4008. Fax 803/771-0495. 72 rms. A/C TV TEL

$ Rates: $89–$109 single or double. AE, DC, DISC, MC, V.

The Whitney is a bit more upscale than some hotels in Columbia, because it is an all-suite hotel with such features as complimentary limousine service to area restaurants and the airport, limited public areas giving it a more residential appeal, an outdoor pool, and a fitness room. All the guest suites have complete kitchens with microwave ovens, stoves, refrigerators, and utensils. Suites also boast washers and dryers, armoires with TVs, butler's tables, and balconies. The small staff is congenial. A little café, or something along that line, is lacking. It's southeast of the center of town, at Devine Street.

MODERATE

CLAUSSEN'S INN, 2003 Green St., Columbia, SC 29205. Tel. 803/ 765-0440. 29 rms. A/C TV TEL
$ Rates: $85–$100 single; $95–$110 double. AE, MC, V.

⭐ This charming hostelry, two miles southeast of downtown, is housed in a former bakery that dates to 1928. Rooms are tastefully decorated and may have watermelon-colored walls, pine armoires, Windsor chairs, and small patios. There are complimentary drinks in the evening.

RESIDENCE INN MARRIOTT, 150 Stoneridge Dr., Columbia, SC 29221. Tel. 803/779-7000, or toll free 800/331-3131. 128 suites. A/C TV TEL **Directions:** Take the Greystone Boulevard exit off I-126.
$ Rates (including continental breakfast): $79 studio suite; $105 penthouse suite. Discounts for stays longer than six nights. AE, DC, DISC, MC, V.

Ⓢ These are lovely, moderately priced, upscale accommodations. Located near the Riverbanks Zoo, the hotel has one- and two-bedroom suites, most of which have fireplaces. There's a pool, whirlpool, barbecue facilities, health club, and coin laundry. Complimentary beer, wine, and snacks are served in the evening Monday through Thursday.

BUDGET

DAYS INN, 7128 Parklane Rd., Columbia, SC 29204. Tel. 803/736- 0000, or toll free 800/325-2525. 135 rms. A/C TV TEL **Directions:** Go two blocks off I-20, exit 74.
$ Rates (including breakfast): $32 single; $37 double. Senior discounts available. AE, DC, DISC, MC, V.
Economy-minded travelers will find this a comfortable, budget-priced place to stay, with a restaurant on the premises.

RED ROOF INN EAST, 7580 Two Notch Rd., Columbia, SC 29223. Tel. 803/736-0850, or toll free 800/843-7663. 109 rms. A/C TV TEL **Directions:** Exit 74 at junction of U.S. 1 and I-20.
$ Rates: $29–$39 single; $33–$41 double. Senior discounts available. AE, DC, DISC, MC, V.
This budget choice offers complimentary coffee and daily newspaper, and there's a good restaurant nearby. The inn has facilities designed for the disabled. Another of this chain's locations, the **Red Roof Inn West,** is located at 10 Berryhill Rd., Columbia, SC 29210 (tel. 798-9220, or toll free 800/843-7663).

TREMONT INN, 111 Knox Abbott Dr., Cayce, SC 29033. Tel. 803/796- 6240. 100 rms. A/C TV TEL **Directions:** Go two miles west of downtown on U.S. 21, 176, and 321.

$ Rates: $32–$38 single; $33–$38 double. AE, DC, MC, V.

Just a mile from the State House, this hotel is set back from the road in wooded, landscaped grounds. It boasts an extremely helpful and friendly staff and oversize beds in the cheerfully decorated rooms. Irons and ironing boards are available, and there's a swimming pool, coin laundry, valet service, babysitting service, children's playground, and complimentary coffee in the lobby.

WHERE TO DINE

Columbia has a host of restaurants and eateries, but many have chain affiliations. The area around Five Points, close to the USC campus, is ideal for snacks, coffee, or even something more substantial.

MODERATE

BAILEY'S IRISH PUB, 741 Saluda Ave. Tel. 799-6303.

Cuisine: PUB. **Reservations:** Not required.

$ Prices: Appetizers $2.50–$5.50; main courses $8–$10. CB, DC, DISC, MC, V.

Open: Mon–Sat 11:30am–10pm. Bar, Mon–Fri 11:30am–2am, Sat 11:30am–midnight.

With a name like this you'd expect green decor (which it has), live music (which it offers), and even a few items from the old country. Shepherd's pie is a staple here, but there is also French dip, sandwiches, and crabcakes. The outside tables are popular for crowd-watching.

GARIBALDI'S, 2013 Greene St. Tel. 771-8888.

Cuisine: ITALIAN/SEAFOOD. **Reservations:** Recommended.

$ Prices: Dinner $6–$20. AE, MC, V.

Open: Mon–Thurs 5:30–10:30pm, Fri–Sat 5:30–11pm.

Garibaldi's, near the university campus, is popular with locals for good food in an art deco decor. In addition to pasta and other Italian specialties, the menu includes seafood, beef, and chicken.

GOURMET SHOP CAFE, 724 Saluda Ave. Tel. 799-3705.

Cuisine: BAKERY/WINE SHOP. **Reservations:** Not accepted.

$ Prices: Sandwiches $4–$5; salads $4–$6. AE, CB, DC, MC, V.

Open: Mon–Fri 9am–3:45pm, Sat 9am–4:45pm, Sun 10am–3:45pm.

Here you'll find a delightful combination of wine and coffee and bakery items. Many students congregate here, and some stop by to shop for supper—maybe for fresh French bread and the perfect bottle of wine. The shop also sells kitchen gadgets for real gourmets. The tables on the sidewalk are particularly inviting.

HENNESSEY'S, 1649 Main St. Tel. 799-8280.

Cuisine: CONTINENTAL. **Reservations:** Recommended.

$ Prices: Lunch $5–$8; dinner $9–$22. AE, MC, V.

Open: Lunch Mon–Fri 11:30am–3pm; dinner Mon–Fri 6–10pm, Sat 6–11pm.

Occupying a converted old hardware store, this atmospheric restaurant is one of Columbia's most interesting. Emphasis here is on seafood and steak, and their cakes deserve top billing. Save room for a home-baked dessert. For lighter fare, there's a good salad bar at lunch.

LE PETIT CHATEAU, 4423 Devine St. Tel. 782-7231.

Cuisine: FRENCH. **Reservations:** Recommended.
$ **Prices:** Dinner $11–$18. AE, DC, MC, V.
Open: Tues–Sat 6–10:30pm. **Closed:** Holidays.

This lovely French restaurant serves such delicacies as roast duckling and veal in various guises. There's also a good wine list at reasonable prices. It's popular with the locals, so it's best to reserve on Friday or Saturday. It's on U.S. 76 at Ft. Jackson Boulevard.

BUDGET

ADRIANA'S, 721 Saluda Ave. Tel. 799-7595.

Cuisine: BISTRO/COFFEEHOUSE. **Reservations:** Not accepted.
$ **Prices:** Coffees $1.50, desserts $1.75–$3.00. No credit cards.
Open: Mon–Sat 9am–midnight, Sun noon–11pm.

There's something quintessentially appealing about a bistro or coffeehouse: You can arrive smartly dressed or shirttails hanging, and no one bats an eye. At Adriana's you'll find black-and-white art on the walls, marble tables, ice cream–parlor chairs, and lots of students. The homemade desserts are delicious. You might want the cheesecake, ice cream, yogurt, or one of the flavorful coffees. Stop in and chill out or warm up.

CALIFORNIA DREAMING, 401 South Main St. Tel. 254-6767.

Cuisine: AMERICAN. **Reservations:** Not accepted.
$ **Prices:** Lunch under $7; dinner under $15. AE, MC, V.
Open: Mon–Fri 11am–3pm and 5–10pm, Sat 11am–11pm, Sun 11am–10pm.

Set in a restored turn-of-the-century railway station, this is a large and popular eatery, usually filled to capacity, especially on Friday and Saturday nights. Specialties are prime rib and seafood, with good salads. It's downtown, two blocks south of Blossom Street.

ZORBA'S, 2628 Decker Blvd. Tel. 736-5200.

Cuisine: GREEK. **Reservations:** Accepted Fri–Sat only.
$ **Prices:** Main courses $4–$15. AE, MC, V.
Open: Mon–Thurs 11am–10pm, Fri–Sat 11am–11pm.

If you've a weakness for Greek food, this is the place to go. The menu also includes a number of Italian selections. There is a second Zorba's in the 7 Oaks Shopping Center (tel. 772-4617), with a similar menu, hours, and prices.

2. EASY EXCURSIONS FROM COLUMBIA

North-central South Carolina was the scene of several significant battles of the American Revolution. Camden was actually the site of Lord Cornwallis's most important garrison for quite some time, and the turning point of the war is believed by many to have been the battle at Kings Mountain. Battles of another sort are regularly waged these days on Darlington's raceway, as stock cars engage in fierce competition.

CAMDEN

The 24-mile drive to Camden, via I-20, will take you straight back to this nation's beginnings. Founded by Irish Quakers back in 1751, it's the state's oldest inland town.

During the Revolution, some 14 battles raged within a 30-mile radius here. General Cornwallis took the town and made it his command post for the British campaign throughout the South—and, despite all the military engagements in the area, Camden remained in British hands until they retreated in 1781, burning the town behind them. During the Civil War, another invader, General Sherman, brought his Union troops to burn the town once more, since it had served the Confederates as a storehouse and as a hospital.

Relics of all that history are everywhere you look, but these days Camden is equally well known for the training of fine thoroughbred horses; the internationally known **Colonial Cup** steeplechase at nearby Springdale Course draws huge crowds of devoted followers.

Make your first stop the **Kershaw County Chamber of Commerce,** 700 W. DeKalb St., Camden, SC 29020 (tel. 803/432-2525). Pick up a guidebook and a self-guided driving tour to point you to 63 historic sites in the area.

✪ **Historic Camden,** South Broad Street (tel. 432-9841), is a Revolutionary War park affiliated with the National Park Service. There are restored log houses with museum exhibits, fortifications, the Cornwallis House, powder magazine, a model of the original town of some 80 buildings, and miniature dioramas depicting military action between 1780 and 1781. The guided tour includes a narrated slide presentation and access to all museums. Hours are Tuesday through Saturday 10am to 4pm, Sunday 1 to 5pm. Adults pay $4.50; students, $1.50; children under 6 enter free. Self-guided tours are free.

At nearby **Goodale State Park,** two miles north of Camden on Old Wire Road (off U.S. 1), you'll find lake swimming and fishing, with pedal and fishing boats for rent. Bring along a picnic and take time to wander the nature trail.

DARLINGTON

Stock-car fans in their thousands invade Darlington (about 70 miles northeast of Columbia via I-20 and U.S. 52/401) in early April for NASCAR's **TransSouth 500** race, and again on Labor Day weekend for the **Southern 500.** The **Darlington County Chamber of Commerce,** 102 Orange St., P.O. Box 274, Darlington, SC 29532 (tel. 803/393-2641), can furnish detailed information on racing activity as well as sightseeing in this area.

If you arrive between the year's two main races, hie yourself over to the **NMPA Stock Car Hall of Fame/Joe Weatherly Museum** (tel. 393-2103) at the Darlington Raceway, one mile west of town on S.C. 34. It holds the world's largest collection of stock-racing cars, including those of such racing greats as Richard Petty, Fireball Roberts, and Bill Elliott. Hours are 8:30am to 5pm daily, and admission is $2.

Take a stroll through **Darlington's historic district** (the Chamber of Commerce can furnish a self-guided walking tour), and take a look at the marvelous mural, painted by Blue Sky, that shows the town square in days gone by (it's on North Main Street).

FLORENCE

Nearby Florence (10 miles south of Darlington via U.S. 52/401) is a railroad town, the home of large railyards and shops. For detailed sightseeing information, contact the **Greater Florence Chamber of Commerce,** 610 W. Palmetto St. (P.O. Box 948), Florence, SC 29501 (tel. 803/665-0515).

Located near the airport, the **Florence Air & Missile Museum** (tel. 665-5118), a World War II fighter-pilot training base, holds more than 38 aircraft, missiles, and rockets. Jet fighters, bombers, tanks, and ground-to-ground rockets are displayed.

The space suit worn by Alan Shepard on his Apollo flight is here, as are Apollo launch computers and many other space-age items. Admission is $5 for adults, $3 for children 4 to 16. It's open daily from 10am to 6pm. Take exit 170 from I-95; there are also easy-to-follow signs from U.S. 74 and U.S. 301.

The **Florence Museum,** 558 Spruce St., at Graham Street (tel. 662-3351), has African and Asian art, Native American pottery collections, and the interesting Hall of South Carolina History. The exhibits change periodically. Admission is free. It's open Tuesday to Saturday 10am to 5pm, Sunday 2 to 5pm.

ROCK HILL

Rock Hill (76 miles north of Columbia via I-77) has many preserved historic homes and neighborhoods. The **Rock Hill Chamber of Commerce,** 115 Dave Lyle Blvd. (P.O. Box 590), Rock Hill, SC 29731 (tel. 803/324-7500), has an easy-to-follow walking-tour map for visitors. The **York County Convention & Visitors Bureau,** 201 E. Main St. (P.O. Box 11377), Rock Hill, SC 29731 (tel. toll free 800/866-5200), can also furnish information on the area. Visit historic Brattonsville, the new Heritage U.S.A. Water Park, and Paramount's Carowinds Theme Park. During the season, take in an AAA baseball game at Knight's Castle or visit azalea gardens at Glencairn. Antique shops, outlet stores, and specialty shops are sure to please avid shoppers.

Take Exit 82A off I-77 to reach the **Museum of York County,** 4621 Mt. Gallant Rd. (tel. 329-2121). This modern structure holds the world's largest collection of mounted hooved African mammals, as well as art galleries, a planetarium, and the new Vernon Grant Gallery, which features works by the artist who created Kellogg's Snap, Crackle, and Pop characters. The museum store sells Catawba pottery, and the planetarium offers free shows on weekends. Picnic facilities are available, and everywhere is handicapped-accessible. Museum hours are Tuesday 9am to 9pm, Wednesday through Saturday 9am to 5pm, Sunday 1 to 5pm. Planetarium hours are Saturday at 11am, 2, 3, and 4pm. Admission to both is $3 adults, $2 students and seniors, free for children under 5.

DINING NOTE This is fish-camp country—very often you'll run across terrific fish dinners (all you can eat for practically nothing) in rustic cafés down unpaved side roads. Stop at a gas station, grocery store, or some other local establishment, and just ask—everybody has a favorite, and believe me, if you like this sort of thing, it's worth a detour to find a hospitable fish-camp eatery. To get you started, here are three fish camps in the area. It's a good idea to call ahead both for hours and for specific driving directions: **Shell Inn Fish Camp,** Rte. 6, Porter Road, Rock Hill (tel. 324-3823); **Catawba Fish Camp,** S.C. 9, Fort Lawn (tel. 872-4477); and **The Fish House,** Hickory Grove (tel. 925-2603).

YORK

York is about 15 miles northwest of Rock Hill via S.C. 5. Arm yourself in advance with detailed information on this historically rich region from the **Greater York Chamber of Commerce,** P.O. Box 97, York, SC 29745 (tel. 803/684-2590), or stop by the chamber office in York for self-guided walking-tour maps of the 340-acre York historic district. Among the more than 180 historical structures and landmarks here are beautifully preserved and restored homes.

Nearby **Historic Brattonsville,** 1444 Brattonsville Rd., McConnells (tel. 803/684-2327), is a restored Southern village of 18th- and 19th-century buildings. To reach it, take U.S. 321 from York, or S.C. 322 from Rock Hill. Restorations include the dirt-floor "Backwoodsman" cabin, a 1750s frontier home; an authentic antebellum plantation home; hand-hewn log storage buildings; a brick slave cabin; and many other restorations. Hours Tuesday and Thursday are 10am to 4pm, Saturday and Sunday 2 to 5pm. Adults pay $4, students $2. Tours are self-guided.

KINGS MOUNTAIN

On I-85, just across the border from North Carolina, the **Kings Mountain National Military Park** (from York, take S.C. 5 northwest for about 20 miles) marks the site of a Revolutionary War battle that some historians label crucial to the eventual American victory. The southern Appalachians had been virtually undisturbed by the war until 1780, when British Maj. Patrick Ferguson, who had threatened to "lay the country waste with fire and sword," set up camp here with a large loyalist force. The local backwoodsmen recruited Whigs from Virginia and North Carolina to form a largely untrained, but very determined, army to throw the invaders out. The ill-trained and outnumbered colonists converged on Kings Mountain and kept advancing on Ferguson's men—in spite of wave after wave of bayonet charges—until they took the summit. Ferguson was killed in the battle, and the Appalachians were once more under colonial control. You can see relics and a diorama of the battle at the visitors' center. It's open every day of the year except Thanksgiving Day, Christmas Day, and New Year's Day, from 9am to 5pm; admission is free.

3. AIKEN THOROUGHBRED COUNTRY

The international horse set hangs out in the country around Aiken, where horse training and racing are major preoccupations. It's a fairly common driving experience to share the road with a horse and its mount: There's even a stoplight just for horses on Whiskey Road! Nearly a thousand horses winter and train in this area, and Aiken has two racetracks, as well as polo grounds.

WHAT TO SEE & DO

Aiken lies right at the Georgia–South Carolina border, some 75 miles southwest of Columbia. Without doubt, the three weekends of horse racing in March that make up the **Aiken Triple Crown** are the highlight of the year. Even nonhorsey folks, however, will delight in the lovely old homes in the town's historic district. By contacting **Thoroughbred Country,** P.O. Box 850, Aiken, SC 29802 (tel. 803/649-7981), before you come, you may be able to arrange visits to some of the private stables around Aiken. For self-guided walking and driving tours, go by the **Aiken Chamber of Commerce,** 400 Laurens St. NW (tel. 803/641-1111).

AIKEN COUNTY HISTORICAL MUSEUM, 433 Newberry St. SW. Tel. 642-2015.

This museum occupies part of a former "Winter Colony" millionaire's estate. Of special interest are Native American artifacts, an oldtime drugstore from a little South Carolina town that no longer exists, a 19th-century schoolhouse, and early firefighting equipment.

Admission: By donation.

Open: Tues–Fri 9:30am–4:30pm, first Sun of month 2–5pm.

HOPELANDS GARDENS, 149 Dupree Place. Tel. 648-5461.

⭐ This is one of Aiken's loveliest attractions. The grounds hold the **Thorough-bred Racing Hall of Fame** in a restored carriage house. The gardens have one trail, dubbed the "touch and scent" trail, which has plaques in standard type and in braille to identify the plants and to lead visitors, blind or sighted, to a performing arts stage. There, open-air concerts are performed Monday evenings in summer, and theatrical productions are offered periodically. It's at the corner of Whiskey Road and Dupree Place.

Admission: Free.

Open: Gardens, daily 10am–dusk; Hall of Fame, Tues–Sun 2–5pm.

WHERE TO STAY

Aiken is an easy day trip from Columbia—but this part of the state is so beguiling that you may want to settle in here for a day or so. Note that when special events are on (horse races, the Masters Golf Tournament in neighboring Augusta, Georgia, etc.), rates in the Aiken area often carry a surcharge; always inquire when booking. Be sure, too, to ask about golf, honeymoon, or family package rates.

BEST WESTERN EXECUTIVE INN, 3560 Augusta Rd., Aiken, SC 29801. Tel. 803/649-3968. 60 rms. A/C TV TEL

$ Rates: $44 single; $48 double. AE, DC, MC, V.

This attractive Best Western has in-room movies, an exercise room, indoor pool, whirlpool, and a nice cocktail lounge. It's two miles west of town on U.S. 1/78.

DAYS INN, 2660 Columbia Hwy., Aiken, SC 29801. Tel. 803/642-5692, or toll free 800/325-2525. 78 rms. A/C TV TEL

$ Rates: $34–$38 single or double. AE, DC, DISC, MC, V.

⑤ Guest rooms are standard for this chain (which means more than just acceptable). While there's no restaurant, there's one within easy distance; and there is a pool. It's at the junction of I-20 and U.S. 1.

HOLLY INN, 235 Richland Ave., Aiken, SC 29801. Tel. 803/648-4265. 35 rms. A/C TV TEL

$ Rates: $32–$45 single or double. AE, MC, V.

The Holly Inn encloses a courtyard and pool in the very center of Aiken's historic district. The inn dates from 1929, and the tastefully decorated guest rooms have high ceilings typical of that era. Some have fireplaces. The new Holly House next door has suites.

WILLCOX INN, 100 Colleton Ave., Aiken, SC 29801. Tel. 803/649-1377. 30 rms. A/C TV TEL

$ Rates: $80–$105 single; $95–$120 double. Weekly rates available. AE, MC, V.

⭐ Top honors go to the present reincarnation of an 1897 inn (Winston Churchill was a guest here in days gone by). Guest rooms are individually decorated, and all have ornamental fireplaces. The lobby has the distinctive air of an English country home. Second Empire furnishings are used liberally throughout. The dining room serves all three meals, as well as an excellent Sunday brunch.

WHERE TO DINE

WILLCOX INN, 100 Colleton Ave. Tel. 649-1377.

Cuisine: AMERICAN. **Reservations:** Recommended.

$ Prices: Lunch under $10; dinner $12–$20. AE, DC, MC, V.

Open: Breakfast daily 7–10am; lunch daily 11:30am–2pm; dinner Mon–Sat 6–9:30pm.

This is your best bet. The cuisine is pleasingly eclectic, and the Southern breakfasts are a standout. Jackets are required for men.

CHAPTER 10

SOUTH CAROLINA'S UP COUNTRY

1. SPARTANBURG
2. GREENVILLE
3. ALONG THE
   CHEROKEE
   FOOTHILLS SCENIC
   HIGHWAY

South Carolina's northwest, or "up country," is a land of scenic wonders: miles and miles of peaks and waterfalls, unspoiled forests, and mountain hamlets. It was in this region that American patriots trounced vastly superior British forces at the Cowpens, one of the most decisive battles of the southern campaign during the Revolution.

1. SPARTANBURG

106 miles NW of Columbia; 226 miles NW of Charleston

GETTING THERE By Plane   The Greenville-Spartanburg Airport is served by American and American Eagle (tel. toll free 800/433-7300); Delta and Delta Connection (tel. toll free 800/221-1212); Northwest Airlink (tel. toll free 800/225-2525); USAir and USAir Express (tel. toll free 800/428-4322); and United Express (tel. toll free 800/241-6522).

By Train   For **Amtrak** information, call toll free 800/USA-RAIL.

By Bus   For local **Greyhound/Trailways** information, call 803/779-0650.

By Car   I-26 runs from Columbia to Spartanburg; I-85 reaches the city from the northeast and southwest. AAA services are available through **Carolina Motor Club,** 828 E. Main St., Spartanburg 29301 (tel. 803/583-2766).

ESSENTIALS   The **area code** is 803. The **Spartanburg Tourism and Convention Bureau,** P.O. Box 1636, Spartanburg, SC 29301 (tel. 803/594-5050; fax 803/594-5055), can furnish detailed brochures on sightseeing, accommodations, and dining.

Named for the Spartan Regiment, which marched off to battle from the town during the Revolutionary War, Spartanburg is today a leading textile center in the South. It also lays claim to being the world's largest exporter of peaches, and visitors can visit packing sheds from June through August. From Spartanburg, it's easy driving to attractions in the up country. The city is only a short distance off the Cherokee Foothills Scenic Highway.

WHAT TO SEE & DO

SIGHTS IN TOWN

REGIONAL MUSEUM OF SPARTANBURG COUNTY, 501 Otis Blvd. Tel. 596-3501.

✪ This museum features a permanent collection of exhibits depicting the Battle of Cowpens and the founding of the city, as well as an extensive doll collection. Periodic exhibits deal with up-country life.

Admission: $1 adults, 50¢ children under 12.
Open: Daily 10am–noon and 3–5pm.

NEARBY PLANTATIONS

WALNUT GROVE PLANTATION, 1200 Ott's Shoal Rd., Roebuck. Tel. 576-6546.

✪ A short drive south from Spartanburg, you'll find a superb example of a colonial plantation house—not the stately columned sort found in the low country, but a large, simple farmhouse typical of landowner's homes in this region. Built in 1765 on a land grant from King George III, the house itself is fascinating, with its authentic furnishings (and its separate kitchen filled with early-vintage gadgets). Outbuildings include a barn that holds a Conestoga-type wagon.

Admission: $3.50 adults, $2 students.
Open: Apr–Oct, Tues–Sat 11am–5pm, plus year-round Sun 2–5pm. **Closed:** Major holidays. **Directions:** Go 9½ miles south of I-85 on I-26, one mile from the intersection with U.S. 221.

THOMAS PRICE HOUSE, 1200 Oak View Farms Rd., Woodruff. Tel. 476-2483.

Also south of Spartanburg, this imposing house was built in 1795 from bricks made right on the premises. They were laid in a distinctive Flemish bond, which—along with the inside end chimneys and steep gambrel roof—gives the house a style seldom seen in these parts. Its builder was a gentleman farmer, but an enterprising one: He ran a general store and the post office and even had a license to feed and bed stagecoach travelers in his home, licensed as a "house of entertainment." Furnishings, while not the originals, are all authentic items of the period.

Admission: $2.50 adults, $1.50 students and seniors.
Open: Apr–Oct, Tues–Sat 11am–5pm, Sun 2–5pm; Nov–Mar, Sun 2–5pm.
Directions: Go seven miles south on I-26 to exit 35, then west via signposted county roads 50 and 86.

AN EXCURSION TO THE COWPENS NATIONAL BATTLEFIELD

If time won't permit a drive down the Cherokee Foothills Scenic Highway (see below), you can visit the ✪ **Cowpens National Battlefield,** only 18 miles north of Spartanburg, by taking I-85 north to its junction with U.S. 221, then on to S.C. 11 (the Scenic Highway) and its junction with S.C. 110.

A decisive colonial victory was won here in January 1781. Gen. Nathanael Greene, who headed the American forces in the South, sent a force under Daniel Morgan to divert the attention of British General Cornwallis from Greene's reorganization of colonial troops. When General Morgan threatened the British fort at Ninety Six,

Cornwallis dispatched a large number of infantry and dragoons to repulse the backwoods army, and the two forces met at the Cowpens (named for a nearby natural cattle enclosure). When the British were at last defeated, they had suffered 110 men killed, 200 wounded, and another 550 captured—while Morgan lost 12 men and counted 60 wounded! This defeat of a corps of professional British Regulars was not only important militarily, it also spurred some doubting patriots into action. Make your first stop the visitors' center to watch "Daybreak at the Cowpens," a multi-image slide presentation about the battle. The battlefield is open daily from 9am to 8:30pm from Memorial Day to Labor Day. The visitors' center is open all year from 9am to 5pm.

WHERE TO STAY

HOTELS

DAYS INN, 578 N. Church St., Spartanburg, SC 29303. Tel. 803/585-4311, or toll free 800/325-2525. 80 rms. A/C TV TEL **Directions:** Take exit 72C from I-85, then go two miles east on S.C. 56.
$ Rates: $38 single; $42 double. Senior discount available. AE, DC, MC, V.
Guest rooms here meet the usual high standards of this chain. In addition, there's in-room cable TV and movies, a pool, and a coffee shop.

HAMPTON INN, 4930 College Dr., Spartanburg, SC 29301. Tel. 803/576-6080, or toll free 800/426-7866. 112 rms. A/C TV TEL **Directions:** Take exit 69 from I-85.
$ Rates (including continental breakfast): $42 single; $48 double. Children under 12 stay free with parents. Senior discount available. AE, DC, DISC, MC, V.
Rooms here are attractive and comfortable, and if you need a crib, it's free. There's cable TV and a pool.

RAMADA INN, 1000 Hearon Circle, Spartanburg, SC 29303. Tel. 803/578-7170, or toll free 800/228-2828. 198 rms. A/C TV TEL **Directions:** Go northbound on I-85 and take exit 72C to Frontage Road; then go southbound to exit 73A.
$ Rates: $45 single; $54 double. AE, DC, DISC, MC, V.
Some rooms here have whirlpool baths and/or extra-large beds, and free coffee is dispensed in the lobby. There's a pool, whirlpool, sauna, health club, and playground, as well as a good restaurant and a cocktail lounge with dancing and entertainment Monday through Saturday.

RESIDENCE INN BY MARRIOTT, 9011 Fairforest Rd. (P.O. Box 4156), Spartanburg, SC 29305. Tel. 803/576-3333, or toll free 800/331-3131. 88 suites. A/C TV TEL **Directions:** Take exit 71 from I-85.
$ Rates: $79–$95 single or double studio suite; $99–$125 penthouse suite. Discounts for stays over six nights. AE, DC, MC, V.
This upscale hostelry offers studio suites and two-story penthouse suites. All have separate living and sleeping quarters and kitchens (the inn even provides grocery-shopping service). Guests can enjoy a pool, whirlpool, health club, sports court, barbecue and picnic facilities, coin laundry, and a complimentary hospitality hour Monday through Thursday. No-smoking suites are available. Half of the suites now have VCRs.

CAMPING

The **Foothills KOA of Spartanburg,** 600 Campground Rd., Spartanburg, SC 29303 (tel. 803/576-0970), signposted from exit 69 on I-85 and exit 17 on I-26, offers 125 sites, both shaded and open, on exceptionally well-maintained grounds. There are groceries and propane, a coin laundry, pool, recreation room, playground, and a nature trail for end-of-the-day walks. Pets are welcome. Rates are $20 to $25 for two, $4 for each additional person.

In wooded grounds set back from the highway, **Pine Ridge Campground,** 199 Pine Ridge Campground Rd., Roebuck, SC 29376 (tel. 803/576-0302), has 45 shaded sites. There's a pool, recreation room, playground, and fishing. Pets are accepted. Rates run $9 to $16 for up to four people, $2 for each additional person.

WHERE TO DINE

PICCADILLY CAFETERIA, 166 Westgate Mall. Tel. 574-2044.
 Cuisine: AMERICAN. **Reservations:** Not accepted.
$ **Prices:** Lunch and dinner $5–$10. AE, CB, DC, DISC, MC, V.
 Open: Daily 11am–8:30pm.

Piccadilly Cafeteria is a good place to feed the entire family without busting the budget. Home-cooked entrées of chicken, beef, and fish here are a cut above the usual cafeteria fare.

2. GREENVILLE

90 miles NW of Columbia; 215 miles NW of Charleston;
243 miles NW of Myrtle Beach; 141 miles NE of Atlanta

GETTING THERE   By Plane   See "Getting There," Chapter 6.

By Train   Amtrak stops daily at 1120 W. Washington St. (tel. toll free 800/USA-RAIL).

By Bus   For **Greyhound/Trailways** information, call 803/232-7378.

By Car   I-395 begins at Greenville and goes southeast towards Columbia; I-85 passes through the city and goes northeast to Charlotte or southwest to Atlanta.

ESSENTIALS   The **area code** is 803. The **Greater Greenville Convention & Visitors Bureau** is at 500 E. North St. (P.O. Box 10527), Greenville, SC 29603 (tel. 803/233-0461, or toll free 800/476-8687).

H alfway between Charlotte, N.C. and Atlanta, Ga., Greenville is an inviting upstate city situated in the foothills of the Blue Ridge Mountains. Sharing the limelight with its neighbors, Spartanburg and Anderson, the area is populated by more than 840,000 people.

In the 1700s, Greenville was occupied by the Cherokee Indians. As the area grew more populated, it became known as a resort for low-country planters during the antebellum era and later was introduced to the textile industry when the Huguenot Mill opened in the 1870s. Today, it enjoys a reputation for its more high-tech advancements—and it has friendly folks who welcome visitors warmly, as you'll see.

WHAT TO SEE & DO

Greenville has much to offer visitors. **Nippon Center Yagoto** is a complex of buildings constructed in the Shoin Zukuri style, which means the interiors were built without nails. The furniture has as many as 20 coats of the traditional Japanese black cashew coating, mixed with black or orange-red pigment. The **Rope Mountains Science Center** is open to the public on the second Saturday of each month. Also on those grounds are the **Daniel Observatory, Hooper Planetarium,** and **Living History Farm. Furman University** is a private liberal arts college on 750 acres.

Also, be sure to check out the city's historical buildings: the **Beattie House,** 8 Bennett St.; the pre–Civil War **Christ Episcopal Church,** 10 N. Church St.; the **Kilgore-Lewis House,** 560 N. Academy St.; the **John Wesley United Methodist Church,** 101 E. Court St.; and **Whitehall,** Earle St., the 1813 summer home of a South Carolina governor that's listed in the National Register of Historic Places.

For sports enthusiasts, Greenville and its environs offer golf at a number of public courses, bicycling, horseback riding, and tennis.

On the cultural side, you must stop at **Bob Jones University** to see its fine art collection. For information on the **Greenville Ballet,** write to P.O. Box 8702, Greenville, SC 29604, or call 803/235-6456, or 803/467-3000. The new **Peace Center for the Performing Arts** is home to the Greenville Symphony Orchestra and other nationally known artists.

WHERE TO STAY

EXPENSIVE

EMBASSY SUITES GOLF AND CONFERENCE CENTER, 670 Verdae Blvd., Greenville, SC 29607. Tel. 803/676-9090, or toll free 800/ EMBASSY. 268 suites. A/C MINIBAR TV TEL **Directions:** Take I-385 to the Roper Mountain Road exit.

$ Rates: $109 single; $119 double; $79 weekends. AE, CB, DC, DISC, MC, V.

This is the first Embassy Suites in the Greenville area, and I'll confess that it was still under construction when I toured it. The nine-story atrium design must be pleasing guests by now because it was poised to open shortly. If you've ever stayed at an Embassy before, you probably know the routine: lovely suites in contemporary colors with separate living and sleeping areas, wet bars, microwave ovens, refrigerators, two remote-control TVs, modern baths, and sofabeds in the living rooms. An indoor pool, outdoor pool, and fitness room are part of the amenities, too. The signature cooked-to-order full breakfasts are served in the atrium, amid trees, plants, and twinkling lights. The concept is a popular one. Embassy was first with the idea, which explains why they are the best in the business.

GREENVILLE HILTON AND TOWERS, 45 W. Orchard Park Dr., Greenville, SC 29615. Tel. 803/232-4747, or toll free 800/445-8667. Fax 803/235-6248. 256 rms. A/C TV TEL

$ Rates: $90–$110 single or double. AE, CB, DC, DISC, ER, MC, V.

Three miles out of the center of town, the Hilton is a major player in the local hotel game and is a rather impressive deluxe choice. The beautiful glass motor entry leads to an equally striking lobby faced with marble and appointed with rich detail, custom fixtures, and expensive furniture. The lounge hops to the beat of Top 40, while another bar is more appealing to the pin-striped crowd. For leisure, you might sweat it out in an aerobics class, the sauna, or in the fitness room, or you might take a swim in the indoor pool or whirlpool. Rooms all have mirrored closet doors, remote-control TV, and colonial-modern appointments. For even more comfort, the executive level includes a private lounge where continental breakfast is served.

GREENVILLE-SPARTANBURG AIRPORT MARRIOTT, One Parkway

East, Greenville, SC 29615. Tel. 803/297-0300, or toll free 800/228-9290. 204 rms. A/C TV TEL **Directions:** Take I-85 to the Pelham Road exit.
$ Rates: $99 single, $119 double. AE, CB, DC, DISC, ER, MC, V.

⭐ Many consider the Marriott to be the best of Greenville's best. It has luxurious style, as evidenced by the tons of marble throughout, the elegant restaurant, the smartly dressed staff, and the leisure facilities—which include both indoor and outdoor swimming pools, a sauna, and a whirlpool. You can book a room with two queen-size beds or one king-size bed, contemporary decor, remote-control TVs, desks, and attractive baths. It's two miles from the airport.

HYATT REGENCY GREENVILLE, 220 N. Main St., Greenville, SC 29601. Tel. 803/325-1234, or toll free 800/228-9000. 330 rms. A/C TV TEL
$ Rates: $75–$125 single; $80–$130 double. AE, CB, DC, DISC, MC, V.
Can you name a hotel lobby that is actually a designated city park? Right. The Hyatt Regency Greenville. Hey, these folks know what they're doing, and they have fun doing it—but they should, since they're the only game in town, rather downtown (all the competition is a couple miles away). Free parking is available next door in the handy garage, and there is valet parking too. The trademark atrium lobby is here along with other Hyatt touches: terrace dining, Regency Club floor, and meeting space to beat the band—in fact, they sometimes have a band, too. The rooms are first class, the style is modern, and some pretty good deals can be had on weekends.

MODERATE

COURTYARD BY MARRIOTT, 70 Orchard Park Dr., Greenville, SC 29615. Tel. 803/234-0300, or toll free 800/321-2211. Fax 803/234-0296. 146 rms. A/C TV TEL
$ Rates: $69 single; $79 double. AE, CB, DC, DISC, MC, V.

⑤ When Marriott Hotels came up with this format to appeal to both business and leisure travelers, they probably had no idea the concept would be so successful. The blueprint format is followed throughout the chain, and it is a model for the hotel industry for its efficiency, comfort, and upscale ambience at affordable prices. The low-rise construction gives the impression of a homey hotel where you don't feel overwhelmed by all of the features, such as the outdoor pool and indoor whirlpool. All the accommodations are bright and inviting with contemporary colors, pile carpet, and modern baths. It's off I-385.

HOLIDAY INN, 4295 Augusta Rd., Greenville, SC 29605. Tel. 803/277-8921, or toll free 800/465-4329. 153 rms. A/C TV TEL **Directions:** Take exit 45A off I-85 at Augusta Road.
$ Rates: $39–$85 single or double. AE, CB, DC, DISC, MC, V.

⑤ You'll get your money's worth at this Holiday Inn, which has a restaurant and lounge popular with the local folks. The hotel's decor has been updated, and it features an outdoor pool, but not much else. However, you can use the YMCA for free with your room key. More attention to detail has been paid to the guest rooms here than at most Holiday Inns.

RESIDENCE INN, 48 McPrice Court, Greenville, SC 29615. Tel. 803/297-0099, or toll free 800/331-3131. Fax 803/288-8203. 96 suites. A/C TV TEL
Directions: Take I-385 to Haywood Road; McPrice Court is off Orchard Park Dr.
$ Rates (including continental breakfast): $59–$79 single or double. AE, CB, DC, DISC, ER, MC, V.
The familiar Residence Inn concept offers guests the comforts of condominium living with the conveniences of a hotel. The inn offers a hospitality hour Monday through

Thursday, free newspapers, an outdoor whirlpool and swimming pool, fitness rooms, a sports court, and laundry. Accommodations are suites with full kitchens, living rooms, and one or two beds. Most suites have wood-burning fireplaces. This is an excellent value, especially for families.

BUDGET

QUALITY INN HAYWOOD, 50 Orchard Park Dr., Greenville, SC 29615. Tel. 803/297-9000, or toll free 800/228-5151. Fax 803/297-8292. 146 rms. A/C MINIBAR TV TEL **Directions:** Take I-85 to I-385 at Haywood Road; you can see the hotel at the exit.

$ Rates: $43 single; $49 double. AE, CB, DC, DISC, ER, MC, V.

Ⓢ The rates here alone are enough to catch your eye, but there are also solid accommodations and facilities to consider. All the rooms have coffeemakers and double, queen-size, or king-size beds. The restaurant serves all meals, and you can relax out by the pool if the weather cooperates. Other restaurants are in the neighborhood, too.

TRAVELODGE GREENVILLE [HAYWOOD], 830 Congaree Rd., Greenville, SC 29607. Tel. 803/288-6221, or toll free 800/255-3050. Fax 803/288-2778. 125 rms. A/C TV TEL **Directions:** Take I-395 to Roper Mountain Road (exit 37); the hotel is right there.

$ Rates (including continental breakfast): $30–$37 single or double. AE, CB, DC, DISC, ER, MC, V.

This five-story hotel caters to budgeting motorists, features an outdoor pool, and provides free passes to a nearby fitness center. Rates include free local phone calls. As the rates indicate, rooms are modest but comfortable.

WHERE TO DINE

ADDY'S DUTCH CAFE & RESTAURANT, 17 E. Coffee St. Tel. 232-ADDY.
   Cuisine: EUROPEAN/CONTINENTAL. **Reservations:** Recommended.
$ Prices: Main courses $9–$16. AE, DC, MC, V.
   Open: Mon–Fri 4:30pm–2am, Sat 4:30pm–midnight.
Between Main and Brown Streets, Addy's enjoys a good reputation among knowledgeable purists—those who love a bit of Europe in their backyard. The atmosphere is distinctly European and fun with more than 40 labels of beer offered, not to mention all the cheeses.

McGUFFYS, 711 Congaree Rd. Tel. 288-3116.
   Cuisine: AMERICAN. **Reservations:** Not required. **Directions:** Take I-385 to Roper Mountain Road (exit 37); it's near the Travelodge.
$ Prices: Appetizers $3–$5; main courses $5–$13; dinner for two $20–$25. AE, DISC, MC, V.
   Open: Mon–Fri 11am–1:30am, Sat 11am–midnight, Sun 11am–10pm.
They pack them in at McGuffys. The bar is as popular as the restaurant, or more so. TV monitors, natural woods, green decor, and brass trim are combined for the party atmosphere that twenty-somethings enjoy. If you want to eat, the menu includes pasta, fish, steaks, and freshly prepared vegetables.

OMEGA DINER/STAX'S BAKERY, 72 Orchard Park Dr. Tel. 297-6639.
   Cuisine: AMERICAN/BAKERY. **Reservations:** Not accepted.
$ Prices: Appetizers $1.95–$4.50; main courses $6.25–$11.95; dinner for two $22; light fare $1.65–$4.15. AE, CB, DC, MC, V.

Open: Sun–Wed 6:30am–11pm, Thurs 6:30am–2am, Fri–Sat 6:30am–4:30am.

The Omega Diner is a great place for after-hours. You can choose from waffles, biscuits, French toast, pancakes, sandwiches, and burgers. It's always busy—it's sort of an upscale Denny's without all the charmless chain trimmings. The decor includes brass, tile, and oak woods. The bakery will no doubt catch your eye.

SEVEN OAKS, 104 Broadus Ave. Tel. 232-1895.
   Cuisine: AMERICAN/SOUTHERN. **Reservations:** Recommended.
$ Prices: Appetizers $3.50–$5.50; main courses $14–$27; dinner for two $45. AE, MC, V.
   Open: Dinner Mon–Sat 6–10:30pm.

For a special evening out, Seven Oaks is the place to come. The beautiful white clapboard mansion with its grand veranda and outside table service will likely please the most discriminating diner. The atmosphere is upbeat, the service is attentive, and the Southern menu is both appetizing and enterprising. The veranda offers a romantic mixture of gardens, elegant table settings, and candlelight.

3. ALONG THE CHEROKEE FOOTHILLS SCENIC HIGHWAY

S.C. 11, known as the Cherokee Foothills Scenic Highway, curves 130 miles through the heart of South Carolina's Blue Ridge Mountain foothills, stretching in an arc from I-85 at Gaffney, near the North Carolina border, almost to the Georgia border at Lake Hartwell State Park, where it links up once more with I-85. The drive is a beautiful one on its own merits, but the rewards are plentiful for those who veer off the highway. There are no less than 10 state parks and 5 recreational areas along the way, as well as many county-operated parks. Anglers note: Bring your gear, as fish are just waiting for the bait in local streams and lakes. And historians will be happy to find a Revolutionary War battlefield; South Carolina's only covered bridge; a Native American museum; and the Pendleton historic district, one of the nation's largest.

INFORMATION   The **South Carolina Department of Parks, Recreation and Tourism,** P.O. Box 71, Columbia, SC 29202 (tel. 803/734-0122), can furnish a detailed route map and an informative brochure. For details on state parks, some of which allow camping, contact the **South Carolina Division of State Parks,** 1205 Pendleton St., Columbia, SC 29201 (tel. 803/734-0159).

FROM GAFFNEY TO LAKE HARTWELL STATE PARK

Join the highway at Gaffney (a short drive north on I-85 from Spartanburg). You'll know you're there when you see the town's huge water tower, dubbed the Peachoid because it looks just like a gigantic peach.

As you travel south, look for signs leading to a turnoff for **Campbell's Bridge,** which dates to 1909 and is the only covered bridge still standing in the state. The bridge is south of the highway; to the north, at about the same turnpoint, detour to see the 1,000-foot, sheer rock face of **Glassy Mountain.**

There are numerous overlooks along the highway that afford breathtaking views. On Caesar's Head Mountain, in Caesar's Head State Park, an easy-to-walk, two-mile trail takes you to **Raven Cliff Falls,** where you can view the spectacle from a wood deck. **Sassafras Mountain,** north of the highway in Table Rock State Park (Rte. 3, Pickens; tel. 878-9813), near the little town of Rocky Bottom, is the highest in South Carolina, with an elevation of 3,548 feet. At the nature center, look for exhibits on the park's flora, fauna, and geology. The park opens at 6am daily, with seasonal closing hours.

Plan a stop at the **Keowee-Toxaway State Park,** on the shores of Lake Keowee (108 Residence Dr., Sunset; tel. 868-2605), to spend some time at the interesting **Cherokee Indian Museum,** and to walk a short trail along which kiosks house exhibits about Cherokee lifestyles. The park is open daily from 9am to sunset, the museum until 5pm, with no admission. There are also rental cabins, campsites, and picnic areas.

You may want to linger a few days at ✪ **Lake Hartwell State Park,** the southern terminus of the Cherokee Foothills Scenic Highway. It's a good base for several interesting day trips, and the park itself offers a host of activities. For details on recreation and accommodations, contact the Division of State Parks (see "Information," above).

PENDLETON

The little town of Pendleton, a short drive north from Lake Hartwell, is headquarters for the ✪ **Pendleton District Commission,** which covers three adjoining counties. For advance information, contact the **Pendleton District Historical, Recreational, and Tourism Commission,** 125 E. Queen St. (P.O. Box 565), Pendleton, SC 29670 (tel. 803/646-3782). The official tourism season begins with the award-winning **Historic Pendleton Spring Jubilee,** the first weekend in April. Across from Pendleton's village green, stop by **Hunter's Store,** an 1850s restoration that now serves as a visitors' center. They can furnish cassette-tape tours of the town and maps and information for the entire district. Allow time to browse through the gift shop, which stocks local handmade arts and crafts.

WHERE TO STAY & DINE

LIBERTY HALL INN, 621 S. Mechanic St., Pendleton, SC 29670. Tel. 803/646-7500, or toll free 800/643-7944. 10 rms. A/C TV
$ Rates (including breakfast): $52–$62 single; $57–$67 double. Weekly rates available. AE, DC, DISC, MC, V.

This charming 1840s building began life as a private home. Guest rooms (in which smoking is prohibited) are individually decorated with antiques and ceiling fans. Even if you don't stay here, consider making a reservation for dinner (Monday through Saturday 6 to 9pm). A four-course meal can be had for $11 to $16 (around $9 from the children's menu) in one of two candlelit dining rooms or on the garden deck or one of the verandas. Dinners come complete with fresh vegetables and rice pilaf, and specialties include beef tenderloin marinated in port wine, soy sauce, and herbs; veal Lombardy; and Trout Italiano. They also have a quite respectable wine list. The inn is a short walk from the town square, six miles from I-85.

AN EXCURSION TO NINETY SIX NATIONAL HISTORIC SITE

Farther afield, ✪ **Ninety Six National Historic Site** (tel. 803/543-4068) is well worth a visit. Drive south via U.S. 178 to Greenwood; the site is on S.C. 248 two miles south of Ninety Six. This was a frontier trading post, and served as a fort during the French and Indian War before South Carolina's first Revolutionary War battle erupted here. The visitors' center, operated by the National Park Service, has loads of information on the archeological digs and the restoration work now afoot. Along the one-mile foot trail, you'll see the old earthworks, traces of the old village, a reconstructed stockade, and an early log cabin. The park is open from dawn to sunset; the visitors' center is open 8am to 5pm daily. Admission is free.

CHAPTER 11
PLANNING A TRIP TO GEORGIA

Georgia is not only the largest state east of the Mississippi, it is also one of the most varied and complex. Though it is often thought of as a sleepy bastion of the Old South, home of Tara-like plantations and a slow-moving social life, Georgia from the beginning has had a bustling commerce. Savannah, surrounded by cotton and rice plantations, was an enterprising seaport, and its plantation owners were as much involved in shipping and trade as in overseeing their land holdings. Atlanta began as a railroad terminal, and Columbus came into being because of the water power of the Chattahoochee and its nine-foot-deep channel—navigable all the way to the Gulf of Mexico—that provided easy access to the world's markets. Industry, agriculture, social graciousness, and business activity have all been woven together to create the character of a state that very often surprises visitors.

That same diversity characterizes Georgia's recreation and sightseeing attractions. The beaches and creature comforts of the Golden Isles lie not far from Brunswick and Savannah, cities rich in historical sights. The big-city excitement of Atlanta has its own special lure. If you're looking for that antebellum Old South, Thomasville's plantation country is perfect. Outdoorsmen can fish and hunt, whitewater enthusiasts will have no trouble finding canoe trails down the state's rushing rivers, and golfers will bump into excellent courses all over the state, if they're not busy gaping at the world's finest players in the Masters Golf Tournament in April at Augusta. I just can't think of any kind of traveler who won't find something exciting in Georgia.

1. GETTING TO KNOW GEORGIA

GEOGRAPHY

Georgia's terrain slopes down to the sea, from the Blue Ridge Mountains in the north

WHAT'S SPECIAL ABOUT GEORGIA

Historic Cities

- [ ] Atlanta, the state's capital, played a vital role as an important rail center in the Civil War.
- [ ] Savannah was the setting for the state's birth and today is a model of historic restoration and preservation.
- [ ] Macon, with its 70,000 cherry trees.

Sea Islands

- [ ] Known collectively as the Golden Isles, St. Simons, Jekyll, and Sea islands have magnificent beaches and are accessible by automobile.
- [ ] Cumberland Island, a designated National Seashore with broad sandy beaches, is a haven for wildlife, as well as for people who look for a respite from resort development.

Mountains

- [ ] The Blue Ridge Mountains near Georgia's northwest border mark the beginning of the Appalachian Trail.
- [ ] Brasstown Bald Mountain, near the North Carolina border, rises to 4,784 feet, the highest elevation in the state.
- [ ] Stone Mountain, near Atlanta, with its recreational and historic park, is a massive granite dome on whose face are sculpted the figures of Jefferson Davis, Gen. Stonewall Jackson, and Gen. Robert E. Lee, all on horseback.

Recreation and Scenic Areas

- [ ] The Chattahoochee National Forest, a setting of great scenic beauty along the state's northern border.

- [ ] Between Macon and Athens, the Oconee National Forest is popular for its natural beauty and for its recreational sites.

Historic Sites

- [ ] The Martin Luther King, Jr., National Historic Site in Atlanta is a memorial to one of the state's greatest black leaders.
- [ ] Kennesaw Mountain National Battlefield Park, northwest of Marietta, was the site of an 1864 battle that almost halted Sherman's march through Georgia.
- [ ] The Andersonville National Historic Site commemorates the Civil War's most infamous prison camp.

Plantations

- [ ] The Antebellum Plantation complex in Stone Mountain Park, near Atlanta, features a plantation home, an overseer's dwelling, slave cabins, and other typical outbuildings of an early 19th-century plantation.
- [ ] The Hofwyl-Broadfield Plantation, near Brunswick, is a rice plantation carved from swampland whose grounds are now designated a wildlife preserve.
- [ ] Thomasville is surrounded by several splendid antebellum plantations.

central and northeast border regions, to the rolling piedmont southeast of the mountains, and on to the coastal plain, ending on the shores of the Atlantic. A network of important navigable rivers—the Chattahoochee, the Ocmulgee, the Oconee, and the Savannah—originates chiefly in the piedmont section. In the southeast, the Okefenokee Swamp is one of the country's last remaining natural swamp areas.

DATELINE

- **1540** De Soto explores region of today's Georgia.
- **1565** Spanish soldiers arrive, but are forced by combined French and Indian resistance to retreat to the sea islands.
- **1732** King George II of England grants royal charter for the Georgia territory. Gen. James Oglethorpe sails in November with 114 settlers.
- **1736** Fort Frederica is built on St. Simons Island; the first golf course in Georgia is constructed by wealthy Scots landowners at the site of present-day Darien.
- **1742** British defeat the Spanish in the Battle of Bloody Marsh.
- **1773** Georgia's slave population grows to over 15,000.
- **1776** British warships arrive at Savannah; three Georgia delegates sign the Declaration of Independence in Philadelphia.
- **1778** Savannah falls to the British.
- **1782** British forces surrender at Savannah.

(continues)

HISTORY

In 1540, Hernando de Soto became the first European to explore Georgia and the Southeast. Spanish missions had settled in Georgia by 1566, but not to stay. In 1733, the English arrived in the person of Gen. James Oglethorpe and his small band of settlers. It was only after a back-and-forth, four-year struggle called the War of Jenkins' Ear (1739–1743) was settled by Oglethorpe's decisive victory at the Battle of Bloody Marsh that the English future of the colony was secured. From 1745, when Oglethorpe and his trustees surrendered their charter to the English king, until the Revolution, the region was a royal province.

As news of Georgia's wealth of natural resources spread, it drew new settlers from the north and from all over Europe; Germans, Scots highlanders, Swiss, Welsh, French, and Irish all arrived with a driving industriousness. They followed the rivers inland, explored and settled the rolling piedmont, and pushed on into the western mountains. As the Revolution approached, those in the north agitated for freedom from the British, and were in bitter conflict with the entrenched loyalists along the coast. Eventually, however most of Georgia's residents came together in support of the fight for independence.

Just prior to the Civil War, there was division and conflict among Georgians again over the issue of slavery; the state seceded from the Union and joined the Confederacy in 1861. The war was a complete disaster for Georgia. Its manufacturing plants lay in ruins, plantations and small farms alike were burned over, and most young men were either killed or suffered lifelong wounds. It remained for the older leaders to rebuild a shattered economy. What had been large plantations, useless without slave labor, became small, privately owned farms. Out of the ashes of Atlanta rose an even greater metropolis, its economy still based on transportation.

In the years since, manufacturing plants have sprouted all over the state; the textile industry has become important as a means of converting one of the state's most important crops into finished products; and Jimmy Carter went from peanut farming to the governor's chair, then on to the U.S. presidency. Today's Georgia is a state that cherishes its past but looks to the future.

FAMOUS GEORGIANS

Conrad Potter Aiken (1889–1973) Savannah-born poet, novelist, and short-story writer; winner of Pulitzer prize in 1930.

Thomas Green Bethune (1849–1907) Born a slave near Columbus, he became an internationally famous pianist and composer known as "Blind Tom."

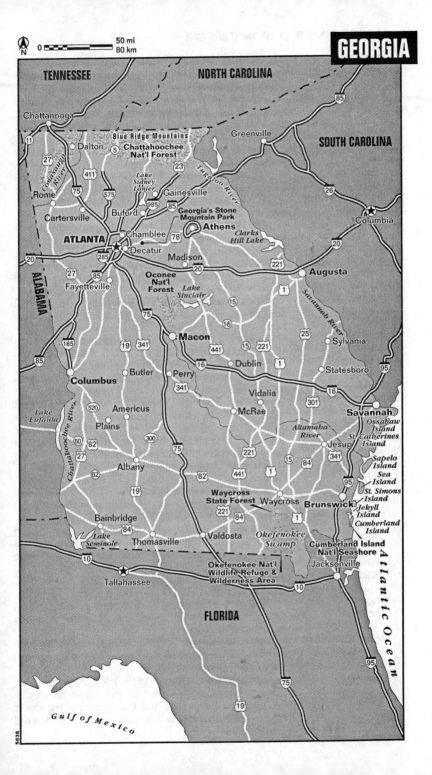

GEORGIA

N

0 — 50 mi
0 — 80 km

TENNESSEE

NORTH CAROLINA

SOUTH CAROLINA

Chattanooga

11

27

Dalton

Blue Ridge Mountains

5

Chattahoochee Nat'l Forest

Greenville

85

411

Coosawattee River

23

26

Rome

75

575

Lake Sidney Lanier

Gainesville

Tugaloo River

Cartersville

Buford

985

85

Georgia's Stone Mountain Park

Columbia

ATLANTA

Chamblee

78

Athens

Clarks Hill Lake

20

285

Decatur

Madison

20

221

Augusta

ALABAMA

27

85

Fayetteville

Oconee Nat'l Forest

Lake Sinclair

1

Savannah River

185

75

15

25

85

19

341

Macon

441

16

15

221

Sylvania

95

Columbus

Butler

Perry

16

Dublin

1

Statesboro

520

341

Vidalia

16

Americus

300

McRae

301

Savannah

Lake Eufaula

Plains

75

Altamaha River

Ossabaw Island

50

82

Albany

82

441

15

84

Jesup

341

St. Catherines Island

27

62

19

221

1

Sapelo Island

Sea Island

Waycross State Forest

Waycross

95

St. Simons Island

Bainbridge

84

221

84

1

Brunswick

Jekyll Island

Lake Seminole

Thomasville

Valdosta

Okefenokee Swamp

Cumberland Island

10

Okefenokee Nat'l Wildlife Refuge & Wilderness Area

Cumberland Island Nat'l Seashore

Jacksonville

Tallahassee

10

95

Chattahoochee River

FLORIDA

Atlantic Ocean

75

19

Gulf of Mexico

5636

Erskine Preston Caldwell (1903–) Noted novelist born in White Oak. Best known for his novels *Tobacco Road* and *God's Little Acre*.

James Earl ["Jimmy"] Carter, Jr. (1924–) Born in Plains, he went on to become a nuclear physicist, naval officer, peanut farmer, state senator, governor, and 39th president of the United States.

Ray Charles (1932–) Noted blind pianist and singer born in Albany.

Tyrus Raymond ["Ty"] Cobb (1886–1961) Baseball Hall of Famer born in rural Banks County. His 4,191 hits during his 1905 to 1928 career remained a long-standing record.

Melvyn Douglas (1901–1981) Academy Award winner (twice), born in Macon. His best-known performances were in *Hud* and *Being There*.

Joel Chandler Harris (1848–1908) Born in Eatonton, he is best remembered as creator of the beloved Uncle Remus stories.

John Henry ["Doc"] Holliday (1852–1887) Born in Georgia, he migrated to Texas at an early age for health reasons and became a friend of lawman Wyatt Earp.

Robert Tyre ["Bobby"] Jones, Jr. (1902–1971) Atlanta-born golfer won the U.S. Amateur championship five times and the U.S. Open three times.

Stacy Keach (1941–) Popular television and movie actor best known for his *Mike Hammer* series.

Martin Luther King, Jr (1929–1968) Civil rights leader who organized some of the earliest protest marches, including the march on Washington in 1963. He was shot down in Memphis in 1968, but remains a dominating figure in African-American affairs.

Gladys Knight (1944–) Popular singer and recording artist born in Atlanta.

Carson Smith McCullers (1917–1967) Noted author and playwright, born in Columbus and best remembered for her 1946 play *Member of the Wedding*.

Margaret Mitchell (1900–1949) Atlanta-born author of *Gone With the Wind*, written when she was recuperating from a serious illness. The book sold more than one million copies its first six months of publication. The Georgia Legislature named her "Georgia's most famous person" in 1985.

Mary Flannery O'Connor (1925–1964) Savannah-born novelist and short-story writer who won international acclaim.

Burt Reynolds (1936–) Popular movie actor born in Waycross, who has been a leader in developing local stage companies in Florida.

Jackie Robinson (1919–1972) Born in Cairo, Georgia, he became the first African-American to play major league baseball in the United States. His career spanned 1947 to 1956, and he was elected to the Baseball Hall of Fame.

Dean Rusk (1909–) Canton-born secretary of state in the Johnson administrations, as well as longtime president of the Rockefeller Foundation.

Joanne Woodward (1930–) Born in Thomasville, this noted film and television actress won the 1957 Academy Award for her role in *The Three Faces of Eve.*

Andrew Jackson Young, Jr. (1932–) Civil rights leader whose political career includes service as U.S. ambassador to the United Nations in the Carter administration and the mayoralty of Atlanta.

RECOMMENDED BOOKS

GENERAL

Atlanta: A City of Dreams (Peachtree Publishers, 1990). A futuristic look at the Atlanta of 1996.

Bailey, Sue, and William H Bailey. *Cycling Through Georgia* (Susan Hunter Publishing, 1989).

Black, Denise, and Janet Schwartz. *Around Atlanta with Children* (Sigma Publishing, 1990). A guide for family activities.

Bridges, Herb. *Frankly, My Dear,———*(Mercer University Press, 1986). *Gone With the Wind* memorabilia.

Cochran, Glenda. *Cumberland Island: A National Seashore* (Island House, 1988). Explores this wildlife refuge and its protected inhabitants of the animal world.

Crutchfield, James A., ed. *The Georgia Almanac and Book of Facts* (Rutledge Hill, 1986).

Hepburn, Lawrence R. *Contemporary Georgia* (Carl Vinson Institute of Government, 1987).

Mitchell, William. *Gardens of Georgia* (Peachtree Publishers, 1989).

Schemmel, William. *Georgia: Off the Beaten Path* (Globe Pequot Press, 1990). A colorful and informative guide to unique places.

Sojourn in Savannah (Printcraft Press, 1986). An official guidebook and map to Georgia's birthplace.

HISTORY

Bell, Malcolm. *Historic Savannah* (Historic Savannah Foundation, 1981). A literate and entertaining history of the city.

Bryan, T. Conn. *Confederate Georgia* (University of Georgia Press, 1953). A close look at Georgia during the Civil War.

Cate, Margret Davis. *Early Days of Coastal Georgia* (Fort Fredrica Assoc., 1955). A fascinating look at Georgia's beginnings along the coast.

Cromie, Alice. *A Tour Guide to the Civil War* (Rutledge Hill, 1986). A detailed and authoritative guide to important sites of the war.

Merritt, Carole. *Historic Black Resources* (Historic Preservation Society, 1984). An invaluable guide to the history of blacks in Georgia.

ARCHITECTURE & PHOTOGRAPHY

Georgia From the Mountains to the Sea (Aerial Photography Services, 1987). A beautiful and informative picture book.

DATELINE

Wind premieres in Atlanta.
- **1973** Maynard Jackson, Jr., is elected Atlanta's first black mayor.
- **1974** Hank Aaron hits his record-breaking 715th home run in Atlanta.
- **1976** James Earl Carter is elected U.S. president.
- **1990** Atlanta awarded 1996 Summer Olympics.

Gleason, David King. *Antebellum Homes of Georgia* (LSU Press, 1987).
Lane, Mills. *Architecture of the Old South Georgia* (Beehive Press, 1986).
Martin, Van Jones, and William Robert Mitchell, Jr. *Landmark Homes of Georgia* (Gold Coast Publishing, 1982).

2. INFORMATION & MONEY

TOURIST INFORMATION

For advance reading and planning, contact the **Division of Tourism,** Georgia Department of Industry, Trade & Tourism, P.O. Box 1776, Atlanta, GA 30301 (tel. 404/656-3590, or toll free 800/VISIT-GA). Ask for information on specific interests, as well as a complete calendar of events for the year of your visit—some pretty special things happen around the state all during the year.

State information centers are located near Augusta, Columbus, Kingsland, Lavonia, Ringgold, Plains, Savannah, Sylvania, Tallapoosa, Valdosta, and West Point. They're open daily from 8:30am to 5:30pm.

MONEY

The following chart should help you plan your daily budget.

WHAT THINGS COST IN GEORGIA	U.S. $
Taxi from Atlanta airport to downtown (1 passenger)	15.00
Fare between any MARTA stops	1.25
Local telephone call	.25
Double at Ritz Carlton Atlanta (deluxe)	155.00
Double at Courtyard by Marriott (moderate)	89.00
Double at Fairfield Inn by Marriott Airport in Atlanta (budget)	43.00
Lunch for one at Aunt Fanny's Cabin in Atlanta (moderate)	9.00
Lunch for one at The Varsity in Atlanta (budget)	3.00
Dinner for one, without wine, at Nikolai's Roof in Atlanta (deluxe)	60.00
Dinner for one, without wine, at Niko's Greek Restaurant in Atlanta (moderate)	15.00
Dinner for one, without wine, at Mick's in Atlanta (budget)	8.00
Bottle domestic beer	2.40
Bottle imported beer	3.00
Coca-Cola	1.15
Cup of coffee	1.10
Roll of ASA 100 Kodacolor film, 36 exposures	6.79
Concert/theater tickets	18.50
Movie ticket	5.50

3. WHEN TO GO — CLIMATE & EVENTS

CLIMATE

The average high and low temperatures at coastal Savannah and central Atlanta show that "low-country" areas are somewhat warmer year-round than those farther inland. Winter temperatures seldom drop below freezing anywhere in the state. Spring and fall are the longest seasons, and the wettest months are December through April.

GEORGIA AVERAGE TEMPERATURES (IN FAHRENHEIT)

	High	Low
Savannah	91	40
Atlanta	88	36
Columbus	92	37

GEORGIA CALENDAR OF EVENTS

JANUARY

☐ **King Week,** Atlanta. A commemoration of the birthday (January 15) of slain civil rights leader Dr. Martin Luther King, Jr. January 8 to 18.

FEBRUARY

☐ **St. Patrick's Festival,** Dublin. A three-week festival, culminating on St. Patrick's Day with Irish food, concerts, and a parade. February 27 to March 17.
☐ **Atlanta Flower Show** The premier gardening event in the Southeast, featuring landscaped gardens, educational seminars, and exhibits. Late February.

MARCH

☐ **Savannah St. Patrick's Day Parade** The coastal city's large Irish population turns everything green on their patron saint's day and puts on one of the country's largest parades. March 17.
☐ **Callaway Gardens Azalea Festival,** Pine Mountain. See more than 700 varieties of azaleas in bloom, as well as craft demonstrations, storytelling, and continuous entertainment. Late March to early April.
☐ **Cherry Blossom Festival,** Macon. Join the tens of thousands who come to this city to see the 170,000 cherry trees in bloom. Mid- to late March.

APRIL

☐ **Seafood Festival,** Riverfront Plaza, Savannah. Delicacies from local waters are featured in traditional coastal dishes. The festival includes arts, crafts, and entertainment. First weekend in April.

☐ **Dogwood Festival,** Atlanta. Celebrating the profusion of snowy dogwood blossoms around the city. There are tours, hot air balloons, art shows, dinners, and special entertainments. Mid-April.

☐ **Confederate Memorial Day,** statewide. The Civil War remembered in the state that suffered severely during the conflict. Late April.

☐ **Rose Festival,** Thomasville. The "City of Roses" celebrates with a rose show, arts and crafts, tours, and the Rose Festival Parade. Third week in April.

MAY

☐ **Plains Country Days.** Plains. Take a hayride or run the 5K race. There's a street dance and lots of food. Early May.

JUNE

☐ **Bluegrass Festival** Music from Georgia's mountains presented in marathon performances from noon till midnight. Dahlonega. Mid-June.

☐ **Georgia Peach Festival,** Fort Valley. Georgia's famous peaches star in a festival featuring music, arts and crafts, and parades. Mid-June.

AUGUST

☐ **Theater Festival,** Madison. An opening-night gala, professional productions of two plays, after-theater cabarets, historic home tours, basket lunches, and barbecue dinners. Early August.

☐ *The Reach of Song,* Georgia Mountain Fairground, Hiawassee. Georgia's official state drama depicting the life of poet Byron Herbert Reece in an outstanding outdoor production. Late August.

SEPTEMBER

☐ **Oktoberfest** Georgian-German hospitality reigns supreme in the Bavarian Alpine-style village of Helen, nestled in the Georgia mountains. Each year brings nearly a million people to taste traditional German food and dance the polka. Mid-September to early October.

☐ **Arts Festival,** Piedmont Park, Atlanta. Craftspersons from all over the country display and sell their work. Musical, theatrical, and dance performances punctuate each day. The second or third week in September.

OCTOBER

☐ **Powers Cross Roads Country Fair and Art Festival,** Newnan. More than 300 artists and craftspeople from around the country exhibit their work. Early October.

☐ **Historic Festival,** Andersonville. Hundreds of volunteers reenact Civil War battles, and the play *The Andersonville Trial* is performed. Plus balloon rides, arts and crafts, and country and bluegrass music. Early to mid-October.

☐ **Gold Rush Days** Your chance to pan for gold in Dahlonega, site of one of the earliest gold strikes in the United States. There's also country cooking, arts and crafts exhibits, and old-time beard-growing and tobacco-spitting contests. October 19 to 20.

DECEMBER

☐ **Christmas in the City** A variety of downtown Atlanta events celebrating the season—the Festival of Trees, Breakfast with Santa, lots of children's activities, and performances by the Atlanta Symphony and professional theatrical groups. All month.

☐ **Christmas Island,** Jekyll Island. A joyous holiday celebration in beautifully decorated homes of this island retreat's early millionaires. All month.

☐ **Peach Bowl Classic,** Atlanta-Fulton County Stadium. Two of the country's top collegiate football teams battle it out annually. December 29.

4. TIPS FOR THE DISABLED, SENIORS, SINGLES, FAMILIES & STUDENTS

FOR THE DISABLED Many hotels and restaurants in Georgia provide easy access for the handicapped, and some display the international wheelchair symbol in their brochures. However, it's always a good idea to call ahead before you book and travel.

For information on associations for the disabled, see "Tips for the Disabled, Seniors, Singles, Families, and Students," in Chapter 1. The Georgia's Governor's Developmental Disabilities Council (tel. 404/853-9113) may also be of help. Traveler's Aid (tel. 404/527-7400) also offers assistance to visitors. The Georgia Department of Industry, Trade & Tourism publishes a guide *Georgia On My Mind* that lists attractions and accommodations with access for the disabled. To receive a copy, call toll free 800/VISIT-GA, ext. 1903, or write Tour Georgia, P.O. Box 1776, Atlanta GA 30301.

For transportation within Atlanta, disabled persons may call Rent A Van of Atlanta (tel. 404/422-9025), Wheelchair Getaways, Inc. (tel. 404/467-9851), or Handicare LTD, a taxi service (tel. 404/981-0563).

FOR SENIORS The tourism arm of the State of Georgia publishes a guide called *The Georgia Interstate—A Traveler's Directory,* which details information for seniors and families on services and attractions along the interstate highway system.

FOR SINGLES Single travelers should look for *Atlanta Singles Magazine* on newstands throughout Atlanta for information on events and activities.

FOR FAMILIES All Georgia visitors' centers offer discount coupons for families as well as the *Atlanta Street Map & Visitors Guide.* Families might also pick up the book, *A Guide for Family Activities,* by Denise Black, which offers a host of ideas and activities for children in the Metro Atlanta area. Another local guide is called *Fun Family Vacations—Southeast.*

FOR STUDENTS See also "Tips for the Disabled, Seniors, Singles, Families, and Students," in Chapter 1. Student Assistant Services (tel. 921-0606) helps students with problems and offers services to them. Student Camp & Trip Advisors will help students plan excursions and trips; call 404/951-8747. The YMCA of Metro Atlanta offers special rates to students; contact them at 588-9622.

5. ALTERNATIVE/ADVENTURE TRAVEL

See "Alternative/Adventure Travel," in Chapter 1 for general pointers on educational and outdoor travel in the region.

There are 44 state parks in Georgia that welcome campers to sites that rent for $8 and up per night. Some 25 parks have vacation cottages that rent for $40 to $70 per night, depending on the number of rooms. All rates are in-season, and drop other months. Reservations must be made at each park. For more information on these and other park facilities and programs, contact the **Georgia Department of Natural Resources,** Office of Information, 205 Butler St. SE, Suite 1352, Atlanta, GA 30334 (tel. 404/656-3530).

6. GETTING THERE

BY PLANE Virtually every major national airline flies into Georgia through Atlanta's **Hartsfield International Airport,** (see "Orientation" in Chapter 13), 13 miles south of downtown, off I-85 and I-280. From Atlanta, there are connecting flights to points around the state. Travel agents or any of the leading airlines can furnish specific information about airlines currently serving Atlanta's airport.

BY TRAIN Amtrak (tel. toll free 800/USA-RAIL) has stops in Atlanta, Savannah, Jesup, Gainesville, and Toccoa. Bargain fares are sometimes in effect for limited periods; you should always check for the most economical way to schedule your trip.

BY BUS **Greyhound/Trailways** reaches most cities and towns in Georgia. Like Amtrak, the bus line runs periodic special rates that are real money-savers, so check with your nearest Greyhound/Trailways office. In Georgia, call 404/522-6300 (Atlanta) or 912/233-7723 (Savannah).

BY CAR Georgia is crisscrossed by major interstate highways: I-75 bisects the state from Dalton in the north to Valdosta in the south; I-95 runs north and south along the eastern seaboard. East-west routes are I-16, with exits to Dublin, Macon, and Savannah; and I-20 runs east and west with exits to Atlanta, Augusta, Carrollton, and Madison. I-85 runs northeast-to-southwest in the north half of the state. State-run welcome centers at all major points of entry are staffed with knowledgeable, helpful Georgians who can often advise you as to time-saving routes.

7. GETTING AROUND

BY PLANE From Atlanta, there are connecting flights into Augusta, Savannah, Albany, Brunswick (for the Golden Isles), and (by commuter line) into several smaller cities around the state. Check with travel agents or major airlines for specific flight information to these destinations.

BY TRAIN Amtrak (see "Getting There," above) runs from Toccoa to Gainesville and Atlanta, as well as from Savannah to Jesup, and **Georgia Railroad** operates between Atlanta and Augusta.

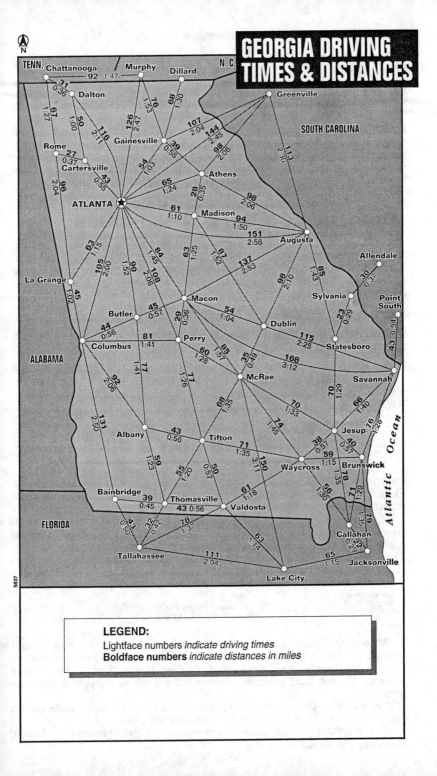

BY BUS **Greyhound/Trailways** serves most locations in the state. See "Getting There," above.

BY CAR In addition to the interstates that make it easy to get around the state, U.S. 84 crosses from the Alabama state line southeast to Macon and Valdosta and on south to Florida, and U.S. 441 runs from the North Carolina border south to Athens, Dublin, and the Florida state line. For 24-hour road conditions' information, call 404/656-5267. **AAA** services are available in Atlanta, Augusta, Columbus, Macon, Savannah, Smyrna, and Tucker (see following chapters for addresses and telephone numbers in Atlanta and Savannah; consult local telephone directories in other locations).

8. SUGGESTED ITINERARIES

If You Have One Day Depending on your personal interests, see coastal Savannah, with its wealth of historic sightseeing and lighthearted riverfront, or cosmopolitan, sophisticated Atlanta. Neither can be truly explored in the space of one day, but you *can* catch a bit of the flavor of either.

If You Have Two Days See Savannah or Atlanta in more depth.

If You Have One Week Spend **Days 1 through 4** in Atlanta, **Days 5 through 7** in Savannah.

If You Have Two Weeks Spend **Days 1 through 7** as above, **Days 8 and 9** in the Golden Isles. **Day 10,** drive to Macon or Columbus. **Days 11 through 14,** make day trips to Callaway Gardens in Pine Mountain, to the Little White House in Warm Springs, and to Plains and Andersonville.

9. WHERE TO STAY & DINE

For tips on smart accommodations and dining see "Where to Stay and Dine," in Chapter 1. For information on camping and cabin accommodations in state parks and recreational areas, see "Alternative/Adventure Travel," above.

For tips on smart dining and general details of the Southern cuisine you'll find in Georgia and the Carolinas, see Chapter 1. Many traditional Georgia dishes have their origins in the state's early history, and *Georgia's Historic Restaurants and Their Recipes,* by Dawn O'Brien and Jean Spaugh (John F. Blair Publishing, 1987), is a good read for any visitor interested in food.

 GEORGIA

American Express American Express services are available in Georgia through agencies in Albany, Atlanta (five locations; see "Fast Facts: Atlanta" in Chapter 13), Augusta (two locations), Columbus, Dalton, Duluth, Macon, and Valdosta. Consult local telephone directories for local addresses and telephone numbers.

Area Code Georgia area codes are: Savannah, 912; Brunswick and the Golden Isles, 912; Atlanta, 404; Columbus and Pine Mountain, 404.

Car Rentals Major national car-rental firms have branches in Atlanta, Savannah, and Albany.

Climate See "Climate," earlier in this chapter.

Crime Travel in Georgia is, for the most part, quite safe. When walking in major cities such as Atlanta or Savannah, however, it is best to walk with a companion. Both cities are carefully patrolled, especially during large conventions or special events, and other cities are extremely safe and friendly. I would urge, however, that you take the same precautions you would at home—lock car and hotel room doors, leave valuables in hotel safes, and don't carry large amounts of cash on your person.

Emergencies For medical, police, or fire emergency, dial 911.

Liquor Laws If you're 21 or over, you can buy alcoholic beverages in package stores between 8am and 11:45pm (except on Sunday, election days, Thanksgiving, and Christmas). Whether or not you'll be able to buy mixed drinks in lounges and restaurants depends on which county you're in. Beer and wines are available everywhere.

Newspapers/Magazines *The Atlanta Journal-Constitution* is the state's leading daily newspaper; *Southern Living* is a glossy publication concerned mainly with architecture, travel in the South, and gardening, profusely illustrated with color photography.

Police See "Emergencies," above.

Safety See "Crime," above.

Time Georgia is in the eastern standard time zone.

Weather Call 762-1186.

CHAPTER 12

SAVANNAH & THE GEORGIA COAST

- **WHAT'S SPECIAL ABOUT SAVANNAH**
- **SAVANNAH CALENDAR OF EVENTS**
- **1. ORIENTATION**
- **FAST FACTS: SAVANNAH**
- **2. WHERE TO STAY**
- **3. WHERE TO DINE**
- **4. WHAT TO SEE & DO**
- **SUGGESTED ITINERARIES**
- **5. SPORTS & RECREATION**
- **6. SAVVY SHOPPING**
- **7. EVENING ENTERTAINMENT**
- **8. EASY EXCURSIONS**
- **9. FARTHER AFIELD**

Georgia's 150-mile-long coastline is a semitropical, richly historic stretch of seafront. There are moss-draped live oaks and palmettos (some of the prettiest driving in the South is along Georgia's portion of U.S. 17), broad beaches, creeks and rivers, the remains of old plantations, and offshore islands with luxury resort accommodations. Savannah is the foremost Atlantic seaport, and Cumberland Island, the newest National Seashore, is still under development. Since 1540 (when Hernando de Soto became the first European to set foot on what would one day be Georgia), this coast has sheltered Native Americans, Spanish missionaries, British colonists, pirates, cotton growers and shippers, English troops, an "infamous" Union general during the Civil War, wealthy Yankees seeking an unspoiled retreat—and most recently, a former president of the United States.

A BRIEF HISTORY Spanish missions had gained a brief foothold on St. Simons and Jekyll islands as early as 1566, but "civilization" came to stay on this part of the Atlantic coast on February 12, 1733, when Gen. James Oglethorpe arrived at Yamacraw Bluff with 114 English settlers—nonconformist Protestants and former inmates of England's debtor prisons who were looking to the New World for a new beginning. Oglethorpe's idealism encompassed a new future for the unfortunates he'd brought with him. He planned a town that would provide space, beauty, and comfort for every resident of the colony: A settlement of houses, each with its own garden plot, laid out around town squares (there were 24 in the original plan) and with an orderly mercantile section. Thus Savannah was America's very first "planned city."

The natural deep-water harbor soon attracted Spanish, Portuguese, German, Scots, and Irish immigrants, and a lively sea trade brought seafarers from all over the world—along with hordes of pirates who put into the port from time to time. In 1775, when Savannah got word that war had broken out at Lexington, Massachusetts, a patriot battalion was hastily formed. Savannah changed hands frequently during the Revolution. The city was named the state capital following the 1776 Declaration of Independence, and remained so until 1807, when proslavers managed to have the government moved to Milledgeville.

The years between the Revolutionary and Civil wars were a period of great prosperity for Savannah; many of the classic revival, regency, and Georgian colonial homes you'll see restored today were built at that time. It was the era of "King Cotton" and great tobacco farms. Cotton "factors" (brokers) kept track of huge fortunes along River Street on what came to be known as Factors' Walk. Through it

WHAT'S SPECIAL ABOUT SAVANNAH

Historic Sites and Homes

- [ ] More than 800 restored homes, with the Davenport House, Green-Meldrin Home, and the Andrew Low House among the highlights.
- [ ] Factors' Walk, a row of old cotton warehouses along the historic and lively waterfront.
- [ ] The Pirates' House, now a very good restaurant, but the hangout of all sorts of blackguards in its early years.

Museums

- [ ] The Ships of the Sea Maritime Museum on the waterfront, a homage to the city's seafaring past.
- [ ] The Savannah Science Museum, with its hands-on exhibits and outstanding planetarium.

City Squares

- [ ] Johnson, Wright, Chippewa, Madison, and Monterey squares are among the most delightful survivors of General Oglethorpe's original city plan.
- [ ] Forsyth Park, where locals and visitors gather and strolling musicians often entertain.

---

all, builders, merchants, and shippers kept to Oglethorpe's master plan for the city, preserving the parks and squares in the midst of all the commercial hubbub.

When secession rumblings reached fever pitch in 1861, Georgia's governor ordered state troops to seize Fort Pulaski, 15 miles east of Savannah, even though the state did not withdraw from the Union until 16 days later. The war brought devastation to the area, since Sherman ended his "march to the sea" here in December 1864. Sherman marched into Savannah more quietly than was his usual custom, since Confederate General Hardee had evacuated his troops to spare this city the destruction Sherman had left in his wake all across the state.

After the war, Savannah's port was soon humming again. Manufacturing began to take hold, and by the early 1900s there were infant industries that would grow into a boom by the outbreak of World War II. Shipbuilding was a natural here, and led the local economy during both world wars.

Today the economy and much of city life still revolve around port activity. For the visitor, however, it's Old Savannah, in a beautifully restored and maintained historic area, that draws the most attention. For this we can thank seven Savannah ladies who, after watching mansion after mansion be demolished in the name of "progress," managed in 1954 to raise funds to buy the dilapidated Isaiah Davenport house just hours before it was slated for demolition to make way for a parking lot. The women banded together as the Historic Savannah Foundation, then went to work buying up architecturally valuable buildings and reselling them to private owners who would promise to restore them. As a result, more than 800 of the 1,100 historic buildings of Old Savannah have been restored, using original paint colors—pinks and reds and blues and greens. The "living museum" is now the largest urban National Historic Landmark District in the country—some 2½ square miles, including 20 one-acre squares that still survive from Oglethorpe's dream of a gracious city.

SAVANNAH'S ARCHITECTURE Part of what makes Savannah special, is its architecture. In the early days, the city's first carpenters built houses all alike for the new colonists. Then English-inspired designs came to Savannah after the Revolution, when the city grew dramatically. Not far away, Eli Whitney had invented the cotton gin that allowed for the broad-scale processing of cotton. It was 1817 when the cotton merchants brought a fellow, William Jay, from London to build a new breed of palace, or home, for them. He designed the Owens-Thomas House. From that beginning, a bank, school, and theater were constructed along with more elaborate buildings employing the Regency style with stucco, balustrades, and columns. It was after Savannah built a railroad to Georgia's cotton fields in the central part of the state that the rowhouse form of building came to the city. Alongside the Savannah River, kilns fired what was to become known as Savannah grays, the popular brick used in construction. Another part of Savannah's style comes from the use of ironwork, such as that used on the public squares, fountains, monuments, and houses. The wrought-iron work was used in all styles of accommodations—from Greek revival mansions to Romanesque buildings to Gothic villas. The ironwork became more and more popular, and later the ornamental work became a familiar trademark to Savannah's homes, leaving us with the romantic and specialized designs we still enjoy today.

SAVANNAH CALENDAR OF EVENTS

MARCH

☐ **St. Patrick's Day Parade.** Second in size only to New York's. Everybody gets into the act. March 17.
☐ **Annual Tour of Homes.** This four-day event features tours of private homes, churches, museums, and gardens in the historic district. Low-country cuisine and other special events are also staged. Contact Savannah Tour of Homes & Gardens, 18 Abercorn St. (tel. 912/234-8054). Late March.

APRIL

☐ **Savannah Seafood Festival.** Sponsored by the Savannah waterfront Association, this celebrates the coastal culinary heritage with food, entertainment, and crafts. Three days in early April.
☐ **Night in Old Savannah.** Blocks are set aside for what amounts to a massive street fair. For three enchanted days there's ethnic food and entertainment. For specific dates and details, write or call Night in Old Savannah, P.O. Box 14147, Savannah, GA 31416 (tel. 912/355-2422). Late April.

MAY

☐ **First Saturday Festivals.** These begin the first Saturday of this month (and continue every month until October). A joyous street fair along River Street, with food, entertainment, and arts-and-crafts booths.
☐ **Savannah Scottish Games and Highland Gathering.** Dancing, pipe bands, athletic competitions, and Scots foods (for details and exact date, call 912/352-9959). On or about May 6.
☐ **Military Through the Ages Days,** Old Fort Jackson. Exhibits, demonstrations, and military drills. Call 912/232-3945 for exact dates. Last week in May.

JUNE

☐ **Blessing of the Fleet.** Thunderbolt. Annual ceremony to bless local shrimp boats, preceded by three days of colorful religious pageantry, with dances, street fairs, and art exhibits. Third Sunday in June.

□ **Savannah Maritime Festival.** In anticipation of the 1996 Olympic sailing regatta (to be held in Savannah), this festival celebrates the spirit of nautical history with sporting and cultural events. Contact: Savannah Maritime Festival, P.O. Box 9347, Savannah, GA 31401 (tel. 912/236-3959).

SEPTEMBER

□ **Savannah Jazz Festival.** A five-day celebration of this uniquely American music, with nationally known musicians appearing at venues around the city. For specific dates, call 912/944-0456.

OCTOBER

□ **Oktoberfest on River Street.** German food, crafts, and entertainment are featured in this festival, which traditionally runs for three days. Early October.

□ **Savannah Greek Festival.** Three days of Greek food, music, and dancing. For exact dates, call 912/236-8256. Mid-October.

DECEMBER

□ **Christmas Tour of Homes.** Seven homes are shown on each day of the weekend event; candlelight tours, carriage rides, and hand-bell ringers and carolers are also part of the experience. Contact: Downtown Neighborhood Association, 117 W. Perry St., Savannah, GA 31401 (tel. 912/236-TDNA).

□ **Christmas Tour of Historic Inns.** Eleven of Savannah's finest inns are spotlighted in this "on your own" walking or driving tour. Everyone has fascinating stories to tell and refreshments to offer. Contact: Association of Historic Inns of Savannah, 14 E. Oglethorpe Ave., Savannah, GA 31401 (tel. 912/236-1484, or toll free 800/822-4553).

1. ORIENTATION

ARRIVING

By Plane   Savannah International Airport is eight miles west of downtown just off I-16. **American** (tel. toll free 800/433-7300), **Delta** (tel. toll free 800/221-1212), **United** (tel. toll free 800/241-6522), and **USAir** (tel. toll free 800/428-4322) have flights from Atlanta and Charlotte, with connections to other points. Limousine service to downtown locations (tel. 912/966-5364) has a one-way fare of $9; taxi fare is $15 for one person, $3 for each additional passenger.

By Train   The train station is at 2611 Seaboard Coastline Dr. (tel. 912/234-2611), some four miles southwest of downtown. For **Amtrak** schedule and fare information, call toll free 800/USA-RAIL. Cab fare into the city is around $4.

By Bus   Greyhound/Trailways (tel. 912/233-7723) has direct service from Atlanta and other major Georgia cities, with connections to points farther afield.

By Car   From north or south, I-95 passes 10 miles west of Savannah, with several exits to the city, and U.S. 17 runs through the city; from the west, I-16 ends in downtown Savannah and U.S. 80 also runs through the city from east to west. AAA services are available through **AAA Auto Club South,** 712 Mall Blvd., Savannah, GA 31406 (tel. 912/352-8222).

TOURIST INFORMATION

The **Savannah Visitor Center** is located at 301 Martin Luther King, Jr., Blvd., Savannah, GA 31401 (tel. 912/944-0456, or toll free 800/444-2427); it's open Monday through Friday from 8:30am to 5pm, Saturday and Sunday from 9am to 5pm. The staff is friendly and efficient. There's an audio visual presentation for a small fee ($1 adults, 50¢ children); organized tours; and self-guided walking, driving, or bike tours with excellent maps, cassette tapes, and brochures.

Tourist information is also available from the **Savannah Area Convention & Visitors Bureau,** 222 W. Oglethorpe Ave., Savannah, GA 31401 (tel. 912/944-0456, or toll free 800/444-2427). For information on current happenings, call 912/233-ARTS.

Be sure to pick up a copy of *Sojourn in Savannah,* an informative guide to this city and the surrounding area. It's on sale at the visitors' center for $6, or you can order it by sending $8 (including postage and handling) to Sojourn in Savannah, P.O. Box 1628, Savannah, GA 31402.

CITY LAYOUT

The **historic district** is bordered by the Savannah River and Forsyth Park at Gaston Street, and Montgomery and Price Streets. Within its borders, there are more than 1,000 historically and architecturally important restored buildings, as well as 18 of those lovely, restful squares.

The **Victorian district** lies south of the historic district and holds some superb examples of post–Civil War architecture.

The **waterfront** holds Factors' Walk, a string of three-story brick warehouses dating from the early 1800s that now house museums, restaurants, bars, boutiques, and a fascinating museum of nautical artifacts.

GETTING AROUND

On Foot   The grid-shaped historic district is best seen on foot. Leisurely strolls with frequent stops in the many squares is recommended. Johnson Square is the perfect place for a snack, ice cream, or cold soda.

By Bus   You'll need exact change for the 75¢ fare, plus 5¢ for a transfer. For route and schedule information, call **Chatham Area Transit (CAT)** at 233-5767.

By Taxi   The base rate for taxis is 60¢, with a $1.20 additional charge for each mile. For 24-hour taxi service, call **Adam Cab Co.** at 927-7466.

By Car   Although many points of interest outside the historic district can be reached by bus, your own wheels will be much more convenient, and they're absolutely essential for sightseeing outside the city proper. All major car-rental firms have branches in Savannah, but it pays to shop around for those with the best basic rate and unlimited mileage.

FAST FACTS: SAVANNAH

American Express   American Express Travel Service is located at 5500 Abercorn St., Suite 22 (tel. 351-0770).

Area Code   Savannah's area code is 912.
Emergencies   Dial 911 for police, ambulance, or fire emergencies.
Hospitals   There are 24-hour emergency room services at Candler General Hospital, 5353 Reynolds St. (tel. 356-6037), and Memorial Medical Center, 4800 Waters Ave. (tel. 356-8390).
Newspapers   *Savannah Morning News* and *Savannah Evening Press* are both dailies.

2. WHERE TO STAY

The undisputed stars here are the small inns in the historic district, most in lovely old homes that have been renovated with modern conveniences, while retaining every bit of their original charm. Book into one of these if you want to experience Savannah graciousness firsthand.

EXPENSIVE

HOTELS IN TOWN

DESOTO HILTON, 15 E. Liberty St. (P.O. Box 8207), Savannah, GA 31412. Tel. 912/232-9000, or toll free 800/445-8667. Fax 912/232-6018. 254 rms. A/C MINIBAR TV TEL
$ Rates: $68–$118 single; $78–$128 double. Family and weekend rates available. AE, CB, DC, DISC, MC, V. **Parking:** Free underground.
In the heart of town, at Liberty and Bull Streets, the Hilton enjoys a fine commercial reputation. It lacks a waterfront location but tries to make up for it with fine interiors. One of the restaurants is a cheerful number with white wicker furniture; the other is a bit more formal. For a quick sandwich to go, you might try the deli. Hard Hearted Hannah's is a very popular jazz club. On hand is an outdoor pool.

HYATT REGENCY SAVANNAH, 2 W. Bay St., Savannah, GA 31401. Tel. 912/238-1234, or toll free 800/228-9000. 346 rms. A/C TV TEL
$ Rates: $110–$150 single; $135–$175 double; $95 weekends. AE, CB, DC, DISC, MC, V. **Parking:** $7 per day.
The Hyatt is Savannah's most prominent hotel. It sits right on the Savannah River with great views of passing ships and faces the waterfront shops and restaurants. You won't find a better location. Inside, you'll find all the Hyatt-ized touches: an atrium lobby, terrace lounge, a water-view restaurant, and a lounge. Besides the bistro restaurant, you may choose the grill room. Sometimes live entertainment is staged in the lounge. The rooms are standard first class with the usual amenities. Guests may use a nearby health club or the hotel's own indoor pool and small fitness room.

RADISSON PLAZA HOTEL SAVANNAH, 100 Gen. McIntosh Blvd., Savannah, GA. 31401. Tel. 912/233-7722, or toll free 800/333-3333. Fax 912/233-3765. 385 rms. A/C TV TEL
$ Rates: $95–$139 single; $95–$159 double. Children under 12 stay free with parents. AE, CB, DC, DISC, MC, V.
This is the new choice in town, a major competitor of the Hilton and Hyatt. The atrium design keeps everything in full view, and guests are rewarded with views of the river. The decor is done in a trendy commercial style. Extra amenities and breakfasts

are provided on the Club level. The pool and whirlpool are indoors. This brick building features an upscale family restaurant and adjoining parking. It's at the end of East Bay Street, on the waterfront.

SHERATON SAVANNAH RESORT AND COUNTRY CLUB, 612 Wilmington Island Rd., Savannah, GA 31410. Tel. 912/897-1612, or toll free 800/325-3535. Fax 912/897-1613, ext. 7245. 202 rms. A/C TV TEL. **Directions:** On the Intracoastal Waterway, just across the Wilmington River Bridge, 10 miles east of downtown on U.S. 80.

$ Rates: $99 single, $114 double; Golf and honeymoon packages available. Children under 18 stay free with parents. AE, CB, DC, DISC, MC, V.

This hotel has all the amenities of a resort, but it hasn't been properly renovated in years, and it shows. The building itself is rather striking in its Mediterranean style and is resort-like. But hard economic times have obviously hit home. The grounds are beautiful (not so much with flowers and attention but in terms of spaciousness and arrangement), and there are several tennis courts and an 18-hole golf course, not to mention an attractive pool area. This once grand resort still has much potential, but for the time being, it's not one of my top choices.

HISTORIC INNS

BALLASTONE INN, 14 E. Oglethorpe Ave., Savannah, GA 31401. Tel. 912/236-1484, or toll free 800/822-4553. 18 rms (with bath), 4 suites. A/C TV TEL. **Directions:** In historic district.

$ Rates (including continental breakfast): $95–$200 single or double. No children under 16. AE, MC, V.

⭐ This inn is right next door to the Juliette Gordon Low Girl Scout shrine and convenient to everything in the historic district. Rooms are decorated with antiques or authentic reproductions, ceiling fans, and Scalamandre wallpapers. Each has a distinctive decorative theme; some have fireplaces and some have Jacuzzis. If your tastes run to low-ceilinged coziness rather than the more formal elegance of 14-foot ceilings, ask for one of the rustic garden-level rooms in the original servants' quarters, with brick walls, exposed beams, and more casual furnishings. Master rooms are especially large and have a separate dressing room and wet bar. You'll find fresh fruit and flowers in your room on arrival, and a lovely little courtyard where you can sit with the other guests. Coffee or tea is always available in the inviting parlor, and there's also a full-service bar. There's no dining room, but the location is convenient to good restaurants. Complimentary shoeshine and bed turndown with sweets and cordials are available.

ELIZA THOMPSON HOUSE, 5 W. Jones St., Savannah, GA 31401. Tel. 912/236-3620, or toll free 800/348-9378. Fax 912/238-1920. 25 rms. A/C TV TEL

$ Rates (including breakfast): $88–$108 single or double. AE, MC, V.

Looking for a little romance? Here it is and with lots of extras: lovely rooms, great breakfasts, afternoon snacks. There are 14 fireplaces in the inn, and one is burning when you come into the foyer. The rooms may have Charleston Rice beds or other four-poster headboards, fine antique floors, and cozy baths. As an added bonus, Mrs. Wilkes's Dining Room (see "Where to Dine," below) is in the next block; in fact, you'll find some of her delicious breakfast items right here.

FOLEY HOUSE INN, 14 W. Hull St., Savannah, GA 31401. Tel. 912/232-6622, or toll free 800/647-3708. Fax 912/231-1218. 20 rms. A/C TV TEL

$ Rates (including continental breakfast): $85–$185 single or double. AE, MC, V.

This beautifully restored 1880 narrow brick inn on Chippewa Square has a friendly

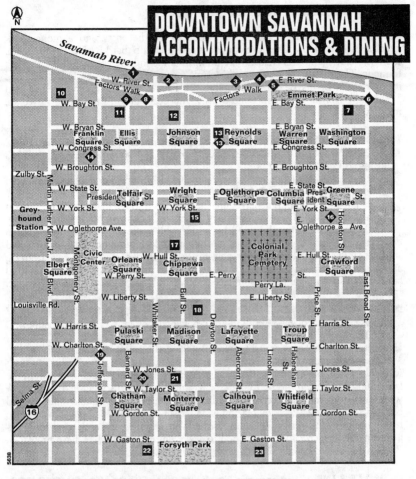

DOWNTOWN SAVANNAH ACCOMMODATIONS & DINING

Savannah River

GEORGIA

Atlanta

Savannah

ACCOMMODATIONS:

Ballastone Inn **15**
Best Western Riverfront Inn **10**
Days Inn Historic District **11**
DeSoto Hilton **18**
Eliza Thompson House **21**
Foley House Inn **17**
The Gastonian **23**
Hyatt Regency Savannah **12**
Magnolia Place **22**
The Mulberry **7**
Planters Inn **13**

DINING:

Bistro Savannah **14**
The Boar's Head **5**
The Chart House **8**
The Crystal Beer Parlor **19**
The Exchange Tavern **3**
Garibaldi's **14**
Huey's **2**
Kevin Barry's Irish Pub **1**
Mrs. Wilkes's Dining Room **20**
The Olde Pink House Restaurant
  and Planters' Tavern **13**
The Pirates' House **6**
River House **9**
The Shrimp Factory **4**
606 East Cafe **14**
Wall's **16**

atmosphere enhanced by the burning fireplace in the entry and a money-back guarantee. (How many places are confident enough to do that?) Besides the main inn, there is a carriage house. Also on the premises are two little courtyards, one with a fountain. There is also an outdoor whirlpool. You can expect to find a four-poster bed in your room or maybe a fireplace, since 16 rooms have them. The ground-level rooms have cozy appointments and a brick-and-beam decor; their wood stoves are inviting, too.

THE GASTONIAN, 220 E. Gaston St., Savannah, GA 31401. Tel. 912/232-2869, or toll free 800/322-6603. Fax 912/234-0006. 10 rms (with bath), 3 suites. A/C TV TEL

$ Rates (including full Southern breakfast): $98–$245 single or double. No children under 12. No smoking. AE, MC, V.

⭐ Hugh and Roberta Lineberger are Californians who fell in love with the city on a visit in 1984. The two four-story Italianate brick town houses that make up the Gastonian are connected by an elevated walkway, with a lovely garden courtyard in between. A hot tub sits on the raised deck outdoors. Guest rooms and suites are individually decorated (French, English, Victorian, etc.), most have Jacuzzis, and all have operating fireplaces. A charming carriage house is now a honeymoon suite. You also get a fruit-and-wine basket on arrival, and nightly turndown service.

MAGNOLIA PLACE, 503 Whitaker St., Savannah, GA 31401. Tel. 912/236-7674, or toll free 800/238-7674 outside Georgia. 13 rms (with bath). A/C TV TEL

$ Rates (including continental breakfast): $89–$195 single or double. AE, MC, V.
Closed: Mid-Jan to mid-Feb.

Magnolia Place, between West Gaston and West Huntington Streets, was built in the late 1800s as a private home for one of Savannah's most distinguished families. A wide, two-story veranda overlooks Whitaker Street; inside, the grand staircase and back parlor—where afternoon tea and wine are served to guests—reflect an elegance hard to come by these days. The house is filled with antiques, and each guest room has a queen- or king-size four-poster bed; 6 have whirlpool baths, 11 have fireplaces. Breakfast is served on the veranda when weather permits.

PLANTERS INN, 29 Abercorn St., Savannah, GA 31401. Tel. 912/232-5678, or toll free 800/554-1187. Fax 912/232-8893. 55 rms. A/C TV TEL

$ Rates (including continental breakfast): $89–$125 single or double. AE, DC, MC, V.

Ⓢ Here is a beautiful inn on Reynolds Square. It opened years and years ago as the John Wesley Hotel and today features a partly marbled two-story lobby where continental breakfast is served. The goodies and cool drinks (or hot ones) are a welcome in the afternoon. Beautiful guest rooms have all the markings of a deluxe inn, such as fine woods in period style, beautiful wallpaper, reproduction antique furniture, remote-control TVs, pretty color schemes, and baths with marbled vanities. You'll appreciate the nightly turndown service and the room service (which is a special treat in an inn). Next door is an excellent (but pricey) restaurant and a more modestly priced tavern.

MODERATE/BUDGET

IN TOWN

THE BEST WESTERN RIVERFRONT INN, 412 W. Bay Rd., Savannah,

GA 31401. **Tel. 912/233-1011,** or toll free 800/334-7234. 142 rms (with bath). A/C TV TEL
$ Rates: $54 single; $60 double. AE, CB, DC, DISC, ER, MC, V.
This inn, at the junction of U.S. 17 and 80, is conveniently located for historic district sightseeing. Rooms are well appointed, with in-room movies. There's a restaurant and outdoor pool.

DAYS INN HISTORIC DISTRICT, 201 W. Bay St., Savannah, GA 31401.
Tel. 912/236-4440, or toll free 800/325-2525. 196 rms (with bath), 57 suites. A/C TV TEL
$ Rates: $67–$79 single; $77–$99 double. Senior discounts and weekly rates available. AE, DC, DISC, MC, V.
When this building was constructed in 1981, it was cited by the Historic Savannah Foundation "for . . . sensitive design of a new hotel within Savannah's historic market district." Indeed, you would be forgiven for taking the new structure for a lovingly restored original. On hand is a restaurant, parking facilities, and a tour service.

THE MULBERRY, 601 E. Bay St., Savannah 31401. Tel. 912/238-1200,
or toll free 800/465-4329. Fax 912/236-2184. 120 rms. A/C TV TEL
$ Rates: $85–$105 single; $100–$120 double. AE, CB, DC, DISC, MC, V.
Close to the waterfront at Washington Square, the Mulberry is a blend of historic inn and hotel. Once a Days Inn and now affiliated with Holiday Inn, it offers all the conveniences of a major hotel in a period atmosphere. There are gas lamps in the courtyard, and the bar is clubby and romantic. There's a restaurant on the premises and a couple of restaurants nearby. The rooms are a bit more traditional, and almost two dozen are more like suites, with wet bars, sitting areas, refrigerators, and more detail. This is a good moderately priced choice.

NEARBY

CLUBHOUSE INN, 6800 Abercorn St., Savannah, GA 31405. Tel.
912/356-1234, or toll free 800/CLUB-INN. Fax 912/925-8424. 138 rms. A/C TV TEL
$ Rates (including breakfast): $56 single; $66 double; $50 weekends. Senior discounts available. AE, DC, DISC, MC, V.
This fast growing chain of blueprint hotels is a great value in a pleasant environment. The two-story hotel wraps around the courtyard with an outdoor pool, gas grill, and indoor whirlpool. Rates also include a nightly manager's cocktail reception. Accommodations are minimally first class with hotel-modern furniture, pleasing colors, and good baths. It's located five to ten minutes south on Abercorn Street from the center of town.

THE COURTYARD BY MARRIOTT, 6703 Abercorn St., Savannah, GA
31405. Tel. 912/354-7878, or toll free 800/321-2211. Fax 912/354-1432. 144 rms (with bath), 12 suites. A/C TV TEL **Directions:** From I-16 take exit 34A to I-516 East, and turn right on Abercorn Street.
$ Rates: $68 single; $78 double, $59 weekends. Children under 16 stay free with parents. Senior discounts available. AE, DC, MC, V.
Built around a landscaped courtyard, it has attractive, renovated rooms with separate seating areas, oversize work desks, and private patios or balconies. There's a pool, whirlpool, health club, coin laundry, restaurant, and bar. The restaurant serves à la carte breakfast only.

FAIRFIELD INN, 2 Lee Blvd., Savannah, GA 31405. Tel. 912/353-7100,

or toll free 800/228-2800. 135 rms. A/C TV TEL **Directions:** From I-16, take exit 34A to I-516 East, turn right on Abercorn Street, then right on Lee Boulevard.
$ Rates: $34–$40 single; $38–$45 double. Senior discounts available. AE, DC, MC, V.

The Savannah location of this reliable budget chain by Marriott has nicely appointed rooms, in-room movies, a large, well-lit work desk, and an outdoor pool. There are several good, moderately priced restaurants nearby.

CAMPING

The **Bellaire Woods Campground,** 805 Fort Argyle Rd., Savannah, GA 31419 (tel. 912/748-4000), is 2½ miles west of I-95, 4½ miles west of U.S. 17, and 12 miles from the Savannah historic district on the banks of the Ogeechee River. There are full hookups, LP gas service, a store, self-service gas and diesel fuel, a dump station, hot showers, a laundry, and a swimming pool. Rates range from $12.50 for tents to $18 for RV hookups, and reservations are accepted with a $10 deposit.

3. WHERE TO DINE

MODERATE

IN TOWN

BISTRO SAVANNAH, 309 W. Congress St. Tel. 333-6266.
   Cuisine: AMERICAN. **Reservations:** Recommended.
$ Prices: Appetizers $4.50–$6.95; soups and salads $2.95–$3.95; main courses $8.95–$10.95; dinner for two $25. AE, MC, V.
   Open: Sun–Thurs 6–10:30pm, Fri–Sat 5:30pm–midnight.
The decor inside Bistro Savannah is upbeat and attractive. Exposed brick is mixed with cane chairs and local art. Local seafood and country game is a specialty that changes daily. Try one of the pastas, or perhaps Shepherd's Pie. It's near the City Market.

THE BOAR'S HEAD, 1 N. Lincoln St. Tel. 232-3196.
   Cuisine: CONTINENTAL/AMERICAN. **Reservations:** Recommended.
$ Prices: Main courses $5.25–$7.75 at lunch, $14.25–$18.25 at dinner; early bird specials (5:30–6:30pm) $9.95. AE, MC, V.
   Open: Daily 11:30am–10:30pm. **Closed:** Major holidays.
In a 200-year-old waterfront warehouse at River Street, the Boar's Head offers a sophisticated atmosphere and excellent cuisine and service. Tables are placed to take advantage of the marvelous river view. Hanging baskets of greenery and soft candlelight create a cozy, intimate mood. The seafood, veal, and steaks are superb. Early bird specials include three choices from the menu.

THE CHART HOUSE, 202 W. Bay St. Tel. 233-6686.
   Cuisine: SEAFOOD. **Reservations:** Recommended.
$ Prices: Appetizers $3.25–$7.45; main courses $17–$23; early bird specials (5:30–6:30pm) $12.95. AE, MC.
   Open: Dinner Sun–Thurs 5–10pm, Fri–Sat 5–11pm.
At River and Barnard Streets, this snug and very nautical seafood restaurant overlooks

the Savannah River and Riverfront Plaza. From the outside deck, you can enjoy the view of passing ships and have an appetizer and cocktail before dinner. Oysters, shrimp, and other local catches are excellent. Also on the menu are halibut steaks and beef steaks. The bar is a cozy meeting place too.

ELIZABETH ON 37TH RESTAURANT AND DESSERT CAFE, 105 E. 37th St. Tel. 236-5547.
Cuisine: SEAFOOD. **Reservations:** Recommended.
$ Prices: Appetizers $6.50–$8.50; main courses $17.50–$24.50. AE, MC, V.
Open: Dinner Mon–Sat 6–10:30pm.

Elizabeth and Michael Terry have added a real charmer to the Savannah restaurant scene. Michael, an ex-attorney, welcomes diners and serves as wine steward, while Elizabeth presides over the kitchen in a charming turn-of-the-century mansion. The duo has earned the praise of many, both regionally and nationally. The menu specializes in fresh seafood from local waters, and for nonseafood lovers, there are outstanding lamb, steak, chicken, and even vegetarian dishes. Appetizers may include Georgia goat cheese salad or southern fried grits with salmon and leeks. There's an excellent wine list, and on Thursday, all wines are sold by the glass. Desserts are something to write home about, and there's a special children's menu. It's at 37th and Drayton Streets.

THE EXCHANGE TAVERN, 201 E. River St. Tel. 232-7088.
Cuisine: SEAFOOD/LOW COUNTRY. **Reservations:** Not required.
$ Prices: Sandwiches $2.95–$4.95; appetizers $3–$5; main courses $8.25–$14.50; children's menu $2.55–$3.95. AE, DC, MC, V.
Open: Mon–Thurs 11am–midnight, Fri–Sat 11am–2:30am, Sun noon–midnight.

There's a great selection of sandwiches and "Low-country Nibblers" here, amid an interesting collection of clocks. The extensive menu also features traditional seafood dishes, steaks, chicken, and shish kebab. A great "drop-in" place for beer, cocktails, and food, it's at the riverfront, east of Bull Street.

GARIBALDI'S, 315 W. Congress St. Tel. 232-7118.
Cuisine: ITALIAN/SEAFOOD. **Reservations:** Not required.
$ Prices: Appetizers $2.75–$5.75, main courses $10.95–$12.95. AE, MC, V.
Open: Sun–Thurs 6–10:30pm, Fri–Sat 5:30pm–midnight.

Like its siblings in Charleston and Columbia, S.C., Garibaldi's has an accent on Italian, but plenty of seafood is on the menu board too. The seafood and veal combination is usually a hit. This is a fine, moderately priced choice near the City Market.

HUEY'S, 115 River St. Tel. 234-7385.
Cuisine: ITALIAN CAFE. **Reservations:** Not required.
$ Prices: Appetizers $1.75–$4.95; sandwiches $4.75–$5.75. AE, DISC, MC, V.
Open: Mon–Thurs 7am–10pm, Fri 7am–11pm, Sat 8am–11pm, Sun 8am–10pm.

This casual eatery on the riverfront offers some water views in an atmosphere of ceiling fans, a red and gray decor, and exposed brick. On the menu are Oyster Po Boy and a blackened chicken sandwich served with fried red beans and rice, plus an array of salads ranging from chicken to shrimp.

KEVIN BARRY'S IRISH PUB, W. River St. Tel. 233-9626.
Cuisine: AMERICAN/INTERNATIONAL. **Reservations:** Not required.
$ Prices: Main courses $9.95–$16.95. AE, DISC, MC, V.
Open: Mon–Sat 11am–2:30am, Sun 12:30pm–2am.

With a name like this, I don't have to tell you what's on the menu or what will be the featured entertainment. The woodsy atmosphere and brick make this a cozy hideaway on the waterfront. Irish folk music will entertain you as you choose between the prime rib, Maine lobster, Irish beef stew, or shepherd's pie. A separate bar menu is also available. They even sell Irish gift items.

THE OLDE PINK HOUSE RESTAURANT AND PLANTERS' TAVERN, 23 Abercorn St. Tel. 232-4286.

Cuisine: SEAFOOD/AMERICAN. **Reservations:** Recommended.
$ Prices: Dinner $13–$21. AE, MC, V.
Open: Dinner daily 5:30–10:30pm.
Built in 1771, this old house has been a private residence, a bank, headquarters for one of Sherman's generals, and a tea room. It's an ideal spot for an elegant candlelight dinner in a lovely colonial room, or in front of the Planters' Tavern's large open fireplaces. Riverfront gumbo, black turtle bean soup, baby flounder stuffed with crab, and Old Savannah trifle are all delicious. It faces Reynolds Square.

THE PIRATES' HOUSE, 20 E. Broad St. Tel. 233-5757.

Cuisine: SEAFOOD. **Reservations:** Recommended, especially in summer.
$ Prices: Full lunch $5–$9; full dinner $13–$17; Sunday brunch $15. AE, DC, MC, V.
Open: Lunch daily 11:30am–2:30pm; dinner daily 5:30–9:45pm; Sun brunch 11am–3pm.
A restaurant, a Treasure Island bar, a gift shop, and a museum share this 1754 inn at Bay Street, once a rendezvous for pirates and sailors. Robert Louis Stevenson used the place as a setting in *Treasure Island*. It's listed as an authentic house museum by the American Museum Society; you'll want to set aside time to explore every one of the 23 fascinating dining rooms. Seafood specialties include oysters Savannah or sherry-flavored shrimp and crabmeat au gratin or you can opt for chicken cordon bleu, duck à l'orange, or a variety of flaming main courses, followed by one of the 36 desserts. Do try the Treasure Island bar—it's entertaining and lively. And bring the children: the friendly staff here will give them special attention. The restaurant is a winner of the National Restaurant Association's Great Menu Award.

RIVER HOUSE, 125 W. River St. Tel. 234-1900.

Cuisine: SEAFOOD. **Reservations:** Recommended.
$ Prices: Main courses $9–$13 at lunch; $17–$21 at dinner. AE, MC, V.
Open: Mon–Fri 11am–10pm, Sat 11am–11pm, Sun noon–11pm.
In a converted cotton warehouse on the riverfront, River House excels in fresh seafood creations; the menu depends on the freshest catches of the day. Other specialties are steaks, sourdough bread, hickory-smoked chicken, and homemade pasta. A marvelous bakery inside the restaurant, the Pecan Pie and Cookie Co., lets you take some of those delicious breads and desserts away for later. It's one block west of the Hyatt Regency.

SHRIMP FACTORY, 313 E. River St. Tel. 236-4229.

Cuisine: SEAFOOD. **Reservations:** Recommended.
$ Prices: Full lunch $6–$11; full dinner $12–$19. AE, MC, V.
Open: Mon–Thurs 11am–10pm, Fri–Sat 11am–11pm, Sun noon–10pm.
In an 1826 cotton warehouse setting of exposed old brick and wooden plank walls, with a marvelous salad bar resting next to a miniature shrimp boat, owner Cheryl Harris serve the freshest seafoods from local waters (their Savannah shrimp créole is peerless), inspired salads, and steak and chicken dishes. Price of entrées includes salad

bar and after-dinner cordial. The pine-bark stew, served in a little iron pot with a bottle of sherry on the side, is a potage of seafoods simmered with a delicate herb seasoning; it comes with French bread and a whipped cheese spread. (You won't have to ask how it came by its peculiar name—the legend is printed right on the menu.) The large bar is a popular hangout before and after dinner. It's located on the riverfront.

A SAVANNAH INSTITUTION

MRS. WILKES'S DINING ROOM, 107 W. Jones St. Tel. 232-5997.
   Cuisine: SOUTHERN. **Reservations:** Not accepted.
$ **Prices:** Breakfast $5; lunch $8. No credit cards.
   Open: Breakfast Mon–Fri 8–9am; lunch Mon–Fri 11:30am–3pm.
Remember the days of the boarding houses, when everybody sat together and food was served in big dishes placed in the center of the table? Mrs. Sema Wilkes has been serving locals and travelers in just that manner since the 1940s. You won't find a sign ("It would look so commercial, not at all like home," according to Mrs. Wilkes), but you probably will find a long line of people patiently waiting for a seat at one of the long tables in the basement dining room of an 1870 gray brick house with curving steps and cast-iron trim. Mrs. Wilkes believes in freshness and plans her daily menu around the seasons. Your food will be a reflection of the cuisine Savannah residents have enjoyed for generations—fried or barbecued chicken, red rice and sausage, blackeyed peas, corn-on-the-cob, and other traditional Southern delicacies. It's west of Bull Street.

NEARBY

THE RIVER'S END, 3122 River Dr. Tel. 354-2973.
   Cuisine: SEAFOOD. **Reservations:** Recommended. **Directions:** Go 5½ miles east on U.S. 80 to Victory Drive, then ½ mile south on River Drive.
$ **Prices:** Full dinner $9–$17. AE, DC, MC, V.
   Open: Dinner Mon–Thurs 5–10pm, Fri–Sat 5–11pm.
Located at Tassie's Pier next door to the Thunderbolt Marina on the Intracoastal Waterway, this is a good place to relax and watch the shrimp-boat and pleasure-boat traffic outside. The fresh seafood comes in a marvelous array of culinary creations. For landlubbers, there are choice steaks. Desserts are homemade and absolutely luscious.

BUDGET

THE CRYSTAL BEER PARLOR, 301 W. Jones St. Tel. 232-1153.
   Cuisine: SEAFOOD/BAR FOOD. **Reservations:** Not accepted.
$ **Prices:** Under $6. AE, DISC, MC, V.
   Open: Mon–Sat, 11am–9pm.
This longtime favorite west of Bull Street, opened its doors in the Depression days of 1933 and sold huge sandwiches for a dime. Prices have gone up since then, but local affection for this plain, unpretentious place has diminished not one whit. Try to go earlier or later than peak lunch or dinner hours (if you get there at noon, you'll be in for a lengthy wait). Inside, you can order draft beer in a frosted mug, and owner Conrad Thomson still serves up great fried oyster and shrimp salad sandwiches, crab stew, and chili. The seafood gumbo is one of the best in the Southern Atlantic region, in my opinion. There's ample parking in the lot off Jones Street.

606 EAST CAFE, 319 W. Congress St. Tel. 233-2887.
  Cuisine: CAFE. **Reservations:** Not required.
$ **Prices:** Chili $1.75–$2.50; burgers and sandwiches $3–$4.75. AE, MC, V.
  Open: Mon–Wed 11am–10pm, Thurs–Sat 11am–11pm, Sun 11am–9pm.
In the City Market area, 606 is a casual and colorful spot for something light. Try the gyro wrap, pita sandwich, or tuna salad plate. Blue plate specials are offered daily. I like the cow motif and the Caribbean colors, but the fish with the big lips is a little garish!

WALL'S, 515 E. York Lane. Tel. 232-9754.
  Cuisine: BARBECUE. **Reservations:** Not accepted.
$ **Prices:** Under $7.50. No credit cards.
  Open: Wed 11am–5pm, Thurs 11am–10pm, Fri–Sat 11am–11pm.
Plastic booths, bibs, Styrofoam cartons, and canned drinks from a fridge set the tone at this delightfully casual eatery that dishes up some of the best barbecue in the South. Spare ribs and barbecue sandwiches star on the menu; deviled crabs are the only nonbarbecue item. It's located between York Street and Oglethorpe Avenue.

---

4. WHAT TO SEE & DO

SUGGESTED ITINERARIES

If You Have One Day   Don't put a foot outside the historic district—even at that, you won't see it all!

If You Have Two Days   Devote both days to the historic district and Factors' Walk along the riverfront.

If You Have Three Days   Spend **Days One and Two** as above; **Day Three,** wander around the Victorian district.

If You Have Five Days   Spend **Days One through Three** as above. **Day Four,** visit Fort Jackson; **Day Five,** drive out to Fort Pulaski.

THE TOP ATTRACTIONS

HISTORIC HOMES

DAVENPORT HOUSE, 324 E. State St. Tel. 236-8097.
   This is where those seven determined ladies started the whole Savannah restoration movement. Built between 1815 and 1820 by master builder Isaiah Davenport, it's one of the truly great federal-style houses in this country, with lovely, delicate ironwork and a handsome elliptical stairway. It's on Columbia Square.
   Admission: $4 adults; $3 children 6 to 18.
   Open: Mon–Wed, Fri–Sat 10am–4pm; Sun 1:30–4:30pm. **Closed:** Major holidays.

GREEN-MELDRIM HOME, 14 W. Macon St. Tel. 233-3845.
   General Sherman headquartered here when his troops occupied Savannah in 1864. It was from this Gothic-style house that the general sent his famous (in Savannah, at least) telegram to President Lincoln offering him the city as a Christmas gift. The house now belongs to St. John's Church, which uses the former kitchen, servants' quarters, and stable as its rectory. The rest of the premises are open to visitors.
   Admission: $3 adults, $1 students; children under 6 free. It's on Madison Square.
   Open: Tues, Thurs–Sat 10am–4pm.

DOWNTOWN SAVANNAH ATTRACTIONS

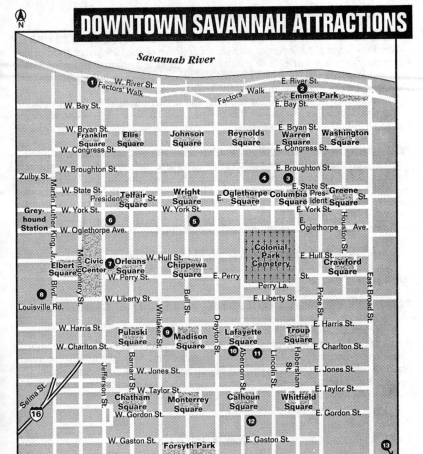

Savannah River

W. River St.
Factors' Walk
Factors' Walk
E. River St.
E. Bay St.
Emmet Park

W. Bay St.

W. Bryan St.
Franklin Square
Ellis Square
Johnson Square
Reynolds Square
E. Bryan St.
Warren Square
Washington Square
W. Congress St.
E. Congress St.

Zulby St.
W. Broughton St.
E. Broughton St.

W. State St.
President Telfair St. Square
Wright Square
Oglethorpe Square
E. State St.
Columbia Pres-Square ident
Greene Square

Grey-hound Station
W. York St.
W. York St.
E. York St.
Houston St.

Chamber of Commerce
W. Oglethorpe Ave.
Oglethorpe Ave.

Montgomery St.
Civic Center
Orleans Square
W. Hull St.
Chippewa Square
Colonial Park Cemetery
E. Hull St.
Crawford Square
East Broad St.

Elbert Square
W. Perry St.
E. Perry
Perry La.
St.

Savannah History Museum
Louisville Rd.
W. Liberty St.
E. Liberty St.
Price St.

W. Harris St.
Pulaski Square
Madison Square
Lafayette Square
Troup Square
E. Harris St.

W. Charlton St.
Abercorn St.
E. Charlton St.
Habersham St.
Lincoln St.

Barnard St.
Whitaker St.
Bull St.
Drayton St.

W. Jones St.
E. Jones St.

Jefferson St.
W. Taylor St.
Chatham Square
Monterrey Square
Calhoun Square
Whitfield Square
E. Taylor St.

Selma St.
16
W. Gordon St.
E. Gordon St.

W. Gaston St.
Forsyth Park
E. Gaston St.

5639

GEORGIA
Atlanta
Savannah

Andrew Low House **10**
Chamber of Commerce **6**
Davenport House **3**
Factors' Walk **1**
Flannery O'Connor Childhood Home **11**
Green-Meldrim Home **9**
J. G. Low's Birthplace **5**
Massie Heritage Interpretation Center **12**
Municipal Auditorium **7**
Owens-Thomas House & Museum **4**
Savannah History Museum **8**
Savannah Science Museum **13**
Ships of the Sea Maritime Museum **2**
Visitors Center **8**

JULIETTE GORDON LOW'S BIRTHPLACE, 142 Bull St. Tel. 233-4501.

On Bull Street at Oglethorpe Avenue, the founder of the Girl Scouts lived in this regency-style house that is now maintained both as a memorial to her and as a National Program Center. The Victorian additions to the 1818 house were made in 1886, just before Juliette Gordon married William Mackay Low.

Admission: $4 adults, $3 for those 18 and under; discount for Girl Scouts.

Open: Mon–Tues, Thurs–Sat 10am–4pm, Sun 12:30–4:30pm. **Closed:** Some Sun in Dec–Jan, and major holidays.

THE ANDREW LOW HOUSE, 329 Abercorn St. Tel. 233-6854.

After her marriage, Juliette Low lived in this house built in 1848, and it was here that she actually founded the Girl Scouts. She died here in 1927. The classic mid–19th-century house is of stucco over brick with elaborate ironwork, jalousied porches, carved woodwork, and crystal chandeliers. William Makepeace Thackeray visited twice (the desk at which he worked is in one bedroom), and Robert E. Lee was entertained at a gala reception in the double parlors in 1870. It faces Lafayette Square.

Admission: $3.50 adults, $2 students, $1 children 6 to 12.

Open: Mon–Wed, Fri–Sat 10:30am–4pm; Sun 12–4pm. **Closed:** National holidays.

FLANNERY O'CONNOR CHILDHOOD HOME, 207 E. Charlton St. Tel. 233-6014.

This Savannah-born writer is best known for her novels and short stories. She won the O. Henry Award three times for best short story, and her portraits of the South have earned her much acclaim. Between October and May, the association holds readings, films, lectures, and seminars about her and other Southern writers. The home is on Lafayette Square.

Admission: Free.

Open: Fri–Sun 1–4pm.

MUSEUMS

SAVANNAH HISTORY MUSEUM, 303 Martin Luther King, Jr., Blvd. Tel. 238-1779.

Housed in the restored train shed of the old Central of Georgia Railway station, behind the visitors' center at Liberty Street and Martin Luther King, Jr., Boulevard, this museum is a good introduction to the city. In the theater, the **Siege of Savannah** is replayed. In addition to the theatrics, there's an exhibition hall displaying memorabilia from every era of Savannah's history.

Admission: $3 adults, $1 senior citizens and children 6 to 12; $10 family rate.

Open: Daily 8:30am–5pm.

SAVANNAH SCIENCE MUSEUM, 4405 Paulsen St. Tel. 355-6705.

This museum features hands-on exhibits in natural history, astronomy, and science. Reptiles and amphibians of Georgia are also featured, and planetarium shows realistically re-create night skies every Sunday at 3pm. There are ramps for wheelchair access. It's located one mile southeast of downtown Savannah.

Admission: Museum, $2.50 adults, $1.50 senior citizens and children 12 and under; planetarium show $1.50.

Open: Tues–Sat 10am–5pm; Sun 2–5pm. **Closed:** Major holidays.

SHIPS OF THE SEA MARITIME MUSEUM, 503 E. River St. Tel. 232-1511.

Located in a renovated waterfront building, it has beautifully constructed models of seagoing vessels from Viking warships right up to today's nuclear-powered ships. There's also a marvelous collection of ships in a bottle.

Admission: $3 adults; $1.50 ages 7 to 12, children under 7 free.

Open: Mon–Sun 10am–5pm. **Closed:** Major holidays.

A WALKING TOUR

Before starting your walk around Savannah, it's a good idea to stop in at the **Savannah Visitor Center** at 301 Martin Luther King, Jr., Blvd. (see "Orientation," above), which is actually one of the city's major sightseeing attractions. It's in the restored Central of Georgia Railroad passenger station, dating from the late 1850s, part of a 35-acre railroad-yard complex that once bustled with train traffic. The mid-Victorian building is decorated with "Savannah colors" (the Factors' red, Tabby white, and Geechee teal, among others). The train shed out back houses the **Savannah History Museum** (see "The Top Attractions," above).

There's so much to see in Savannah that it's really hard to say where to start, but I like to head for the **waterfront.** On the way there, take a walk past **Ellis and Franklin squares,** where Savannah's history comes full circle. Back in 1954, the demolition here of the century-old City Market—to build a parking garage—outraged Savannahians and sparked the "restoration rebellion." The result is the **New City Market.** The four-block market is filled with interesting little eateries, shops, and antique dealers.

Find your way to River Street and walk west to **Factors' Walk.** These old buildings are not set aside as museums. They still make up a lively commercial center—only now there are charming boutiques, restaurants, and taverns in what used to be brokers' offices and warehouses. Strung along a high bluff at the river's edge, the brick buildings rise three (sometimes more) stories above River Street and date from the early 1800s. Each level has its own street—River Street, Lower Factors' Walk, Upper Factors' Walk—and there are bridgeways connecting each level to streets along the bluff. The entrance ramps, from Bay Street down to River Street, are paved with cobblestones that crossed the Atlantic as ballast in sailing ships. If you happen to be there on the first Saturday of any month, you'll be swept up in a River Street festival, with live entertainment, street vendors, and sidewalk artists and craftspeople.

Incidentally, that statue at the foot of the East Broad Street ramp, of a young girl waving toward the harbor, is in memory of Florence Martus, who (so they say) fell in love with a sailor. She promised to greet every ship until he returned to marry her. For 44 years, she waved a white cloth by day and a lantern by night to every ship entering the harbor past the Elba Island Light, where she lived with her brother. Greatly loved and looked for eagerly by seamen, she never missed an arriving ship (she said she could "feel" them approaching), and assisted in at least one heroic rescue. Her own sailor never returned.

Bull Street, stretching south from the river, was named for Col. William Bull, an aide to General Oglethorpe. It holds five of those lovely squares. Revolutionary War hero Nathanael Greene is buried in **Johnson Square,** the first of the five, between Bryan and Congress Streets, where food carts offer a variety of snacks. **Wright Square,** between York and State, holds a large memorial honoring Tomochichi, the Yamacraw chief without whose friendship the Oglethorpe settlement might have perished. A bronze figure of Oglethorpe himself stands in **Chippewa Square** (between Perry and Hull). Continuing on Bull Street, you'll pass through **Madison Square** and **Monterey Square** and come to **Forsyth Park.** The white, cast-iron fountain here is a focal point for Savannah residents, who sit on its railing, feed pigeons, and listen to strolling musicians.

After you rest in the park, continue to wander the district. Look for **Gordon Row,** with its town houses with graceful curving stair rails made from ornate ironwork; and the handsome brick homes on **Marshall Row** facing a broad avenue with grass and trees down its center. If you can, spend the day walking—along the waterfront, through the squares, and along the streets—in order to get an overall picture of what the city is all about.

ORGANIZED TOURS

A delightful way to see Savannah is by horse-drawn carriage. An authentic antique carriage carries you over cobblestone streets as the coachman spins a tale of the town's history. The one-hour tour ($9.50 for adults, $4.50 for children) covers 15 of the 20 squares. Reservations are required; contact **Carriage Tours of Savannah** (tel. 236-6756).

    Colonial Tours (tel. 233-0083) operates tours of the historic district, with pickups at most downtown inns and hotels ($9 for adults, $5 for children under 12), as well as a one-hour **Haunted History** tour detailing Savannah's ghostly past (and present!). Call to reserve for all tours.

    Gray Line Savannah Tours (tel. 236-9604) have joined forces with **Historic Savannah Foundations Tours** (tel. 234-TOUR) to feature narrated bus tours of museums, squares, parks, and homes. Reservations must be made for all tours, and most have starting points at the visitors' center and pickup points at various hotels and motels.

    The **Negro Heritage Trail Tour,** 502 E. Harris St. (tel. 234-8000), offers organized tours ($10 adults, $5 children) from the African-American perspective. The trail is sponsored by the King-Tinsdell Cottage Foundation.

COOL FOR KIDS

MASSIE HERITAGE INTERPRETATION CENTER, 207 E. Gordon St. Tel. 232-1693.

    Here's a stop in the historic district for the kids. Geared to school-age children, the center features various exhibits about Savannah, including such subjects as the city's Greek, Roman, and Gothic architecture; the Victorian era; and a history of public education. Other exhibits include a period costume work room and a 19th-century classroom, where children can experience a classroom environment from days gone by.

    Admission: $1.50 donation requested.

    Open: Mon–Fri 9am–4pm, weekends by appt.

NEARBY ATTRACTIONS

About 2½ miles east of downtown Savannah via Islands Expressway is **Fort Jackson** (tel. 232-3945), with a nine-foot-deep tidal moat around its brick walls. Built by the U.S. Army Corps of Engineers between 1809 and 1879 at a strategic point on the Savannah River, this is the fort that Georgia troops occupied before the outbreak of the Civil War and held until Sherman arrived in 1864. Its arched rooms (designed to support the weight of heavy cannon mounted above, which commanded the harbor entrance) hold 13 exhibit areas. The Fort is open daily from 9am to 5pm, with a $2.50 admission fee (discounted for seniors, children and retired military personnel).

    Fort McAllister (tel. 727-2339) is 10 miles east of U.S. 17 at Richmond Hill, on the banks of the Great Ogeechee River, and was a Confederate earthwork fortification. There's a visitors' center with historic exhibits, and there's a $1.50 fee for adults, 75¢ for children. It's open Tuesday through Saturday from 9am to 5pm and on Sunday from 2 to 5:30pm. There are also walking trails and campsites (call for booking information).

Fort Pulaski, a national monument, is 15 miles east of Savannah off U.S. 80 on Cockspur and McQueens islands at the very mouth of the Savannah River. It took 18 years to complete the massive, pentagonally shaped fort, with its casemate galleries and drawbridges crossing the moat. It was captured by Union troops in 1862 after a 30-hour bombardment, and you can still see shells from that battle embedded in the walls. There are exhibits on the fort's history in the visitors' center (tel. 786-5787) which is open every day except Christmas Day from 8:30am to 5:15pm (to 6:45pm in summer). Admission is $2 per person, free to those 16 and under and 62 and over, with a $4 maximum per car.

There's a quiet little beach over on **Tybee Island,** 18 miles east of Savannah via U.S. 80 (Victory Drive). Oglethorpe built a lighthouse here in 1736, which was destroyed by a storm and replaced in 1773 by a structure you can visit and even climb (if you're up to 178 steps). Pirates sought haven on Tybee Island, and it was a favorite place for duels between Savannah gentlemen—but today it's a relaxing memorial park playground, with a fishing pier, and marina, and the **Tybee Museum** in the lighthouse, featuring historical dioramas, documents, relics, and artwork. There are also scores of motels should you decide to stay overnight. For more information, contact **Tybee Visitor Information,** 222 West Oglethorpe Ave., Savannah, GA 31499 (tel. toll free 800/444-CHARM).

5. SPORTS & RECREATION

Savannah is a terrific cycling city, and you can rent bikes through the Hyatt Regency. Golfers can head for courses in Bacon Park on Skidaway Road (tel. 354-2625) or the Mary Calder course, Bay Street Extension (tel. 238-7100). Public tennis courts are at Bacon Park on Skidaway Road (tel. 354-5925) and Forsyth Park, Drayton and Gaston Streets (tel. 354-5925). The Savannah Downtown Athletic Club, 7 E. Congress St. (tel. 236-4874), opens its superbly equipped health club to the public for a fee.

Swimming, fishing, surfing, and other beach activities are best at Tybee Island (see "Nearby Attractions," above), and deep-sea fishing can be arranged from early spring through late fall with Salt Water Charters, 111 Wickersham Dr. (tel. 598-1814). There are fishing piers at Bull River (U.S. 80 East), at the Frank W. Spencer Park near the Intracoastal Waterway on Islands Expressway, and at Morgan Bridge on Old Hwy. 204 at the Ogeechee River.

6. SAVVY SHOPPING

Factors' Walk, on River Street, is a shopper's delight, with some nine blocks (including Riverfront Plaza) of interesting shops offering everything from crafts to clothing to souvenirs. The **City Market,** between Ellis and Franklin squares on W. St. Julian Street, has art galleries, boutiques, and sidewalk cafés. **Oglethorpe Mall,** at 7804 Abercorn St. Ext., has more than 100 specialty shops and four major department stores as well as restaurants and fast-food outlets. Bookstores, boutiques, and antique shops are located between Wright Square and Forsyth Park.

If you're walking about on the riverfront, drop in to **River House Candles,** 121 W. River St. (tel. 233-7179), for a demonstration of candle-making. The assortment is excellent, and you'll probably find the process fascinating. They are open Sunday through Thursday 9:30am to 10pm and Friday and Saturday 9:30am to 11pm.

7. EVENING ENTERTAINMENT

Check both daily newspapers for goings-on during your stay in Savannah.

THE PERFORMING ARTS   The **Savannah Symphony Orchestra** performs at the Savannah Civic Center, Orleans Square (tel. 236-9536), which is also home to ballet, musicals, and Broadway shows. Tickets cost $9.75 to $32.

The **Savannah Theater,** Chippewa Square (tel. 233-7764) presents contemporary plays, drama, and comedy.

THE CLUB & MUSIC SCENE   As in so many Southern cities, Savannah's nightlife is largely to be found in motel or hotel lounges or restaurants that offer dinner dancing. A more lively nighttime Savannah is to be found in the taverns on the waterfront.

Hard Hearted Hannah's in the DeSoto Hilton offers the city's best jazz. Dancing is offered at **Johnny Harris's** popular restaurant on Victory Drive. But stick to the riverfront for the most concentrated entertainment. There is also a dance bar near the Days Inn and the City Market open to the wee hours. Check out **Kevin Barry's** on the riverfront too (see "Where to Dine," above).

Be sure to stop by **Wet Willie's,** at 101 E. River St. (tel. 233-5650). They have a branch of this bar in Florida, but it can't be any more popular than here. The sign behind the bar says "Attitude Improvement," while another says they'll call a taxi when it's time to go home. Wet Willie's is a combination of Dairy Queen and liquor on tap. The specialty drinks on "tap" are tasty and colorful—sort of a rum and sherbert in a glass. Among the ever-changing favorites: Bahama Mama, Blue Hawaiian, Jungle Juice, Monkey Shine, and Sex on the Beach. No admission is charged. They are open Monday through Thursday 10:30am to 1am, Friday and Saturday 10:30am to 2am, and Sunday 12:30pm to 1am.

8. EASY EXCURSIONS

BRUNSWICK

The Colonial Council of the Royal Province of Georgia laid out Brunswick's streets back in 1771, making it another of early Georgia's planned cities. It has always been an important port, with a natural harbor that can handle oceangoing ships. It's a very pretty town, with palms, flowering shrubs, and moss-draped live oaks all over the place. Watching the large fleet of shrimp boats (Brunswick calls itself "Shrimp Capital of the World") put in on a sunny afternoon is a favorite pastime with both locals and visitors.

Among the sights are the **James Oglethorpe Monument** (a statue of Georgia's founder) in Queens Square on the east side of Newcastle Street; the **Lover's Oak,** a giant, 900-year-old oak at Albany and Prince Streets; **Lanier's Oak** (honoring the poet), half a mile south of town on U.S. 17; and **Bay Street** (between Third and Gloucester), lined with seafood processing plants, where you can watch the shrimp boats dock beginning about 3pm—a lively, interesting spectacle.

GETTING THERE & GETTING AROUND   Brunswick is just 81 miles south of Savannah (I-95 is quicker; U.S. 17 more beautiful). A stopover at Midway, some 30 miles south of Savannah, is worthwhile if only to see the **Midway Church,** built in 1792 after an earlier version burned, with its large slave gallery, high pulpit, and colonial-era headstones in the tiny graveyard.

INFORMATION The **Brunswick–Golden Isles Welcome Center,** Rte. 10, Box I-95, Brunswick, GA 31520 (tel. 912/264-0202), is on I-95 southbound between exits 8 and 9. The friendly staff can give you area information, and if (God forbid!) you come without reservations, can book a room for you at one of more than 20 nearby hotels and motels. There's also a welcome center at 2000 Glynn Ave. (tel. 264-5337).

THE OKEFENOKEE SWAMP

A longer trip is the one inland to Fargo to visit the Okefenokee Swamp (Fargo, GA 31631; tel. 912/637-5274). This is the largest freshwater swamp still preserved in the United States, some 700 square miles. There is a half-mile nature trail with a boardwalk, three daily swamp tours by boat, year-round interpretive programs, a museum, a picnic area, camping, and boat rentals. The boat tours ($7 for adults, $5 for children under 12) are a two-mile trip along waterways lined with thickly tangled growth and alive with alligators and lovely white blossoms of water plants.

You can also visit the **Okefenokee Heritage Center,** two miles west of Waycross on U.S. 82 (tel. 912/285-4260), to see a restored 1912 steam locomotive and depot, an "operating" 1890 print shop, the restored 1840 Gen. Thomas Hilliard House, and general exhibits on local history. There's a small admission fee, and hours are Tuesday through Saturday 9am to 5pm, and on Sunday 1 to 5pm.

At that same site, there's the **Southern Forest World** (tel. 912/285-4056), a museum depicting the development and history of the forest industry in the South. The collection includes a logging train, tools, and other forestry-related artifacts, as well as a variety of audiovisuals to expound on the subject. Hours are the same as at the Heritage Center. Admission is $3 for adults, $1 children.

9. FARTHER AFIELD

THE GOLDEN ISLES

Brunswick is also the gateway to Georgia's "Golden Isles" (a local appellation), the three best known of a string of lush, semitropical islands that runs the length of the state's coastline. Sea Island and St. Simons are just across the Torras Causeway (which passes over the famous "Marshes of Glynn" immortalized by poet Sidney Lanier, who came from these parts), and Jekyll Island is south of town across the Lanier Bridge, then south on Ga. 50 (large signs point the way). Together, they form one of the loveliest resort areas along the entire Atlantic coast.

The islands haven't always been dedicated to fun in the sun, however. The Spanish had missions here as early as 1566, and anthropologists say there were Creek tribal settlements here from 2500 B.C. St. Simons was the scene of the small but important Battle of Bloody Marsh in 1742, which probably determined once and for all the southern part of the country would remain under British, not Spanish, domination. General Oglethorpe had built Fort Frederica on the west side of St. Simons and a smaller battery, Fort St. Simons, on the south end as a defense against the Spanish, who were entrenched in nearby Florida and had a greedy eye on the lands to their north.

After the Revolution, the islands were world-famous for their Sea Island cotton, grown on huge plantations supported mainly by slave labor. The last slaver, the *Wanderer,* landed its cargo of Africans on Jekyll Island as late as 1858. The importing of slaves was by that time illegal, and the crew was promptly arrested. After the Civil War, without their large labor force, the plantations languished and finally disappeared. There was a brief period of prosperity based on a lumber mill on St. Simons (from the 1870s to 1903), and the first daily postal service began in 1876.

In the late 1880s, the Golden Isles got into the resort business when a group of Yankee millionaires "discovered" Jekyll Island and decided it was the ideal retreat from northern winters. They bought the island for $125,000 and built "cottages" there with anywhere from 15 to 25 rooms, and a clubhouse large enough to accommodate up to 100 members. From then until 1947, when second-generation members of the Jekyll Island Club sold the property to the state of Georgia for $675,000, the "Millionaires' Village" was so exclusive that no uninvited guest ever set foot on the place, and even invited guests were limited to visits of no more than two weeks if they stayed in the clubhouse. Many of the "cottages" are open to visitors today, and all the attractions that drew the wealthy are now public property, with plenty of accommodations to take care of us "ordinary" folk.

Sea Island was purchased back in 1927 by Howard Coffin (he already owned another "golden isle," Sapelo Island), who built a causeway from St. Simons to reach the five-mile-long barrier island, then set about developing what has become a world-famous resort, the Cloister, which opened in October 1928.

Where you stay will probably depend on how long you plan to visit the islands. If this is only a way station for you, then your best bet is to stop at one of the motels clustered at the U.S. 341/I-95 interchange, where restaurants, service stations, stores, gift shops, and easy access to the islands' causeway add up to real convenience. It's a different story, of course, if a few days' escape from the cares of civilization in an island setting is what you're after.

Gourmet dining reigns supreme at most of the hotels listed for all three islands; however, excellent dining at less expensive prices is also available on St. Simons. After dark, social life centers around motel lounges, and you should check with the information center on Jekyll Island to see what's going on when you're there.

INFORMATION Sources for helpful information in advance are: **Jekyll Island Convention and Visitors Bureau,** 901 Jekyll Island Causeway, Jekyll Island, GA 31527 (tel. 912/635-3636, or toll free 800/841-6586) and **St. Simons Chamber of Commerce,** Neptune Park, St. Simons Island, GA 31522 (tel. 912/638-9014). Jekyll Island charges a $2 "parking" fee to all visitors at a toll gate on the island.

JEKYLL ISLAND

Golfers can pretend they're Jekyll Island millionaires and play the **Oceanside Nine,** patterned after the course at St. Andrews, Scotland, or one of the three 18-hole golf courses on the island: **Oleander, Pine Lakes,** and **Indian Mound.** Also on Jekyll Island are outdoor and indoor tennis courts, bicycle rentals and bike paths, pier fishing (at no charge), and charter boats for offshore and inlet fishing. No license is required for saltwater fishing; freshwater licenses cost $6 for five days and can be obtained at most hardware or sporting goods stores or at the **Howard Coffin Recreational Park** in Brunswick (freshwater fish around here include bream, red breast, crappie or white perch, shad, bass, and trout).

The **Aquarama,** on Beachview Drive and Parkway, is a modernistic structure with a circular ballroom for dancing and an Olympic-size outdoor swimming pool overlooking the ocean. Check when you get there about dancing times and charges.

You can visit the **Jekyll Island Club Historical District** and the **Millionaires' Village** "cottages" on a 1½-hour tour. It starts at the orientation center on Stable Road (tel. 635-2762, or 635-4036). Highlights include a stained-glass window that Louis Comfort Tiffany installed in Faith Chapel in 1904 and a cottage once owned by William Rockefeller. Adults pay $7; students 6 to 18 years, $5; and children under 6, free.

Jekyll is also the site of Georgia's first brewery (on the northwest end of the island), started by General Oglethorpe, who evidently knew how to "put first things first" for his settlers. Very near the brewery stand the ruins of a home built in 1738 by William Horton, one of Oglethorpe's captains. It was constructed of "tabby," a mortar made of lime, sand, oyster shells, and water, and much used in coastal areas during colonial times.

Where to Stay

Jekyll Island cottage rental rates and availability can be obtained through **Parker-Kaufman Realtors,** Beachview Drive (P.O. Box 3126), Jekyll Island, GA 31527 (tel. 912/635-2512). They'll send a color brochure upon request.

The **Jekyll Island Campground,** North Beachview Drive, Jekyll Island, GA 31527 (tel. 912/635-3021), is managed by the Jekyll Island Authority and is the only island campground in the Golden Isles. On its 18 wooded acres are more than 200 sites, nestled among live oaks and pines. Facilities include bathhouses, showers, laundry, camping equipment, pure tap water, grocery store, garbage pickup, LP gas, and bike rentals. Tent sites cost $10; regular sites, $13; full hookup sites, $15.

THE CLARION RESORT BUCCANEER, 85 Beachview Dr., Jekyll Island, GA 31520. Tel. 912/635-3230, or toll free 800/228-5150. Fax 912/635-3230. 213 rms, 64 kitchenettes. A/C TV TEL

$ Rates: Mar to mid-Aug $89–$119 single or double; $99–$169 kitchenette. Children under 19 stay free with parents. Lower rates other months. Discount packages available. AE, CB, DC, DISC, MC, V.

This oceanfront resort is in a setting of lush tropical foliage ½ mile south of S.R. 50. Rooms all have a private balcony or terrace and are exceptionally nice. For families, there are kitchenettes, a children's playground, and a year-round recreation program. There are bike rentals, and golfers and tennis buffs will find a home here. In addition to that gorgeous beach, there's a pool and oceanfront hot tub. The oceanview restaurant features very good regional cooking.

THE COMFORT INN ISLAND SUITES, 711 Beachview Dr., Jekyll Island, GA 31520. Tel. 912/635-2211, or toll free 800/228-5150. Fax 912/635-3230. 180 suites, 78 kitchenettes. A/C TV TEL

$ Rates (including breakfast): $75–$109 single or double, $109 kitchenette. Children under 17 stay free with parents. Package discounts and weekly or monthly rates available. AE, DC, DISC, MC, V.

This oceanfront resort is on beautifully landscaped grounds 1½ miles north of S.R. 50. Suites include double or king-size beds, and some have kitchenettes or private whirlpools overlooking the ocean. There are two outdoor hot tubs, pool, playground, and an arbor area for outdoor dining. There's also a good moderately priced restaurant next door.

JEKYLL ISLAND CLUB HOTEL, 371 Riverview Dr., Jekyll Island, GA 31520. Tel. 912/635-2600, or toll free 800/333-3333. 136 rms and suites. A/C TV TEL

$ Rates: $75–$119 single or double; $140–$199 suite. Children under 16 stay free with parents. Lower rates Labor Day–early May. AE, DC, DISC, MC, V.

This is the undisputed star of Jekyll Island accommodations. In the heyday of Jekyll's millionaires, the rambling, turreted club was the center of social activities, and provided deluxe lodgings for Morgans, Vanderbilts, and Rockefellers. In 1987 it reopened as a Radisson Hotels Resort. It has access to shopping areas, as well as 10 miles of beaches.

You'll love the caramel- and vanilla-colored exterior and the fine hardwood floors and exposed beams inside. The dining room is softly lit and elegantly furnished; the fluted columns are beautiful, and the service excellent. There's also a delightful deli/café. About a mile away is the hotel's beach club. Besides the outdoor pool, you can play tennis at nine courts or even try croquet. If you want to treat yourself, this is it. It's located in the historic district.

Where to Dine

BLACKBEARD'S, 200 N. Beachview Dr. Tel. 635-3522.
Cuisine: SEAFOOD/STEAK. **Reservations:** Not required.
$ Prices: Lunch $3.50–$24.95; dinner $9.95–$24.95. Children's menu. MC, V.
Open: Daily 11am–10pm. **Closed:** Christmas Day.

For hearty eaters, this is the place to dine. Seafood is fresh from local waters, and steaks come cooked precisely to order. The ocean view is gorgeous, and in fine weather there's outdoor dining.

GRAND DINING ROOM, JEKYLL ISLAND CLUB, 371 Riverview Dr. Tel. 635-2600.
Cuisine: SEAFOOD/STEAK. **Reservations:** Recommended. **Directions:** in the historic district.
$ Prices: Breakfast $5.50–$9.95; lunch $6.95–$12.95; dinner $14.95–$24.95; children's plate available. AE, DC, DISC, MC, V.
Open: Daily 7–10am, 11am–2pm, 6–9:30pm.

In this lovely room with crystal wall lamps and pillared fireplace, fresh seafood comes in a wide variety of preparations, depending on catches of the day; steaks are first rate. They do their own baking here. In the evening, there's a strolling guitarist, and valet parking is free. It's located ½ mile north of S.R. 50 (Ben Fortson Parkway) in the historic district.

ZACHRY'S, 44 Beachview Dr. Tel. 635-3128.
Cuisine: SEAFOOD. **Reservations:** Not required.
$ Prices: Breakfast 95¢–$6.95; lunch and dinner $1.75–$12.95. Children's menu. MC, V.
Open: Fri–Mon 8–11am; daily 11am–10pm.

Excellent seafood specialties are prepared by the chef of this rather casual eatery; the menu also includes selections of steak and chicken, and there's a very good salad bar.

ST. SIMONS ISLAND

St. Simons Island is real sightseeing territory. No tourist would miss **Fort Frederica National Monument** (tel. 638-3639), on the northwest end of the island. About all that's left of the original construction is a small portion of the king's magazine and the barracks tower, but archeological excavations have unearthed many foundations, and the visitors' center has a film on the history of the fort and the town. There's a $4 per vehicle charge, and it's open every day from 8am to 5pm, later during the summer.

My favorite attraction on St. Simons is the **Museum of Coastal History** (tel. 638-4666), in the restored lighthouse keeper's house next to the St. Simons Light at 101 12th St. There is a gallery with information about the coastal region, and upstairs is a re-creation of what the lighthouse keeper's dwelling was like from the 1870s to the 1900s. Hardy souls will want to climb the lighthouse's 129 steps for a spectacular view of the Golden Isles. Admission ($3 for adults, $1 for children 6 to 12) includes the museum and the lighthouse. Hours are Tuesday through Saturday 10am to 5pm and Sunday 1:30 to 5pm.

Then there's the **Coastal Center for the Arts** (tel. 634-0404), on Demere Road near the airport, where local and "traveling" art and craft exhibits are displayed, and there are lectures, films, concerts, classes, and demonstrations. It is open Monday through Saturday from 10am to 5pm year-round, and there's no admission.

Scattered from end to end of St. Simons are ruins of the plantation era: **Hampton Plantation** (where Aaron Burr spent a month after his duel with Alexander Hamilton) and **Cannon's Point** on the north; **West Point, Pines Bluff,** and **Hamilton Plantations** on the west along the Frederica River; **Harrington Hall** and **Mulberry Grove** in the interior; **Lawrence, St. Clair, Black Banks, The Village,** and **Kelvyn Grove** on the east; and **Retreat Plantation** on the south end. Ruins are about all you'll see today, but there's a restored chapel on the West Point Plantation (made of tabby, the mortar turned pink because of an unusual lichen; natives say it reflected blood on the hands of Dr. Thomas Hazzard, who killed a neighbor in a land dispute and built the chapel after being so ostracized by island society that he would not attend Christ Church), along with some restored slave cabins.

Christ Church, 6329 Frederica Rd., at the north end of the island, was built in 1820. It was virtually destroyed when Union troops camped here during the Civil War, burning pews for firewood and butchering cattle in the chapel. In 1886, Anson Greene Phelps Dodge, Jr., restored the church as a memorial to his first wife, who had died on their honeymoon. It's a serene white wooden building nestled under huge old oaks. The doors are open every day from 2 to 5pm during daylight saving time, 1 to 4pm other times, and there is no charge to go inside.

Where to Stay

In addition to the accommodations listed below, private cottages are available for weekly or monthly rental on St. Simons. You can get an illustrated brochure with rates and availability information from **Parker-Kaufman Realtors,** 1699 Frederica Rd., St. Simons Island, GA 31522 (tel. 912/638-3368).

THE KING AND PRINCE BEACH RESORT, 201 Arnold Rd., St. Simons Island, GA 31522. Tel. 912/638-3631, or toll free 800/342-0212. Fax 912/634-1720. 170 rms, 49 villas. A/C TV TEL
$ Rates: Mid-Mar to early Nov, $99–$145 single or double; $233–$283 villa. AE, CB, DC, MC, V.
At Arnold Road and Downing Street, The King and Prince is a casual, yet elegant first-class resort with a mission-style roof and skylighted lobby. French doors and an attractive decor make the dining room a lovely spot for dinner or for buffets in summer. The beach is beautiful, and there are lighted tennis courts, watersports, several pools, three whirlpools, and a fitness room. Accommodations range from standard guest rooms to three-bedroom condominiums.

QUEEN'S COURT MOTEL, 437 Kings Way, St. Simons Island, GA 31522. Tel. 912/638-8459. 23 rms, suites, and kitchenettes. A/C TV TEL
$ Rates: $45 single; $50 double; $55 suite; $61 kitchenette. MC, V.
This complex of two-story buildings surrounding a shaded, grassy lawn is in the village center. Rooms have one double bed or two single beds, and there are suites with two double beds and a large sitting room, as well as kitchenette units. Drapes and spreads are new. No pets allowed.

SEA GATE INN, 1014 Ocean Blvd., St. Simons Island, GA 31522. Tel. 912/638-8661. 34 rms, 8 efficiencies, 6 kitchenettes. A/C TV TEL
$ Rates: $45 single or double; $85–$230 efficiency; $75–$100 kitchenette. AE, MC, V.

All rooms are bright and colorful, and some have kitchens, private patios, or balconies, including some oceanfront rooms. There's free coffee and doughnuts for all; restaurants are only three blocks away. Eighteen units are oceanfront. It's half a mile east of the village.

SEA PALMS GOLF AND TENNIS RESORT, 5455 Frederica Rd., St. Simons Island, GA 31522. Tel. 912/638-3351. Fax 912/638-3351, ext. 529. 207 rms and villas. A/C TV TEL

$ Rates: Mar–Oct, $99–$250 single or double; $119–$279 villa. Children under 14 stay free with parents. Lower rates other months. Golf, tennis, and honeymoon packages available. AE, DC, MC, V.

Covering some 800 acres that accommodate both permanent residents and vacationers, this is more a community than a resort. There are fully furnished villas overlooking the golf course and the Marshes of Glynn, as well as the newer, very posh Sea Marsh Villas.

Recreational facilities include a dozen clay tennis courts, private beach, indoor and outdoor pool, playground, putting green, health club, and 27 holes of golf.

Where to Dine

BLANCHE'S COURTYARD, 440 Kings Way. Tel. 638-3030.
Cuisine: SEAFOOD. **Reservations:** Recommended.
$ Prices: Dinner $12–$17. AE, DC, MC, V.
Open: Summer, daily 5:30–10pm; winter, daily 5:30–9:30pm. **Closed:** Holidays.
Blanche's has a Victorian atmosphere, with lots of old brickwork, antiques, and a private patio. Try their broiled seafood spiced up cajun-style. On Saturday, there's entertainment (dress is casual).

THE CRAB TRAP, 1209 Ocean Blvd. Tel. 638-3552.
Cuisine: SEAFOOD. **Reservations:** Not required.
$ Prices: Dinner $9–$14. MC, V.
Open: Mon–Sat 5–10:30pm; Sun 5–10:30pm in season. **Closed:** Holidays.
No fancy trappings, but the seafood is superb. Fresh local shrimp, oysters, and scallops come with coleslaw and hush puppies.

EMMELINE AND HESSIE, 100 Marina Dr. Tel. 638-9084.
Cuisine: SEAFOOD. **Reservations:** Not required.
$ Prices: Lunch $6–$10; dinner $10–$20. AE, MC, V.
Open: Daily 11:30am–10pm.
Named after two ferries that once plied the waters between Brunswick and St. Simons, it overlooks the Intracoastal Waterway and St. Simons Bay at the Brunswick/ St. Simons Island causeway, in Marina Village. Inside, its ship decor is cozied up by plants. There's specialty shrimp dishes and an excellent oyster bar. They do their own baking and dish up homemade soup and sauces.

LITTLE ST. SIMONS ISLAND

The ideal place to savor the wild beauty of Georgia's coast still untouched by commercial development. Reached by boat from St. Simons, Little St. Simons, P.O. Box 1078, St. Simons Island, GA 31522 (tel. 912/638-7472), is a 10,000-acre privately owned sanctuary that offers you the uncrowded run of six miles of undeveloped beaches, fishing, swimming, horseback riding, and birdwatching for 200 species. Accommodations, under the caring management of Debbie McIntyre, are in comfortable lodges, some built before 1920, some opened in the past few years.

Meals, served family style, feature locally caught seafoods and Southern staples like fried chicken and barbecue. Rates range from $200 to $400, depending on accommodations, including all meals and activities. Many of the cozy public areas have been upgraded.

SEA ISLAND

Since the late 1920s, Sea Island, northernmost of the Golden Isles and connected by bridge to St. Simons Island, has meant just one thing—the Cloister Hotel. Although there is little else for the visitor, the hotel is a destination by itself.

Where to Stay and Dine

CLOISTER HOTEL, Sea Island, GA 31561. Tel. 912/638-3611, or toll free 800/SEA-ISLAND in Georgia. Fax 912/638-5159. 264 rms. A/C TV TEL **Directions:** Nine miles east of U.S. 17.

$ Rates (per person per night, including meals): Mar 15–Nov, $220–$398 single, $270–$448 double (plus tax and service); other months, $166–$194 single, $216–$244 double. 6% state tax, 15% service charge. Golf, tennis, and honeymoon packages available. No credit cards.

The world-famous Cloister, a Moorish-style complex roofed with red tile, has a main building as well as newer low-rise hotel structures with gardenlike surroundings, all offering the ultimate in luxury and convenience. This elegant place has been family-owned since it opened in 1928; with a staff ratio of three employees to every two guests, you'll begin to feel pampered the minute you register.

Guests enjoy the Sea Island Beach Club, with luxurious dining rooms right at the ocean's edge, and the particularly charming Spanish Lounge, with three cloister windows, high wooden ceilings, wood-burning fireplaces, and oversize armchairs. There's dancing every night, and special events feature plantation suppers, cookouts, musical happenings, and al fresco dinner dances.

Guests have use of the diving pool, heated swimming pool, wading pool, sundecks, full-service spa with health and fitness facilities, golf (54 holes), tennis (17 all-weather courts), riding stables, skeet and trap shooting, fishing and boating docks, bicycles, croquet, shuffleboard, and chip-and-putt.

CUMBERLAND ISLAND

Nowhere else on the East Coast are the island qualities—peace, unspoiled natural surroundings—so perfectly preserved as at Cumberland Island. Since 1972, most of this island has been a National Seashore administered by the National Park Service.

To step onto Cumberland Island, just 16 miles long and 3 miles across at its widest point, is to step into a wilderness of maritime forest (with tunnel-like roads canopied by live oaks, cabbage palms, magnolia, holly, red cedar, and pine), salt marshes alive with waving grasses, sand dunes arranged by wind and tide into a double line of defense against erosion, and gleaming sand beaches that measure a few hundred yards in width at low tide. It is to enter a breathtaking world of animal life, where alligators wallow in marshes, white-tail deer bound through the trees, wild pigs snuffle in the undergrowth, armadillos and wild turkeys roam freely about, over 300 species of birds wheel overhead, and wild horses canter in herds or pick their way peacefully to watering holes.

GETTING THERE There's an airstrip for small planes near the Greyfield Inn (see below), and air-taxi arrangements can be made from Jacksonville or St. Simons Island (call the inn for details). The only public transport to the island is via the ferry from St. Mary's on the mainland; you must book ahead (contact National Park Service, Cumberland Island National Seashore, Box 806, St. Mary's, GA 31558; tel. 912/882-4335). There are two trips daily from mid-May through Labor Day, and every day except Tuesday and Wednesday other months. In summer months, book as far in advance as possible. The fare is $10 for adults, $7 for children 6 to 12, $8 for seniors.

If you plan to stay overnight, the best way to reach Cumberland is by the inn's ferry, the *Lucy R. Ferguson,* which maintains a regular schedule to Fernandina Beach, Florida. Reservations are necessary, and must be made through the inn (see below). I strongly urge that you bring your bicycle, since there's no public transportation on the island. You can, however, safely leave your car in the Fernandina Beach parking lot across from the police station.

WHAT TO SEE & DO

Don't look for a swimming pool, tennis courts, or a golf course—Cumberland's attractions are a different sort. The inn is just a short walk from those high sand dunes and a wild, undeveloped beach. Beachcombing, swimming, shelling, fishing, and exploring the island are high on the list of activities.

There are no signs left of the Native Americans who lived here some 4,000 years ago, nor of the Franciscan missionaries who came to convert them during the 1500s. No ruins exist of the forts built at each end of the island by Gen. James Oglethorpe in the 1700s, and the only thing that remains of his hunting lodge is its name, Dungeness: On the same site, Gen. Nathanael Greene's post-Revolutionary tabby mansion (which burned to the ground after the Civil War) and its successor, a massive Carnegie mansion, both inherited the name.

What you will find as you poke around this fascinating island are the ruins of Carnegie's **Dungeness** (which burned in 1959); the **Greene-Miller cemetery** (Phineas Miller was Mrs. Greene's second husband), which first held the remains of Henry "Lighthorse Harry" Lee before they were removed to Virginia and still holds inhabitants from Revolutionary times through the Civil War era; **Stafford plantation house** and, down the lane a bit, **"the chimneys,"** a melancholy post–Civil War ruin (ask at the inn for the full story); **Plum Orchard,** a magnificent Carnegie mansion, fully furnished but unoccupied and now the property of the National Park Service; and most of all, the hushed solemnity of island roads, pathways, and fields being reclaimed by native plants and wildlife.

WHERE TO STAY & DINE

There's only one hotel on Cumberland, and it's no less enchanted than the island itself.

GREYFIELD INN, P.O. Box 900, Fernandina Beach, FL 32035. Tel. 904/261-6408. 9 rms (with shared baths).
$ Rates (including meals): $275–$315 double. 50% deposit required. 6% gratuity and 17% tax will be added to your bill. MC, V.
The only commercial building (if you can call it that) in the area is a three-story plantation mansion with a wide, inviting veranda set in a grove of live oaks. Built shortly after the turn of the century as a summer retreat by Thomas Carnegie (Andrew's brother and partner), Greyfield has remained family property ever since. Guests today are treated very much as family visitors were in years past: The extensive and very valuable library is open for your perusal; furnishings are those the family has always used; the bar is an open one, operated on an honor system (you simply pour your own and note it on a pad); meals are served and you dine at the long family table, adorned with heirloom silver candlesticks. You're at liberty to browse through old

family photo albums, scrapbooks, and other memorabilia scattered about the large, paneled living room (if the weather is cool, there'll be a fire in the oversize fireplace). Soft chimes announce meals (dinnertime means "dress"—informal dresses and jackets, no shorts or jeans). If beachcombing or exploring is what you have in mind for the day, the inn will pack a picnic lunch for you to carry along. Guest rooms vary in size; bathrooms are shared and still hold the original, old-fashioned massive fittings. Reservations must be made well in advance. Children under 6 are not accepted.

CHAPTER 13

ATLANTA &
ENVIRONS

Atlanta began life as a railroad city. For a long time it had no name except "The Terminus," since it was the southern end of a Western and Atlantic Railroad spur linking the state with Tennessee and points west. A civil engineer who had surveyed the rail route is said to have predicted that it would "be a good location for one tavern, a blacksmith shop, a grocery store, and nothing else." That was back in 1837 (the first run on the line did not come until 1842). The little settlement of dirt-floored shacks and wide-open bars kept its "work camp" atmosphere through two name changes—first to Marthasville, then to Atlanta (a female form of the "Atlantic" in the railroad's name)—and a municipal charter in 1847 that made it a legitimate town.

As more and more rail lines met at the junction, however, life became more civilized, and businessmen arrived to attend to the warehousing, distributing, and wholesaling of freight. When the Confederacy came into being, Atlanta was an important supply and arms center. Gen. William T. Sherman fought a long, bitter battle to win the city for the Union, then kept it under harsh military rule from September to November of 1864. Once he had evacuated civilian Atlantans, he burned all but 400 of the city's 3,600 homes and destroyed its railroads before setting out on his "march to the sea."

Only four years later, however, Atlanta had recovered sufficiently to be named the state capital (partly because of its accessibility, through rebuilt railroads, to all parts of the state). The collapse of a slavery-based plantation economy proved a boon to this trade-oriented city, and its growth hasn't faltered since those Reconstruction recovery days. It has enlarged its rail transportation system, brought in six interstate highways (the trucking industry is now an important part of the local economy), and acquired an airport second in traffic only to Chicago's O'Hare. Four hundred fifty of the Fortune 500 corporations have offices here, and many have moved their home offices to the city.

The effect of all this commerce with the outside world has been to breed in Atlantans a cosmopolitanism that keeps them constantly working to bring culture to their city. Atlanta today is visibly alive with cultural activity. There are concerts and cabarets, ballets and bar-lounges, art galleries and avant-garde "happenings"—and

WHAT'S SPECIAL ABOUT ATLANTA

Historic Sites

- ☐ Martin Luther King, Jr., Historical Site, the two-block area dedicated to the memory of the beloved Nobel Peace Prize winner and civil rights leader.
- ☐ Wren's Nest, a mecca for lovers of the Old South tales of Uncle Remus—Joel Chandler Harris, who made his home here.
- ☐ Underground Atlanta, site of the city's first rail terminus, now a complex of restaurants and nightclubs, shops, and Heritage Row, which depicts Atlanta's history from the earliest Indian settlement to the present.

Museums

- ☐ Museum of the Jimmy Carter Library, whose exhibits include a full-scale replica of the Oval Office.
- ☐ High Museum of Art, a treasure trove of European and African art collections.
- ☐ Georgia State Museum of Science and Industry, which features a diorama of Georgia industry, as well as wildlife exhibits, rocks, fossils, and minerals.

the influx of European-cuisine restaurants has made it harder and harder to find fried chicken, country ham, hot biscuits, and grits. Today's Atlantans will tell you that their town is the "New York of the South"—and then proceed to take you by the hand and prove it.

ATLANTA CALENDAR OF EVENTS

JANUARY

- ☐ **Martin Luther King Week.** Celebrates the civil rights leader's life with musical tributes, seminars, films, plays, and tributes from celebrities and civil rights leaders. Second week in January.

FEBRUARY

- ☐ **Atlanta Flower Show.** Atlanta Apparel Mart and Inforum. Four days (usually centered around Valentine's Day) of flower and vegetable garden displays, as well as gardening demonstrations. Mid-February.

MARCH

- ☐ **St. Patrick's Day Parade.** More than 7,000 marchers; bands, drill teams, bagpipe players, and cloggers. Downtown and Buckhead parades. March 17.

APRIL

- ☐ **Antebellum Jubilee,** Stone Mountain Park. Regional arts and crafts demonstrations, folk music concerts, and the re-creation of a Civil War encampment. Early April.

☐ **Atlanta Dogwood Festival,** Piedmont Park. A week of art shows, open-house tours, concerts, children's activities, food booths, and environmental displays. Mid-April.

MAY

☐ **Springfest,** Stone Mountain Park. Folk and country music, arts and crafts displays, children's events, and traditional Southern food. One weekend, early May.

JUNE

☐ **Atlanta Jazz Series,** Grant Park. Free weekend concerts from 4 to 10pm, with big-name performers usually appearing in the evenings. First weekend in June.

☐ **Stone Mountain Village Annual Arts and Crafts Festival.** Displays by more than 200 craftspeople and antiques dealers, free entertainment, food booths. Mid-June.

JULY

☐ **July 4th Celebrations.** Downtown parade; Stone Mountain Park celebration.

SEPTEMBER

☐ **Georgia Music Festival,** World Congress Center. Statewide competitions and concerts culminate with the Georgia Music Hall of Fame Awards concert and banquet. Mid-September.

☐ **Atlanta Greek Festival,** Greek Orthodox Cathedral. Greek food, dancing, and ethnic crafts, as well as lectures on subjects of Hellenic interest. Late September.

NOVEMBER

☐ **Veteran's Day Parade.** A major Atlanta event, with a gigantic contingent of floats, drill teams, and color guards led by a celebrity grand marshal. November 11 (or closest Monday or Saturday).

☐ **Lighting of the Great Tree,** Underground Atlanta. Beloved Atlanta tradition. Late November.

DECEMBER

☐ **Country Christmas,** Atlanta Botanical Garden. Popcorn stringing, entertainment by strolling musicians and mimes, caroling, and wreath-making. First Sunday in December.

1. ORIENTATION

ARRIVING

BY PLANE Atlanta's **Hartsfield International Airport** (tel. 404/530-6600) is the home of **Delta Airlines** (tel. toll free 800/221-1212) and served by more than a dozen other carriers, including **American** (tel. toll free 800/433-7300), **Continental** (tel. toll free 800/525-0280), **Northwest** (tel. toll free 800/225-2525), **TWA** (tel. toll free 800/221-2000), **United** (tel. toll free 800/241-6522), and **USAir** (tel. toll free 800/428-4322).

Atlanta Airport shuttle (tel. 524-3400, or toll free 800/842-2770) connects the airport to downtown and major hotels between 7am and 11pm, with a $8 fare ($12 to Lenox Square and Emory University). MARTA's rapid rail trains run from 4:35am to 1:42am, with a downtown fare of $1.25. Taxi fare is $15 for one passenger, $8 each for two, $6 each for three. A word of warning: be *sure* the taxi driver knows how to get to where you want to go before you leave the airport.

BY TRAIN Amtrak (tel. 800/USA-RAIL) trains arrive at Brookwood Railway Station, 1688 Peachtree St., providing daily service to and from Washington, New York, Boston, and intermediate points to the northeast, and New Orleans and intermediate points to the southwest.

BY BUS Bus service to Atlanta is provided by **Greyhound/Trailways Bus Lines,** 81 International Blvd., Atlanta, GA 30303 (tel. 404/522-6300).

BY CAR Atlanta is accessible by car via three interstate highways: I-75, which runs north/south from Tennessee to Florida; I-85, northeast to southwest from South Carolina to Alabama; and I-20, east and west from South Carolina to Alabama. I-285, more commonly known as the Perimeter Highway, circles the Atlanta metropolitan area.

TOURIST INFORMATION

The **Atlanta Convention and Visitors Bureau,** 233 Peachtree St. NE, Suite 2000, Atlanta, GA 30303 (tel. 404/521-6600), can supply a wealth of information on sightseeing, accommodations, dining, cultural happenings, and special interests.

After your arrival, stop by one of the helpful ACVB **visitor information centers,** at the following locations: Peachtree Center Mall (downtown), 231 Peachtree St.; Lenox Square Shopping Center (Buckhead), 3393 Peachtree Rd.; and Underground Atlanta, 65 Upper Alabama St.

For a more in-depth exploration of the city, *Frommer's Atlanta* (Prentice Hall Travel),a comprehensive guide, is available at many bookstores.

CITY LAYOUT

MAIN ARTERIES AND STREETS To a stranger, Atlanta's street "system" is a perplexing maze that seems to have no particular plan. Here are some tips that might help you make some sense of Atlanta's streets. In the center of the downtown area, Peachtree, Marietta, Decatur, Edgewood, and Whitehall Streets come together at Five Points Intersection; and all those NE, NW, SE, and SW addresses fan out from this point. Peachtree runs north and south through the city, North and Ponce de Leon Avenues run east and west, and I-75 and I-85 (the Northeast Expressway) run through downtown. I-20 (the East and West expressways) runs through the city center. Don't be misled by the word "expressway," however: At rush hours, these arteries are as clogged as city streets, so plan accordingly. Another thing to remember is that "Peachtree" doesn't always mean Peachtree Street (which is the real main street in Atlanta). There are 26 "Peachtree"s: If the name is followed by Drive, View, Circle, Avenue, or anything else, it isn't *the* Peachtree Street!

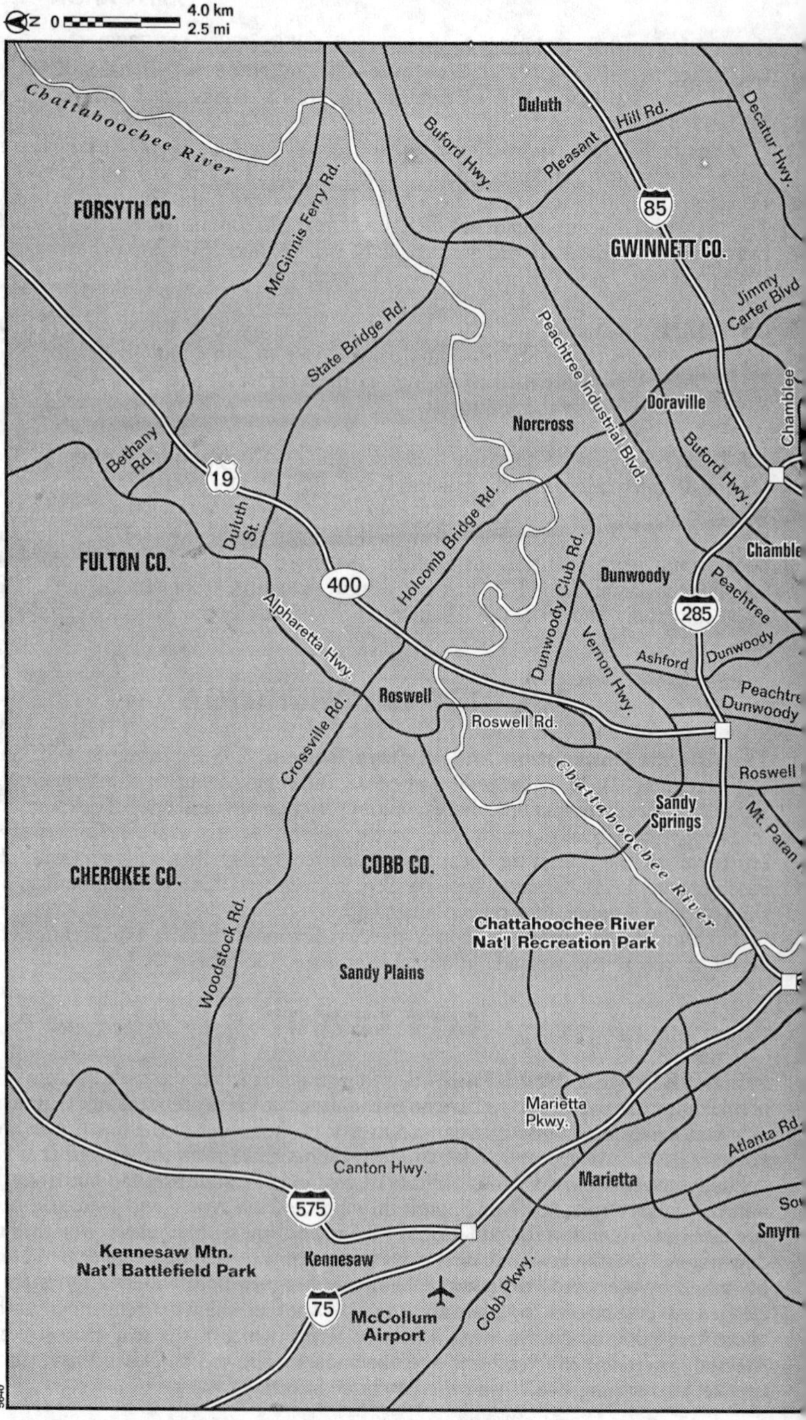

N
0
4.0 km
2.5 mi
Chattahoochee River
FORSYTH CO.
McGinnis Ferry Rd.
Buford Hwy.
Duluth
Pleasant Hill Rd.
Decatur Hwy.
85
GWINNETT CO.
Jimmy Carter Blvd
State Bridge Rd.
Peachtree Industrial Blvd.
Chamblee
Doraville
Norcross
Bethany Rd.
19
Buford Hwy.
Duluth St.
Holcomb Bridge Rd.
Chamble
FULTON CO.
400
Dunwoody Club Rd.
Dunwoody
Peachtree
285
Alpharetta Hwy.
Vernon Hwy.
Ashford
Dunwoody
Peachtre
Dunwoody
Roswell
Crossville Rd.
Roswell Rd.
Roswell
Chattahoochee River
Sandy Springs
Mt. Paran
CHEROKEE CO.
COBB CO.
Woodstock Rd.
Chattahoochee River
Nat'l Recreation Park
Sandy Plains
Marietta Pkwy.
Atlanta Rd.
Canton Hwy.
Marietta
575
So
Smyrn
Kennesaw Mtn.
Nat'l Battlefield Park
Kennesaw
75
McCollum
Airport
Cobb Pkwy.
5640

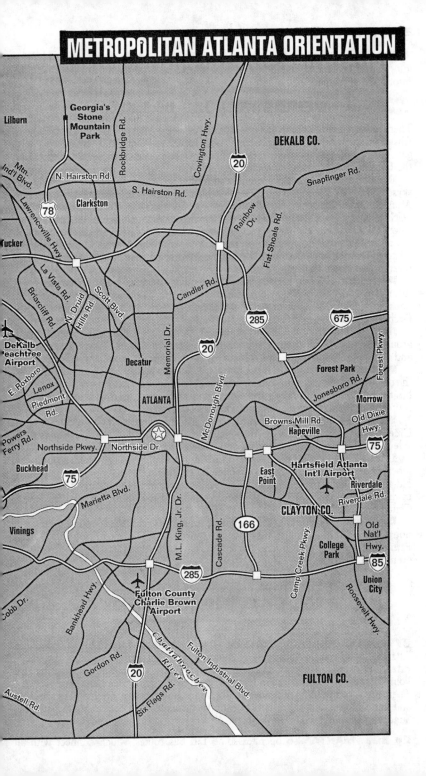

METROPOLITAN ATLANTA ORIENTATION

MAPS The best inner-city and metropolitan area maps are those supplied by the information centers of the Atlanta Convention and Visitors Bureau (see "Tourist Information," above).

NEIGHBORHOODS IN BRIEF

There are seven rather clearly defined sections of metro Atlanta: downtown, midtown, Ansley Park, Buckhead, Virginia-Highland, Little Five Points, and Decatur. To help get your bearings, think of the metropolitan area as a huge curve, with downtown at the bottom and Buckhead at the top.

Downtown Atlanta's commercial center is home to numerous gleaming skyscrapers, the most outstanding of which is Peachtree Center. Underground Atlanta, Omni Coliseum, the Georgia World Congress Center, department stores (Rich's, Macy's, etc.), the downtown branch of High Museum of Art (in the Georgia-Pacific Center), Grant Park (with its zoo and Cyclorama), and the state capitol are all in this area. Adjacent to central downtown is the Martin Luther King, Jr., Historic District, a predominantly black neighborhood that bred and nurtured the revered civil rights leader.

Midtown North of downtown, extending roughly from Ponce de Leon Avenue to 26th Street. Major attractions include the Woodruff Arts Center, which houses the High Museum of Art, the Alliance Theatre, and the Atlanta Symphony Orchestra; and the Fox Theatre.

Ansley Park Adjacent to midtown. Designed by Frederick Law Olmsted around the turn of the century, it is chiefly a residential area of landscaped greenery, and also houses Colony Square, a complex of shops, restaurants, and offices.

Buckhead About six miles north of downtown is Atlanta's affluent district, the setting of gorgeous mansions surrounded by landscaped gardens, posh shops and boutiques, some of the city's top hotels and restaurants, and two top-of-the-line shopping centers, Lenox Square and Phipps Plaza.

Virginia-Highlands Northeast of downtown, this is to Atlanta what Greenwich Village is to New York—an area of quirky little shops, bookstores, sidewalk cafés, art galleries, bistros, and some of the liveliest bars in the city.

Little Five Points Just beyond Virginia-Highlands, centered around the junction of Euclid and Moreland Avenues. After a period of deterioration, the lovely old Victorian homes here became the renovation craze of city residents and now shine in their original glory. This is also where you'll find the Jimmy Carter Presidential Center and Library.

Decatur A charming village, dating from 1823, clustered around the courthouse square, a 15-minute drive east of downtown. The huge, bustling Dekalb Farmer's Market, is found here. Decatur is also the setting for a variety of cultural events and festivals.

2. GETTING AROUND

BY PUBLIC TRANSPORTATION By Subway MARTA (Metropolitan Atlanta Rapid Transit Authority), is Atlanta's rapid-rail system, with 29 stations. It extends north to the airport, and east-west and north-south lines intersect at the Five Points Station in downtown. Hours are 5:30am to 1am, and the regular fare is $1.25. There are token vending machines at all stations, and transfers are free. For schedule and route information, call 848-4711 Monday through Friday 6am to 10pm, Saturday, Sunday, and holidays 8am to 4pm.

By Bus MARTA also operates some 150 bus routes, which connect with all

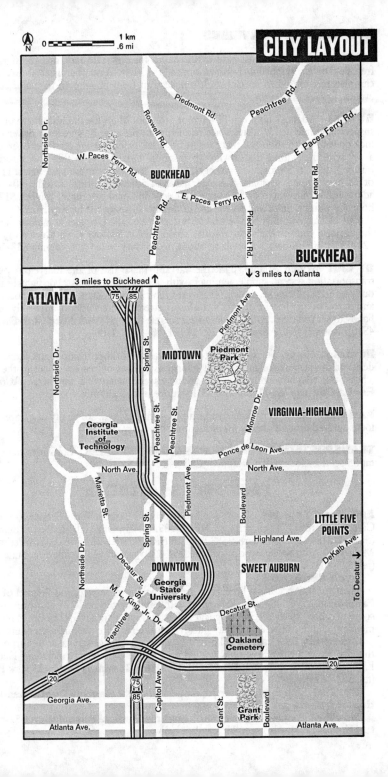

CITY LAYOUT

1 km
0   .6 mi
N

BUCKHEAD

Northside Dr.

Piedmont Rd.

Roswell Rd.

Peachtree Rd.

W. Paces Ferry Rd.

E. Paces Ferry Rd.

BUCKHEAD

Peachtree Rd.

E. Paces Ferry Rd.

Lenox Rd.

Piedmont Rd.

BUCKHEAD

3 miles to Buckhead ↑

↓ 3 miles to Atlanta

ATLANTA

75 85

Northside Dr.

Spring St.

MIDTOWN

Piedmont Ave.

Piedmont Park

VIRGINIA-HIGHLAND

Monroe Dr.

Georgia Institute of Technology

W. Peachtree St.

Peachtree St.

Ponce de Leon Ave.

North Ave.

North Ave.

Piedmont Ave.

Boulevard

Marietta St.

Spring St.

LITTLE FIVE POINTS

Highland Ave.

DeKalb Ave.

Northside Dr.

Decatur St.

DOWNTOWN

Georgia State University

SWEET AUBURN

To Decatur →

M. L. King, Jr., Dr.

Decatur St.

Peachtree

Oakland Cemetery

20

75 85

Georgia Ave.

Capitol Ave.

Grant St.

Grant Park

Boulevard

20

Atlanta Ave.

Atlanta Ave.

rapid-rail stations. You must have exact change for the $1.25 fare, and transfers are free. For route and schedule information, call the MARTA number listed above. They can also tell you when special shuttle buses run from downtown to major sports events.

BY TAXI   Atlanta's taxis can be a major problem. Many are unclean, mechanically suspect, and manned by drivers not familiar with the city. Be sure your driver has a lock on your destination and that the fare is settled before setting off. Fares operate on a set schedule within the downtown business district and within the Buckhead business district: $4 for one passenger, $2 each for two or more passengers. For all other destinations, a single passenger pays $1.50 for the first ⅙ mile, 20¢ each additional ⅙ mile; there's a $1 charge for each additional passenger. You pay $12 per hour for waiting time, and $5 for use of additional space for luggage. Taxis usually cannot be flagged down on the streets, but must be called, or met at major hotels or the airport. One of the most reliable companies is **Yellow Cab Company** (tel. 521-0200). If you have a complaint about taxi service, voice it by calling 658-7600.

BY CAR   Within Atlanta, park the car and make use of the marvelous public transportation system, supplementing it with taxis when you must. For sightseeing in outlying areas, of course, driving is easily the most convenient mode of transportation, and if you *do* get lost in Atlanta's confusing streets, there's usually a friendly native handy to set you right. AAA services are available through **AAA Auto Club South,** 4S40B Roswell Rd., Atlanta, GA 30343 (tel. 404/843-4500).

Rentals   **Hertz, Avis, Budget, National,** and other major rental firms have desks at the airport for pickup and return, as well as offices elsewhere in the city (check the telephone directory for addresses and telephone numbers). **Atlanta Rent-a-Car** (tel. 763-1160), with 11 locations is a locally run company.

Parking   On-street parking can be a problem, but there are plenty of garages and lots scattered around almost every section of the city.

TRANSPORTATION FOR THE HANDICAPPED   MARTA provides transportation services for the handicapped. Call 848-5440 for details.

FAST FACTS: ATLANTA

American Express   There are five American Express Travel Service locations: Colony Square, 1173 Peachtree St. NE (tel. 892-8175); One Galleria Pkwy., Suite 74 (tel. 952-2484); Lenox Square, 3393 Peachtree Rd. NE (tel. 262-7561); 1052 Perimeter Mall, 4400 Ashford-Dunwoody Rd. (tel. 395-1305); and 133 Peachtree St., Suite 315, (tel. 523-8055).

Area Code   404.

Babysitters   Most hotels can arrange babysitter service, and **Friend of the Family** (tel. 255-2848) is a reliable firm with carefully screened, 21-and-over sitters, some of whom speak foreign languages. Twenty-four-hour advance notice is recommended, and if you wish you may interview a sitter before making a commitment.

Currency Exchange   There's a currency exchange service at the airport. In the city, downtown offices of major banks provide the service, including Nations Bank, 35 Broad St. NW (tel. 581-2009); and **Trust Company Bank,** 25 Park Place (tel. 588-7694).

Dentist   A free referral service is operated by the **Georgia Dental Association of Atlanta** (tel. 458-6166).

Doctor   For physician referrals, contact the **Medical Association of Atlanta** (tel. 752-1564). Also see "Hospitals," below.

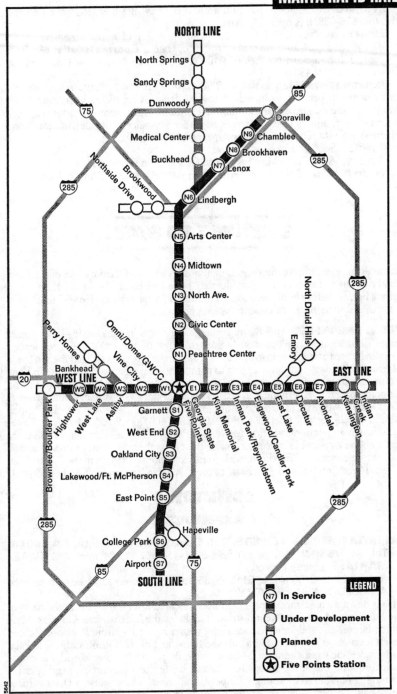

MARTA RAPID RAIL

NORTH LINE

- North Springs
- Sandy Springs
- Dunwoody
- Medical Center
- Buckhead

- Doraville
- (N9) Chamblee
- (N8) Brookhaven
- (N7) Lenox
- (N6) Lindbergh

Brookwood
Northside Drive

- (N5) Arts Center
- (N4) Midtown
- (N3) North Ave.
- (N2) Civic Center
- (N1) Peachtree Center

Perry Homes
Omni/Dome/GWCC
Vine City
Bankhead
Highower
West Lake
Ashby

WEST LINE
(W5) (W4) (W3) (W2) (W1) ★ (E1) (E2) (E3) (E4) (E5) (E6) (E7)

Brownlee/Boulder Park

Georgia State
Five Points
King Memorial
Inman Park/Reynoldstown
Edgewood/Candler Park
East Lake
Decatur
Avondale
Kensington
Indian Creek

North Druid Hills
Emory

EAST LINE

- Garnett (S1)
- West End (S2)
- Oakland City (S3)
- Lakewood/Ft. McPherson (S4)
- East Point (S5)
- Hapeville
- College Park (S6)
- Airport (S7)

SOUTH LINE

LEGEND
- (N7) In Service
- ◯ Under Development
- ◯ Planned
- ★ Five Points Station

5642

Drugstores They're plentiful around the city. Big B, 1026 Ponce de Leon Ave. (tel. 876-0381), is open 24 hours.

Emergencies Call **911** and explain the nature of your emergency.

Hospitals 24-hour emergency rooms operate at **Georgia Baptist Medical Center,** 300 Boulevard NE (tel. 653-4000), and **Grady Memorial Hospital,** 80 Butler St. (tel. 589-4307).

Newspapers/Magazines *The Atlanta Journal-Constitution* is the major daily newspaper. Others include *Atlanta Business Chronicle* and *Atlanta Daily World. Atlanta* magazine is an excellent reference for information on current cultural, entertainment, and sightseeing activities. Other periodicals include *Atlanta Now, Business Atlanta, Dining Out* magazine, and *Where* magazine.

Police See "Emergencies," above.

Safety See "Crime" in "Fast Facts: Georgia," in Chapter 11.

Transit Info Call the **Metropolitan Atlanta Rapid Transit Authority,** at 848-4711.

3. WHERE TO STAY

Atlanta can provide accommodations of almost every variety, from some of the finest luxury hotels in the country to moderately priced motels to bed-and-breakfasts in private homes. Before booking, check "Frommer's Smart Traveler: Hotels" in Chapter 1 for useful hints on accommodations shopping.

BED & BREAKFAST B&Bs are available in Atlanta in grand style—host homes range from modest, middle-class houses to some of the city's finest residences. They're located in the downtown area, in suburban neighborhoods, and even in Stone Mountain. If this is your favorite way to get to know an area, you're sure to find one convenient to your personal interests. As a bonus, local hosts often clue you in on shopping bargains, entertainment, etc. As far in advance as possible, contact **Bed & Breakfast Atlanta,** 1801 Piedmont Ave., Suite 208, Atlanta, GA 30324 (tel. 404/875-0525, or toll free 800/96-PEACH; fax 404/875-9672). Madalyne Eplan, the efficient and enthusiastic manager, will carefully screen all host homes and place you as close as possible to the section of the city you prefer. Rates run $40 to $60 including a continental breakfast, with some exceptional lodgings in the $70 to $120 range. There's no fee, and American Express, MasterCard, and VISA are accepted.

DOWNTOWN

EXPENSIVE

ATLANTA HILTON & TOWERS, 255 Courtland St., Atlanta, GA 30043. **Tel. 404/659-2000,** or toll free 800/445-8667. 1,224 rms. A/C TV TEL **MARTA:** Peachtree Center.
$ Rates: $115–$165 single; $115–$185 double. Children stay free with parents. AE, CB, DC, DISC, ER, MC, V.

This is downtown Atlanta's only resort hotel, located just off I-75/85, in the heart of the business and entertainment district. It includes the International Shopping Mall, which houses gift and variety shops along with a high-tech business support center. Seven restaurants and lounges include the four-star Nikolai's Roof, Café de la Paix, and Trader Vic's restaurants, a 24-hour coffee shop, and Another World, the exotic nightclub atop the hotel. Guests have use of lighted tennis courts, a jogging track, swimming pool, exercise room, whirlpool, and sauna. There is also a Delta Airlines desk, business center, gift shops, toy store, hairstylist, and airport shuttle.

HYATT REGENCY, 265 Peachtree St. NE, Atlanta, GA 30303. Tel. 404/577-1234, or toll free 800/233-1234. 1,279 rms. A/C MINIBAR TV TEL **MARTA:** Peachtree Center.
$ Rates: $160 single, $185 double. Children under 18 stay free with parents. Weekend rate (Fri–Sun) on availability. AE, CB, DC, DISC, ER, MC, V. **Parking:** $9.

⭐ The first of Atlanta's "super hotels." Its 23-story atrium lobby is somewhat subdued, although definitely striking, with a gold and silver aluminum and stainless-steel sculpture that extends from the 2nd level to the 12th, much greenery, and glass elevators. There are several lounges and four restaurants, including the blue-domed Polaris rooftop revolving restaurant and cocktail lounge. Facilities include an outdoor pool and hot tub, full health club, barber shop, and beauty salon.

OMNI INTERNATIONAL, 1 CNN Center, Atlanta, GA 30335. Tel. 404/659-0000, or toll free 800/843-6664. 469 rms and suites. A/C MINIBAR TV TEL **MARTA:** Omni.
$ Rates: $155–$195 single; $175–$225 double. AE, DISC, ER, MC, V.
You'll find this hotel within a modernistic megastructure that also houses Ted Turner's CNN headquarters. Its soaring marble lobby and tastefully luxurious guest rooms are as modern as their setting, and glass elevators climb the entire 15 stories. Some guest rooms have balconies overlooking the lobby, and there's a VIP floor for the ultimate in luxury and service. The coffee shop, two restaurants (Bugatti's is a local favorite), a disco, and three bars will keep you busy, and 24-hour room service is provided. Convention facilities, concierge, shopping arcade, drugstore, and tennis and golf privileges are on hand.

RITZ-CARLTON ATLANTA, 181 Peachtree St. NE, Atlanta, GA 30303. Tel. 404/659-0400, or toll free 800/241-3333. 447 rms. A/C MINIBAR TV TEL **MARTA:** Peachtree Center.
$ Rates: $149–$249 single or double. AE, CB, DC, DISC, ER, MC, V.

⭐ This small personal-service hotel is tops in my book. Located in the heart of the business district on the corner of Peachtree and Ellis Streets, it is a 25-story rose-marble structure whose interior projects an old-world graciousness and charm very rare in modern hotels. The sunken lobby features Oriental rugs, paneled walls, touches of bronze, and fine antique furnishings interspersed with comfortable seating. Even the elevators exude elegance.

Guest rooms are restful refuges of traditional furnishings, bay windows, fresh flowers, and marble bathrooms. Both the 24th and 25th floors have been set apart as The Club, where guests enjoy a private lounge with complimentary refreshments and the services of a personal concierge. Personal service, however, is not limited to those floors: Under the watchful eye of the concierge, every guest has access to a bevy of friendly, efficient assistants who happily arrange for, among other things, tickets to local events and a personal shopping service.

Up the dramatic stairway, beyond the clublike, intimate lounge, is the elegant dining room called simply The Restaurant, where gourmet-quality lunches and dinners (with a special fitness-cuisine menu recommended by the American Heart Association) are accompanied by sophisticated piano music. The Café, just off the lobby, serves lighter fare, and a small lobby lounge offers continental breakfasts, afternoon tea, and cocktails. Guests have use of a nearby fitness club.

MODERATE

There is little to distinguish the chain outlets from one another except location, although facilities do vary slightly. Those listed here can be assumed to have the

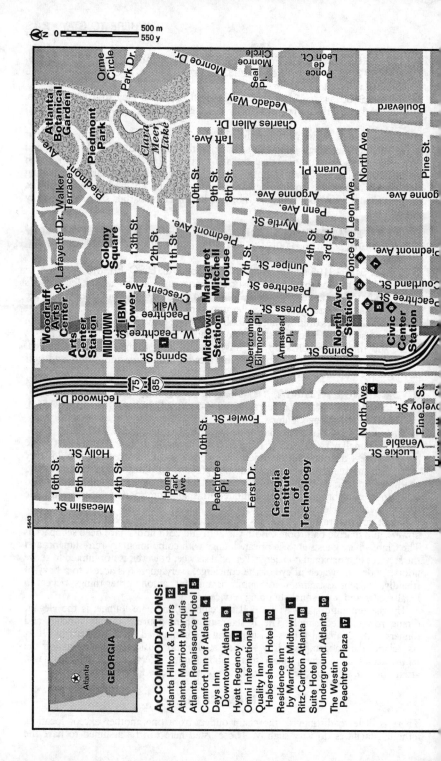

ACCOMMODATIONS:

Atlanta Hilton & Towers **12**
Atlanta Marriott Marquis **11**
Atlanta Renaissance Hotel **5**
Comfort Inn of Atlanta **4**
Days Inn
Downtown Atlanta **9**
Hyatt Regency **11**
Omni International **14**
Quality Inn
Habersham Hotel **10**
Residence Inn
by Marriott Midtown **1**
Ritz-Carlton Atlanta **18**
Suite Hotel
Underground Atlanta **19**
The Westin
Peachtree Plaza **17**

CENTRAL ATLANTA ACCOMMODATIONS & DINING

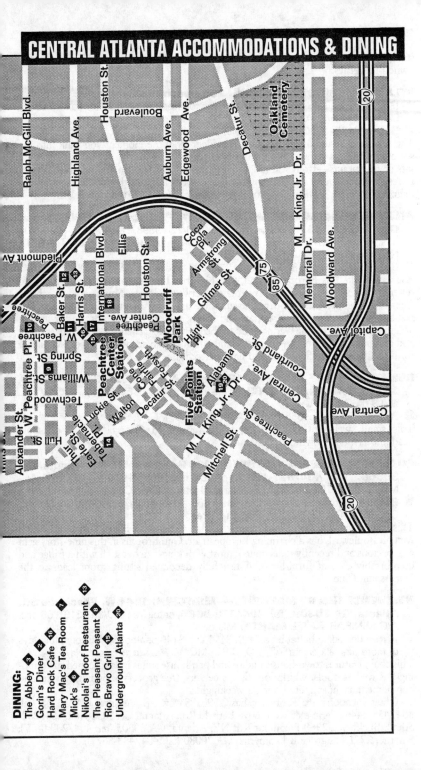

DINING:
The Abbey ③
Gorin's Diner ②
Hard Rock Cafe ⑩
Mary Mac's Tea Room ⑦
Mick's ⑥
Nikolai's Roof Restaurant ⑬
The Pleasant Peasant ⑧
Rio Bravo Grill ⑮
Underground Atlanta ⑳

standard, motel-quality rooms and decor, and I've added some of the nicer locally owned hostelries.

ATLANTA MARRIOTT MARQUIS, 265 Peachtree Center Ave., Atlanta, GA 30303. Tel. 404/521-0000, or toll free 800/228-9290. Fax 404/586-6299. 1,671 rms. A/C TV TEL **MARTA:** Peachtree Center.

$ Rates: $175–$200 single or double; $94 weekends. AE, CB, DC, DISC, MC, V.

The futuristic design of the Marriott is evident from the moment you walk into the seemingly endless atrium. With 46 floors, it rises dramatically skywards. There are lots of restaurants—from seafood and continental to Mexican and gourmet. Take a refresher at the sports bar or enjoy the indoor pool and health club. The rooms are deluxe, and extra services are provided for the executive on the club levels.

ATLANTA RENAISSANCE HOTEL, 590 W. Peachtree St. NW, Atlanta, GA. Tel. 404/881-6000, or toll free 800/228-9898. Fax 404/815-5010. 504 rms. A/C MINIBAR TV TEL **Directions:** Take exit 100 off I-75/85. **MARTA:** North Ave.

$ Rates: $150 single; $165 double; $72–$95 weekends. AE, DC, DISC, MC, V.

You might like this European hotel, in a high rise that has previously been several different hotels. It's conveniently situated between Colony Square and Peachtree Center. I like the ultra-modern designs and art deco overtones. There are two restaurants: one casual for breakfast and lunch, the other more upscale for dinner. You might elect to try the German pub for beer or snacks. There's a small fitness room and an outdoor pool on the premises, and a health club across the street is available for a fee. Rooms are first class and have balconies.

COMFORT INN OF ATLANTA, 120 North Ave. at I-75/85, Atlanta, GA 30313. Tel. 404/441-6788, or toll free 800/228-5150. 64 rms. A/C TV TEL **MARTA:** North Ave.

$ Rates: $50 single; $55 double. AE, DC, DISC, MC, V.

This small, well-kept chain motel is convenient to Georgia Tech, Coca-Cola headquarters, and downtown Atlanta.

QUALITY INN HABERSHAM HOTEL, 330 Peachtree St. NE, Atlanta, GA 30308. Tel. 404/577-1980, or toll free 800/241-4288. 91 rms. A/C MINIBAR TV TEL **MARTA:** Peachtree Center or Civic Center.

$ Rates (including continental breakfast): $69–$149 single; $79–$159 double. AE, CB, DC, DISC, ER, MC, V. **Parking:** Free.

This small, well-run hotel in downtown Atlanta, between Baker Street and Ralph McGill Boulevard, has a charming European air. Guest rooms in this nine-story gem are spacious and recently redecorated, most with king-size beds, all with a fridge and comfortably elegant furnishings. A tastefully decorated sitting room leads to the Habersham Club.

RESIDENCE INN BY MARRIOTT—MIDTOWN, 1041 W. Peachtree St., Atlanta, GA 30309. Tel. 404/872-8885, or toll free 800/331-3131. 66 rms. A/C MINIBAR TV TEL **MARTA:** Midtown.

$ Rates (including buffet breakfast): $119 apt, $149 penthouse. Discount for stays of more than six nights. AE, DC, DISC, MC, V. **Parking:** Free.

This chain features town-house studios and penthouse suites in landscaped surroundings, as well as pools, whirlpools, fitness centers, free grocery-shopping service, and complimentary hospitality hour on weeknights.

Other locations are Perimeter East, 1901 Savoy Dr., Atlanta, GA 30341 (tel. 404/455-4446); Perimeter West, 6096 Barfield Rd., Atlanta, GA 30328 (tel. 404/252-5066); Buckhead, 2960 Piedmont Rd. NE, Atlanta, GA 30305 (tel. 404/239-0677); Smyrna, 2771 Hargrove Rd., Smyrna, GA 30080 (tel. 404/433-8877).

SUITE HOTEL UNDERGROUND ATLANTA, 54 Peachtree St., Atlanta, GA 30303. Tel. 404/223-5555, or toll free 800/477-5549. Fax 404/223-0467. 150 suites. A/C TV TEL **MARTA:** Five Points.

$ Rates: $120–$140 single or double; $109 weekends. AE, DC, DISC, MC, V.

With the popularity of Underground Atlanta, it seemed logical to erect a hotel on top. This all-suite building with limestone and brick construction is a handsome addition to the hotel scene. The formal interior is a nice change of pace from the hectic commercial tones of many nearby hotels. The hotel is more residential than others. The decor is soft, tasteful, and plush. Quilted bedspreads, bed ruffles, armoires, refrigerators, and wet bars are some of the regular appointments. Sleeping and living areas are separate. Buffet breakfasts are served each morning. You can use a health club nearby.

THE WESTIN PEACHTREE PLAZA, 210 Peachtree St. NE, Atlanta, GA 30303. Tel. 404/659-1400, or toll free 800/228-3000. 1,074 rms. A/C MINIBAR TV TEL **MARTA:** Peachtree Center.

$ Rates: $155–$200 single; $180–$225 double. AE, DC, DISC, MC, V. **Parking:** $10 valet.

Atlanta's most famous hotel is probably the Westin, because it's the most striking—it should be, since the hotel is the tallest in North America. Inside you'll be dazzled by the spectrum of restaurants and lounges. On the roof is the revolving restaurant, a grand spectacle for a special evening on the town. More traditional food outlets are dotted around the hotel, including a fine seafood restaurant. Rooms on the hotel's executive floors offer even more amenities than the regular rooms. Try to get a room high up, because the view is wonderful. And if you're not afraid of heights, you'll want to ride in the glass elevator that goes up the side of the building.

BUDGET

CAMPGROUNDS About 16 miles east of the city, the **Family Campground,** P.O. Box 778, Stone Mountain, GA 30086 (tel. 404/498-5600), at Stone Mountain Park has 400 wooded sites with facilities for tents and RVs. There are full hookups, LP gas, showers, a laundry, supply store, restaurant, minigolf, swimming, boating, and fishing. Rates for two people begin at $12 for tent sites, $14 for full hookup; $2 for each additional person. Take I-285 to the Stone Mountain exit, then drive 7½ miles east on Ga. 78 to Stone Mountain Park.

DAYS INN DOWNTOWN ATLANTA, 300 Spring St. (at Baker), Atlanta, GA 30303. Tel. 404/523-1144, or toll free 800/325-2525. 262 rms. A/C TV TEL **MARTA:** Peachtree Center.

$ Rates: $59–$99 single; $69–$109 double. AE, DC, DISC, MC, V. **Parking:** $4. This conveniently located motel is directly across from the Atlanta Merchandise Mart, only four blocks from the World Congress Center. Guest rooms are comfortable, and it also features a restaurant and a pool.

IN BUCKHEAD

The affluent Buckhead area is home to upscale shopping—Phipps and Lenox Square Malls—and a number of luxury hotels. Here's a sampling.

HOTEL NIKKO ATLANTA, 3300 Peachtree Rd., Atlanta, Ga 30305. Tel. 404/365-8100, or toll free 800/645-5687. Fax 404/233-5686. 462 rms. A/C MINIBAR TV TEL **MARTA:** Lenox.

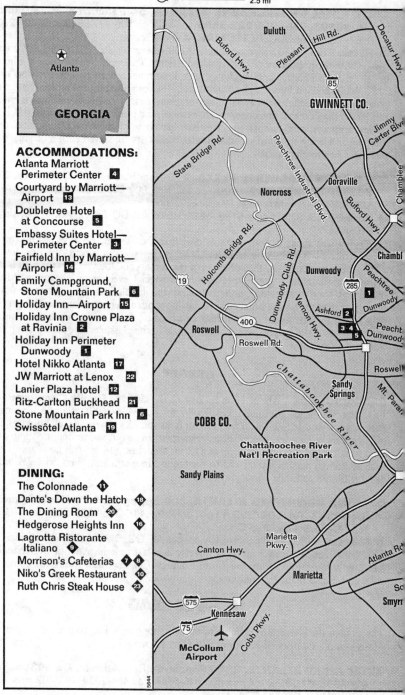

4.0 km
2.5 mi

GEORGIA

★ Atlanta

ACCOMMODATIONS:
Atlanta Marriott
  Perimeter Center **4**
Courtyard by Marriott—
  Airport **13**
Doubletree Hotel
  at Concourse **5**
Embassy Suites Hotel—
  Perimeter Center **3**
Fairfield Inn by Marriott—
  Airport **14**
Family Campground,
  Stone Mountain Park **6**
Holiday Inn—Airport **15**
Holiday Inn Crowne Plaza
  at Ravinia **2**
Holiday Inn Perimeter
  Dunwoody **1**
Hotel Nikko Atlanta **17**
JW Marriott at Lenox **22**
Lanier Plaza Hotel **12**
Ritz-Carlton Buckhead **21**
Stone Mountain Park Inn **6**
Swissôtel Atlanta **19**

DINING:
The Colonnade **11**
Dante's Down the Hatch **18**
The Dining Room **20**
Hedgerose Heights Inn **16**
Lagrotta Ristorante
  Italiano **9**
Morrison's Cafeterias **7 8**
Niko's Greek Restaurant **10**
Ruth Chris Steak House **23**

5644

Duluth

Buford Hwy.

Pleasant Hill Rd.

Decatur Hwy.

85

GWINNETT CO.

Jimmy Carter Blvd.

State Bridge Rd.

Peachtree Industrial Blvd.

Doraville

Chamble

Norcross

Buford Hwy.

Holcomb Bridge Rd.

Chambl

Dunwoody

Peachtree

19

Dunwoody Club Rd.

Vernon Hwy.

285

1

Dunwoody

Ashford **2**

3 4

400

5

Roswell

Roswell Rd.

Peacht
Dunwood

Chattahoochee River

Roswell

Mt. Para

Sandy
Springs

Mt. Para

COBB CO.

Chattahoochee River
Nat'l Recreation Park

Sandy Plains

Marietta
Pkwy.

Atlanta Rd

Canton Hwy.

Marietta

575

Smyr

So

75

Kennesaw

Cobb Pkwy.

✈
**McCollum
Airport**

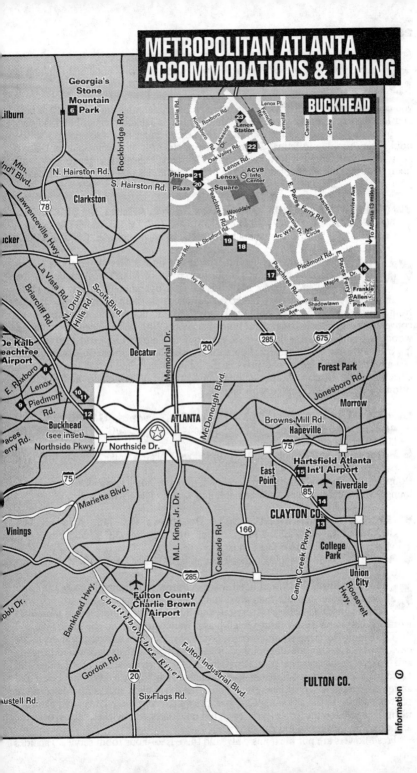

METROPOLITAN ATLANTA ACCOMMODATIONS & DINING

BUCKHEAD

Information ⓘ

$ Rates: $140–$195 single or double. AE, DC, DISC, MC, V.

I remember seeing the construction rise in this towering hotel and thinking it was going to look like where the Wizard lived in Oz. But the rotunda faced with marble is a powerful architectural statement. Come here for a drink even if you can't stay here. You'll find Japanese and French restaurants and a handful of bars and lounges. A Japanese garden (remember, this is a Japanese chain hotel) adjoins the outdoor pool. You can work out in the fitness center that also sports a whirlpool, steam room, and sauna. All the latest equipment is in the fitness area. Deluxe guest rooms are fitted with armoires, thick carpets, expensive appointments, and luxury baths. This is one of the handful of Atlanta hotels that deserves to be called luxurious.

JW MARRIOTT AT LENOX, 3300 Lenox Rd. NE, Atlanta, Ga 30326. Tel. 404/262-3344. Fax 404/262-8689. 371 rms. A/C TV TEL **MARTA:** Lenox.

$ Rates: $135–$180 single or double; $99–$114 weekends. AE, CB, DC, DISC, ER, MC, V.

Wow. What a splash this hotel makes. It was once a Westin and today enjoys great success as a gleeming gem in the crown of Marriott. Attached to the yuppie-scale Lenox Square Mall, it is a deluxe operation in an area with other superlative hotels—the Ritz and Nikko for starters. A phantom V Rolls-Royce sits out front. Inside, everything is posh and quiet. You're not apt to find hordes of conventioneers wearing badges and funny hats here. With coffered ceilings, polished wood walls, inlaid marble floors, thick carpets, and Chinese Chippendale armchairs, it's truly a deluxe establishment. I particularly like the English garden theme in the restaurant and the pianist who plays in the lobby lounge. You'll find jazz here too. Check out the rooms: two-poster beds, minibars, wingback chairs and matching ottomans, and baths trimmed with marble.

LANIER PLAZA HOTEL, 418 Armour Dr., Atlanta, GA 30324. Tel. 404/873-4661, or toll free 800/554-8444. 350 rms. A/C TV TEL **MARTA:** Lindbergh Center.

$ Rates: $79–$109 single; $89–$119 double. Children under 17 stay free with parents. CB, DC, DISC, ER, MC, V.

Rooms here are very attractively decorated, and the hotel has a pool, restaurant, lounge with entertainment, coin laundry, and health club privileges.

RITZ-CARLTON BUCKHEAD, 3434 Peachtree Rd. NE, Atlanta, GA 30326. Tel. 404/237-2700, or toll free 800/241-3333. 553 rms. A/C MINIBAR TV TEL **MARTA:** Lenox.

$ Rates: $149–$215 single or double. AE, CB, DC, DISC, ER, MC, V. **Parking:** $10.

This "uptown" Buckhead hotel was extensively refurbished in early 1987 and now is more splendid than ever. Public areas and dining rooms are rich with Italian marble, mahogany, crystal, and rare African woods, and a museum's worth of 18th- and 19th-century English and French art adds to the luster.

The Dining Room restaurant is much favored by Atlantans as well as visitors to the city, with gourmet cuisine and polished, friendly service. With its dark-wood paneling and cheery fireplaces, the new Ritz-Carlton Bar is reminiscent of Claridge's in London. The three-tiered Café, an all-day dining room, is also a repository of art and antiques. Brunch is served here every Sunday, and late-night snacks and desserts are offered nightly. In the adjoining Café bar, there's dancing every Friday and Saturday night. Espresso, on the lower level, serves full breakfasts, sandwiches, salads, desserts, and of course, espresso and cappuccino.

Fresh flowers are put in rooms daily, and there is 24-hour room service. Facilities include a fitness center, pool, whirlpool, business center, gift shop, beauty salon, and tobacconist.

SWISSOTEL ATLANTA, 3391 Peachtree Rd. NE, Atlanta, GA 30326. Tel. 404/365-0065. Fax 404/365-8787. 364 rms. A/C MINIBAR TV TEL
MARTA: Lenox.
$ Rates: $145–$195 single or double; $109 weekends. AE, DC, DISC, MC, V.
Here's a hotel that would ordinarily stand head and shoulders above others in usual circumstances. But here in Buckhead, the Swissotel is hard-pressed to keep up with the Jones's—in this case Ritz, JW Marriott, and Nikko. Still, it is very first class and has a European flavor to it. When it's busy, it's very busy, and you'll be glad to retire to your room. The café is charming but can be distracting with all the hubbub nearby from the lounge. The health club features a sauna, steam room, lap pool, whirlpool, and workout equipment. Rooms have all the extras you'd expect from a deluxe hotel.

AT THE AIRPORT

Atlanta Airport is swarming with hotels for all the chains: Hilton, Holiday Inn, Marriott, Ramada, Renaissance, and Sheraton. Take your pick. Most offer great rates if you come at the right time. They also tend to be sold out if weather is bad and air traffic gets backed up, so you might plan ahead.

COURTYARD BY MARRIOTT—ATLANTA AIRPORT, 2050 Sullivan Rd., College Park, GA 30337. Tel. 404/997-2220, or toll free 800/321-2211. 144 rms. A/C TV TEL
$ Rates: Sun–Thurs $79 single; $89 double. Fri–Sat $59 single or double. Senior discounts available.
This is one of six Courtyard by Marriott hotels in the metro Atlanta suburbs. Rooms are spacious, attractively furnished, and offer guests the use of swimming pools, restaurants, and lounges.
Other area locations include: Northlake, 4083 Lavista Rd. at I-285, Tucker, GA 30084 (tel. 404/938-1200); Peachtree Corners, 3209 Holcomb Bridge Rd., Norcross, GA 30092 (tel. 404/446-3777); Peachtree-Dunwoody, 5601 Peachtree-Dunwoody Rd., Atlanta, GA 30342 (tel. 404/843-2300); Windy Hill Road, 2045 S. Park Pl., Atlanta, GA 30339 (tel. 404/955-3838); and Executive Park, 1236 Executive Park Dr. at I-85 North, Atlanta, GA 30329 (tel. 404/728-0708).

FAIRFIELD INN BY MARRIOTT—AIRPORT, 2451 Old National Parkway, College Park, GA 30349. Tel. 404/761-8371, or toll free 800/228-2800. 132 rms. A/C TV TEL
$ Rates: $36 single; $43 double. Discounts for seniors available. AE, CB, DC, DISC, MC, V.
Guest rooms feature well-lit work desks, separate vanity areas, and two double or one king-size bed. A restaurant is next door. Other area locations are: Gwinnett Mall, I-85 at Pleasant Hill Road, Duluth, GA 30136; Northlake, 2155 Ranchwood Dr., Northlake, GA 30345; Northwest, 2191 Northwest Pkwy., Marietta, GA 30067; and Peachtree Corners, Peachtree Ind. Blvd. at Jones Mill Road, Norcross, GA 30092.

HOLIDAY INN—AIRPORT, 1380 Virginia Ave., Atlanta, GA 30344. Tel. 404/762-8411, or toll free 800/HOLIDAY. 500 rms. A/C MINIBAR TV TEL
$ Rates: $84–$92 single; $96–$104 double. Children under 18 stay free with parents. AE, DC, DISC, MC, V.

At the airport, this hotel tries to adapt to the times. It has eliminated its lounge and has incorporated a sports bar with a wide-screen TV instead. They offer free shuttle service to the airport. The rooms were renovated in October 1992. Other facilities include a restaurant open between 6am and 11pm. For leisure, you may choose from the tennis court, pool, or sauna.

IN THE PERIMETER AREA

The Perimeter Area, bounded by I-285 circling Atlanta, is a great place to find deals on hotel rates—especially on weekends. The area is growing and houses the bulk of the shopping malls.

ATLANTA MARRIOTT PERIMETER CENTER, 246 Perimeter Center Pkwy. NE, Atlanta, GA 30346. Tel. 404/394-6500, or toll free 800/228-9290. Fax 404/394-4338. 404 rms. A/C TV TEL **Directions:** Take I-285 to the Ashford-Dunwoody Road exit.
$ Rates: $109 single or double; $79 weekends. AE, DC, DISC, MC, V.
This solid business hotel has great weekend rates from time to time. You might consider the sibling hotel of this property, the Marriott Suites, if you don't get space here. Service is swift and friendly. You'll like the restaurant with its fireplace and good American menu. Live music plays in the bar, decorated in Christmas colors, and there's an indoor-outdoor pool, sauna, lighted tennis courts, and whirlpool to help you unwind.

DOUBLETREE HOTEL AT CONCOURSE, 7 Concourse Pkwy., Atlanta, GA 30328. Tel. 404/395-3900. Fax 404/395-3935. 374 rms. A/C MINIBAR TV TEL **Directions:** Take I-285 to the Ashford-Dunwoody Road exit.
$ Rates: $139 single; $149 double; $65 weekends. AE, DC, DISC, ER, MC, V.
The Doubletree is a snappy deluxe hotel that is for those who like a zing in their surroundings. The winding driveway sprinkled with waterways alone will put the most tense guest at ease. From the café, you can see the fountain and small lake. An American menu is served in the formal dining room. With a glass-enclosed whirlpool, steam room, fitness rooms, sauna, and lap pool, you'll be treated royally. The rooms are spacious and classy with dark wooded appointments, live plants, desks, and king-size or double beds.

EMBASSY SUITES HOTEL ATLANTA-PERIMETER CENTER, 1030 Crown Pointe Pkwy., Atlanta, GA 30338. Tel. 404/394-5454. Fax 404/396-5167. 241 rms. A/C TV TEL **Directions:** Take I-285 to the Ashford-Dunwoody Road exit.
$ Rates: $105–$125 single or double; $69 weekends. AE, DC, DISC, MC, V.
The accent at this hotel is softer than at other Embassy hotels. It's smartly done with granite at the registration, glass elevators in the trademark atrium, and a mirror adding light to the restaurant serving lunch and dinner. Embassy is known for its cooked-to-order breakfasts prepared in the atrium amid lush foliage and upscale appointments. Look for the whirlpool under a skylight or take a swim in the indoor pool. All the suites have two phones, two TVs, a wet bar, a refrigerator, and a microwave oven. Living and sleeping areas are separate.

HOLIDAY INN CROWNE PLAZA AT RAVINIA, 4355 Ashford-Dunwoody Rd., Atlanta, GA 30346. Tel. 404/395-1234. Fax 404/392-9503. 492 rms. A/C MINIBAR TV TEL **Directions:** Take I-285 to the Ashford-Dunwoody Road exit.
$ Rates: $124–$154 single; $134–$164 double; $79–$94 weekends. AE, DC, DISC, MC, V.

This just might be my favorite hotel in Atlanta. It sits next to the Perimeter Mall, so you can hop over there to visit its great food court and to go wandering around. Inside, the atrium is like a park with flowing water, exotic birds, flowers, and plants. The café and gourmet room, which have excellent service and fine avant garde cuisine, are excellent. The setting is woodsy, with trees in the back; you'd never know you were attached to highrise office buildings. Rooms are excellent, and there is a club or executive level, too. You can always be sure the service will be in top form because Holiday Inn's world headquarters is next door (the staff never knows when a bigwig might pop in).

HOLIDAY INN PERIMETER DUNWOODY, 4386 Chamblee Dunwoody Rd., Atlanta, GA 30341. Tel. 404/457-6363. 252 rms. A/C TV TEL
   Directions: Take the I-285 Chamblee-Dunwoody Road exit.
$ Rates: $75–$79 single; $85–$89 double. AE, CB, DC, DISC, MC, V.
What makes this Holiday Inn so popular is its style wrapped in a small package. The brick building always looks up to date, and the interiors are always fresh. With only five stories, it's a manageable size. At the end of the lobby is an attractive bar under a skylight; you'll pass a baby grand piano on your way there. The restaurant is French. In the health club is a whirlpool, swimming pool, sauna, and workout facility. Again, in the shadow of the world headquarters of Holiday Inn, this is better than the vast majority and really a delight to the business market. Good rates can be had weekends.

AT STONE MOUNTAIN

STONE MOUNTAIN PARK INN, Jefferson Davis Rd. (P.O. Box 775), Stone Mountain Park, Stone Mountain, GA 30086. Tel. 404/469-3311, or toll free 800/277-0007. 92 rms. A/C TV TEL
$ Rates: $49–$75 single; $49–$90 double. AE, DC, DISC, MC, V.
Although this attractive inn is some 16 miles east of the city, it is worth the trip. The inn, situated inside Georgia's Stone Mountain Park, faces the north side of the mountain with its stone face carving. In summer, a laser light show is presented on the carving with seating available on the lawn across from the inn. Rooms are especially comfortable and nicely decorated in an 18th-century rustic style. Buffets in the restaurant are all-you-can-eat. Liquor is available in the restaurant. There's a heated pool with a wading section for the kids and beverage service for the grown-ups.

4. WHERE TO DINE

It's a point of pride among Atlantans that their town has so many fine restaurants; and yet real *Southern* cooking is surprisingly hard to come by in the city's eateries. What there is tends to be overdone and soggy, a far cry from the cuisine of Southern homes. The two establishments that do a good job in this department are Aunt Fanny's Cabin, see "In Smyrna," and Mary Mac's Tea Room, see "Downtown," below. These top my list of places to eat, even though neither is expensive or flashy.

For general tips on how to get the most out of your Atlanta culinary exploration, see "Frommer's Smart Traveler: Restaurants," in Chapter 1.

DOWNTOWN
EXPENSIVE

THE ABBEY, 163 Ponce de Leon Ave. NE. Tel. 876-8532.

Cuisine: CONTINENTAL. **Reservations:** Recommended. **MARTA:** North Ave.

$ Prices: Main courses $16.95–$24.95. AE, DC, DISC, V.

Open: Dinner daily 6–11pm. **Closed:** Major holidays.

Located in a renovated church, this restaurant has won numerous culinary awards. It's lovely, with lots of stained glass, waiters in monks' robes, and candlelight giving a soft glow to the whole scene. Contemporary continental and American cuisine dominates the menu, and specialties include mahi mahi, grilled venison loin, and zinfandel onion confit. The wine cellar is outstanding.

NIKOLAI'S ROOF RESTAURANT, atop Atlanta Hilton, 255 Courtland St. at Harris. Tel. 659-2000.

Cuisine: CONTINENTAL/RUSSIAN. **Reservations:** Required. **MARTA:** Peachtree Center.

$ Prices: Fixed-price five-course dinner $60. AE, DC, MC, V.

Open: Daily 6:30–9:30pm.

For sheer elegance, hardly any Atlanta restaurant outdoes this one. Decor, cuisine, and service are all well nigh perfect. Cuisine varies according to season, but it's basically continental, with Russian specialties. The wine list is one of the best in the city.

MODERATE

HARD ROCK CAFE, 215 Peachtree St. NE. Tel. 688-7625.

Cuisine: AMERICAN. **Reservations:** Not required. **MARTA:** Peachtree Center.

$ Prices: Appetizers $2.95–$5.95; main courses $5.95–$8.95. AE, DC, MC, V.

Open: Daily 11am–2am.

Just like its sibling cafés around the United States and the world, the Hard Rock Café has the accent on rock, with memorabilia from rock's famous past and present. There's a full bar that is often busy. On the menu are sandwiches, burgers, fajitas, a fresh daily catch, and chicken salad. It's downtown across from the Westin.

MALIBU JACKS, Kenny's Alley, Underground Atlanta. Tel. 577-9544.

Cuisine: LIGHT FARE. **Reservations:** Accepted. **MARTA:** Five Points.

$ Prices: Salads $3.95–$7.50; burgers $5.75–$5.95. AE, DC, DISC, MC, V.

Open: Mon–Thurs 11:30am–11pm, Fri–Sat 11:30am–2am, Sun 11:30am–6pm.

The atmosphere here is upscale beachy, and the California theme is carried off well. You'll find the food named after California landmarks: Frisco fries, Golden Gate chicken salad, and Pebble Beach club sandwich. For dessert, try apple cobbler with vanilla ice cream.

MARY MAC'S TEA ROOM, 224 Ponce de Leon Ave. NE at Myrtle St. Tel. 876-6604.

Cuisine: SOUTHERN. **Reservations:** Not required. **MARTA:** North Ave.

$ Prices: Lunch $6–$8; dinner $8–$13. 10% discount for students with ID. No credit cards.

Open: Lunch Mon–Fri 11am–4pm; dinner Mon–Fri 5–8pm.

On the northern edge of the downtown section, Mary Mac's has been run for more than a quarter of a century by Mrs. Margaret Lupo, now assisted by two of her six offspring. She advertises "Southern hospitality with damyankee efficiency." Serving 2,000 people daily, Mary Mac's has to be efficient, but that doesn't seem to diminish either the hospitality or the quality of food. Fried chicken and country ham are really good here, as are the fresh vegetables and hot breads.

THE PLEASANT PEASANT, 555 Peachtree St., between Linden and Merritts Aves. Tel. 874-3223.
   Cuisine: CONTINENTAL. **Reservations:** Not accepted. **MARTA:** North Ave.
$ **Prices:** Appetizers $7–$9; main courses $10–$20. AE, DC, MC, V.
   Open: Lunch Mon–Fri 11:30am–2:30pm; dinner daily 5:30pm–midnight.
Located in a renovated Victorian ice-cream parlor, the Pleasant Peasant is adorned with plants and antiques in an intimate atmosphere. It's crowded, but the service is consistently good. The daily special such as apple barbecue lamb often heads a menu that regularly includes calypso grouper and Oriental plum pork. There is full bar service and a respectable wine list.

RIO BRAVO GRILL (Downtown), 240 Peachtree St., NE. Tel. 524-9224.
   Cuisine: SOUTHWEST. **Reservations:** Accepted. **MARTA:** Peachtree Center.
$ **Prices:** Appetizers $4.25–$7.95; main courses $6.95–$8.95. AE, DC, DISC, MC, V.
   Open: Mon–Thurs 11am–10pm, Fri–Sat 11am–11pm, Sun 4–10pm.
I think the southwest decor at Rio Bravo is wonderful. So is the menu. This is a popular and growing collection of restaurants—there are several others sprinkled around the city. At happy hour, you can enjoy free tacos with your drinks weekdays between 4 and 6pm. Look for mesquite grill, Santa Fe chicken, salmon San Antonio, and smoked Chile pasta.

BUDGET

GORIN'S DINER, 1170 Peachtree St. Tel. 892-2500.
   Cuisine: DINER. **Reservations:** Not accepted. **MARTA:** Arts Center.
$ **Prices:** Burgers $5.75–$5.95; shakes and malts $2.95. AE, MC, V.
   Open: Mon–Thurs 7am–midnight, Fri 7am–2am, Sat 7:30am–2am, Sun 7:30am–midnight.
I love a diner that's open late. Gorin's is fun, upbeat, and uptown—in the trendy Colony Square area. The menu is 1950s diner. Besides the staples, you can order Death By Chocolate, key lime pie, and a root-beer float. Blue, green, and yellow neon trims this stainless steel diner on the outside, and it is adjacent to the locally famous Gorin's Ice Cream shop.

MICK'S, 557 Peachtree St. Tel. 875-6425.
   Cuisine: AMERICAN. **Reservations:** Not accepted. **MARTA:** North Ave.
$ **Prices:** Main courses $6–$10, children's menu $3. AE, DC, MC, V.
   Open: Sun–Thurs 11am–midnight, Fri–Sat 11am–1am; breakfast menu Sat–Sun 9am–noon.
The tile floor, leather booths, and counter stools here are straight out of a movie set of the 1950s. The menu, too, has overtones of those more innocent years: You can order a cherry Coke, banana split, chicken pot pie, or meatloaf. Mick's, however, also offers hickory-grilled pork chops and linguine. Desserts include cream pies, strawberry shortcake, banana split, and hot-fudge sundae.

IN BUCKHEAD

EXPENSIVE

THE DINING ROOM, Ritz-Carlton Buckhead, 3434 Peachtree Rd. NE. Tel. 237-2700.

Cuisine: CONTINENTAL. **Reservations:** Required. **MARTA:** Lenox.
$ Prices: Dinner for two with wine $80–$100. AE, CB, DC, MC, V.
Open: Lunch Mon–Fri 11:30am–2:30pm; dinner Mon–Sat 6–10pm. **Parking:** Complimentary valet parking.

Atlanta's most fashionable hotel boasts one of its loveliest dining rooms. Award-winning chef Guenther Seeger creates nouvelle cuisine with celestial finesse and style in this beautiful, romantic room, with its fresh flowers and English hunting portraits. The sauces, and even Seeger's luscious-looking desserts, are so light you may sample several dishes and still leave feeling comfortable.

HEDGEROSE HEIGHTS INN, 490 E. Paces Ferry Rd. NE, Buckhead. Tel. 233-7673.
Cuisine: INTERNATIONAL. **Reservations:** Recommended. **MARTA:** Lindbergh Center.
$ Prices: Main courses $16–$24; dinner for two with wine $85–$120. AE, DC, MC, V.
Open: Dinner Tues–Sat 6:30–10pm. **Closed:** Sun, Mon, and major holidays.

Old-world grandeur, attentive service, and imaginative American, Swiss, and French cuisine by owner Heinz Schwab make Hedgerose a memorable dining experience. The 1915 house has been lovingly restored and proudly displays its English-style woodwork. There's an excellent wine cellar. Jackets required for men.

LAGROTTA RISTORANTE ITALIANO, 2637 Peachtree Rd. NE. Tel. 231-1368.
Cuisine: ITALIAN. **Reservations:** Required. **MARTA:** Lindbergh Center.
$ Prices: Appetizers $5.95–$7.25; main courses $7.25–$22.95; dinner for two with wine $60–$80. AE, DC, MC, V.
Open: Mon–Sat 6–10:30pm.

Northern Italian pastas, seafood, veal, and chicken dishes are at their absolute finest in this lively subterranean dining room that crackles with confidence and good cheer. Small wonder this establishment has been voted the best Northern Italian restaurant for the past 10 years.

RUTH CHRIS STEAK HOUSE, 950 E. Paces Ferry Rd., Buckhead. Tel. 365-0660.
Cuisine: STEAK. **Reservations:** Required. **MARTA:** Lenox.
$ Prices: Dinner for two with wine $70–$80. AE, DC, DISC, MC, V.
Open: Mon–Fri 11:30am–11pm, Sat 5–11pm, Sun 5–10pm.

In this stunning contemporary dining room, aged prime strips, filets, and ribeyes are served on sizzling hot platters. The menu also features seafood (Maine lobster) excellent side dishes, a large wine list, and super desserts like blueberry cheesecake and New Orleans–style praline freezes.

MODERATE

THE COLONNADE, 1879 Cheshire Bridge Rd. NE. Tel. 874-5642.
Cuisine: SOUTHERN. **Reservations:** Not accepted. **MARTA:** Lindbergh Center.
$ Prices: Main courses $8–$11. No credit cards.
Open: Lunch daily 11am–2:30pm; dinner Sun–Wed 5–9pm, Thurs–Sat 5–11pm.

An Atlanta favorite for more than 30 years, this friendly place is located between Wellborne Drive and Manchester Street. The Colonnade, like a cheerful American restaurant of the 1950s, serves inexpensive steaks, chops, seafood, Southern fried chicken, and vegetables.

NIKO'S GREEK RESTAURANT, 1789 Cheshire Bridge Rd. Tel. 872-1254.
   Cuisine: GREEK. **Reservations:** Not required. **MARTA:** Lindbergh Center or Lenox.
$ Prices: Main courses $8–$14. Children's menu available. AE, MC, V.
   Open: Tues–Sat 11am–2:30pm, 5–11pm. **Closed:** Sun–Mon.

Niko Letsos, his wife Anna, and their three daughters run this marvelous place in northeast Atlanta, creating an atmosphere which is relaxing and zestful at the same time. Begin with specialties like the saganaki appetizer, which is flamed at your table with accompanying shouts of *"Opa!"* from waiters and other diners. The Zorba Special—a combination plate of moussaka, pastitsio, and dolmades served with Greek beans and Greek salad—will bring you to your feet with shouts of your own. Then there are those luscious Greek desserts like baklava and rizogalo, all to the accompaniment of Greek music.

IN SMYRNA

AUNT FANNY'S CABIN, 2155 Campbell Rd., Smyrna. Tel. 436-5218.
   Cuisine: SOUTHERN. **Reservations:** Not required.
$ Prices: Main courses $13.95–$16.95. AE, DC, MC, V.
   Open: Lunch Mon–Fri 11:30am–2:30pm; dinner Mon–Fri 6–10pm, Sat 6–10:30pm, Sun noon–10pm.

Atlanta's best Southern restaurant isn't in Atlanta at all, but in nearby Smyrna. The restaurant, in a former slave cabin over 130 years old, has a decided "plantation days" atmosphere in both the cuisine and its presentation. There really was an "Aunt Fanny" Williams, and this was her home. She was in her 70s when she first began serving meals to the public in 1941. She bustled around the kitchen as long as she was able, then took to a rocking chair to personally greet guests. The fireplaces, the antique furniture, the old copper cookware hanging about, and the soft glow of candlelight all combine to re-create the world in which Aunt Fanny grew up (she died in 1949). People from 59 different countries have dined here over the years, including foreign ministers, cabinet members, state governors, senators, and countless entertainment personalities.

The food is straight out of the Old South (in fact, many of the recipes were Aunt Fanny's). The menu is limited: fried chicken, Smithfield ham, charcoal-broiled steak, and fresh rainbow trout. Vegetables are fresh, with a true home-cooked flavor—the baked squash belongs in a culinary hall of fame, as far as I'm concerned! All dishes are served family-style, coming to the table in large dishes; and if there's food left on the platter at the end of a meal, brown bags appear for you to take the remains home. Beer and wine are served, and there's a bar offering mint juleps and other cocktails.

SPECIALTY DINING

DINING COMPLEXES If you're a born shopper and plan to spend a lot of time in Atlanta's fabulous malls, eating won't break the budget. At **Lenox Square,** there are simply too many eateries to name—just look around when your feet begin to hurt and you're sure to spot one.

۞ Underground Atlanta, bounded by Peachtree, Wall, and Washington Streets, and Martin Luther King, Jr., Drive (tel. 523-2311; see "What to See and Do," below), is home to more than 16 restaurants and nightclubs centered around its Kenny's Alley; most are open nightly until around midnight.

LOCAL FAVORITES The menus at both locations of **۞ Dante's Down the**

Hatch, at 3380 Peachtree Rd. in Buckhead, across the street from Lenox Square (tel. 266-1600), and in Kenny's Alley, Underground Atlanta (tel. 577-1800), are made up largely of cheese trays and cheese and beef fondues. If you are a dedicated cheese-lover, as I am, Dante's should top all other eating spots on your Atlanta list. Never mind the unique settings, service by people who know and care about cheeses, and superb entertainment (see "Evening Entertainment," below)—it's the cheeses under discussion here. Even the brie—the most temperamental of all cheeses—has never arrived at my table here runny and overripe. In fact, it has always been worthy of a poetic hymn of praise, and I have it on good authority that when the brie doesn't measure up, it comes off the menu. For my money, that speaks volumes for these two places. Fondues are prepared with imported cheeses and loving care, and if you're in the mood for meat, the quality of beef is just as good as that of the brie.

Hours at Buckhead are Monday to Thursday from 4pm to midnight, Friday and Saturday from 4pm to 1am, and Sunday from 4 to 11pm. At Underground Atlanta, the hours are Monday to Thursday from 2pm to midnight, Friday and Saturday from 2pm to 1am, and Sunday from 2 to 11pm.

LIGHT, CASUAL & FAST FOOD If you're fond of Southern barbecue keep an eye out for the four Atlanta locations of the **Old Hickory House,** all serving barbecued pork, beef, chicken, and ribs. I've had better barbecue in the South, but the Hickory House brand is above average. All locations feature a rustic decor and prices that range from $4 to $10; most are open daily 6am to 10pm.

Just a couple of blocks from the Georgia Tech campus (alongside I-75 and I-85 where North Avenue crosses over the highway) is an Atlanta institution—the **☼ Varsity Drive-In,** 61 North Ave. (tel. 881-1706). For budget eating, you just can't beat the Varsity, and some 16,000 people a day agree with me. The hot dogs, hamburgers, and french fries are good, service (both carside and inside, where they have seats and stand-up eating counters) is excellent and very fast, and prices are definitely low. Open Sunday through Thursday from 8am to 12:30am, Friday and Saturday from 8am to 2:30am.

There are an even dozen **Morrison's** cafeterias around town. Locations include 1025 Virginia Ave., near Hartsfield International Airport (tel. 761-8066); and Ansley Mall, Piedmont Avenue and Monroe Drive (tel. 872-8091). They're open seven days, with continuous service from lunch through dinner.

5. WHAT TO SEE & DO

SUGGESTED ITINERARIES

IF YOU HAVE ONE DAY Allow yourself time for a meaningful visit to a few selected sights; my own list would include Underground Atlanta, the Martin Luther King, Jr., Historic District, and the Jimmy Carter Library and Museum.

IF YOU HAVE TWO DAYS To those attractions you've visited on Day 1, add one or two more that match your interests (the High Museum of Art, the CNN Center, etc.). Reserve part of the day for Grant Park and the fascinating Cyclorama. After dark, dip into Atlanta's lively nightlife and treat yourself to a different cultural or social experience each night.

IF YOU HAVE ONE WEEK You'll have enough breathing space in a week to get around to most of the major city attractions and intersperse Atlanta sightseeing with

DID YOU KNOW . . . ?

- A Creek Indian settlement called Standing Peachtree stood on the site of modern-day Atlanta until 1813, and the city's confusing street system follows many old Indian trails.
- Metropolitan Atlanta includes some 83 municipalities, happily occupied by more than two million people.
- The first Coca-Cola was served in Jacob's Pharmacy in 1886—as a headache cure.
- The first scheduled passenger air service to Atlanta was inaugurated in 1930. Today, its airport is the world's largest and third-busiest.
- The 1996 Summer Olympics will be held in Atlanta, as will the 1994 Super Bowl.

one day at Six Flags Over Georgia, another at Stone Mountain Park, or make an excursion to Juliette and the Whistle Stop Café.

THE TOP ATTRACTIONS

THE SIGHTS

The ✪ **Carter Presidential Center,** 1 Copenhill Ave., at North Highland and Cleburne Avenues (tel. 331-3942), is a "must-see" for every visitor. Two miles east of downtown, with the skyline as dramatic backdrop, the center's four contemporary circular buildings are set among 30 acres of trees, gardens, lakes, and waterfalls. Inside are thousands of documents, photos, gifts, and memorabilia of Jimmy Carter's White House years. You may walk into a full-scale reproduction of the Oval Office. On a keyboard and video monitor, choose your response to a terrorist crisis, and watch as President Carter spells out the consequences. Photos follow Carter from his boyhood in Plains, through his navy career, state politics, and the presidency. A display of gifts received by Carter ranges from splendid silver, ivory, and crystal from heads of state, to paintings and peanut carvings from admirers around the world. "Presidents," a 30-minute film, looks at the crises and triumphs that hallmarked past administrations. You may have a light lunch, with a view of the gardens, in the center's restaurant. Open Monday through Saturday from 9am to 4:45pm, Sunday from noon to 4:45pm. Adults pay $2.50 admission, seniors $1.50; those under 16, enter free.

The ✪ **Martin Luther King, Jr., National Historic District,** 449 Auburn Ave. (tel. 524-1956, or 331-3919), includes major landmarks of the civil rights leader's life. His white marble tomb, with an eternal flame symbolizing his dream of a brotherhood of mankind, is the heart of the **Freedom Hall** complex. You may also view a multimedia presentation on his life; tour **Ebenezer Baptist Church,** where he was pastor and where his funeral service was held; and walk one block east to the Victorian home where he was born on January 15, 1929. National Park Service rangers, headquartered across the street from Freedom Hall, lead half-hour walking tours of the neighborhood. The tomb and other outdoor areas may be visited without charge, but donations are requested at Ebenezer Church, the birthplace, and the film. The church is open for tours Monday to Friday 9am to 4:30pm and Saturday 10am to 2:30pm. The house is open daily 10am to 5pm, and the hall is open daily 9am to 8pm.

Right in the center of town, a four-block tract of Atlanta's history lies beneath newer city streets. ✪ **Underground Atlanta** is the city's birthplace, where the Zero Milepost of the Western & Atlantic Railroad was planted in 1837. In post–Civil War days, railroad viaducts were built over its rococo buildings, which then lay deserted for the better part of a century. Then a group of farsighted Atlanta businessmen decided to restore the crumbling area, and the result was an authentic, completely charming picture of Atlanta in the 1800s. Over the years, the historic "city beneath a city" has suffered some ups and downs. In the mid-1980s, it was closed for a massive redevelopment, and in 1989 it reopened with more than 200 establishments, including shops, restaurants, and nightspots. Along with all the other Underground attractions, there's the three-story, multimedia **World of Coca-Cola,** dedicated to

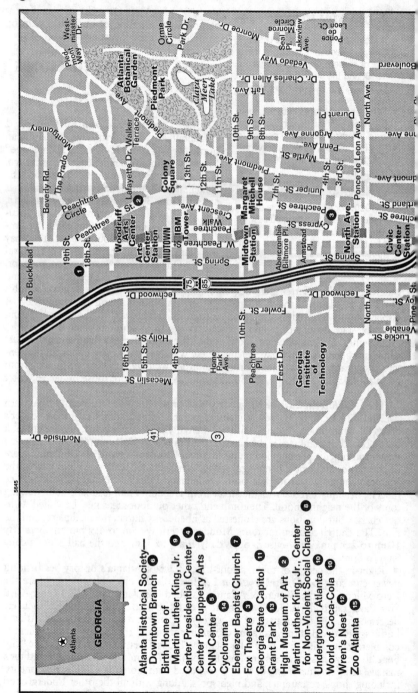

GEORGIA

Atlanta

Atlanta Historical Society—
Downtown Branch **6**
Birth Home of
Martin Luther King, Jr. **9**
Carter Presidential Center **4**
Center for Puppetry Arts **1**
CNN Center **5**
Cyclorama **14**
Ebenezer Baptist Church **7**
Fox Theatre **3**
Georgia State Capitol **11**
Grant Park **13**
High Museum of Art **2**
Martin Luther King, Jr., Center
for Non-Violent Social Change **8**
Underground Atlanta **10**
World of Coca-Cola **10**
Wren's Nest **12**
Zoo Atlanta **15**

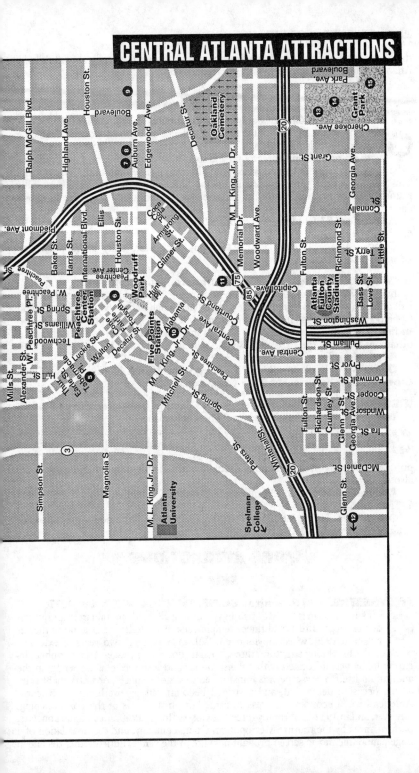

CENTRAL ATLANTA ATTRACTIONS

the history and international appeal of this native drink. You really shouldn't leave Atlanta without at least one visit to the Underground.

MUSEUMS

CYCLORAMA, 800 Cherokee Ave., in Grant Park. Tel. 624-1071.

★ For a breathtaking view of the Battle of Atlanta, go by the neoclassical building that houses this 42-foot-high, 356-foot-circumference, 100-year-old painting with a 3-dimensional foreground and special lighting, music, and sound effects. When you see the monumental work, you'll know why Sherman said, "War is hell." This is one of only three cycloramas in the U.S., and it has recently been fully restored—an artistic and historical treasure not to be missed. There are 15 shows daily.

Admission: $3.50 adults, $3 seniors, $2 children 6 to 12; free for children under 6.

Open: May–Sept, daily 9:30am–5:30pm. Oct–Mar, daily 9:30am–4:30pm. **Closed:** Major holidays.

GEORGIA STATE CAPITOL, Capitol Square. Tel. 656-2844.

Built in 1884, it has a gold-topped dome standing 237 feet above the city. Besides a hall of fame (with busts of famous Georgians), and a hall of flags (with U.S., state, and Confederate battle flags), it houses the **Georgia State Museum of Science and Industry,** which has collections of Georgia minerals and Indian artifacts, dioramas of famous places in the state, and fish and wildlife exhibits.

Admission: Free.

Open: Mon–Fri 8am–5:30pm. Tours weekdays 10 and 11am and 1 and 2pm. **Closed:** Major holidays. **MARTA:** Georgia State.

HIGH MUSEUM OF ART, Woodruff Arts Center, 1280 Peachtree St. NE. Tel. 892-3600, or 892-HIGH for 24-hour information.

★ This marvelous museum houses impressive collections of Western and African art, and first-rate traveling exhibitions. Permanent exhibits include Italian art from the 14th to the 18th centuries, 19th-century French art, and photographs, prints, and an extensive collection of decorative arts. Paintings by American artists are also on display.

Admission: $5 adults, $3 seniors and students, $1 children 6 to 17. Free Thurs 1–5pm.

Open: Tues–Thurs, Sat 10am–5pm, Fri 10am–9pm, Sun noon–5pm. **Closed:** Major holidays. **MARTA:** Arts Center.

MORE ATTRACTIONS

SIGHTS

FOX THEATRE, 660 Peachtree St. NE. Tel. 876-2040, or 881-1977.

★ This extravaganza of Moorish-Egyptian fantasy, with its minarets and onion domes, began life as a Shriners' temple back in 1916. Its life as a movie theater began in 1929, when movie mogul William Fox, after two years of extensive work on the blocklong structure, threw open its doors to an eager Atlanta public. Its exotic lobby was decorated with goldfish ponds and lush Oriental carpeting; in the auditorium itself, a skyscape was transformed to sunrise, sunset, or starry night skies as the occasion demanded, and a striped bedouin canopy overhung the balcony. America's worst economic depression came hot on the heels of the Fox's opening, however, and in 1932 bankruptcy forced its closing. In the 1940s, occasional concerts, performances by the touring Metropolitan Opera company, and the installation of a huge panoramic movie screen brought new life to the venue, until another decline in the 1970s, when the doors were closed once more. The Fox was slated for demolition to make room for a modern office building—but Atlantans, not about to give up their treasured showplace, raised $1.8 million to save the old movie palace. Since then, restored to its former glory, it has positively thrived as a venue for live entertainment.

Admission: $5 per person for tours.

Open: Tours Feb–Nov, Mon and Thurs 10am, Sat 10 and 11:30am; Dec–Jan, Mon and Thurs 10am only. **MARTA:** North Ave.

CNN CENTER, One CNN Center, (Marietta St. and Techwood Dr.). Tel. 827-2300.

Ted Turner's Cable News Network is headquartered in this multilevel structure, which also houses his entertainment networks, and stations TBS and TNT. If you've ever wanted to see the making of an up-to-the-minute news broadcast, this is the place to do it; a 45-minute tour takes you through the entire process as you view the news team at work just beyond a glassed-in viewing room. Also, one of the six theaters on the premises shows *Gone With the Wind* twice every day. There are frequent special events in the large atrium lobby, and a dozen or so restaurants and casual eateries are on hand to take care of hunger pangs.

Admission: $5 adults, $3.50 seniors, $2.50 students under 12, free for children 5 and under.

Open: Tours every 30 minutes, daily 9am–5pm. **Closed:** Major holidays. **MARTA:** Omni.

WREN'S NEST, 1050 Ralph D. Abernathy Blvd. SW. Tel. 753-8535.

Joel Chandler Harris, who created the "Uncle Remus" character in whose voice he retold African-American folk tales, lived at the Wren's Nest (named for the wrens who nested in his mailbox). The beautiful Victorian house is now a National Historic Landmark containing original family furnishings, photographs, and memorabilia. Guided tours are given on the hour and half-hour. The Wren's Nest also sponsors special storytelling programs for the public.

Admission: $3 adults, $2 seniors and teens, $1 children 4 to 12.

Open: Tues–Sat 10am–4pm, Sun 1–4pm. **Closed:** Major holidays. **Directions:** Two blocks from Ashby St.

NEIGHBORHOODS

If you come looking for the antebellum Atlanta of Margaret Mitchell's *Gone With the Wind,* you won't find it; General Sherman burned it all down in 1864. It's worth the time and effort, however, to drive five miles or so northwest out Peachtree Street to Peachtree Battle Avenue, then left to Habersham Drive, Northside Drive, and West Paces Ferry Road (that's the Governor's Mansion at no. 391, by the way, open Tuesday through Thursday 10 to 11:45am at no charge), to **Tuxedo Road.** This residential area can, despite its more recent vintage, rival any antebellum section, with dogwoods, azaleas, magnolias, and some of the most beautiful private residences you could find anywhere in the country.

A short drive to the little community of **Roswell,** just north of Atlanta, will also take you back to pre–Civil War days. A number of homes here of that vintage have either been preserved through continuous residency or restored by enthusiastic and appreciative new owners. The childhood home of President Theodore Roosevelt's mother, **Bulloch Hall,** is in Roswell. There's a visitors' center at 617 Atlanta St. (tel. 640-3253).

COOL FOR KIDS

You will enjoy **Grant Park,** between Cherokee Avenue and Boulevard SE, as much as the young fry. There are miles and miles of walkways and roads through the park, some of them along the breastwork built for the city's defense in 1864. In the park, you'll find ✪ **Zoo Atlanta,** 800 Cherokee Ave. (tel. 624-5678), a 40-acre zoo with habitats simulating the animals' native environments. There's an African rain forest with resident gorilla families and a walk-through aviary; and an East African savanna, with lions, giraffes, rhinos, ostriches, and other species. Admission is $7 for adults, $4.50 for kids 3 through 11, free for those under 3 (you can rent strollers). Hours are daily 10am to 5pm, till 6pm during daylight savings time; closed Martin Luther King, Jr., Day, Thanksgiving Day, Christmas Day, and New Year's Day.

Parents should also plan to join in the fun at the ✪ **Center for Puppetry Arts,** 1404 Spring St. (tel. 873-3391). Its home, once an elementary school, now houses a 300-seat theater, two galleries, a museum, lecture hall, education room, reference library, and gift shop. Call to see what they're presenting—and *do* plan to include adults as well as kids. More than 200 puppets are on display, and there are shows and other activities regularly planned. You can even make a puppet. Limited free parking is available.

About 12 miles west of downtown, just off I-20 West, the **Six Flags Over Georgia** theme park, 7561 Six Flags Pkwy. (tel. 739-3400), is one of the best in the country. There are more than 100 rides, a multitude of shows, and several restaurants. The $25 admission charge covers all rides and shows (except for concerts in the amphitheater) for one day ($27 for two days). Adults 55 and over and children 42 inches tall and under pay $12. It's open late May through Labor Day, daily from 10am to 10pm (to midnight Friday and Saturday); early September through October and April and May, weekends only (closed November to February). Call 948-9290, or 739-3400 for specific information; or write P.O. Box 43187, Atlanta, GA 30378. The park's name refers to Gerogia's history under the flags of England, France, Spain, the Confederacy, Georgia, and the United States. Hours and prices are subject to change, so call to check.

Off U.S. 78 (Stone Mountain Freeway), 16 miles east of downtown, ✪ **Stone Mountain Park** (tel. 498-5600) is one of the Southern Atlantic region's premier attractions. Millions flock to the 3,200-acre park each year to enjoy a wealth of attractions and recreation. Foremost, of course, is Stone Mountain, the world's largest granite monolith, which rises from a five-mile circumference to 825 feet. Carved on its sheer north flank is the world's largest sculpture, a 90-by-190-foot carving of Confederate heroes Robert E. Lee, Thomas "Stonewall" Jackson, and President Jefferson Davis. You can take a skylift to the top, or hike up an easy trail on the other side. Elsewhere in the park you can play golf, swim from a sand beach, visit an authentic antebellum plantation or an antique auto and music museum, and ride around the mountain's base on a steam locomotive. There's also an ice skating rink, biking, fishing, and campgrounds. Admission is $5 per car, $20 for an annual permit. The six major attractions—skylift, auto/music museum, railroad, riverboat, plantation, and wildlife trails—are each $3 for adults, $2 for children ages 4 to 11. Admission to the beach complex is $4. Accommodations are available at the Stone Mountain Park Inn or the Family Campground (see "Where to Stay," above). The park is open year-round daily from 6am to midnight.

ORGANIZED TOURS

Gray Line, 3745 Zip Industrial Blvd. (tel. 767-0594), has a **Grand Circle** full-day tour that takes in Peachtree Street; Peachtree Center; the Capitol; Georgia Tech; Coca-Cola corporate headquarters; the Governor's Mansion; the Martin Luther King, Jr., Historic District; the High Museum of Art; Swan House; Cyclorama; the city's most beautiful residential sections; Five Points; the CNN television complex; Underground Atlanta; and Stone Mountain. Adults pay $25, children $18. Call for exact departure times and booking. If you don't have a full day, the 3½-hour **All**

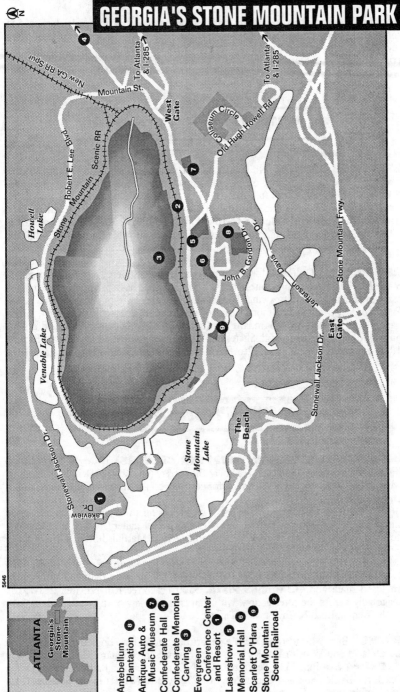

GEORGIA'S STONE MOUNTAIN PARK

New GA RR Spur

Mountain St.

West Gate

Coliseum Circle

To Atlanta & I-285

To Atlanta & I-285

Old Hugh Howell Rd.

Robert E. Lee Blvd.

Stone Mountain Scenic RR

Howell Lake

Venable Lake

Stonewall Jackson Dr.

Lakeview Dr.

Stone Mountain Lake

The Beach

John B. Gordon Dr.

Davis

Jefferson

Stone Mountain Frwy.

Stonewall Jackson Dr.

East Gate

7 **2** **5** **8** **6** **3** **9** **1**

ATLANTA

Georgia's Stone Mountain

Antebellum Plantation **8**
Antique Auto & Music Museum **7**
Confederate Hall **4**
Confederate Memorial Carving **3**
Evergreen Conference Center and Resort **1**
Lasershow **5**
Memorial Hall **6**
Scarlett O'Hara **9**
Stone Mountain Scenic Railroad **2**

5646

Around Atlanta excursion covers many of these same attractions, with fares of $15 for adults, $10 for children. The 3½-hour **Black Heritage Tour** (for the same fares) tours the Martin Luther King, Jr., Historic District, as well as the Atlanta University complex, one of the largest centers of higher education for African-Americans in the world.

6. SPORTS & RECREATION

SPECTATOR SPORTS No matter which season finds you in Atlanta, there's likely to be something going on in professional sports. You can call the **Atlanta-Fulton County Stadium** (tel. 522-1967) or the **Omni Coliseum** (tel. 681-2100) for information on what's scheduled currently. For seasonal schedules call **Braves baseball** at 522-7630, **Falcons football** at 261-5400, or **Hawks basketball** at 827-3800. Dates and tickets for sports events are also available through **SEATS** (tel. 577-2626).

RECREATION Golfers will want to play the 18-hole Robert Trent Jones–designed Stone Mountain Park Golf Course (tel. 498-5717), which has a pro on hand to provide assistance with that faulty swing. For tennis buffs, there are public courts at Lenox Park, Grant Park, and Piedmont Park; for information, contact Tennis Tech, Lenox Park Tennis Center, 3375 Standard Dr. (tel. 237-7339). Swimmers will find a huge public pool in Piedmont Park. Skates and bicycles can be rented from Skate Escape, 1086 Piedmont Ave. NE, at 12th Street (tel. 892-1292), directly across from the park.

7. SAVVY SHOPPING

DEPARTMENT STORES & SHOPPING CENTERS **Macy's Peachtree** (formerly Davison's), 180 Peachtree St., at Ellis Street (tel. 221-7221), is truly dazzling. Macy's Cellar is a fun place to browse for gourmet cookware and fancy foods, and to enjoy a deli lunch.

The **Mall at Peachtree Center**, two blocks north of Macy's, has numerous small shops and eateries tucked into the three-level gallery, which connects via covered bridge with the Hyatt Regency and Marriott Marquis hotels. There's also a Peachtree Center MARTA rapid-rail station.

Buckhead, a little north of the downtown area, has **Lenox Square Mall**, 3393 Peachtree Rd. NE, at Lenox Road (tel. 233-6767), with more than 130 stores in its enclosed mall; and ○ **Phipps Plaza**, 3500 Peachtree Rd. NE (tel. 261-7910), diagonally across the intersection, with branches of New York stores such as Saks Fifth Avenue, Lord & Taylor, and Tiffany & Co.

BOOKS Both **Macy's** and **Rich's** department stores have book departments, and **B. Dalton** and **Waldenbooks** have branches in Lenox Square Mall.

Oxford Books, 2345 Peachtree Rd. NE, at Peachtree Battle Avenue, in the Peachtree Battle Shopping Center (tel. 364-2700), is the largest in the Southeast. It's hard to imagine a fiction or nonfiction title they won't have in stock. In addition, they carry out-of-town newspapers and magazines. At **Oxford Too**, also in this shopping center, comic books and secondhand or remaindered books are featured. There's another Oxford Books in Buckhead at 360 Pharr Rd., between Peachtree and Piedmont Roads (tel. 262-3333), which also sells CDs, videotapes, and sheet music. The main branch is open Sunday through Thursday 9am to midnight, Friday and Saturday 9am to 2am.

8. EVENING ENTERTAINMENT

If there is one thing in which Atlanta is rich, it's nightlife. There is theater, symphony, ballet, lounge music (country-and-western, jazz, and rock-and-roll), cabaret, and almost any other kind of nocturnal entertainment you could name. Most hotels and motels distribute free the publications *Where, Key: This Week in Atlanta,* or *After Hours,* all good guides for where to find what; and the Saturday edition of the *Atlanta Constitution* has a "Weekend" section to fill you in further. Should you *still* be at a loss as to how to spend an evening, take yourself to Kenny's Alley at Underground Atlanta, where you're bound to find some entertainment to suit your fancy.

THE PERFORMING ARTS

CLASSICAL MUSIC & DANCE The ✪ **Atlanta Symphony Orchestra** and the ✪ **Atlanta Opera** usually perform in Symphony Hall at the Woodruff Arts Center, 1280 Peachtree St. NE. (tel. 892-2414). You'll catch **Atlanta Ballet** performances at the Atlanta Civic Center, 395 Piedmont Ave. NE, between Ralph McGill Boulevard and Pine Street (tel. 892-3033).

THEATER The Woodruff Arts Center's ✪ **Alliance Theatre,** 1280 Peachtree St. NE, between 15th and 17th Streets (tel. 892-2414), is home to plays, musicals, and children's theater. Atlanta's **Seven Stages** theater troupe produces experimental plays centered around political, social, and interpersonal themes in the Seven Stages Performing Arts Center, 1105 Euclid Ave. (tel. 523-7647). Performances at Seven Stages cost $8 to $20 and usually run Wednesday through Saturday at 6pm and Sunday at 3pm.

Broadway hits are a regular feature of Atlanta's entertainment scene. You'll find them at the **Fox Theatre,** 660 Peachtree St. NE, at Ponce de Leon Avenue (tel. 881-2000, or 577-9600 for SEATS), or the **Atlanta Civic Center,** 395 Piedmont Ave. NE, between Ralph McGill Boulevard and Pine Street (tel. 523-6275).

THE CLUB & MUSIC SCENE

In addition to the following, some of Atlanta's best bars are to be found in deluxe hotels, and many have live piano music during the cocktail hour and early evening.

POPULAR ENTERTAINERS

The **Fox Theatre** and the **Atlanta Civic Center** (see above) both host performers such as Stevie Wonder, Ray Charles, and Liza Minnelli. In addition, there are concerts at the **Omni Coliseum,** 100 Techwood Dr. NW (tel. 681-2100). Rock stars who draw huge crowds are usually accommodated in the **Atlanta-Fulton County Stadium,** 521 Capitol Ave. SW, between Fulton Street and Georgia Avenue (tel. 522-1967).

JAZZ/FOLK GUITAR

DANTE'S DOWN THE HATCH, across from Lenox Square Mall, 3380 Peachtree Rd. Tel. 266-1600.

Dante's design has created the illusion of a pirate ship tied up to an old Mediterranean wharf, and the result is an engaging spot that combines fun with sophistication. In the "wharf" section, there is jazz, classical, and flamenco guitar until 8pm nightly. The Paul Mitchell Trio is on hand in the "ship" section. Mitchell is a jazz pianist who ranks with the greats, and his sidemen match his brilliant artistry. As for the "crew," most have been aboard for a long time, and all really make you feel cared for. Then, of course, there are those cheeses, fondues, special drinks, and an excellent wine list. Dante himself is always on hand to see that you have a good time. It's so popular that reservations are really a "must."

A second Dante's, in Kenny's Alley, Underground Atlanta (tel. 577-1800), was actually the first of the two, but lay dark for several years during the Underground's decline and closure. The setting and the entertainment are much the same as at the Peachtree Road location, with only slight variations in hours and prices. Call for details.

Cover charge: Entertainment charge $4 after 8pm on the ship deck ($5 Fri–Sat) No charge on the wharf.

Open: Mon–Thurs 4pm–midnight, Fri–Sat 4pm–1am, Sun 4–11pm. Jazz, Tues–Thurs and Sun 8pm–midnight, Fri–Sat 8pm–1am; folk guitar, Mon 5:30–11:30pm, Tues–Thurs and Sun 5:30–8pm, Fri 5–6:30pm.

BLUES

BLUES HARBOR, 2293B Peachtree Rd., Tel. 524-3001.

Forget geography—Blues Harbor has moved a bit of Chicago a few hundred miles south. The club itself has lots of wrought-iron grillwork, and the menu features po-boy sandwiches and other specialties. Some of the country's leading blues musicians play here.

Cover charge: $5–$6.

Open: Dinner daily 6–9pm; 3 shows per night from 9:30pm.

COMEDY

THE PUNCH LINE, 80 Hildebrand Ave., Sandy Springs. Tel. 252-LAFF.

The Punch Line keeps 'em laughing with locally and nationally known comedians, with five or more comics and other entertainers each evening. There's a limited deli menu described by the owners as "upscale gourmet."

Cover charge: $7–$15 for most shows, depending on performers.

Open: One show Sun–Thurs, two shows Fri–Sat.

9. NETWORKS & RESOURCES

FOR STUDENTS The quickest way to link up with Atlanta's student life is to call the two universities and ask for Student Union or other on-campus organizations: **Georgia Institute of Technology** (tel. 894-2000), and **Georgia State University** (tel. 651-2000).

FOR GAY MEN & LESBIANS Look for the publication *ETC*, which lists bars and restaurants that welcome gay men and lesbians. You can also contact the publishers directly by calling 525-3831.

FOR WOMEN If you run into travel or emotional difficulties, contact the **Travelers Aid Society,** which has three Atlanta locations: 40 Pryor St. SW, near Underground Atlanta, between Decatur and Wall Streets (tel. 527-7400); the Greyhound/Trailways Terminal, 81 International Blvd., at Williams Street (tel. 527-7411); and at the airport (tel. 766-4511).

FOR SENIORS Atlanta's seniors are an active bunch. You'll find an entire page of resources in the "Community Interest" pages of the telephone directory. Two useful organizations are **Downtown Atlanta Senior Services,** 607 Peachtree St. NE (tel. 872-9191), and **North Atlanta Senior Services,** 3003 Powell Mill Rd. NW (tel. 237-7307). In addition, there are three publications for seniors: *Senior News* (tel. 231-3560), *Senior Tribune* (tel. 971-0197), and *Seniority Magazine* (tel. 350-9889).

10. EASY EXCURSIONS

MADISON, WASHINGTON & CRAWFORDVILLE

If you looked for antebellum Georgia around Atlanta, you were in the right church but the wrong pew. The state's pre–Civil War moonlight-and-magnolias romance lives on, and you'll find it some 60 to 100 miles east of Atlanta in charming towns with patriotic names like Washington, Madison, Monticello, Milledgeville, and Eatonton.

MADISON

✪ **Madison** is off I-20 an hour's drive east from Atlanta. Late in 1864, with Atlanta in flames, Gen. William T. Sherman's Union juggernaut reached Madison's outskirts. Happily for us, they were met by former U.S. Senator Joshua Hill, a secession opponent who'd known Sherman in Washington. Old ties prevailed, and the town was spared.

What to See and Do

Stop first at the **Madison-Morgan Cultural Center,** 434 S. Main St. (U.S. 441; tel. 342-4743). The red-brick schoolhouse, circa 1895, features a history museum on the Piedmont region of Georgia, an 1895 classroom museum, art galleries with changing exhibits, and an auditorium for presentations. Live programs range from Shakespeare and symphony chamber orchestra to gospel singing and ballet. Open Tuesday through Saturday 10am to 4:30pm, Sunday 2 to 5pm. Adults pay $2, students $1.

Pick up a self-guided walking-tour map and other information at the center and walk past the majestic Greek Revival, federal, Georgian, neoclassical, and Victorian homes lining Main Street, Academy Street, Old Post Road and the pretty courthouse square. You'll find plenty of places to purchase antiques and handcrafts.

You can temper all this history with delicious relaxation at ✪ **Hard Labor Creek State Park** (tel. 706/557-3001), near Madison. Leave town via I-20 West and take exit 49 into Rutledge, then drive two miles on Fairplay Road to the park. *Golf* magazine rates the park's 18-hole course as one of the finest public courses in

America. You can also swim at a sand beach, fish for bass and catfish, and hike the 5,000 wooded acres. The park has 51 campsites with electricity, water, rest rooms, and showers for $10 a night, and 20 fully furnished two-bedroom cottages at $50 (Sunday through Thursday) and $60 (Friday and Saturday) a night.

Where to Dine

YE OLD COLONIAL RESTAURANT, on the square, Madison. Tel. 706/ 342-2211.
  Cuisine: SOUTHERN. **Reservations:** Not accepted.
$ Prices: Lunch under $10, dinner under $15. No credit cards.
  Open: 5:30am–8:30pm.
When you're famished, stop by this Victorian bank building for excellent Southern cooking at very modest prices.

A Side Trip to Eatonton and Milledgeville

South of Madison on U.S. 441, **Eatonton** was the birthplace of author Joel Chandler Harris. Look for the statue of Br'er Rabbit on the courthouse lawn. The ✪ **Uncle Remus Museum** has a wonderful collection of memorabilia about Br'er Rabbit, Br'er Fox, and Harris's other storybook critters. The log cabin is the combination of two former slave cabins. In each window are scenes of a southern plantation during the antebellum days. The museum is open Monday through Saturday 10am to 5pm (except one hour for lunch), Sunday 2 to 5pm. Closed Tuesday from September through May.

   Milledgeville, south of Eatonton, was Georgia's capital from 1803 to 1868 and today is considered the Antebellum Capital. Like Madison, it was miraculously spared Sherman's wrath, and today is a treasure trove of antebellum architecture. Take a guided trolley tour (Tuesday and Friday at 10am) or walk about the historic district. The **tourist information center,** 200 W. Hancock St., can provide maps and other information. Hours are Monday through Friday 9am to 5pm, Saturday 10am to 2pm. Call 912/452-4687, or toll free 800/653-1804. The **Old Governors Mansion,** a pink marble Palladian beauty at 120 S. Clark St. (tel. 912/453-4545), has been exquisitely restored and refurnished as the home of the president of Georgia College. You may tour the antique-rich public rooms Tuesday through Saturday 9am to 5pm, Sunday 2 to 5pm. Admission is $3 for adults, $1 for children 12 to 17. Fans of the late Flannery O'Connor (author of *The Violent Bear It Away* and "A Good Man Is Hard to Find") should see her memorial room in the library of Georgia College.

WASHINGTON

Northeast of Madison, about 100 miles from Atlanta on U.S. 78, **Washington** has even more antebellum homes. Landmarks include the **Washington-Wilkes Historical Museum,** 308 E. Robert Toombs Ave. (tel. 706/678-2105), open Tuesday through Saturday 10am to 5pm. Adults pay $1, children 50¢. Also, check out the home of **Robert Toombs,** the Confederacy's flamboyant secretary of state, at 216 Robert Toombs Ave. (tel. 706/678-2226), open Tuesday through Saturday 9am to 5pm, Sunday 2 to 5:30pm. Admission is $1.50 for adults, 75¢ for children.

CRAWFORDVILLE

Just 20 miles southeast of Washington, **Liberty Hall,** at sleepy little **Crawfordville,** was the home of Confederate Vice President Alexander Hamilton Stephens. The adjoining **Confederate Museum** (tel. 706/456-2221) has an extensive collection of

Civil War memorabilia. Open Tuesday through Saturday 9am to 5pm, Sunday 2 to 5pm. Adults pay $1.50; children 75¢.

DAHLONEGA & THE NORTHEAST MOUNTAINS

For a metropolitan area of 2½ million, Atlanta is amazingly close to nature. Within 70 to 120 miles, city dwellers can hike through national forests and test their mettle on the rugged Appalachian Trail, scale Georgia's highest peak, fish trout streams, and canoe and swim in mountain lakes. At dusk, they can return home, or stay over in a comfortable lodge, a country inn, or a fully furnished state-park cottage or campground.

DAHLONEGA

About 70 miles north of Atlanta on U.S. 19, **Dahlonega** is ideal as a one-day mini-adventure, or as the start of a longer exploration. *Dahlonega* is a Cherokee word meaning "precious yellow." In 1828, according to legend, a trapper named Benjamin Parks stubbed his toe on a rock and uncovered a vein of gold here that quickly brought prospectors streaming into these hills. Although prospecting hasn't been a major industry here since the Civil War, enough gold is still around to periodically re-leaf the dome of Georgia's State Capitol, and to intrigue visitors who pan for it at **Crisson's Mine,** outside town (tel. 706/864-6363). Dahlonega's public square sports a rustic look. Old galleried buildings and stores have been turned into shops purveying gold-panning equipment, gold jewelry, mountain handcrafts, antiques, ice cream, and fudge. In the center of the square, the red-brick **Gold Museum** chronicles the history of the gold rush and the many mines that flourished in these parts. A 28-minute film is especially worthwhile. The museum is open Monday through Saturday 9am to 5pm, Sunday 10am to 5pm. Adults pay $1.50, students 6 to 18, 75¢. For information on the museum, call the Chamber of Commerce at 864-3711.

Where to Stay and Dine

Just off the square, the ○ **Smith House Restaurant, Inn, and Country Store,** 202 S. Chestatee St., Dahlonega, GA 30533 (tel. 706/864-3566, or toll free 800/852-9577), is renowned for its monumental family-style Southern buffets that include fried chicken, ham, roast beef, barbecue, a dozen or more vegetables, relishes, cornbread, and biscuits. Adults pay $12.30; children 4 to 9 $5.85, 10 to 12 $8–$9. The 16 comfortably furnished guest rooms, although remodeled, still reflect the days of the inn's beginning in the late 1800s. Rates run from $30 to $72 single or double (including a continental breakfast), depending on the season.

A SCENIC DRIVE FROM DAHLONEGA

From Dahlonega, U.S. 19 winds north into the mountains, toward one of the state's prettiest parks. At Neel's Gap, take a break at the **Mountain Crossing/Walasi-Yi Center.** The stone-and-log building is a legacy of the Depression-era Civilian Conservation Corps, and a landmark on the **Appalachian Trail,** which crosses here on its way to Maine. You can sip cider at the little snack bar, and purchase mountain crafts and guidebooks. Five miles farther north, about 20 miles from Dahlonega, **Vogel State Park,** in Blairsville (tel. 706/745-2628), invites you to hike around pretty Lake Trahlyta; fish for bass, trout, and bream; and in summer have a refreshing swim. There are campsites with power and water hookups, hot showers, and laundry facilities ($10 a night for tent and pop-up camping as well as for RV hookups). Cottages are comfortably furnished, with wood-burning fireplaces ($40 to $50 a night for a one-bedroom, $50 to $60 for a two-bedroom, $60 to $70 for a three-bedroom).

From Vogel, drive north five miles on U.S. 19 and head east on Ga. 180. At the junction of Ga. 180 and Ga. 348, either continue east to **Brasstown Bald Mountain,** or head south on Ga. 348 across the spectacular **Richard Russell Scenic Highway.** If you choose to do both, drive on to Brasstown first and take the paved road to within 930 yards of the summit of Georgia's highest mountain (4,784 feet). At the parking area, you'll find picnic tables, vending machines, and scenic overlooks. The most panoramic views are from the very top, reached by hiking a woodland trail, or in summer by riding a minibus. The glass-enclosed visitors' center on top has displays of mountain flora and fauna; on clear days you can see across northern Georgia into Tennessee and the Carolinas.

After exploring Brasstown, backtrack on Ga. 180 and head south on the Richard Russell Scenic Highway. The drive is especially breathtaking in fall, when hardwoods blaze with colors. At 3,500-foot Tesnatee Gap, the highway crosses the Appalachian Trail.

Follow Ga. 348 to its end at Ga. 75-Alt; then turn left and drive 2.3 miles to its end at Ga. 17/75. Go right .3 miles, then left on Ga. 356, and 1½ miles into **Unicoi State Park,** P.O. Box 256, Helen, GA 30545 (tel. 706/878-2201). Unicoi is even more beautiful than Vogel. **Anna Ruby Falls** is the scenic high point of the 1,600-acre Chattahoochee National Forest recreation area adjoining Unicoi. From a paved parking area ($2 parking fee), it's an easy and very beautiful half-mile walk through the woods, by a rushing white-water stream, to an observation platform at the base of 153- and 50-foot cascades.

From Unicoi, drive two miles south into **Helen.** Once a quiet Appalachian village, Helen has been turned into a bit of Bavaria in the Georgia hills. Main Street buildings have red roofs, flower boxes, balconies, and murals. You can shop for sweaters, porcelains, cuckoo clocks, and Christmas ornaments; enjoy wurst and beer to oompah music at an outdoor beer garden; and in September and October join the revelry of Oktoberfest. Numerous alpine-style hotels have comfortable accommodations and restaurants.

Where to Stay

UNICOI STATE PARK LODGE, P.O. Box 849, Helen, GA 30545. Tel. 706/878-2824. Fax 706/878-1897. 100 rms (with bath). A/C TV TEL **Directions:** Two miles N of Helen on GA 356.

$ Rates: $30–$50 single, $36–$56 double. AE, DC, DISC, MC, V.

Set on a pristine lake in the midst of 1,000 acres of woodland, this is the heart of the park. Warm and wood-beamed, the lodge has an excellent cafeteria-style dining room serving three meals a day at very modest prices. There's also a gift shop stocked with mountain arts and crafts. Furnished cottages and campsites are tucked into the wooded hillsides.

STOVALL HOUSE, Rte. 1, Box 1476, Sautee, GA 30571. Tel. 706/878-3355. 5 rms (with bath). A/C TV TEL **Directions:** Two miles SW of Helen on S.R. 75 and S.R. 17.

$ Rates: $40 single, $70 double. Children 12 and under stay free with parents. Advance deposit required. MC, V.

One of the prettiest country inns you'll ever happen onto. Under the stewardship of affable Ham Schwartz, the circa-1837 farmhouse has five lovely guest rooms, furnished with antiques and all the modern comforts (no smoking allowed in rooms). Amenities include a wide veranda for leisurely rocking, and a restaurant serving first-rate Southern, American, and continental dishes at moderate prices.

HELENDORF INN, P.O. Box 305, Main St., Helen, GA 30545. Tel. 706/878-2271. 93 rms (with bath). AC TV TEL **Directions:** Town Center on S.R. 17 and S.R. 75.

$ Rates: $35–$79 single or double. $5 per day for pets. Weekly rates available. Reserve deposit required. MC, V.

⭐ Overlooking the Chattahoochee River, the Helendorf is an idyllic base for exploring the region. Most guest rooms have either a balcony or a patio. Fishing is just outside in the river. A restaurant is next door.

MACON

From an architectural standpoint, Macon, 84 miles southeast of Atlanta, probably sits right behind Savannah for its striking buildings and beauty. Macon proudly boasts more than 400 white-columned buildings and 90 parks. What comes as a huge surprise to visitors is that Macon has 170,000 cherry trees—and they are a remarkable sight in late March when they bloom. Compare Washington, D.C.'s famous Cherry Blossom Festival (with a mere 3,000 trees), and you'll understand how wonderful that time of year is in Macon.

In the city's early days, Macon was home to ancient Native American tribes, cotton barons, and explorers. The city founders designed their new town in the 1800s to be like the ancient Gardens of Babylon. Today, that heritage has been preserved. The wide avenues and streets are lined with gorgeous mansions. It's more than a river town today with many cultural and educational outlets, such as Macon College, Georgia College Macon Campus, Mercer University, and Wesleyan College.

As you'll see below, Macon has a wealth of historic significance, a handful of delightful—in one case truly grand—places to stay, and hospitality for which the South is known.

TOURIST INFORMATION   The **Macon-Bibb County Convention and Visitors Bureau,** 200 Cherry St., Macon, GA 31201 (tel. 912/743-3401), will provide you with information on Macon, such as accommodations, sightseeing, festivals, and concerts. If you're traveling southbound, north on Macon, on I-75, there is a welcome center and rest area; it's open daily 9am to 5:30pm, and they provide area information. The downtown welcome center is located at the foot of Cherry Street in the historic Macon Terminal Station. You can drop in there for information when you get into town. Hours are Monday through Saturday 9am to 5:30pm.

WHAT TO SEE & DO

You don't have to take an organized tour in Macon, but it helps. Instead, you might drive up and down the city's streets to look at the architecture. Be sure to get a map from the welcome center and ask them to highlight the historic areas—don't depend on finding the best of Macon by chance. Be sure to have College Street and Bond Street on your list.

The **Cherry Blossom Festival** is traditionally held about the last 10 days in March. During that time, 200 activities are planned around the city. You'll find everything from hot air ballooning to a giant parade with 100 bands, floats, and other marching units. Many events are held in the city parks. The residential areas are filled with lovely Yoshino cherry trees. For more information, contact the Macon, Ga. Cherry Blossom Festival, Inc., 749 Cherry St., Macon, GA 31201 (tel. 912/751-7429).

Macon Terminal Station, 200 Cherry St. (tel. 912/743-3401), is home to the visitors' center today but in its early days, dating back to 1916, it hosted more than 100 trains a day. At **Central City Park,** a 250-acre recreational area, you can enjoy ongoing events. Dr. Martin Luther King, Jr. made his only major speech in Georgia in 1957 at the **Steward Chapel of the African Methodist Episcopal Church,** 887 Forsyth St. (tel. 742-4922). The **Ocmulgee National Monument,** 1207 Emery

Hwy., celebrates 10,000 years of Southeastern Native American heritage and is free and open daily. African-American history in Macon is displayed at the **Harriet Tubman Historical and Cultural Museum,** 340 Walnut St. (tel. 743-8544). You can see the slate roof of the restored apartments at the **Slate House,** 931–45 Walnut St., built in 1845 by James B. Ayers who also built the Hay House (see below).

TOURS There are a handful of areas in the city where walking tours are most fun. Stop at the tourist office (see above) for route maps for the following self-guided tours. The **Victorian Walking Tour** includes stops at Magnolia Street to see Victorian cottages, the Hill-O'Neal Cottage, Washington Memorial Library, and the New Federal Building and Post Office. Other stops include the Lanier Cottage, home of poet Sidney Clopton Lanier, St. Joseph's Catholic Church, Clifford Anderson-Dickey House, and several other significant churches. The **Historic Downtown Walking Tour** includes City Hall, the Municipal Auditorium, Mulberry Street Parks, Washington Block where the stagecoach once stopped, Baber House (1830), and the Grand Opera House. Almost 25 stops are listed in this walking tour. The **White Columns Walking Tour** will highlight the best of Macon's columned buildings and homes. Some of the stops include the Carmichael House, Edward Dorr Tracy House, old Cannonball House (see below), Hay House (see below), the Woodruff House, the Greek Revival Randolph-Whittle-Davis-Smith House with its round and square portico columns, and the 1842 Inn (see "Where to Stay", below).

Organized tours are offered by the very popular **Sidney's Old South Historic Tours,** Terminal Station Building, 200 Cherry St. (tel. 743-3401), or **Col. Bond's Carriage Tours** (tel. 749-7267). Col. Bond's horse-drawn carriages are a romantic way to see the area.

CANNONBALL HOUSE & CONFEDERATE MUSEUM, 856 Mulberry St. Tel. 745-5982.

In the Civil War, Union forces led by Gen. George Stoneman struck this building with a cannonball on July 30, 1864. The cannonball is on the floor in the entryway today. The building is an authentic example of Greek Revival design and is on the National Register of Historic Places.

Admission: $3 adults, $2.50 seniors, $1 children over 12, 50¢ children under 12.
Open: Tues–Fri 10am–1pm and 2–4pm, Sat–Sun 1:30–4:30pm.

GRAND OPERA HOUSE, 651 Mulberry St. Tel. 749-6580.

The Academy of Music was constructed in 1884 and later became known as the Grand Opera House. Such oldtimers as Will Rogers, Sarah Bernhardt, Dorothy Lamour, Burns and Allen, and the Gish sisters have performed here. With seating for 1,057, it also boasts one of America's largest stages—big enough to accommodate a production of "Ben Hur" with its stage machinery and treadmills for the chariot races.

Admission: $3 per person.
Open: Mon–Fri tours at 10am, noon, and 2pm.

HAY HOUSE, 934 Georgia Ave. Tel. 742-8155.

Built between 1855 and 1860, this extravagant home of Italian Renaissance Revival design was the home of William Butler Johnston. Johnston was the keeper of the Confederate treasury in the mid-1800s. The interiors are nothing short of spectacular—like European palaces. More than 20 rooms in the house are not fully restored, but those that are complete are breathtaking. The house is on the register as a National Historic Landmark. If you see nothing else in Macon, see the Hay House.

Admission: $6 adults, $5 seniors, $2 students, $1 children 6 to 12.
Open: Mon–Sat 10am–5pm, Sun 1–5pm. **Closed:** Holidays.

SIDNEY LANIER COTTAGE, 955 High St. Tel. 743-3851.

This 1842 Victorian cottage was home to Sidney Lanier, one of Georgia's most famous citizens, a poet who is best known for "Song of the Chattahoochee" and "The Marshes of Glynn." Behind the house is a garden. The house is outfitted in furnishings of the period and is home to the Middle Georgia Historical Society.

Admission: $2.50 adults, $1 students, 50¢ children under 12.

Open: Mon–Fri 9am–1pm and 2–4pm, Sat 9:30am–12:30pm. **Closed:** Holidays.

WHERE TO STAY

Along I-75 are many middle-grade hotels and motels including such chain names as Howard Johnson, Comfort Inn, Holiday Inn, Hampton Inn, and Courtyard by Marriott. Off I-475 are Ramada Inn, Travelodge, and a Holiday Inn. The best place in town is the 1842 Inn (see below). On the commercial side of things, the Radisson Hotel Macon, downtown, is an upscale business hotel close to everything.

1842 INN, 353 College St., Macon, GA. 31201. Tel. 912/741-1842, or toll free 800/336-1842. Fax 912/741-1842. 21 rms. A/C TV TEL

Directions. Take exit 52 off of I-75, then go four blocks to the center of the historic district.

$ Rates: $75–$109 single; $85–$119 double. AE, MC, V.

The 1842 Inn is reason enough to come to Macon. It's one of only a handful of places in Georgia that might be called truly special and is one of my favorite inns south of the Mason-Dixon line. The inn is romantic, upscale, and delightfully charming. You're likely to find a working fireplace in your room along with the antiques, expensive fabrics, four-poster beds, and maybe even a whirlpool. At night, the grounds are bathed in artistic lighting. You can enjoy some sherry or wine in one of the parlor rooms in front of the fire. Across the courtyard is a carriage house with more rooms. Come to Macon and add your name to the list of celebrities, such as Dr. Ruth and Barbara Walters, who have stayed here.

WHERE TO DINE

LEN BERG'S RESTAURANT, Old Post Office Alley. Tel. 742-9255.

Cuisine: AMERICAN/DINER. **Reservations:** Not required.

$ Prices: Lunch $4–$7; dinner $6–$9. No credit cards.

Open: Lunch daily 11:15am–2:30pm; dinner daily 5–9:30pm.

An institution in Macon, Len Berg's has home-cooking. Pure and simple. And it's in a simple building—no columns or architectural merit—just a single-story cinderblock structure. It is well known for its fresh peach ice cream. Other menu items include salmon croquettes and cream-topped macaroon pie for dessert. It's located between Walnut and Mulberry Streets, behind the old post office.

A SIDE TRIP TO JULIETTE

An easy trip for lunch is north to Juliette, home of the **Whistle Stop Café** (tel. 912/994-3670), where the hit movie *Fried Green Tomatoes* was filmed. The old town has gained a new lease on life since it was invaded by Hollywood, and the tourists keep coming.

The little café is right out of a Hollywood movie set. Inside business is brisk. The decor has a country flavor with ceiling fans, a U-shaped wooden counter, old signs, farm tools hung on the walls, and a handful of booths. Everyone's ordering up fried green tomatoes and many race outdoors or to the windows when a train blows its whistle and chugs by, just a few feet away.

Owner Ms. Jerie Williams oversees everything. The food is made from scratch and the menu is written on a recipe card. When I visited, the daily special ($5.95) was baked or barbecue chicken or a smoked pork chop, and it included three vegetables from a choice of eight. Bread, tea, and dessert were also included. Fried green tomatoes as a side dish costs $2.25. Dessert consisted of a choice of peach cobbler or carrot cake. Hours are Monday through Saturday 8am to 2pm and Sunday noon to 7pm.

Juliette is just a fleck on a map. To get there, take I-75 North out of Macon and go 22 miles to exit 61. Then go right (east) on Route 23/87 for 8.2 miles (set your odometer) until you reach a blinker and stop sign; look for the café one-quarter mile ahead on the right.

CHAPTER 14

COLUMBUS & ENVIRONS

**1. COLUMBUS &
WESTVILLE VILLAGE**

**2. CALLAWAY GARDENS
& WARM SPRINGS**

**3. PLAINS &
ANDERSONVILLE**

Southwestern Georgia is the land of peach orchards, pecan groves, and Jimmy Carter. It is also a land of giant textile mills, pulp and paper plants, and manufacturing centers for automobiles, metal, chemicals, and furniture that bear the definite stamp of the New South. Which is not to say that this part of the state does not retain and value its Old South heritage—it does. Primarily, though, this region looks forward, not backward.

1. COLUMBUS & WESTVILLE VILLAGE

Columbus was the last frontier town of the original 13 colonies, and its wide streets, shaded by marvelous old trees, still reveal much of the original city plan of 1828. Nearby Westville Village re-creates pioneer life in this region.

COLUMBUS

Situated on the Chattahoochee River at the foot of a series of falls, Columbus early on utilized its water supply to become an important manufacturing center, supplying swords, pistols, cannon, gunboats, and other articles of war to the Confederate Army during the Civil War. It fell to Union forces in April of 1865 in one of the last battles of the war. Today there's a lovely riverside walkway, the **Columbus Chattahoochee Promenade**, with gazebos and historical displays, stretching from the Columbus Iron Works Trade and Convention Center to Oglethorpe Bridge.

TOURIST INFORMATION The **Convention and Visitors Bureau,** 801 Front Ave., P.O. Box 2768, Columbus, GA 31902 (tel. 706/322-1613, or 24 hours 706/322-3181), and the **Georgia Visitors Center,** 1751 Williams Rd., Columbus, GA 31902 (tel. 706/649-7455), can furnish detailed sightseeing information. Ask for days and hours of **Heritage Tours,** two-hour guided tours of Heritage Corner. The **Historic Columbus Foundation,** 700 Broadway (tel. 322-0756), can furnish self-guided tour brochures outlining walking and/or driving tours. The Foundation is worth a visit on its own merits—its home dates from 1870 and has period antique furnishings.

WHAT TO SEE & DO

One of Columbus's more interesting attractions is the **Springer Opera House,** a restored 1871 theater in which Edwin Booth and other distinguished actors performed. For guided tour hours, call 324-1100 or 327-3688.

The ○ **Columbus Museum,** 1251 Wynnton Rd. (tel. 649-0713), exhibits prehistoric Native American relics along with artifacts of regional history, works of art from the late 1800s and the 1900s, decorative arts displays, and a restored log cabin. It's open Tuesday through Saturday 10am to 5pm, Sunday 1 to 5pm, closed major holidays. Admission is free.

Fort Benning (tel. 545-2958) is five miles south of the city on U.S. 27. The interesting **National Infantry Museum** reflects the history of the foot soldier from Revolutionary days to the present. It's free, open Monday through Friday 8am to 4:30pm, Saturday and Sunday 12:30 to 4:30pm. Admission is free.

WHERE TO STAY

COLUMBUS HILTON, 800 Front Ave., Columbus, GA 31901. Tel. 706/ 324-1800. 178 rms. A/C MINIBAR TV TEL
$ Rates: $75–$95 single; $95–$105 double. Family and weekend rates available. AE, CB, DC, DISC, MC, V.

The Hilton adjoins the century-old Iron Works Convention Center; one wing was part of the brick and wood-beamed Empire Mills complex. Rooms are of the high Hilton standards, and the luxury level provides concierge services, a private lounge and honor bar, and whirlpool in suites. There's a heated pool, a good restaurant, and a bar with entertainment nightly except Sunday.

COMFORT INN, 3343 Macon Rd., Columbus, GA 31907. Tel. 706/568-3300, or toll free 800/228-5150. 66 rms. AC TV TEL
$ Rates: (including continental breakfast): $44 single; $50 double. Senior discounts available. AE, DC, DISC, MC, V.

Rooms at this attractive motel are nicely done up and very comfortable; four come complete with whirlpool at a small additional charge. Facilities include a pool and exercise room. It's located one block east of I-85 at exit 4.

WESTVILLE VILLAGE

An intriguing excursion from Columbus is the 35-mile drive south on U.S. 27 to Lumpkin, home to ✪ **Westville Village** on South Mulberry Street, a restored 1850s town with unpaved streets, 19th-century buildings and homes, and craftspeople who demonstrate such old-time skills as syrup-making, cotton-ginning, and blacksmithing. It's open (closed major holidays) Tuesday through Saturday 10am to 5pm, Sunday 1 to 5pm. Admission is $6 for adults, $5 for seniors, $3 for students, and free for preschoolers.

2. CALLAWAY GARDENS & WARM SPRINGS

CALLAWAY GARDENS

Callaway Gardens, 50 miles north of Columbus on U.S. 27 at Pine Mountain, were begun back in the 1930s. Every cent of profit generated by the resort is plowed back into development. The Callaway family, which built this beautiful place, derives no private gain at all from its operation. All monies are administered by a nonprofit, state-chartered foundation. The gardens themselves are a complete collection of native plants and flowers, to which experimental gardening adds an exotic note. And all this on 2,500 acres of what used to be abandoned, worn-out farmland.

This lovely resort is the result of one man's efforts to restore the natural beauty of the region and create a restful, scenic recreational environment for Georgia residents.

Cason Callaway, head of one of Georgia's most prosperous textile mills, once said, "All I've done is try to fix it so that anybody who came here would see something beautiful wherever he might look." Callaway set about rebuilding the soil, nurturing and importing plant life, building the largest man-made inland beach in the world, providing inn and cottage accommodations, and opened it all to people of modest means. By the time of his death in 1961 thousands of people from all over the world were walking the nature trails and making full use of the facilities.

TOURIST INFORMATION   The best place to start any exploration of the gardens is the information center near the entrance, where an eight-minute slide show lets you get your bearings as to what is here, as well as giving you the fascinating history of this place.

WHAT TO SEE & DO

The gardens include floral and hiking trails and acres of picnic grounds. Spring is especially lovely, with more than 750 varieties of azaleas, but it doesn't matter what season it is when you enter the five-acre **John A. Sibley Horticulture Center,** an innovative indoor-outdoor complex. **Mr. Cason's Vegetable Garden** comprises 7½ acres planted with fruits and vegetables, and the 160-year-old **Pioneer Log Cabin,** with authentic furnishings, paints a vivid picture of early settler life. The nondenominational **Ida Cason Callaway Memorial Chapel** (named for Cason Callaway's mother) is a lovely native fieldstone structure by a waterfall on a small lake, with stained-glass windows depicting the seasons at the gardens. Organ concerts are scheduled here throughout the year and weddings take place here occasionally. The chapel is open for a moment of quiet meditation at all times. Admission to the garden is $7 for adults, $1 for children 6 to 11, free for children under 6 and for guests at the inn or cottages.

The ◯ **Country Store,** close by the entrance to the gardens, is a great place to buy country-cured bacon and ham, preserves, grits, water-ground cornmeal, and hundreds of other items, both locally made and imported. You can even have slabs of their marvelous bacon mailed to your home.

SPORTS & RECREATION

If you're a day visitor in the summer, the charge is $15 for adults, $7 for kids 6 to 11 (no charge for those under 6), for admission to the **Robin Lake Beach.** That one price entitles you to swim, play miniature golf, canoe, use paddleboats, and ride a riverboat or train. These facilities, like the gardens, are free to guests at the inn or cottages.

Golfers will find three 18-hole courses as well as one 9-hole executive (par-31) course, with two pro shops and fees that run as follows: $38–$48 for daily greens fees, $32 for a power cart for 18 holes. These courses serve as the site of the PGA National Junior Championships and the PGA Club Professional Championships. Tennis courts cost $12 to $14 per hour.

Fishing (with artificial lures only) is available at $20 per person for a half day (includes boat with electric trolling motor), $25 for two people.

Hunters can go for quail on a large preserve that's open from October 1 to March 31 if they have the required Georgia hunting license—and there's skeet and trap shooting every day at the hunting preserve. The ranges are also lit for night shooting.

WHERE TO STAY

The best possible place to stay is at the gardens themselves. However, because of their popularity, reservations must be made at least a month in advance.

CALLAWAY GARDENS RESORT, U.S. 27, Pine Mountain, GA 31822.

Tel. 706/663-2281, or toll free 800/282-8181. Fax 404/663-5080. 793 rms, suites, cottages, and villas. A/C TV TEL

$ Rates: $115 single or double; $200–$350 suite; $160–$550 one- or two-bedroom cottage; $230–$605 one- to four-bedroom villa. Children under 18 stay free with parents. Weekly and monthly rates, and golf and tennis packages available. AE, DC, MC, V.

⭐ Rooms are spacious with a bright, homey decor that seems just right for this setting; some feature balconies or patios. Cottages, fully furnished and equipped, are available on a per-day basis except in summer, when they are reserved for families only on a weekly basis. Villas have fireplaces, screened porches or patios, all cooking utensils and dishes, linens, and outdoor grills. They are beautifully situated on wooded sites and make a great stopover on an extended trip or an ideal "home away from home" on a "stay put" vacation in this area. There's a good grocery store less than a mile away. For in-house dining, there are seven restaurants. And for leisure time, the staff plans children's activities. There's also an exercise room, two pools, a wading pool, bicycles, a beach (included in rates), fishing, boating, tennis, golf, hunting, and skeet and trap shooting. It's one mile south of Ga. 18.

VALLEY INN RESORT, 14420 Hwy. 27, Hamilton, GA 31811-9601 Tel. 706/628-4454. 24 rms, plus cottages and mobile homes. AC TV TEL

Directions: 3 miles south of Callaway Gardens.

$ Rates: Rooms $60–$85 single or double; $85–$95 cottage. Call for mobile home rates. Weekly rates available. MC, V.

This is a small, well-run motel with accommodations that are comfortably furnished, some with kitchens. You can bring your own RV to park in their Travel Trailer Park or rent one of their two-bedroom mobile home units that sleep up to six. There's a good restaurant, open Friday and Saturday only, with home-cooking at moderate rates, as well as a pool and a lake with good fishing. Rates include admission to Callaway Gardens three miles away.

WHITE COLUMNS MOTEL, Hwy. 27 South, P.O. Box 531, Pine Mountain, GA 31822. Tel. 706/663-2312. 13 rms. A/C TV

$ Rates: $33–$45 single or double. AE, DISC, MC, V.

⭐ Very close to Callaway Gardens, this small family-owned-and-operated motel is within walking distance of two good, moderately priced restaurants and is in a convenient location near the beach at Callaway Gardens. Rooms are attractive and come with cable TV. Pets are accepted.

WHERE TO DINE

There are five places to eat in the gardens themselves, all very good, with quite moderate prices. Address and telephone number is the same for all: **Callaway Gardens Resort (tel. 706/663-2281).** All accept American Express, MasterCard, and VISA. In addition, the golf and tennis pro shops both have snackshops, with hot dogs, hamburgers, soft drinks, etc., at budget prices.

The ✪ **Plantation Room** specializes in Southern cuisine, and is tastefully decorated in a country-dining-room style. The menu includes baked ham, fried chicken, roast beef, and the like, but the place outdoes itself in the three buffets each day. For breakfast there's an array of bacon, sausage, ham (all homemade), eggs, French toast, their own speckled-heart grits, fresh berries, and fruits (according to season), and the beverage of your choice, for $8.95. The lunch and dinner buffets not only offer the meats mentioned above, but sometimes throw in continental dishes like crêpes and quiche. On Friday evening, the Captain's Galley seafood buffet can only be called sumptuous. Vegetables are the freshest, especially during the summer, when they come to the table just one or two hours after being picked in Mr. Cason's Vegetable Garden. If you've never eaten corn just pulled from the stalk, you'll find that it's quite different from the "store-bought" kind pulled days before. Lunch will run about $10, dinner $18. Breakfast is served from 7:30 to 10am, lunch from 11:30am to 2pm, and dinner from 6:30 to 10pm.

The ✪ **Georgia Room,** is an elegant setting for intimate, candlelit dinners, with a gourmet menu of continental cuisine and soft piano music. Specialties are pheasant, seafood, lamb, and home-baking, and there's a good wine list. Prix fixe dinners will cost $37, while an à la carte dinner (without wine) will average $15 to $18. Open Monday through Saturday 6:30 to 10pm.

The **Gardens Restaurant** overlooks Mountain Creek Lake and the Lake View Golf Course. Lunch is sometimes a soup-and-salad buffet (salads are a specialty in this room, with ingredients coming from the vegetable garden in the summer), and there's always a good variety of hot dishes. The star of the menu is the French onion soup—delicious! Entrées usually include baked ham, chicken in one form or another, and perhaps veal or lamb. Lunch (daily 11:30am to 2pm) averages $6–$10; dinner (daily 6:30 to 9:30pm) ranges from $10–$18.

The ⑤ **Veranda** offers dinner in a setting of casual charm, with chiefly American cuisine and prices under $15. Open daily 6:30 to 10pm.

The ⑤ ✪ **Country Kitchen,** in the country store, only serves breakfast and lunch in a cozy, old-fashioned atmosphere. The ham, bacon, and sausage are homemade, and the speckled-heart grits are a trademark of the gardens and the Country Kitchen. Try the many varieties of Callaway Gardens muscadine sauces, jams, and jellies that you'll find on your table. The luncheon menu features generous salads and juicy hamburgers. Prices are well under $10, and hours are 8:30am to 5pm daily.

WARM SPRINGS

Just 17 miles from Callaway Gardens (take Ga. 190 and follow the signs) is the simple wooden house that was Franklin Roosevelt's **"Little White House."** FDR discovered Warm Springs in 1924, shortly after he contracted polio, when he went there for the beneficial effect of swimming in the warm spring water. In 1926 he bought the springs, hotel, and some cottages and began developing facilities to help paralytic patients from all over the country through the Georgia Warm Springs Foundation, which he founded. When he became president, this was the retreat he loved most, and the house today is much as he left it when he died here while sitting for a portrait in 1945. The unfinished portrait (by artist Elizabeth Shoumatoff), his wheelchair, Fala's dog chain, ship models, sea paintings, and gifts from citizens are preserved as he last saw them.

Next door, the **Franklin D. Roosevelt Museum** (tel. 706/655-3511) holds more memorabilia and shows a 12-minute movie depicting FDR's life in Warm Springs. The Little White House is open daily 9am to 5pm (closed Thanksgiving, Christmas, and New Year's days); admission is $4 for adults, $2 for children 6 to 18.

3. PLAINS & ANDERSONVILLE

PLAINS

Jimmy Carter, 39th president of the United States, was born 80 miles southeast of Callaway Gardens (via U.S. 27 south to Columbus, then Ga. 280 east). You'll know Plains by the little green-and-white train depot, its water tower brightly painted with the stars and stripes. Despite the fame of its most outstanding citizens, a small-town charm still clings to Plains and its people. The early-1900s buildings are much like they were before the Depression forced their closing (most were used as warehouses until Jimmy Carter's campaign brought business back to town). Plains has preserved the surroundings from which a rural peanut grower went out and became president of the United States.

INFORMATION If you stand in the middle of it, you can almost see the whole town, but for do-it-yourself walking or driving tours of points of interest, go by the **Plains Visitor Center,** P.O. Box 69, Plains, GA 31780, east of Plains on U.S. 280, where Sibyl McGlaun and her very friendly staff will furnish maps and brochures. In Plains itself, the **railway depot** (built in 1888) now houses a visitors' center (tel. 824-3413) and a gift and book shop, but its looks haven't changed a great deal. Two publications I particularly liked—"Plains, Carter Country U.S.A." and "Armchair Tour of Jimmy Carter Country"—are available at the depot, as are self-guided walking-tour brochures, as well as a cassette tape for an auto tour ($1 charge for the latter).

WHAT TO SEE & DO

The one-story, ranch-style brick house that is the **Carter home** is on Woodland Drive, and when the Carters are in residence, there are Secret Service booths at this entrance and at the one on Paschal Street (you can get a pretty good look at it by walking or driving west on Church Street). Then there's the **Plains Methodist Church,** at the corner of Church and Thomas, where Jimmy asked Rosalynn for their first date. When he's in town, Jimmy teaches Sunday school at **Maranatha Baptist Church.** Visitors are invited—check the notice in the window of Hugh Carter's Antiques on Main Street. **Archery,** a 2½-mile drive west of town on U.S. 280, is where Jimmy Carter lived as a child when his father operated a country store. Anybody in Plains can give you explicit directions.

In nearby **Americus,** on the grounds of Georgia Southwestern College, Wheatly and Glessner streets (tel. 912/928-1273), the ✪ **James Earl Carter Library** holds a permanent display of memorabilia of the Carter family.

WHERE TO STAY

PLAINS BED & BREAKFAST INN, P.O. Box 217, Plains, GA 31780. Tel. 912/824-7252. 4 rms (all with bath). A/C TV TEL
$ Rates (including breakfast): $50 double. No credit cards.

✪ This is the Victorian home where Jimmy Carter's parents spent their early married life. Now operated by affable Grace Jackson, the inn has turn-of-the-century furnishings throughout. Grace can arrange meals with advance notice. It's located in the town center across from the depot.

ANDERSONVILLE

Twenty miles northeast of Plains (U.S. 280 to Americus, then Ga. 49 north) is the site of the most infamous of Confederate prison camps. **Andersonville** was built to hold 10,000, but had at one time a prisoner population of over 32,000 struggling to survive on polluted water (from a creek) and starvation rations. Nearly 15,000 prisoners died here. The commander, Capt. Henry Wirtz, although powerless to prevent the fatalities, was tried and hanged after the Civil War on charges of having conspired to murder Union prisoners. Today you can visit the ✪ **Drummer Boy Civil War Museum** (open daily 10am to 4pm with a $1.50 admission fee) and see slide shows on the camp's sad history, as well as the remains of wells and escape tunnels, and **Providence Springs,** which legend says gushed up in answer to prayers of prisoners during the drought of 1864. The Andersonville National Historic Site is open daily 8am to 5pm; admission is free.

After visiting the historic site, browse the antique shops in the adjacent village of Andersonville. Stop by the **Andersonville Guild Welcome Center** (tel. 912/924-

2558) in the old train depot and meet Peggy Sheppard, a gregarious transplanted New York who spearheaded the village's rejuvenation.

WHERE TO DINE

ANDERSONVILLE RESTAURANT, Andersonville, GA 31711. Tel. 928-2980.

Cuisine: COUNTRY BUFFET.

$ Prices: $5 for complete country meal buffet. No credit cards.

Open: Lunch Tues–Sat 11:30am–2pm; dinner Fri 5–9pm.

This is a real "down home" restaurant, with a buffet groaning under the weight of Southern fried chicken, ham, and other meats; fresh vegetables; homemade biscuits; and desserts. Your $5 entitles you to one meat, three vegetables, biscuits, beverage, and dessert—a real bargain in anyone's book. It's in the town center.

FOR THE FOREIGN VISITOR

The information below will be familiar to you if you are coming to the Carolinas and Georgia from another U.S. destination. If not, however, it is meant to clarify details that can often be bewildering to newcomers.

PREPARING FOR YOUR TRIP

ENTRY REQUIREMENTS

DOCUMENTS   Canadian nationals need only proof of Canadian residence to visit the United States. Citizens of Great Britain and Japan need only a current passport. Citizens of other countries, including Australia and New Zealand, usually need two documents: a valid **passport** with an expiration date at least six months later than the scheduled end of their visit to the United States and a **tourist visa** available at no charge from a United States embassy or consulate.

To get a tourist or business visa to enter the United States, contact the nearest American embassy or consulate in your country; if there is none, you will have to apply in person in a country where there is a U.S. embassy or consulate. Present your passport, a passport-size photo of yourself, and a completed application, which is available through the embassy or consulate. You may be asked to provide information about how you plan to finance your trip or show a letter of invitation from a friend with whom you plan to stay. Those applying for a business visa may be asked to show evidence that they will not receive a salary in the United States. Be sure to check the length of stay on your visa; usually it is six months. If you want to stay longer, you may file for an extension with the Immigration and Naturalization Service once you are in the country. If permission to stay is granted, a new visa is not required unless you leave the United States and want to reenter.

MEDICAL REQUIREMENTS   No inoculations are needed to enter the United States unless you are coming from, or have stopped over in, an area known to be suffering from an epidemic, particularly cholera or yellow fever.

If you have a disease requiring treatment with medications containing narcotics or drugs requiring a syringe, carry a valid signed prescription from your physician to allay any suspicions that you are smuggling drugs.

CUSTOMS REQUIREMENTS   Every adult visitor may bring in, free of duty: 1 liter of wine or hard liquor; 200 cigarettes or 100 cigars (but no cigars from Cuba) or 3 pounds of smoking tobacco; and $100 worth of gifts. These exemptions are offered to travelers who spend at least 72 hours in the United States and who have not claimed them within the preceding 6 months. It is altogether forbidden to bring into the country foodstuffs (particularly cheese, fruit, cooked meats, and canned goods) and plants (vegetables, seeds, tropical plants, and so on). Foreign tourists may bring in or take out up to $10,000 in U.S. or foreign currency with no formalities; larger sums must be declared to Customs on entering or leaving.

INSURANCE

Unlike most other countries there is no national health system in the United States. Because the cost of medical care is extremely high, every traveler should secure health coverage before setting out. You may want to take out a comprehensive travel policy that covers (for a relatively low premium) loss of, or theft of, your baggage; trip-cancellation costs; guarantee of bail in case you are arrested; sickness or injury costs (medical, surgical, and hospital); and costs of accident, repatriation, or death. Such packages (for example, "Europe Assistance" in Europe) are sold by automobile clubs at attractive rates, as well as by insurance companies and travel agencies.

INSURANCE FOR BRITISH TRAVELERS Most big travel agents offer their own insurance, and will probably try to sell you their package when you book a holiday. Think before you sign. Britain's Consumers' Association recommends that you insist on seeing the policy and reading the fine print before buying travel insurance.

You should also shop around for better deals. Try **Columbus Travel Insurance Ltd.** (tel. 071/375-0011) or, for students, **Campus Travel** (tel. 071/730-3402). If you're unsure about who can give you the best deal, contact the **Association of British Insurers,** 51 Gresham St., London EC2V 7HQ (tel. 071/600-333).

SAFETY

GENERAL While tourist areas are generally safe, crime is on the increase everywhere, and U.S. urban areas tend to be less safe than those in Europe or Japan. Visitors should always stay alert. This is particularly true of large U.S. cities. It is wise to ask the city or area's tourist office if you are in doubt about which neighborhoods are safe. Avoid deserted areas, especially at night. Don't go into any city park at night unless there is an occasion that attracts crowds—for example, New York City's concerts in the parks. Generally speaking, you can feel safe in areas where there are many people, and many open establishments.

Avoid carrying valuables with you on the street, and don't display expensive cameras or electronic equipment. Hold on to your pocketbook, and place your billfold in an inside pocket. In restaurants, theaters, and other public places, keep your possessions in sight.

Remember also that hotels are open to the public, and in a large hotel, security may not be able to screen everyone entering. Always lock your room door; don't assume that once inside your hotel you are automatically safe and need no longer be aware of your surroundings.

DRIVING Safety while driving is particularly important. Question your rental agency about personal safety, or ask for a traveler safety tips brochure when you pick up your car. Obtain written directions, or a map with the route marked in red, from the agency showing how to get to your destination. And, if possible, arrive and depart during daylight hours.

Recently more and more crime has involved cars and drivers. If you drive off a highway into a doubtful neighborhood, leave the area as quickly as possible. If you have an accident, even on the highway, stay in your car with the doors locked until you assess the situation, or until the police arrive. If you are bumped from behind on the street or are involved in a minor accident with no injuries and the situation appears to be suspicious, motion to the other driver to follow you. *Never* get out of your car in such situations. You can also keep a pre-made sign in your car which reads: "PLEASE FOLLOW THIS VEHICLE TO REPORT THE ACCIDENT." Show the sign to the other driver and go directly to the nearest police precinct, well-lighted service station, or all night store.

If you see someone on the road who indicates a need for help, do not stop. Take note of the location, drive on to a well-lighted area, and telephone the police by dialing 911.

Park in well-lighted, well-traveled areas if possible. Always keep your car doors locked, whether attended or unattended. Look around you before you get out of your car, and never leave any packages or valuables in sight. If someone attempts to rob you or steal your car—do not try to resist the thief/carjacker—report the incident to the Police Department immediately.

The Crime Prevention Division of the Police Department, City of New York, publishes a "Safety Tips For Visitors" brochure. It is translated into French, Spanish, Hebrew, German, Japanese, Dutch, Italian, Russian, Chinese, Portuguese, and Swedish and contains general safety information. For a copy write to: Crime Prevention Division Office of D.C.C.A., 80–45 Winchester Blvd., Queens Village, NY 11427.

GETTING TO THE U.S.

Travelers from overseas can take advantage of the **APEX (Advance-Purchase Excursion) fares** offered by all the major U.S. and European carriers.

At the time of writing, **Delta Airlines** (tel. toll free 800/221-1212) offers a discounted "Discover America" airfare that allows unlimited travel within the continental United States. It *must be purchased through travel agents before entering the United States,* and can be bought in 3 to 10 segments, ranging in price from $449 to $789. Some restrictions apply, and you should be sure to ask for a clear explanation before you buy the pass. **Continental Airlines** (tel. toll free 800/525-0280) has a similar program (at presstime it's in conjunction with Air Canada), called "Visit U.S.A.," offering three to eight segments for travel ranging in price from $379 to $669. This must be purchased abroad. Call Continental for details.

Some large American airlines (for example, TWA, American Airlines, Northwest, United, and Delta) offer travelers—on their transatlantic or transpacific flights—special discount tickets under the name **Visit USA,** allowing travel between any U.S. destinations at minimum rates. They are not on sale in the United States, and must, therefore, be purchased before you leave your foreign point of departure. This system is the best, easiest, and fastest way to see the United States at low cost. You should obtain information well in advance from your travel agent or the office of the airline concerned, since the conditions attached to these discount tickets can be changed without advance notice.

The visitor arriving by air, no matter what the port of entry, should cultivate patience and resignation before setting foot on U.S. soil. Getting through immigration control may take as long as two hours on some days, especially summer weekends. Add the time it takes to clear Customs and you will see that you should make very generous allowance for delay in planning connections between international and domestic flights—an average of two to three hours at least.

In contrast, for the traveler arriving by car or by rail from Canada, the border-crossing formalities have been streamlined practically to the vanishing point. And for the traveler by air from Canada, Bermuda, and some places in the Caribbean, you can sometimes go through Customs and Immigration at the point of departure, which is much quicker and less painful.

For further information, see the "Planning a Trip" chapters for each state.

FAST FACTS FOR THE FOREIGN TRAVELER

Auto Clubs and Car Rentals See Chapter 1, "Getting There," for names and toll-free telephone numbers of leading U.S. car-rental firms. Members of automobile clubs abroad should also check with the **American Automobile Association (AAA)**, 8111 Gatehouse Rd., Falls Church, VA 22047 (tel. 703/222-6000), regarding membership reciprocity or a temporary AAA membership. One of their most valuable services is the 24-hour toll-free telephone number (tel. 800/336-4357) set up exclusively to deal with road emergencies.

Business Hours   Banks open weekdays from 9am to 3pm; although there's 24-hour access to the automatic tellers (ATMs) at most banks and other outlets. Generally, offices open weekdays from 9am to 5pm. Stores are open six days a week with many open on Sunday, too; department stores usually stay open until 9pm one day a week.

Currency   The U.S. monetary system has a decimal base: one American dollar ($1) = 100 cents (100¢).

Dollar bills commonly come in $1 ("a buck"), $5, $10, $20, $50, and $100 denominations (the last two are not welcome when paying for small purchases and are not accepted in taxis or at subway ticket booths).

There are six coin denominations: 1¢ (one cent or "penny"); 5¢ (five cents or "nickel"); 10¢ (ten cents or "dime"); 25¢ (twenty-five cents or "quarter"); 50¢ (fifty cents or "half dollar"—rare); and the very rare—and prized by collectors—$1 piece (both the older, large silver dollar and the newer, small Susan B. Anthony coin).

Traveler's checks denominated in U.S. dollars are accepted without demur at most hotels, motels, restaurants, and large stores. But as any experienced traveler knows, the best place to change traveler's checks is at a bank.

Credit Cards are the method of payment most widely used: VISA (BarclayCard in Britain), MasterCard (EuroCard in Europe, Access in Britain, Diamond in Japan), American Express, Diners Club, Carte Blanche, Discover, and Transmedia, in descending order of acceptance. You can save yourself trouble by using "plastic" rather than cash or traveler's checks in 95% of all hotels, motels, restaurants, and retail stores. A credit card can serve as a deposit for renting a car, as proof of identity (often carrying more weight than a passport), or as a "cash card," enabling you to draw money from banks that accept them. When a credit card is used, the transaction is posted using the world-rate conversion. This is a good tool to use when local exchange rates are bad.

Currency Exchange   Thomas Cook Currency Services (formerly Deak International) offers a wide variety of services: more than 100 currencies, commission-free traveler's checks, drafts and wire transfers, check collections, and precious metal bars and coins. Rates are competitive and service excellent. Call toll free 800/582-4496 for information. Many hotels will exchange currency if you are a registered guest.

Note: The "foreign-exchange bureaus" so common in Europe are rare even at airports in the United States and nonexistent outside major cities. Try to avoid changing foreign money, or traveler's checks denominated in other than U.S. dollars, at small-town banks, or even at branches in a big city; in fact leave any currency other than U.S. dollars at home—it may prove more nuisance to you than it's worth.

Drinking Laws   The legal age for drinking in public places is 21 in all 50 states. Other rules and regulations are governed by local county, city, and community authorities.

Electric Current   The United States uses 110-120 volts, 60 cycles, compared to 220-240 volts, 50 cycles, as in most of Europe. Besides a 100-volt converter, small appliances of non-American manufacture, such as hairdryers or shavers, will require a plug adapter, with two flat, parallel pins.

Embassies/Consulates   Embassies for all countries are located in the national capital, Washington, D.C. Here is a partial list: The **Australian** embassy is at 1601 Massachusetts Ave. NW, Washington, DC 20036 (tel. 202/797-3000); the **Canadian** embassy is at 501 Pennsylvania Ave. NW, Washington, DC 20001 (tel. 202/682-1740); the **Irish** embassy is at 2234 Massachusetts Ave. NW, Washington,

DC 20008 (tel. 202/462-3939); the **New Zealand** embassy is at 37 Observatory Circle NW, Washington, DC 20008 (tel. 202/328-4800); and the **United Kingdom** embassy is at 3100 Massachusetts Ave. NW, Washington, DC 20008 (tel. 202/462-1340). For information on other embassies, call directory assistance in Washington, D.C. at 202/555-1212.

Consulates are maintained in major U.S. cities, and in these three states, most are located in Atlanta, Georgia. Check telephone directories in the other two state capitals (Raleigh in North Carolina and Columbia in South Carolina). If you do not find your country's consulate listed, call Washington, D.C. directory assistance at 202/555-1212 for the telephone number of your embassy, which can give you the location of your country's nearest consulate.

Here is a partial list of consulates located in Atlanta: **Canadian Consulate General,** Suite 400, South Tower, One CNN Center, Atlanta, GA 30303 (tel. 404/577-6810); **Consulate of France,** 285 Peachtree Center Ave., Suite 2800, Atlanta, GA 30303 (tel. 404/522-4226); **Consulate General of the Federal Republic of Germany,** 229 Peachtree St. NE, Suite 1000, Atlanta, GA 30303-1618 (tel. 404/659-4760); **British Consulate General,** 245 Peachtree Center Ave., Marquis One Tower, Suite 2700, Atlanta, GA 30303 (tel. 404/524-5856); **Honorary Consulate of Italy,** 1106 W. Peachtree St. NW, Atlanta, GA 30309 (tel. 404/875-6177); and the **Consulate of Mexico,** One CNN Center, 410 South Tower, Atlanta, GA 30303 (tel. 404/688-3258). For complete information, contact the **Atlanta Chamber of Commerce,** P.O. Box 1740, Atlanta, GA 30301 (tel. 404/586-8470).

Emergencies Throughout the United States, you can telephone for emergency assistance (police, hospital, ambulance, etc.) by dialing 911. If theft or accident has left you stranded, or you meet with an emergency not covered by local government agencies, Travelers Aid is a nationwide organization dedicated to helping travelers in distress; check the local telephone directory, or dial "0" for directory assistance. In Atlanta, the Georgia Council for International Visitors, 999 Peachtree St. NE (tel. 404/873-6170), can provide a wide variety of help to foreign visitors in more than 42 languages.

Holidays On the following national legal holidays, banks, government offices, post offices, and many stores, restaurants, and museums are closed: January 1 (New Year's Day), third Monday in January (Martin Luther King, Jr., Day), third Monday in February (Presidents Day), last Monday in May (Memorial Day), July 4 (Independence Day), first Monday after first Sunday in September (Labor Day), second Monday in October (Columbus Day), November 11 (Veterans Day/Armistice Day), fourth Thursday in November (Thanksgiving Day), and December 25 (Christmas Day).

The Tuesday following the first Monday in November, Election Day, is a legal holiday in presidential-election years.

Legal Aid If you are stopped for a minor infraction (for example, of the highway code, such as speeding), never attempt to pay the fine directly to a police officer; you may be arrested on the much more serious charge of attempted bribery. Pay fines by mail, or directly into the hands of the clerk of the court. If accused of a more serious offense, it is wise to say and do nothing before consulting a lawyer.

Mail Mailboxes are blue, and carry the inscription "U.S.MAIL."

Newspapers/Magazines Leading U.S. national newspapers, published daily, are *The New York Times, USA Today, The Wall Street Journal,* and the *Christian Science Monitor.* You'll find leading state newspapers listed under "Fast Facts" for each state.

Postal Rates Within the United States, postage is 15¢ for postcards and 29¢ for letters; to Canada, it's 30¢ for postcards, 40¢ for letters; for all other international mail, rates are 40¢ for airmail postcards, 50¢ for airmail letters.

Radio/Television Most states have two or more radio stations broadcasting from the capital city, with local stations (most with limited broadcast range) in smaller towns and communities. The leading national television networks are ABC, CBS, NBC, PBS (Public Broadcasting System), and the cable network CNN. Channels and schedules are published in local newspapers and the local edition of *TV Guide* (in larger cities only).

Safety   See "Safety" earlier in this section under "Preparing for Your Trip."

Taxes   In the United States there is no VAT (Value-Added Tax) or other indirect tax at a national level. Every state, and each city in it, is allowed to levy its own local tax on all purchases, including hotel and restaurant checks, airline tickets, and so on. These taxes are not refundable.

Telephone, Telegraph, Telex, and Fax   Pay phones can be found on street corners, as well as in bars, restaurants, public buildings, stores, and service stations. Local calls cost 20¢ to 25¢.

For long-distance or international calls, stock up with a supply of quarters; the pay phone will instruct you when you should put them into the slot. For long-distance calls in the United States, dial 1 followed by the area code and number you want. For direct overseas calls, first dial 011, followed by the country code (Australia, 61; Republic of Ireland, 353; New Zealand, 64; United Kingdom, 44; and so on), and then by the city code (for example, 71 or 81 for London, 21 for Birmingham) and the number of the person you wish to call.

Before calling from a hotel room, always ask the hotel phone operator if there are any telephone surcharges. These are best avoided by using a public phone, calling collect, or using a telephone charge card.

For reversed-charge or collect calls, and for person-to-person calls, dial 0 (zero, not the letter "O") followed by the area code and number you want; an operator will then come on the line and you should specify that you are calling collect, or person-to-person, or both. If your operator-assisted call is international, ask for the overseas operator.

For local directory assistance ("Information"), dial 411; for long-distance information dial 1, then the appropriate area code and 555-1212.

Like the telephone system, telegraph and telex services are provided by private corporations like ITT, MCI, and above all, Western Union (there are hundreds across the country), or dictate it over the phone (tel. toll free 800/325-6000). You can also telegraph money, or have it telegraphed to you very quickly over the Western Union system.

Most hotels have fax machines available to their customers (ask if there is a charge to use it). You will also see signs for public faxes in the windows of small shops.

Time   The United States is divided into six time zones. From east to west, these are: Eastern Standard Time (EST), Central Standard Time (CST), Mountain Standard Time (MST), Pacific Standard Time (PST), Alaska Standard Time (AST), and Hawaii Standard Time (HST). Always keep the changing time zones in mind if you are traveling (or even telephoning) long distances in the United States. For example, noon in Boston (EST) is 11am in Chicago (CST), 10am in Denver (MST), 9am in Los Angeles (PST), 8am in Anchorage (AST), and 7am in Honolulu (HST). When it is noon in London (GMT, or Greenwich Mean Time), it is 7am in Boston. Georgia and the Carolinas fall into the Eastern Standard Time zone.

Daylight Saving Time   is in effect from 1am on the first Sunday in April until 2am on the last Sunday in October, except in Arizona, Hawaii, part of Indiana, and Puerto Rico.

Tipping   Contrary to the practice in many foreign countries, you will seldom, if ever, encounter an added service charge (tip) added to a hotel, restaurant, or other bill. Tipping is the norm, and the amount you tip is strictly up to you, although woe be to those who undertip! You are not, however, expected to tip in self-service restaurants, gas (petrol) stations, and similar establishments.

The following will serve as guidelines: **Bartenders:** 10% to 15%. **Bellhops and Porters:** 50¢ to $1 per piece of luggage (or $3 to $5 for an extra large amount of baggage), and $1 for each room service call or other service performed by bellhops. **Cab drivers:** 15% of the metered fare, up to 20% in some large cities. **Chamber service and sleeping-car attendants:** $1 per day except in luxury hotels in large cities, where you should leave a minimum of $2 per day. **Checkroom attendants:** 50¢ per coat, $1 in large cities. **Doormen:** Tip at your own discretion (usually $1) if they hail a cab for you or perform any other service. Otherwise, no tip is necessary. **Hairdressers:** 15% to 20%. **Parking lot attendants:** 50¢ to $1. **Restaurants and nightclubs:** 15% to 20% of the bill.

Toilets Often euphemistically referred to as "restrooms," public toilets are nonexistent on the streets of American cities. They can be found, though, in bars, restaurants, hotel lobbies, museums, department stores, and service stations—and will probably be clean (although ones in the last-mentioned sometimes leave much to be desired). Note, however, that some restaurants and bars display a notice TOILETS ARE FOR USE OF PATRONS ONLY. You can ignore this sign, or better yet, avoid arguments by paying for a cup of coffee or soft drink, which will qualify you as a patron. The cleanliness of toilets at railroad stations and bus depots may be questionable; some public places are equipped with pay toilets that require you to insert one or two dimes (10¢) or a quarter (25¢) into a slot on the door before it will open. In restrooms with attendants, leaving at least a 25¢ tip is customary.

Yellow Pages The local phone company provides two kinds of telephone directory. The general directory, called the "white pages," lists subscribers (business and personal residences) in alphabetical order. The inside front cover lists emergency numbers for police, fire, and ambulance, and other vital numbers (such as the Coast Guard, poison control center, crime-victims hotline, and so on). The first few pages have community-service numbers, and a guide to long-distance and international calling, complete with country codes and area codes.

The second directory, the "yellow pages," lists all local services, businesses, and industries alphabetically by type, with an index at the back. The listings cover not only such obvious items as automobile repairs by make of car, or drugstores (pharmacies), often by geographical location, but also restaurants by type of cuisine and geographical location, bookstores by special subject and/or language, places of worship by religious denomination, and other information that the tourist might otherwise not readily find. The yellow pages often also include city plans or detailed area maps, often showing postal ZIP codes and public transportation.

THE AMERICAN SYSTEM OF MEASUREMENTS
LENGTH

1 inch (in.)			=	2.54cm	
1 foot (ft.)	=	12 in.	=	30.48cm	= .305m
1 yard (yd.)	=	3 ft.			= .915m
1 mile	=	5,280 ft.			= 1.609km

To convert miles to kilometers, multiply the number of miles by 1.16. Also use to convert speeds from miles per hour (m.p.h.) to kilometers per hour (kmph).

To convert kilometers to miles, multiply the number of kilometers by .62 Also use to convert kmph to m.p.h.

CAPACITY

1 fluid ounce (fl. oz.)			=	.03 liters			
1 pint	=	16 fl. oz.	=	.47 liters			
1 quart	=	2 pints	=	.94 liters			
1 gallon (gal.)	=	4 quarts	=	3.79 liters	=	.83 Imperial gal.	

To convert U.S. gallons to liters, multiply the number of gallons by 3.79.
To convert liters to U.S. gallons, multiply the number of liters by .26.
To convert U.S. gallons to Imperial gallons, multiply the number of U.S. gallons by .83.
To convert Imperial gallons to U.S. gallons, multiply the number of Imperial gallons by 1.2.

WEIGHT

1 ounce (oz.)			=	28.35g			
1 pound (lb.)	=	16 oz.	=	453.6g	=	.45kg	
1 ton			=	2,000 lb.	=	907kg	= .91 metric tons

To convert pounds to kilograms, multiply the number of pounds by .45.
To convert kilograms to pounds, multiply the number of kilograms by 2.2.

AREA

1 acre			=	.41ha		
1 square mile	=	640 acres	=	259ha	=	2.6km²

To convert acres to hectares, multiply the number of acres by .41.
To convert hectares to acres, multiply the number of hectares by 2.47.
To convert square miles to square kilometers, multiply the number of square miles by 2.6.
To convert square kilometers to square miles, multiply the number of square kilometers by .39.

TEMPERATURE

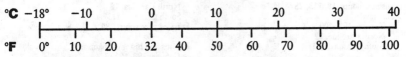

To convert degrees Fahrenheit to degrees Celsius, subtract 32 from °F, multiply by 5, then divide by 9 (example: 85°F − 32 × 5/9 = 29.4°C).
To convert degrees Celsius to degrees Fahrenheit, multiply °C by 9, divide by 5, and add 32 (example: 20°C × 9/5 + 32 = 68°F).

INDEX

GENERAL INFORMATION

DESTINATIONS

NORTH CAROLINA

Key to abbreviations: *B* = Budget; *CG* = Campground; *E* = Expensive; *M* = Moderate; * = Author's Favorite; *$* = Super Value Choice.

SOUTH CAROLINA

GEORGIA

Please Send Me the Books Checked Below:

FROMMER'S COMPREHENSIVE GUIDES
(Guides listing facilities from budget to deluxe,
with emphasis on the medium-priced)

	Retail Price	Code		Retail Price	Code
☐ Acapulco/Ixtapa/Taxco 1993–94	$15.00	C120	☐ Jamaica/Barbados 1993–94	$15.00	C105
☐ Alaska 1994–95	$17.00	C130	☐ Japan 1992–93	$19.00	C020
☐ Arizona 1993–94	$18.00	C101	☐ Morocco 1992–93	$18.00	C021
☐ Australia 1992–93	$18.00	C002	☐ Nepal 1994–95	$18.00	C126
☐ Austria 1993–94	$19.00	C119	☐ New England 1993	$17.00	C114
☐ Belgium/Holland/ Luxembourg 1993–94	$18.00	C106	☐ New Mexico 1993–94	$15.00	C117
☐ Bahamas 1994–95	$17.00	C121	☐ New York State 1994–95	$19.00	C132
☐ Bermuda 1994–95	$15.00	C122	☐ Northwest 1991–92	$17.00	C026
☐ Brazil 1993–94	$20.00	C111	☐ Portugal 1992–93	$16.00	C027
☐ California 1993	$18.00	C112	☐ Puerto Rico 1993–94	$15.00	C103
☐ Canada 1992–93	$18.00	C009	☐ Puerto Vallarta/Manzanillo/ Guadalajara 1992–93	$14.00	C028
☐ Caribbean 1994	$18.00	C123	☐ Scandinavia 1993–94	$19.00	C118
☐ Carolinas/Georgia 1994–95	$17.00	C128	☐ Scotland 1992–93	$16.00	C040
☐ Colorado 1993–94	$16.00	C100	☐ Skiing Europe 1989–90	$15.00	C030
☐ Cruises 1993–94	$19.00	C107	☐ South Pacific 1992–93	$20.00	C031
☐ DE/MD/PA & NJ Shore 1992–93	$19.00	C012	☐ Spain 1993–94	$19.00	C115
☐ Egypt 1990–91	$17.00	C013	☐ Switzerland/Liechtenstein 1992–93	$19.00	C032
☐ England 1994	$18.00	C129	☐ Thailand 1992–93	$20.00	C033
☐ Florida 1994	$18.00	C124	☐ U.S.A. 1993–94	$19.00	C116
☐ France 1994–95	$20.00	C131	☐ Virgin Islands 1994–95	$13.00	C127
☐ Germany 1994	$19.00	C125	☐ Virginia 1992–93	$14.00	C037
☐ Italy 1994	$19.00	C130	☐ Yucatán 1993–94	$18.00	C110

FROMMER'S $-A-DAY GUIDES
(Guides to low-cost tourist accommodations and facilities)

	Retail Price	Code		Retail Price	Code
☐ Australia on $45 1993–94	$18.00	D102	☐ Mexico on $45 1994	$19.00	D116
☐ Costa Rica/Guatemala/ Belize on $35 1993–94	$17.00	D108	☐ New York on $70 1992–93	$16.00	D016
☐ Eastern Europe on $30 1993–94	$18.00	D110	☐ New Zealand on $45 1993–94	$18.00	D103
☐ England on $60 1994	$18.00	D112	☐ Scotland/Wales on $50 1992–93	$18.00	D019
☐ Europe on $50 1994	$19.00	D115	☐ South America on $40 1993–94	$19.00	D109
☐ Greece on $45 1993–94	$19.00	D100	☐ Turkey on $40 1992–93	$22.00	D023
☐ Hawaii on $75 1994	$19.00	D113	☐ Washington, D.C. on $40 1992–93	$17.00	D024
☐ India on $40 1992–93	$20.00	D010			
☐ Ireland on $40 1992–93	$17.00	D011			
☐ Israel on $45 1993–94	$18.00	D101			

FROMMER'S CITY $-A-DAY GUIDES
(Pocket-size guides with an emphasis on low-cost tourist accommodations and facilities)

	Retail Price	Code		Retail Price	Code
☐ Berlin on $40 1994–95	$12.00	D111	☐ Madrid on $50 1992–93	$13.00	D014
☐ Copenhagen on $50 1992–93	$12.00	D003	☐ Paris on $45 1994–95	$12.00	D117
☐ London on $45 1994–95	$12.00	D114	☐ Stockholm on $50 1992–93	$13.00	D022

FROMMER'S WALKING TOURS
(With routes and detailed maps, these companion guides point out
the places and pleasures that make a city unique)

	Retail Price	Code		Retail Price	Code
☐ Berlin	$12.00	W100	☐ Paris	$12.00	W103
☐ London	$12.00	W101	☐ San Francisco	$12.00	W104
☐ New York	$12.00	W102	☐ Washington, D.C.	$12.00	W105

FROMMER'S TOURING GUIDES
(Color-illustrated guides that include walking tours, cultural and historic
sites, and practical information)

	Retail Price	Code		Retail Price	Code
☐ Amsterdam	$11.00	T001	☐ New York	$11.00	T008
☐ Barcelona	$14.00	T015	☐ Rome	$11.00	T010
☐ Brazil	$11.00	T003	☐ Scotland	$10.00	T011
☐ Florence	$ 9.00	T005	☐ Sicily	$15.00	T017
☐ Hong Kong/Singapore/			☐ Tokyo	$15.00	T016
Macau	$11.00	T006	☐ Turkey	$11.00	T013
☐ Kenya	$14.00	T018	☐ Venice	$ 9.00	T014
☐ London	$13.00	T007			

FROMMER'S FAMILY GUIDES

	Retail Price	Code		Retail Price	Code
☐ California with Kids	$18.00	F100	☐ San Francisco with Kids	$17.00	F004
☐ Los Angeles with Kids	$17.00	F002	☐ Washington, D.C. with Kids	$17.00	F005
☐ New York City with Kids	$18.00	F003			

FROMMER'S CITY GUIDES
(Pocket-size guides to sightseeing and tourist accommodations and
facilities in all price ranges)

	Retail Price	Code		Retail Price	Code
☐ Amsterdam 1993–94	$13.00	S110	☐ Montreál/Québec		
☐ Athens 1993–94	$13.00	S114	City 1993–94	$13.00	S125
☐ Atlanta 1993–94	$13.00	S112	☐ New Orleans 1993–94	$13.00	S103
☐ Atlantic City/Cape			☐ New York 1993	$13.00	S120
May 1993–94	$13.00	S130	☐ Orlando 1994	$13.00	S135
☐ Bangkok 1992–93	$13.00	S005	☐ Paris 1993–94	$13.00	S109
☐ Barcelona/Majorca/			☐ Philadelphia 1993–94	$13.00	S113
Minorca/Ibiza 1993–94	$13.00	S115	☐ Rio 1991–92	$ 9.00	S029
☐ Berlin 1993–94	$13.00	S116	☐ Rome 1993–94	$13.00	S111
☐ Boston 1993–94	$13.00	S117	☐ Salt Lake City 1991–92	$ 9.00	S031
☐ Cancún/Cozumel 1991–			☐ San Diego 1993–94	$13.00	S107
92	$ 9.00	S010	☐ San Francisco 1994	$13.00	S133
☐ Chicago 1993–94	$13.00	S122	☐ Santa Fe/Taos/		
☐ Denver/Boulder/Colorado			Albuquerque 1993–94	$13.00	S108
Springs 1993–94	$13.00	S131	☐ Seattle/Portland 1992–93	$12.00	S035
☐ Dublin 1993–94	$13.00	S128	☐ St. Louis/Kansas		
☐ Hawaii 1992	$12.00	S014	City 1993–94	$13.00	S127
☐ Hong Kong 1992–93	$12.00	S015	☐ Sydney 1993–94	$13.00	S129
☐ Honolulu/Oahu 1994	$13.00	S134	☐ Tampa/St.		
☐ Las Vegas 1993–94	$13.00	S121	Petersburg 1993–94	$13.00	S105
☐ London 1994	$13.00	S132	☐ Tokyo 1992–93	$13.00	S039
☐ Los Angeles 1993–94	$13.00	S123	☐ Toronto 1993–94	$13.00	S126
☐ Madrid/Costa del			☐ Vancouver/Victoria 1990–		
Sol 1993–94	$13.00	S124	91	$ 8.00	S041
☐ Miami 1993–94	$13.00	S118	☐ Washington, D.C. 1993	$13.00	S102
☐ Minneapolis/St.					
Paul 1993–94	$13.00	S119			

Other Titles Available at Membership Prices

SPECIAL EDITIONS

	Retail Price	Code		Retail Price	Code
☐ Bed & Breakfast North America	$15.00	P002	☐ Marilyn Wood's Wonderful Weekends (within a 250-mile radius of NYC)	$12.00	P017
☐ Bed & Breakfast Southwest	$16.00	P100	☐ National Park Guide 1993	$15.00	P101
☐ Caribbean Hideaways	$16.00	P103	☐ Where to Stay U.S.A.	$15.00	P102

GAULT MILLAU'S "BEST OF" GUIDES
(The only guides that distinguish the truly superlative from the merely overrated)

	Retail Price	Code		Retail Price	Code
☐ Chicago	$16.00	G002	☐ New England	$16.00	G010
☐ Florida	$17.00	G003	☐ New Orleans	$17.00	G011
☐ France	$17.00	G004	☐ New York	$17.00	G012
☐ Germany	$18.00	G018	☐ Paris	$17.00	G013
☐ Hawaii	$17.00	G006	☐ San Francisco	$17.00	G014
☐ Hong Kong	$17.00	G007	☐ Thailand	$18.00	G019
☐ London	$17.00	G009	☐ Toronto	$17.00	G020
☐ Los Angeles	$17.00	G005	☐ Washington, D.C.	$17.00	G017

THE REAL GUIDES
(Opinionated, politically aware guides for youthful budget-minded travelers)

	Retail Price	Code		Retail Price	Code
☐ Able to Travel	$20.00	R112	☐ Kenya	$12.95	R015
☐ Amsterdam	$13.00	R100	☐ Mexico	$11.95	R128
☐ Barcelona	$13.00	R101	☐ Morocco	$14.00	R129
☐ Belgium/Holland/ Luxembourg	$16.00	R031	☐ Nepal	$14.00	R018
☐ Berlin	$13.00	R123	☐ New York	$13.00	R019
☐ Brazil	$13.95	R003	☐ Paris	$13.00	R130
☐ California & the West Coast	$17.00	R121	☐ Peru	$12.95	R021
☐ Canada	$15.00	R103	☐ Poland	$13.95	R131
☐ Czechoslovakia	$15.00	R124	☐ Portugal	$16.00	R126
☐ Egypt	$19.00	R105	☐ Prague	$15.00	R113
☐ Europe	$18.00	R122	☐ San Francisco & the Bay Area	$11.95	R024
☐ Florida	$14.00	R006	☐ Scandinavia	$14.95	R025
☐ France	$18.00	R106	☐ Spain	$16.00	R026
☐ Germany	$18.00	R107	☐ Thailand	$17.00	R119
☐ Greece	$18.00	R108	☐ Tunisia	$17.00	R115
☐ Guatemala/Belize	$14.00	R127	☐ Turkey	$13.95	R027
☐ Hong Kong/Macau	$11.95	R011	☐ U.S.A.	$18.00	R117
☐ Hungary	$14.95	R118	☐ Venice	$11.95	R028
☐ Ireland	$17.00	R120	☐ Women Travel	$12.95	R029
☐ Italy	$18.00	R125	☐ Yugoslavia	$12.95	R030